my **revision** notes

AQA A-level
PSYCHOLOGY

Molly Marshall
Susan Firth

HODDER
EDUCATION
AN HACHETTE UK COMPANY

The Publishers would like to thank the following for permission to reproduce copyright material.

Photo credits

p. 19 © Denis Nata – Shutterstock; **p. 135** ©urbenbuzz / Alamy Stock Photo

Every effort has been made to trace all copyright holders, but if any have been inadvertently overlooked, the Publishers will be pleased to make the necessary arrangements at the first opportunity.

Although every effort has been made to ensure that website addresses are correct at time of going to press, Hodder Education cannot be held responsible for the content of any website mentioned in this book. It is sometimes possible to find a relocated web page by typing in the address of the home page for a website in the URL window of your browser.

Hachette UK's policy is to use papers that are natural, renewable and recyclable products and made from wood grown in sustainable forests. The logging and manufacturing processes are expected to conform to the environmental regulations of the country of origin.

Orders: please contact Bookpoint Ltd, 130 Park Drive, Milton Park, Abingdon, Oxon OX14 4SE. Telephone: (44) 01235 827720. Fax: (44) 01235 400454. Email education@bookpoint.co.uk Lines are open from 9 a.m. to 5 p.m., Monday to Saturday, with a 24-hour message answering service. You can also order through our website: www.hoddereducation.co.uk

ISBN: 978 1 4718 8299 9

© Molly Marshall and Susan Firth 2017

First published in 2017 by
Hodder Education,
An Hachette UK Company
Carmelite House
50 Victoria Embankment
London EC4Y 0DZ
www.hoddereducation.co.uk

Impression number   10   9   8   7   6   5   4   3   2   1
Year   2021   2020   2019   2018   2017

Cover photo © Maya Kruchancova - Fotolia

Illustrations by Aptara, Inc.

Typeset in Bembo Std Regular, 11/13 pt by Aptara, Inc.

Printed in Spain by Graphycems

A catalogue record for this title is available from the British Library.

Get the most from this book

Everyone has to decide his or her own revision strategy, but it is essential to review your work, learn it and test your understanding. These Revision Notes will help you to do that in a planned way, topic by topic. Use this book as the cornerstone of your revision and don't hesitate to write in it – personalise your notes and check your progress by ticking off each section as you revise.

Tick to track your progress

Use the revision planner on pages iv and viii to plan your revision, topic by topic. Tick each box when you have:

- revised and understood a topic
- tested yourself
- practised the exam questions and gone online to check your answers and complete the quick quizzes.

You can also keep track of your revision by ticking off each topic heading in the book. You may find it helpful to add your own notes as you work through each topic.

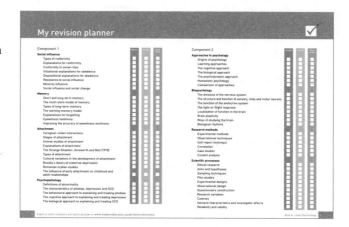

Features to help you succeed

Examiners' tips and summaries

Expert tips are given throughout the book to help you polish your exam technique in order to maximise your chances in the exam. The summaries provide provide a quick-check bullet list for each topic.

Typical mistakes

The author identifies the typical mistakes candidates make and explain how you can avoid them.

Now test yourself

These short, knowledge-based questions provide the first step in testing your learning. Answers are at the back of the book.

Definitions and key words

Clear, concise definitions of essential key terms are provided where they first appear in each component. A comprehensive glossary of terms can be found online.

Revision activities

These activities will help you to understand each topic in an interactive way.

Exam practice

Practice exam questions are provided for each topic. Use them to consolidate your revision and practise your exam skills.

Online

Go online to check your answers to the exam questions and try out the extra *quick quizzes* at **www.hoddereducation.co.uk/myrevisionnotes**

My revision planner

Component 1

REVISED   TESTED   EXAM READY

Component 2

REVISED   TESTED   EXAM READY

Now test yourself answers
Glossary & Exam practice answers
www.hoddereducation.co.uk/myrevisionnotes

Social influence

Types of conformity

REVISED

Internalisation occurs when an individual conforms because he or she believes that a group norm for behaviour or a group attitude is 'right'. If group pressure is removed, this conformity will continue.

Identification occurs when an individual conforms to the role that society expects them to play: the individual does not have to change their private opinion.

Compliance occurs when a person conforms to the majority opinion but does not agree with it. If group pressure is removed, the conformity will cease. Compliance is thought to occur because an individual wishes to be accepted by the majority group.

> **Internalisation:** when an individual conforms because he or she believes that a group norm for behaviour or a group attitude is 'right'.
>
> **Identification:** conforming to the behaviour expected by the majority, such as obeying school rules about uniform, but without enthusiasm.

Explanations for conformity

REVISED

Majority influence (**conformity**) is the process that takes place when an individual's attitudes or behaviour are affected by the views of the dominant group. This may be because of **normative social influence** (the effect of social norms), which occurs when an individual agrees with the opinions of a group of people because he or she wishes to be accepted by them. It can also occur because of informational social influence when the minority yields to group pressure because they think that the majority has more knowledge or information.

Informational social influence occurs when a question asked does not have an obviously correct answer. When this happens, people look to others for information and may agree with the majority view. Informational social influence involves the process of compliance. It also involves internalisation, when an individual conforms because he or she believes that a group norm or opinion is 'right'.

> **Compliance:** when a person conforms to the majority opinion in public but in private does not agree.
>
> **Conformity:** when an individual's attitudes or behaviour are affected by the views of a dominant social group.
>
> **Normative social influence:** when an individual agrees with the opinions of a group of people because he or she wishes to be accepted by them.

Research: Conformity

Conformity as the result of informational social influence (Sherif 1935)

Sherif considered participants who were asked to estimate how far a point of light had moved, first as individuals, then in a group and finally as individuals again. In the group estimate condition they changed their personal estimate and a group norm emerged. Since there was no 'factually correct answer', the group norm emerged as each individual looked to others for information.

Conformity as the result of normative social influence (Asch 1956)

Asch found that when 'real' participants were asked to say out loud which line (A, B or C) matched a stimulus line, they gave incorrect answers that conformed to the majority view 37% of the time. Of the real participants, 75% conformed at least once. When asked why they answered as they did, some said they did not believe the answers given by the others in the group but they had not wanted to look different. This is an example of normative social influence (compliance).

Minority influence is the process that takes place when a consistent minority changes the attitudes and/or behaviour of an individual. Minority influence leads to a change in attitudes and involves the process of conversion. It is the consistency of the minority that is important.

Following Asch's original research, factors such as group size, unanimity and task difficulty were investigated.

Group size

To determine how the size of the majority affects the rate of conformity, group size was varied from 1 confederate to 15 confederates. When there was one confederate, the real participants conformed on just 3% of the critical trials. When the group size increased to two confederates, the real participants conformed on 12.8% of the critical trials. When there were three confederates, the real participants conformed on 32% of the critical trials, which was the same percentage as when there were seven confederates. This suggests that conformity reaches the highest level with just three confederates.

Unanimity

In Asch's original experiment, the confederates all gave the same incorrect answer. In one variation of Asch's experiment, one of the confederates was instructed to give the correct answer throughout and in this variation the rate of conformity dropped to 5%. This demonstrates that if the real participant has support for their belief, they are more likely to resist the pressure to conform. In another variation, when one of the confederates gave a different incorrect answer to the majority, conformity dropped to 9%. This shows that if you break the group's unanimous position, conformity is reduced.

Task difficulty

In Asch's original experiment the correct answer was always obvious. In one of his variations he made the task more difficult by making the difference between the line lengths significantly smaller. In this variation Asch found the rate of conformity increased, probably because of **informational social influence**.

> **Informational social influence:** people may agree with a majority view because when a question asked does not have an obviously correct answer so they look to others for information

Conformity to social roles

REVISED

One explanation for violence and aggression in prisons is that both prisoners and guards have personalities that make conflict inevitable – prisoners lack respect for authority and guards are attracted to the job because of a desire for power. This is a dispositional **hypothesis** and it suggests that both prisoners and guards are inevitably 'evil'. Haney, Banks and Zimbardo (1973) suggested that it was possible to separate the effects of the prison environment from the personalities of the inhabitants to test the dispositional hypothesis and to find out whether conformity is caused by the characteristics of the person (dispositional characteristics) or because of the situation he or she is in (situational factors).

> **Hypothesis:** this states precisely what the researcher believes to be true about the target population and is a testable statement.

The Stanford Prison experiment

In the Stanford Prison experiment, in which male students were allocated the role of prisoner or guard, Haney *et al.* (1973) found strong evidence of conformity to social roles for prisoners and guards. The prison environment had a huge impact on the behaviour of all participants – the prisoners became passive and depressed and the guards became sadistic and oppressive. The conformity was due to the social situation rather than to the personal characteristics of the male student participants. Both guards and prisoners identified with and conformed to the roles they had been allocated.

Zimbardo concluded that identification occurs when an individual conforms to the role that society expects them to play and suggested that three processes could explain the behaviour of the prisoners and guards:
- **Deindividuation:** the prisoners and the guards lost their sense of individuality.
- **Learned helplessness:** the guards' unpredictable decisions led the prisoners to give up.
- **Dependency:** the prisoners depended on the guards and this dependency emasculated them and increased their sense of helplessness.

Situational explanations for obedience

REVISED

Some psychologists explain behaviour as a result of the situation a person is in. For example, behaviour could be the result of social influence, group pressure or group membership. See also Component 3: 'The nature–nurture debate' on page 100.

> **Exam tip**
>
> Make sure you can explain the difference between obedience and conformity.

Research into obedience (Milgram 1963)

Milgram wanted to find out why people obey authority, what conditions foster obedient behaviour and what conditions foster independent behaviour. He asked psychology students to predict how participants would behave if they were ordered to give electric shocks to a stranger. The students had estimated that no more than 3% of the participants would administer a fatal shock of 450 volts. The participants were 40 American men. When asked to play the role of 'teacher' and

administer increasingly strong electric shocks to a stranger, who played the role of a 'learner' (whom they believed was also a participant), although they sweated, trembled, stuttered and quite a few laughed nervously:
- Twenty-six participants (65%) went all the way to 450 volts with the electric shocks.
- Only nine participants (22.5%) stopped at 315 volts.

Variations on Milgram's original experiment

Milgram carried out his experiment in several different situations. The changed factors and percentages who obeyed were as follows:
- Distance order – experimenter instructed 'teacher' by telephone: 23% **obedience**.
- Less prestige – experiment moved from Yale to a scruffy office: 48% obedience.
- Increased proximity – 'teacher' was in the same room as the learner: 40% obedience.
- Social support in disobedience – other 'teachers' refused to give shocks: 10% obedience.
- Reduced responsibility – two 'teachers', one told by the other to give shocks: 92.5% obedience.
- Gender – female participants: 65% obedience.
- Reduced authority – the experimenter was a member of the public: 20% obedience.

> **Obedience:** a change in behaviour so that people do what a person having authority tells them to do.

Milgram concluded that situational factors may determine how people will behave:
- **Legitimate authority.** If the person giving the order has legitimate authority, people transfer the responsibility for their actions to the authority figure.
- **Agentic state.** People act as agents of the legitimate authority and hold the authority figure responsible for their actions.
- **The slippery slope.** People follow a small 'reasonable' order and then feel obliged to continue when the orders gradually become unreasonable.

Dispositional explanations for obedience

REVISED

The authoritarian personality

The authoritarian personality is a dispositional explanation for obedience. The theory of an authoritarian personality was devised in the 1950s to explain the events that led to the slaughter of Jews in Germany in the Second World War. The theory includes the Adorno F-scale (F for Fascist), which supposedly measures Fascist tendencies. T. W. Adorno was one of the most influential philosophers and social critics in Germany after the Second World War. The authoritarian personality was an attempt to explain the conditions that allowed the Nazis to gain a foothold in Europe. The researchers, led by Adorno, used various psychological scales to attempt to explain racism and the atmosphere that led to the slaughter of 6 million Jews and others.

According to Adorno's theory, some of the elements of the authoritarian personality type are:
- blind allegiance to conventional beliefs about right and wrong
- respect for submission to acknowledged authority
- belief in aggression towards those who do not subscribe to conventional thinking
- a need for strong leadership.

According to Adorno, harsh child-rearing practices lead to the authoritarian personality. People with an authoritarian personality are servile to those who have superior status, hostile to people who have inferior status, and support conventional values. Adorno also suggested that authoritarian personalities are more likely to obey those in authority.

Resistance to social influence

REVISED

Situational and personal variables affect the extent to which people conform or obey.
- **Group size:** the bigger the majority, the more influential it is.
- **Gender:** some research suggests that females conform more than males because the norm for female behaviour is to be socially orientated.

- **Personality:** some people are more self-confident and have higher self-esteem than others.
- **Locus of control:** people having an external locus of control believe that events in their life are outside their control, perhaps being controlled by powerful others, and are more likely to conform or obey those having authority. Those having an internal locus of control see themselves as responsible for what happens to them and are more likely to resist pressure to conform/obey.
- **Situational factors:** if we are with others who refuse to obey, we are less likely to obey, but if we are with people who obey, we are more likely to obey.
- **Culture:** people who are raised in collectivist cultures may be more likely to conform than those who are raised in individualist cultures because collectivist cultures value interdependence rather than independence.

Social support

In one of Asch's variations the presence of a confederate who did not conform led to a decrease in the conformity levels in true participants – this is thought to be because the presence of a dissident gave the participant social support and made them feel more confident in their own decision and more confident in rejecting the majority position. Social support also decreases obedience to authority. In a variation of Milgram's study, when there were two other participants (confederates) who acted as 'teachers' who refused to obey, obedience decreased. The presence of others who are seen to disobey the authority figure reduced the level of obedience to 10%.

Differences between obedience and conformity

Obedience:

- occurs within a social hierarchy
- puts the emphasis on social power
- is often different from the behaviour of the authority figure
- has explicit motivation for behaviour
- sees participants explain their behaviour in terms of obedience.

Conformity:

- occurs between people of equal status
- puts the emphasis on social acceptance
- displays the same behaviour as that of the social group
- has implicit motivation for behaviour
- sees participants often deny that their behaviour is motivated by conformity.

Minority influence

REVISED

Moscovici *et al.* (1969) carried out an experiment to find out whether consistency in the minority is an important factor in minority influence. In a **laboratory experiment**, female student participants were randomly allocated to a consistent, inconsistent or control condition. Participants were asked to name the colour of 36 slides, all of which were blue but varied in brightness. In the consistent condition the confederates named all 36 slides as green. In the inconsistent condition the confederates named 24 of the slides as green and 12 slides as blue. Minority influence was measured by the percentage of participants' answers that called the blue slides green (i.e. followed the minority influence). In the consistent condition 8.42% of

> **Revision activity**
>
> Make a wall chart showing all the factors that increase or decrease conformity, obedience or resistance to social influence.

> **Exam tip**
>
> You could be asked to discuss two explanations of resistance to social influence. It might be a good idea to discuss one situational factor that increases independent behaviour and one dispositional characteristic that increases independent behaviour.

> **Typical mistake**
>
> Conformity and obedience are different types of social influence – do not confuse these or use these terms interchangeably.

> **Laboratory experiment:** a method of conducting research in which researchers try to control all the variables except the one that is changed between the experimental conditions.

the participants' answers were green and 32% gave the incorrect answer at least once. In the inconsistent condition 1.25% of the participants' answers were green. The consistent condition showed the greatest conformity to minority influence. The conclusion was that a minority influence is more likely when the minority is consistent, thus, relating to social change, a consistent minority may influence the majority.

The characteristics of influential minorities

Moscovici (1985) suggested five characteristics of the behaviour of influential minorities:
- They are consistent, demonstrating certainty, and they draw attention to their views.
- They enter into discussion and avoid being too dogmatic.
- They take action in support of their principles (for example, take part in protest marches).
- They make sacrifices to maintain their views.
- They are similar in terms of age, class and gender to the population they are trying to influence.

Flexibility and compromise

Some researchers argue that minority influence depends on how the majority interprets consistency. If the consistent minority are seen as inflexible, rigid, uncompromising and dogmatic, they will be unlikely to change the views of the majority. However, if they appear flexible and compromising, they are likely to be seen as less extreme, more moderate and reasonable and will have a better chance of changing majority views.

Nemeth (1986) investigated flexibility and compromise. The experiment was based on a mock jury in which groups of three participants and one confederate had to decide on the amount of compensation to be given to the victim of an accident. When the consistent minority (the confederate) argued for a very low amount and refused to change his position, he had no effect on the majority. However, when he compromised and moved some way towards the majority position, the majority also compromised and changed their view. This suggests that flexibility and compromise are as important as consistency.

> **Revision activity**
>
> Make a list of two or three influential minority groups. Suggest whether each of the groups 'matches' Moscovici's characteristics for an influential minority and suggest how each group has influenced social change.

Social influence and social change

REVISED

The research by Asch, Zimbardo and Milgram can be used to educate people about the danger of 'blind' conformity and/or obedience to authority. Zimbardo and Leippe (1991) proposed that steps can be taken to resist pressure to conform, or pressure to obey an authority figure.
- Trust your intuition if and when you feel there is 'something wrong'.
- Don't just accept the definition of the situation given to you by a person whose interests may conflict with yours.
- Consider what could happen if you obey and act on that possibility.
- Figure out an 'escape plan' and act on this as soon as possible.
- Don't worry about 'what the other person may think of you' – if you are mistaken, you can always apologise.

According to Ross (1988), obedience in Milgram's experiment would have been reduced had there been an 'exit button' visible and in easy reach of the participants, who could have pressed it when they wanted to stop. Think about this 'exit button' idea and mentally rehearse it as it applies to situations in your life.

> **Social influence:** the way that a person or a group of people affect the attitudes and behaviour of another individual.

Evaluation

Sherif (1935): Assessing how far a spot of light has moved is a trivial task and not one that is likely to happen in everyday life. The study has low mundane validity and in real-life situations people may be less likely to be influenced by others.

Asch (1956): The experimental method leads to useful results because there is control over variables so statements can be made about cause and effect and the study can be replicated. However, the biased sample of male American students may not be representative of other populations. The study has low mundane validity; it does not represent a lifelike social situation. People may not change their opinions about social variables as readily as they do about line lengths. The study was unethical because Asch deceived the participants.

Haney et al. (1973): This research is useful as it can be applied to improve the situation in real prisons, for example by training guards to treat prisoners differently. However, the artificial situation may have led to **demand characteristics**. The guards and prisoners may have been acting rather than conforming to their roles. The prisoners and guards were all young and about the same age, and a real prison is an established social community and the prisoners do not all arrive at the same time, so the sample did not represent the population of a real prison.

Milgram (1963): This research is useful as it helps us understand why, in some situations, 'good' people follow orders and do 'bad' things. However, in the 1950s American society was very conformist, and it is possible that participants would be less likely to obey today. The study broke many of today's ethical guidelines.

Moscovici et al. (1969): The experimental method gives control over variables so statements can be made about cause and effect and the study can be replicated. However, the sample is biased and the study has low mundane validity – the experimental procedure does not represent a lifelike social situation. People may not be influenced to change their opinions about social situations as easily as they are about the colour of a slide.

> **Demand characteristics:** aspects of the experiment may act as cues to behaviour that cause the participants (and the experimenter) to change the way they behave.

> **Typical mistake**
>
> Minority influence is not a form of conformity – Moscovici is not an example of research into conformity.

> **Exam tip**
>
> The exams measure knowledge and understanding and to gain high marks you must be able to analyse and evaluate material. Also you must recognise that question commands such as 'Identify, Outline, Describe, Evaluate, Discuss' require different responses. If a question commands you to 'Evaluate', you will not be awarded marks for description.

Summary

You should be able to:
- describe conformity (majority influence) and explain why people conform
- differentiate between informational social influence and normative social influence
- identify, describe and differentiate between types of conformity
- explain the difference between internalisation and compliance
- describe and evaluate research into obedience to authority, including Milgram's work

- identify and explain situational and dispositional reasons for obedience
- identify factors that may increase and explain independent behaviour
- explain why people resist pressures to conform and/or resist pressures to obey authority
- describe and evaluate research into minority influence and identify the characteristics of influential minorities
- discuss, using research evidence, how social influence can affect social change.

Now test yourself

1 (a) Internalisation occurs when ...
   (b) Normative social influence occurs when ...
   (c) Identification occurs when ...
   (d) Majority influence occurs when ...
   (e) Compliance occurs when ...
   (f) Informational social influence occurs when ...
   (g) Minority influence takes place when ...
   (h) Deindividuation occurs when ...
2 Answer TRUE or FALSE to these questions:
   (a) In obedience the emphasis is on social acceptance.
   (b) In obedience the motivation for behaviour is explicit.
   (c) In conformity the motivation for behaviour is implicit.
   (d) In conformity the emphasis is on social acceptance.
   (e) Obedience occurs within a social hierarchy.
   (f) In the Milgram study, 26 of the 40 participants gave 450 volt electric shocks.
   (g) The participants in the Milgram study gave informed consent.
   (h) In an 'agentic state' people hold the authority figure responsible for their action.
   (i) Milgram gave a situational explanation for obedience.
   (j) Adorno agrees with Milgram's explanation of obedience.
3 (a) Identify two characteristics of a person that may influence them to be more obedient.
   (b) Identify two characteristics of a person that may influence them to be less obedient.
   (c) Suggest two factors that may increase conformity.
   (d) Suggest two factors that may decrease obedience.
   (e) When considering resistance to social influence, which one of the following statements is true?
      A An authoritarian personality is more able to resist social influence.
      B A person having an internal locus of control is more able to resist social influence.
      C A person raised in a collectivist culture is more able to resist social influence.
4 (a) Suggest what type of social influence explains the change in public attitudes towards same-sex marriage.
   (b) Identify two characteristics of an influential minority.
   (c) Discuss one limitation of the Moscovici study of minority influence.

Answers on page 232

Typical mistake

Repeating the same 'generic' evaluation point for each research study 'mentioned' in an exam answer, such as 'it lacks ecological validity' or 'it is unethical', is not a good idea. Repeating the same point for every study you mention does not raise the quality of your discussion.

Exam practice

1 Briefly outline and evaluate the findings of any one study of social influence. [4]
2 Social influence research helps us to understand how to change people's attitudes and behaviour: For example, how to persuade people to stop smoking. With reference to this example of social change, explain how psychology might affect the economy. [4]
3 Rosie and Jason were invited to a wedding. Rosie rang all her friends who had been invited to find out ~~~~ wearing a hat. She hadn't planned to wear a hat but when most of her friends said ~~~~ ing one, she changed her mind because she didn't want to look like the 'odd one ~~~~ he had to wear a tie but he refused, saying, 'I don't care what other people think.' ~~~~ nations for conformity. Refer to Rosie and Jason in your discussion. [12]

quick quizzes 1, 2, 3 and 4 online

~~~~wers and quick quizzes at **www.hoddereducation.co.uk/myrevisionnotes**

Memory

Short- and long-term memory

REVISED

Short-term memory (STM) cannot hold much information and has limited capacity. Long-term memory (LTM) can hold an apparently unlimited amount of information and has a vast capacity. See Table 1.1.

George Miller was one of the founders of cognitive psychology and of cognitive neuroscience. Miller is best known for his paper 'The magic number 7 plus and minus 2' (1956), which focused attention on the problem of cognitive overload. He theorised that the capacity of STM is approximately 'seven plus or minus two' pieces of information, but that this capacity can be extended by chunking, or combining, small pieces of information.

> **Capacity:** a measure of how much information can be stored in STM and LTM.
>
> **Duration:** a measure of how long information is held in memory.
>
> **Encoding:** the form in which information is stored in memory.

Table 1.1 Comparison of short- and long-term memory

Comparison	Short-term memory (STM)	Long-term memory (LTM)
Capacity	Limited (7 ± 2 chunks)	Potentially unlimited
Duration	Short (seconds only)	Possibly lifelong
Encoding	Acoustic (sound)	Semantic (meaning)

Research: short term memory

Baddeley (1966) carried out an experiment to show that STM is largely based on acoustic code and found that when testing immediate recall, participants remembered fewer acoustically similar than acoustically dissimilar words.

Jacobs (1987) researched the capacity of STM and found STM has a limited storage capacity of between five and nine items, but learned memory techniques (for example, chunking) may increase capacity as people get older.

Bahrick (1975) studied LTM and found that within 48 years of leaving school, participants could recognise 75% of the faces and names of school friends.

The multi-store model of memory

REVISED

In their **multi-store model of memory**, Atkinson and Shiffrin (1968) suggest that memory comprises three separate stores: the sensory memory store, the STM and the LTM. Each store has a specific function, as shown in Figure 1.1. In the multi-store model, information is rehearsed in the STM and, if rehearsed enough, is transferred to the LTM.

There are three stages of information processing in the multi-store model of memory:
- **Stage 1:** sensory information is perceived (seen, heard, etc.).
- **Stage 2:** the sensory information is transferred to the STM, where it is maintained by rehearsal (if it is not lost or replaced by new, incoming information).
- **Stage 3:** the information is transferred to the LTM.

> **Multi-store model of memory:** the model of memory which proposes that information is passed to a short-term store (STM) where it is held for a brief duration unless rehearsed. Rehearsal leads to transfer to long-term store (LTM).

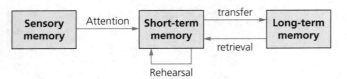

Figure 1.1 The multi-store model

A strength of the multi-store model is that it is simple and can be tested.

In support of the multi-store model of memory, Glanzer and Cunitz (1966) found primacy and recency effects when people were asked to memorise lists of words.

A weakness is that artificial 'free recall' experiments do not replicate the contexts in which memories are created in real life. Also, the model suggests that memory is a passive process, whereas theories of **reconstructive memory** suggest that memory is an active process.

Reconstructive memory: an explanation of how we store and remember long-term memories in terms of social and cultural processes.

Types of long-term memory

REVISED

There are three different types of long-term memory: episodic, semantic and procedural.

Episodic memory is the memory of autobiographical events (times, places, associated emotions, and other contextual who, what, when, where, why knowledge) that can be explicitly stated. Using episodic memory you can remember events and during recollection retrieve contextual information pertaining to a specific event or experience.

Semantic memory refers to the memory of meaning and understanding. Semantic and episodic memory make up the category called declarative memory (explicit memory). With the use of our semantic memory we can give meaning to otherwise meaningless words and sentences.

Procedural memory is a part of the long-term memory that is responsible for knowing how to do things (motor skills). Procedural memory stores information on how to perform certain procedures, such as walking, talking, typing, playing the piano, riding a bike. Procedural memories are implicit and do not involve conscious thought.

The working memory model

REVISED

The Baddeley and Hitch (1974) model of working memory is a model of the STM or, as Baddeley and Hitch call it, working memory. In their model, the STM is an active processor in which the central executive 'attends to and works on' either speech-based information passed to it from the articulatory–phonological loop or visually coded information passed to it by the visual system. The three components of this model, shown in Figure 1.2, are as follows:
- The central executive processes information from all sensory routes. This process is 'attention-like', having limited capacity.
- The articulatory–phonological loop processes speech-based information. The phonological store focuses on speech perception (incoming speech) and the articulatory process focuses on speech production.
- The visuospatial working area (also known as the 'visuospatial sketchpad') is where spatial and visual information is processed.

Exam practice answers and quick quizzes at **www.hoddereducation.co.uk/myrevisionnotes**

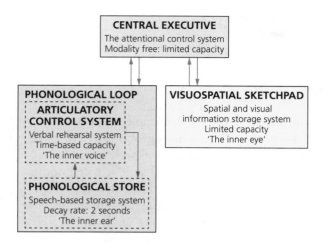

Figure 1.2 The working memory model

The episodic buffer

The working memory model was updated by Baddeley (2000) and an additional component was added called the episodic buffer. The episodic buffer acts as a 'backup' store which communicates with both long-term memory and the components of working memory.

The working memory model can be tested by an interference task technique. This technique is based on the assumption that the articulatory–phonological loop and the visuospatial scratchpad both have limited capacity to process information, so when participants are asked to perform two tasks, using the same system at the same time, their performance is affected.

An advantage of the working memory model is that it suggests that rehearsal is an optional process, which is more realistic than the multi-store model.

The working memory model can explain how we can successfully do two tasks at the same time if the tasks involve different stores, but why we have trouble performing two tasks at the same time if the tasks involve the same stores.

A weakness is that the suggestion that there is a single central executive is theoretical and may be inaccurate.

Explanations for forgetting

REVISED

Interference theory

Memory can be disrupted or interfered with by what we have learned previously or by what we will learn in the future. There are two ways in which interference can cause forgetting:

- **Proactive interference** occurs when you cannot learn a new task because what you already know interferes with what you are currently learning – where old memories disrupt new memories.
- **Retroactive interference** occurs when you forget a previously learned task due to the learning of a new task – in other words, later learning interferes with earlier learning, or new memories disrupt old memories.

> **Revision activity**
>
> Draw and label your own diagram of the working memory model. You may need to do this from memory in an exam.

> **Typical mistake**
>
> Students frequently confuse the working memory model with the multi-store model – remember that the working memory model is a model of the STM.

> **Proactive interference:** occurs when you cannot learn a new task because what we already know interferes with what we are currently learning.
>
> **Retroactive interference:** occurs when you forget a previously learned task due to the learning of a new task.

Proactive and retroactive interference are thought to be more likely to occur where the memories are similar, for example confusing old and new telephone numbers.

Research: Retroactive interference

Postman (1960) investigated how new information interferes with the ability to recall something learned earlier (retroactive interference). In a lab experiment, participants were split into two groups. Both groups had to remember a list of paired words – for example, cat–tree, book–tractor. The experimental group also had to learn another list of words where the second paired word was different – for example, cat–glass, book–revolver. The control group were not given the second list. All participants were asked to recall the words on the first list. The recall of the control group was more accurate than that of the experimental group. Learning items in the second list interfered with participants' ability to recall the list – an example of retroactive interference.

Evaluation

Interference theory does not help us to understand the cognitive processes involved in forgetting. Most research into the role of interference in forgetting has been carried out in a laboratory using lists of words, a situation which is likely to occur fairly infrequently in everyday life (i.e. low ecological validity).

Retrieval failure

When we store a new memory we also store information about the situation, known as retrieval cues. When we come to the same situation again, these retrieval cues can trigger the memory of the situation. Retrieval cues can be:

- **external/context:** cues in the environment, for example smell, place, etc.
- **internal/state:** cues inside us, for example physical, emotional, mood, etc.

Retrieval failure is where the information is in the long-term memory but cannot be accessed (remembered) because the retrieval cues are not present. Information is more likely to be retrieved from the long-term memory if appropriate retrieval cues are present.

Tulving (1974) argued that information is more easily retrieved if the cues present when the information was encoded are also present when the memory is retrieved. The retrieval cues may be information about the physical surroundings (external context) and/or about the physical or psychological state of the person (internal context) at the time the memory was formed. Retrieval cues may be based on context, the setting or situation in which information is encoded and retrieved. Evidence indicates that retrieval is more likely when the context at encoding matches the context at retrieval.

Research: Retrieval

Baddeley (1975) demonstrated the importance of context for retrieval. Baddeley asked deep-sea divers to memorise a list of words. One group did this on the beach and the other group underwater. When they were asked to remember the words, half of the beach learners remained on the beach, the rest had to recall underwater. Half of the underwater group remained there and the others had to recall on the beach. The results show that those who had recalled in the same environment (i.e. context) in which they had learned recalled 40% more words than those recalling in a different environment.

Eyewitness testimony

Loftus and Palmer (1974) researched the accuracy of eyewitness testimony (EWT) by investigating the effect of leading questions. The leading question they asked was based on 'How fast were the cars going when they smashed into each other?' but the verb 'smashed' was varied to lead participants to perceive different speeds for the vehicles.

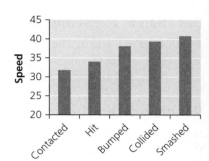

Figure 1.3 Experiment 1: estimated speed for verb used

Experiment 1

Forty-five student participants viewed a short video of a car accident. The participants were divided into five groups of nine. After watching the video, each group was given a questionnaire that included the leading question. However, a different version of the critical question was given to each group, in that the verb varied between 'smashed', 'collided', 'bumped', 'hit' and 'contacted'. As shown in the bar chart in Figure 1.3, the leading question affected the participants' perception of speed.

> **Revision activity**
>
> Explain two differences between Experiment 1 and Experiment 2.

Experiment 2

A group of 150 student participants (three groups of 50) viewed a short video of a car accident. Afterwards they were given a questionnaire. Again, the critical leading question was based on 'How fast were the cars going when they smashed into each other?' However, Group 1 was asked the critical question containing the word 'hit', Group 2 was asked it with the word 'smashed' and Group 3 (the control group) was not asked the leading question. A week later, the participants were asked to return and answer more questions, including 'Did you see any broken glass?' (there was no broken glass in the film clip). The findings are shown in Figure 1.4. Those participants who reported the car was travelling faster (the 'smashed' group) were more likely to report seeing broken glass. This suggests that their memory of a car travelling faster led them to 'invent' a memory in line with this expectation.

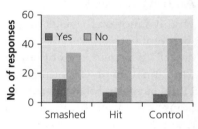

Figure 1.4 Experiment 2: response to 'Did you see any broken glass?'

Case study

Yuille and Cutshall (1986) researched the effect of leading questions on eyewitness accounts of a real event. Twenty-one witnesses to a gun-shooting crime were interviewed by police, and four/five months after the incident, 13 witnesses agreed to be re-interviewed. It was found that misleading questions had no effect.

> **Evaluation**
>
> There is some evidence from real-life studies that recall is not affected by **leading questions** – perhaps because emotional arousal makes the original image stronger. However, the high levels of control in the laboratory experiment meant that it was possible to show clearly that EWT could be affected by the way questions were asked. The results have a useful application in real life – when the testimony of an eyewitness could lead to a person being convicted of a crime.

> **Leading question:** a question that suggests a certain kind of answer.

Factors that may influence eyewitness memory

Estimator and system variables

Estimator variables are factors to do with the witness. They might include levels of stress and whether or not the criminal was carrying a weapon.

System variables are factors where the justice system has some control, such as preventing the use of leading questions.

Duration of event and time of day

The longer we watch, the more likely we are to remember details. Witnesses also remember more when they see something during the day or at night, but remember less when they see something at twilight.

Violence distraction

People have a better memory for non-violent events. Clifford and Scott (1978) showed their participants two short films, one violent and one not, and participants remembered more about the non-violent film.

The amount of time between an event and recall

This will influence memory – the longer the time, the worse the recall. This is known as trace-dependent forgetting. Over time, the memory trace will disappear because when memory circuits are not activated for long periods, the connections between them may weaken to the point where the circuit is broken and the information is lost.

Anxiety (stress)

Highly emotional events may be either more memorable or less memorable than everyday events. **Flashbulb memories** can be described as memories of emotional events that last for a lifetime. Emotional involvement may increase the accuracy of memory, but Freud suggested that **repression** is the way we protect our ego (conscious mind) from unpleasant memories, and that unhappy or traumatic memories are more likely to be forgotten.

Age of a witness

Some research suggests that age affects how well people remember events. Cohen and Faulkner (1989) found that older participants were significantly more likely to be misled by leading questions.

Improving the accuracy of eyewitness testimony

REVISED

The cognitive interview (Geiselman 1985)

The **cognitive interview** is a procedure used by the police to help eyewitnesses recall information more accurately. This type of interview has been found to achieve up to 35% improvement in the accuracy of recall. During the interview the witness is encouraged to:
- report every detail, no matter how seemingly trivial
- recreate the context of the event
- recall the event in different orders (in reverse, partially, etc.)
- recall the event from other perspectives (imagining what someone else may have seen).

While the interview is progressing, the police take care to:
- reduce the anxiety felt by witnesses
- minimise any distractions
- allow the witness to take their time
- avoid interruptions and leading questions.

> **Exam tip**
> Make a note that if an exam question asks you to 'discuss explanations for forgetting' you could argue that the psychodynamic approach gives an alternative explanation for why people forget.

> **Flashbulb memory:** an accurate and long-lasting memory of the details of the context of an event created at a time of intense emotion.
>
> **Repression:** a method of keeping anxiety-provoking information out of conscious awareness – called 'motivated forgetting'.

> **Revision activity**
> Make a chart identifying the factors that influence eyewitness memory and why those factors affect memory.

> **Cognitive interview:** an interview procedure used by the police to help eyewitnesses recall information more accurately.

Fisher *et al.* (1989) found that the cognitive interview gained 47% more facts than were gained in a standard interview and concluded that the cognitive interview is a useful technique for improving EWT.

Summary

You should be able to:

- describe and evaluate the multi-store model of memory
- explain the concepts of memory encoding, capacity and duration
- describe and evaluate the working memory model
- differentiate between the multi-store model of memory and the working memory model
- explain how proactive interference and retroactive interference may lead to forgetting
- suggest how retrieval cues help us remember information

- define what is meant by eyewitness memory
- describe and evaluate research into eyewitness memory
- identify factors affecting the accuracy of EWT
- explain how misleading information and anxiety can affect EWT
- describe psychological research into improving accuracy of EWT
- describe the procedures involved in a cognitive interview and explain why the cognitive interview should increase the accuracy of witness recall.

Now test yourself

TESTED

1 (a) Outline two differences between STM and LTM.
  (b) What is meant by the 'primacy–recency effect'?
  (c) Why does the primacy–recency effect support the multi-store model?
  (d) What is episodic memory?
  (e) What is procedural memory?
  (f) What does semantic memory allow us to do?
  (g) Name the three components of the working memory model.
  (h) Which component of the working memory model processes speech?
  (i) Explain how to use the interference task technique to find evidence to support the working memory model.
2 (a) What do psychologists mean when they say 'he can't remember because of retrieval failure'?
  (b) A class of students was asked to listen to a person reciting a list of two-digit numbers at a rate of one number per second, for example 25, 54, 63, and then asked to write down the numbers they had heard. The average recall of the 15 two-digit numbers recited was 4. Which characteristic of STM best explains why the students remembered so few of the numbers?
  (c) In the morning Ayesha revised for her Spanish exam and after lunch she revised her Italian vocabulary. In the test she did poorly in Spanish but better in Italian. Explain how retroactive interference may have affected her Spanish test.
  (d) What is meant by a 'retrieval cue'?
  (e) Explain the difference between external retrieval cues and internal retrieval cues.
  (f) Twenty students were given the names of 20 cities (for example, Bristol, London, Liverpool, Leeds) to memorise and then given one minute to write down all the names they remembered. Ten students stayed in the same classroom for the memory test but ten were taken to a different room. Explain why the students who stayed in the same room remembered more of the cities.
3 (a) What is a leading question?
  (b) Loftus and Palmer researched the effect of leading questions on eyewitness memory. Outline one of the findings of Experiment 1.
  (c) Loftus and Palmer found that the verb 'smashed' in the leading question created a false memory for seeing broken glass. Explain how the false memory was created.
  (d) List one difference between Loftus and Palmer's Experiment 1 and Experiment 2.
  (e) Suggest one criticism of Loftus and Palmer's research.
  (f) Identify two factors that may influence eyewitness memory.
  (g) Briefly outline how the cognitive interview may trigger memories for an event.

Answers on page 232

Exam practice

1 Read the item and answer the questions:

Twenty student participants were shown a short film of a robbery. They were then divided into two groups and were interviewed about the film. One group was interviewed in the same room where they watched the film and the other group was taken to be interviewed in a different room. The standard interview technique was used. A memory score was calculated for each participant, ranging from 0–20, where a score of 20 meant everything recalled was accurate. The results are shown in Table 1.2.

Table 1.2 Memory scores for the 'same room' and 'different room' condition

Different room	Same room
5	9
6	8
6	10
8	12
6	11
5	14
5	13
4	10
9	18
3	15

(a) Identify an appropriate measure of central tendency for calculating the average of the scores in each of the two groups. Justify your answer. [2]

(b) Calculate the measure of central tendency you identified in (a). [2]

(c) Almost all the participants in the same room condition recalled more information about the filmed car crash than those interviewed in a different room. Using your knowledge of forgetting, explain why this may have occurred. [2]

(d) Jenny has worked in the call centre for five years. While she listens to and responds to each customer she uses her keyboard to enter information to the computer system so that her screen gives her up-to-date information. The trainee at the next screen always asks the customer to wait while he enters the information as he finds it difficult to type, read the screen and listen to what the customer is saying at the same time. How does the working memory model explain the difference between Jenny and the trainee? [4]

(e) During a robbery in a petrol station carried out by two masked men, the cashier was threatened. Afterwards, a person who witnessed the robbery was being questioned. 'Did you see which robber was holding the knife?' asked the police officer. The witness said 'Um, well I think it was the short one, but it was such a shock when they ran in and started shouting and I was scared. I hid behind the DVD display because I didn't want them to notice me.'
Discuss research into factors that affect the reliability of eyewitness testimony. Refer to the information above in your answer. [16]

(f) Describe and evaluate the multi-store model of memory. [16]

Answers and quick quizzes 5, 6 and 7 online

ONLINE

Typical mistake

Students often make the mistake of writing an evaluation that is a 'list' of generalisations about laboratory research lacking ecological validity or samples being unrepresentative, with little attempt at explaining how the evaluative issues raised relate to the context of the question.

Attachment

Schaffer (1993) defines attachment as 'a close emotional relationship between two persons characterised by mutual affection and a desire to maintain closeness'. Attachments are strong emotional bonds that form as a result of interaction between two people.

Caregiver–infant interactions

REVISED

Interaction between caregiver and infant helps to develop and maintain attachment. Interactions include **reciprocity**, imitation, **interactional synchrony** and the use of modified language.

- **Interactional synchrony and reciprocity:** Condon and Sander (1974) analysed the movements of babies while adults were speaking to them. They found that the babies 'moved in time' with the conversation and appeared to 'take turns'. They described this as reciprocal behaviour. Reciprocal behaviour is behaviour that is produced as a response to the behaviour of another person, or behaviour that is produced to elicit a response from another person. Interactional synchrony refers to how a parent's speech and an infant's behaviour become finely coordinated and synchronised so that they are in direct response to one another.
- **Imitation:** Melzoff and Moore (1977) found that 2–3-week-old babies spontaneously imitated adult facial expressions and movements.
- **Modified language:** Caregivers modify their language and use 'motherese' when they speak to young babies. Motherese is a slow, high-pitched repetitive way of speaking in short, simple sentences and varying tone. The use of motherese may contribute to effective turn-taking and aid attachment.

> **Reciprocity:** during caregiver-infant interaction, reciprocal behaviour is behaviour that is produced as a response to the behaviour of another person or behaviour that is produced to elicit a response from another person.
>
> **Interactional synchrony:** the behaviour of caregivers and infants who 'move in time' with each other and who appear to take turns communicating.

Evaluation

Studies with animals (Harlow's monkeys) suggest that infant–caregiver interaction is important for the development of attachment but even if babies do imitate facial expressions this imitation may not be intentional communication, also there is no direct evidence that the use of motherese influences attachment.

Isabella *et al.* (1989) researched interactional synchrony and observed infants at one, three and nine months old while interacting with their caregiver (mother) and found that mother–infant pairs who were developing **secure attachments** were observed to interact in a well-timed, reciprocal and mutually rewarding manner, but those developing insecure relationships were characterised by interactions in which mothers were minimally involved or unresponsive to infant signals.

> **Secure attachment:** a form of attachment which is optimal for healthy cognitive and emotional development.

Stages of attachment

Rudolph Schaffer and Peggy Emerson (1964) studied 60 babies at monthly intervals for the first 18 months of life (a longitudinal study). They discovered that babies' attachments develop in the following sequence:

- **Up to three months of age:** indiscriminate attachments. The newborn is predisposed to attach to any human. Most babies respond equally to any caregiver.
- **After four months:** preference for certain people. Infants learn to distinguish primary and secondary caregivers but accept care from anyone.
- **After seven months:** special preference for a single attachment figure and shows fear of strangers (stranger fear) and unhappiness when separated from a special person (separation anxiety).
- **After nine months:** multiple attachments. The baby becomes increasingly independent and forms several attachments.

Attachments were most likely to form with those who responded accurately to the baby's signals, not the person they spent most time with. Many of the babies had several attachments by ten months old. The mother was the main attachment figure for about half of the children at 18 months old and the father for most of the others.

Animal studies of attachment

Harlow (1958) studied monkeys to identify the mechanisms by which newborn rhesus monkeys bond to their mothers. Infant rhesus monkeys are dependent on their mothers for nutrition, protection, comfort and socialisation and Harlow wanted to find the underlying basis for the attachment. The behavioural theory of attachment suggests that an infant would form an attachment with a carer who provides food. The evolutionary theory suggests that infants have an innate (biological) need to touch and cling to something for emotional comfort.

Infant monkeys reared with surrogate mothers

Eight monkeys were separated from their mothers immediately after birth and placed in cages with access to two surrogate mothers, one made of wire and one covered in soft terry towelling cloth. Four of the monkeys could get milk from the wire mother and four from the cloth mother. The animals were studied for 165 days. Both groups of monkeys spent more time with the cloth mother. The infant would go to the wire mother only when hungry and would return to the cloth mother for most of the day. The cloth mother was more effective in decreasing the youngster's fear. The infant would explore more when the cloth mother was present. This supports the evolutionary theory of attachment, in that it is the sensitive response and security of the caregiver that is important rather than the provision of food. Harlow concluded that for a monkey to develop normally, it must have some interaction with an object to which it can cling during the first months of life (critical period).

Deprivation: in terms of attachment, deprivation refers to the experience of attachment bond disruption as a result of separation from the attachment figure for a period of time.

Lorenz's imprinting theory

Lorenz (1935) took a large clutch of goose eggs which were ready to hatch and placed half under a goose mother and the others beside himself. When the geese hatched (like the one in Figure 1.5), Lorenz imitated a mother goose honking and the young birds regarded him as their mother and followed him accordingly. Lorenz found that geese follow the first moving object they see during a 12–17-hours critical period after hatching. This process is known as imprinting and suggests that attachment is innate and is programmed genetically. Imprinting occurs without any feeding taking place and has consequences both for short-term survival and in the longer term, forming internal templates for later relationships. Research suggests that after 32 hours imprinting is unlikely to occur.

Figure 1.5 A gosling like the one hatched in the Lorenz (1935) study

The evolutionary function of imprinting is probably to enable the animal to recognise close kin because in the natural environment behavioural imprinting results in the formation of a strong bond between offspring and parent. The parent must recognise the offspring in order to not waste energy caring for the young of others. The offspring must recognise its parent because it might be killed by adults of the same species that do not recognise it as their own.

Exam tip

Nature or nurture? When you revise this topic, make a note of this IDA point that can be included in exam answers. According to Harlow, because the infant monkeys explored more when the cloth mother was present, this supports the evolutionary (nature) theory of attachment, in that it is the sensitive response and security of the caregiver that is important rather than the provision of food (nurture). According to Lorenz, the imprinted attachment is innate (nature) and is not learned (nurture).

Explanations of attachment

REVISED

The behavioural explanation (learning theory)

This theory suggests that attachment is learned behaviour (nurture). The basis for the learning of attachments is the provision of food. An infant will initially form an attachment because it learns to associate the feeder (usually the mother) with the comfort of being fed and, through the process of classical conditioning, learns to find contact with the mother comforting.

Behavioural theorists propose that an infant's emotional dependence on, and bond with, its caregiver can be explained in terms of reinforcement arising from the satisfaction of basic physiological needs, such as food and drink. The mother (or caregiver) relieves these needs and thus acquires reward value as the infant learns to associate pleasure with the caregiver.

Based on classical conditioning, receiving food gives the infant pleasure, so when the caregiver feeds him or her, the infant feels pleasure. Thus an association is formed between the caregiver and food, so that whenever the caregiver is near, the infant feels pleasure – expressed as attachment behaviour.

Based on operant conditioning, infants feel discomfort when they are hungry and so desire food to remove the discomfort. They learn that if they cry, their caregiver feeds them and the discomfort is removed. This is negative reinforcement: the consequences of behaviour (crying) lead to something unpleasant ceasing (feeling hungry stops). Thus, proximity-seeking behaviour is reinforced, which in turn leads to the attachment behaviour of distress on being separated from the caregiver.

> ### Evaluation
>
> Feeding cannot fully explain the development of attachments. Harlow's baby monkeys showed a preference for the cloth-covered mother, especially when they were distressed. Harlow also found that, as adults, these monkeys found it difficult to form reproductive relationships and were poor mothers, suggesting that the lack of interaction with a caregiver has a long-term effect and may cause later maladjustment.

> ### Typical mistake
>
> In the exam, students often state that both Harlow and Lorenz challenge the learning theory of attachment – but don't explain why!

The evolutionary explanation

The evolutionary theory of attachment (nature) suggests that infants come into the world biologically pre-programmed to form attachments with others because this will help them to survive. The infant produces innate 'social releaser' behaviours such as crying and smiling that stimulate innate caregiving responses from adults.

Bowlby's theory of attachment (1969)

Bowlby proposed that attachment between human infants and their caregivers is adaptive behaviour (evolutionary explanation). He suggested that there is a sensitive period that ends at around 1–3 years, during which infants develop a special attachment to one individual. Bowlby suggested that social behaviours, such as following, clinging, sucking, smiling and crying, are innate and that infants are born with an innate drive to form attachments, as well as possessing characteristics (social releasers, such as smiles) that facilitate the caregiver's attachment to them. According to Bowlby, attachment is an interactive and innate two-way relationship, in which the caregiver is as attached as the infant. The role of attachment is adaptive, as it promotes survival by (a) maintaining proximity (closeness) between infant and caregiver, (b) assisting cognitive development, and (c) providing the opportunity for learning through imitation.

Bowlby proposed that infants have many attachments but that the one at the top of the hierarchy has special significance for emotional development. The infant becomes most closely attached to the individual who responds in the most sensitive manner, which leads the infant to have one primary attachment object (monotropy). The primary attachment object need not be the infant's biological mother. The child learns from the relationship with the primary caregiver and this relationship acts as a template for future relationships. Bowlby called this an **internal working model** (a cognitive schema) that generates expectations for all future relationships.

Bowlby proposed that the development of attachments follows an innate maturational sequence:

Phase 1: birth to 8 weeks
- Orientation and signals are directed towards people without discrimination.
- Infants behave in friendly ways towards other people but their ability to discriminate between them is limited.

Phase 2: 8–10 weeks to 6 months
- Orientation and signals are directed towards one or more special people.
- There is beginning to be a difference of behaviour towards one primary caregiver.

Phase 3: 6 months to 1–2 years old
- Closeness to a special person is maintained by means of locomotion as well as signals.
- The infant displays separation anxiety, greets the caregiver when he or she returns, and uses the caregiver as a safe base from which to explore.
- The infant selects other people as subsidiary attachment figures but treats strangers with caution (stranger anxiety).

Factors that influence the development of attachments

- **The age of the child:** Bowlby proposed that unless attachments have developed by between one and three years, they will not develop 'normally'.
- **The child's temperament:** some aspects of temperament may be innate and a child's temperament may make it easier or harder for him or her to form attachments.
- **The quality of care:** psychologists suggest that the sensitivity of the caregiver can also affect the development of attachments. Ainsworth *et al.* (1974) proposed that attachment is related to the quality of the interactions between the infant and the caregiver. In support of this theory, Isabella *et al.* (1989) found that responsiveness in the mother towards a one-month-old baby correlated with a close relationship between mother and baby at one year.

The Strange Situation: Ainsworth and Bell (1970)

REVISED

Ainsworth and Bell developed the Strange Situation procedures to measure differences in infant attachment. The Strange Situation involves controlled observation that allows researchers to assess how securely an infant is attached to a caregiver. It comprises seven episodes, each lasting about three minutes:

1 The caregiver carries the infant into a room, puts the infant on the floor and then sits in a chair and does not interact with the infant unless the infant seeks attention.

> **Internal working model:** the first attachment creates an internal working model (a cognitive schema) for all future relationships that gives the child a feel for what a relationship is.

> **Exam tip**
> If, as Bowlby suggests, infant attachment is innate, then stages of development of attachment should be the same in all cultures. In an exam you could show your understanding of research methods by explaining how evidence from cross-cultural research could be used to suggest whether or not attachment is innate.

2 A stranger enters the room and talks with the caregiver, then approaches the infant with a toy.

3 The caregiver leaves. If the infant plays, the stranger observes unobtrusively. If the infant is passive, the stranger tries to interest them in a toy. If the infant shows distress (crying), the stranger tries to comfort them.

4 The caregiver returns and the stranger leaves.

5 After the infant begins to play, the caregiver leaves and the infant is briefly left alone.

6 The stranger re-enters the room and repeats the behaviour as described in step 3.

7 The caregiver returns and the stranger leaves.

The Strange Situation procedure places the infant in a mildly stressful situation in order to observe four types of behaviour:

- Separation anxiety – a securely attached child shows some anxiety but is fairly easily soothed.
- Willingness to explore – a securely attached child explores more when the caregiver is present.
- Stranger anxiety – the degree of security of attachment is related to the degree of stranger anxiety.
- Reunion behaviour – an insecurely attached infant may ignore the caregiver's return.

Research: Strange Situation

Main *et al.* (1985) conducted a longitudinal study. Infants were assessed in the Strange Situation before the age of 18 months with both their mothers and fathers. When the children were re-tested at the age of 6 years, the researchers found considerable consistency in security of attachment to both parents. Of the secure babies, 100% were classified as securely attached to both parents at 6 years and 75% of avoidant babies were reclassified as avoidant at age 6.

Exam tip

You need to be able to describe the four types of behaviour observed in the Strange Situation. In an exam you could be given a description of the behaviour of a young child who has been separated from a caregiver and be asked to suggest whether the child is securely attached or not.

Types of attachment

REVISED

There are individual and cultural differences in styles of attachment. For example, some infants are securely attached whereas others are insecurely attached.

- **Secure attachment:** securely attached infants show some anxiety when their caregiver departs but are easily soothed and greet the caregiver's return with enthusiasm. These infants play independently and return to the caregiver regularly for reassurance. Secure attachment is associated with sensitivity in the caregiver, which teaches the infant to expect the same in other relationships. Secure attachment is generally related to healthy cognitive and emotional development, involving independence, self-confidence and trusting relationships.
- **Insecure–avoidant attachment:** the infant shows indifference when the caregiver leaves and does not display stranger anxiety. At reunion

the infant actively avoids contact with the caregiver. The caregiver tends to be insensitive and may ignore the infant during play. These infants play independently.

- **Insecure–resistant attachment:** the infant is distressed when the caregiver goes and although when the caregiver returns, he or she rushes to the caregiver, the infant is not easily consoled. The infant may resist contact with the caregiver, or may seek comfort and reject it at the same time. These children explore less than other children.

Main and Solomon (1986) added a fourth type of attachment, disorganised attachment, in which there are no set patterns of behaviour at separation or reunion.

Typical mistake

Do not confuse insecure–avoidant attachment with insecure–resistant attachment.

Cultural variations in the development of attachment

REVISED

If infant attachment is innate, then attachment behaviour should be similar in all cultures.

Sagi, van Ijzendoorn and Koren-Karie (1991) studied attachment styles of infants in the USA, Israel, Japan and Germany. They reported as follows:
- **American children:** 71% secure attachment, 12% insecure–resistant, 17% insecure–avoidant.
- **Israeli children:** 62% secure attachment, 33% insecure–resistant, 5% insecure–avoidant. The children in the kibbutz were looked after by adults who were not their family, but they saw few strangers, which may explain why the children were not anxious when their caregiver left but were anxious when the stranger appeared.
- **Japanese children:** 68% secure attachment, 32% insecure–resistant and few insecure–avoidant. It was noted that Japanese children are rarely left by their mother, so the mother leaving during the Strange Situation may have been particularly stressful.
- **German children:** 40% securely attached, 49% insecure–avoidant, 11% insecure–resistant. German children are encouraged to be independent and not to be 'clingy'. The high percentage of insecure–avoidant children may reflect the cultural ethos of valuing independence.

Analysis of Strange Situation studies

Van Ijzendoorn and Kroonenberg (1988) compared the results of 32 Strange Situation studies in eight countries (involving 2,000 children).

Table 1.3 Comparison of Strange Situation studies in various countries

Country	Number of studies	Percentage of each attachment type		
		Secure	Avoidant	Resistant
West Germany	3	57	35	8
Great Britain	1	75	22	3
Netherlands	4	67	26	7
Sweden	1	74	22	4
Israel	2	64	7	29
Japan	2	68	5	27
China	1	50	25	25
USA	18	65	21	14
Average		65	20	14

Criticism

Variations within one **culture** were 1.5 times greater than variations between cultures, which suggests that one culture may comprise several subcultures. Some sample sizes were small, for example only 36 Chinese children were used, and it may be unsafe to generalise the results to all Chinese infants. The Strange Situation is based on US culture and observed behaviour may not have the same meaning in different cultures. The use of procedures developed in one culture may not be a valid measure of behaviour in another culture.

> **Culture:** the beliefs, attitudes, social and child-rearing practices, etc., that people of a group share and that distinguish one group from other groups.

Bowlby's theory of maternal deprivation

Separation is when a child is separated from its attachment figure for a relatively short period of time.

Maternal deprivation occurs when a child has formed an attachment but then experiences the loss of the mother or other attachment figure so that the attachment bond is broken. Bowlby (1953) proposed that long-term maternal deprivation – the loss of the mother figure or other attachment figure – is harmful: 'Mother love in infancy and childhood is as important for mental health as are vitamins and proteins for physical health' (Bowlby 1951).

Bowlby suggested that continuous 'maternal care' is necessary for emotional and cognitive development (maternal care may be provided by a 'mother substitute'). According to Bowlby, deprivation of the primary caregiver during the critical period (before the age of 30 months) has harmful effects on the child's emotional, social and cognitive development. The long-term effects may include separation anxiety, expressed as 'clingy behaviour' and reluctance to attend school, and future relationships may be affected by emotional insecurity.

Maternal **privation** is when a child has never been able to form a close relationship (develop an attachment) with any one caregiver.

> **Revision activity**
>
> In an exam you might be asked to apply Bowlby's theory of maternal deprivation to a hypothetical situation. Make a list of examples in which maternal deprivation could occur.
>
> For example: John is one year old. His mother, who has been his primary caregiver, is injured in a car accident and hospitalised for six months.

Romanian orphan studies

In 1989 the Ceauşescu regime in Romania was overthrown and there were found to be thousands of babies and children in orphanages, many of whom had suffered severe emotional and physical deprivation.

> **Privation:** a lack of any attachment bonds which may lead to permanent emotional damage.

The English and Romanian Adoptee (ERA) project was a longitudinal, multi-method investigation of the development of children adopted into the UK from Romania in the early 1990s. The ERA, led by Professor Michael Rutter and Professor Edmund Sonuga-Barke, followed a random sample of 165 Romanian children, most of whom had spent their early lives in institutions in which conditions were very poor. The aim was to examine the extent to which children could recover when extreme deprivation in early life is followed by a middle childhood within a safe family environment.

Rutter (2007) studied children who had been adopted after having lived with deprivation or privation. Initial findings showed that the children suffered from poor health and also had behaviour issues such as temper tantrums, excessive rocking, insomnia and indiscriminate friendliness. One hundred and eleven Romanian children who were adopted in England before they were two years old were compared with 52 children of similar ages adopted within England. Rutter found that, on adoption, the Romanian children had poor physical health and an average IQ of 63. When these children were assessed again (the children were assessed at the ages of 4, 6 and 11 years), the average IQ for those adopted before the age of 6 months had gone from 63 to 107, but for those adopted after the age of 6 months the average IQ had increased only from 45 to 90. Rutter also studied attachment and did not produce positive findings. Some of the Romanian children continued to experience serious behavioural problems both in general and when it came to the issue of forming a bond with their adoptive parents.

Another study conducted in Canada looked at similar Romanian orphans adopted by Canadian families. This study involved three separate groups of children:
- Canadian children who had not been adopted
- a group of Romanian children whose median age was 18 and a half months
- a group of Romanian children who were adopted before they reached four months old.

The researchers found no difference in the attachments formed by children in Groups 1 and 3. Group 2, however, had attachment difficulties, although most eventually formed attachments with their adoptive parents. The conclusion was that the longer children are institutionalised, the harder it becomes for them to form attachments.

The influence of early attachment on childhood and adult relationships

REVISED

Based on Freud's idea that the mother–child relationship acts as a prototype for all future attachments, Bowlby believed that an attachment creates an internal working model (a cognitive schema) for all future relationships and that this first attachment forms a template or schema that gives the child a feel for what a relationship is. An internal working model is a set of expectations and beliefs about the self, others and the relationship between the self and others. Thus, the internal working model of an individual will contain particular expectations and beliefs about:
- my own and other people's behaviour
- whether or not I am loveable and worthy of love
- whether or not others will help and support me.

Internal working models begin to be formed in early infancy. If the baby finds that his feelings of hunger and his crying behaviour result in a prompt response from a loving adult, he learns that he is loved and nurtured and that he 'deserves' this response. Alternatively, a response that is unavailable or cold will lead to an internal working model of the attachment figure as rejecting and others as not to be relied on for help and support. Children's behaviours become organised around their expectations of themselves and others and these expectations tend to influence the way in which others relate to them.

The internal working model is used in future years to develop other relationships and is particularly important in determining parenting skills in later life. For example, a secure attachment as a child leads to greater emotional and social stability as an adult, whereas an insecure attachment is likely to lead to difficulties with later relationships and is likely to be reflected in the parenting style when the child matures and has children of their own.

Typical mistake

Do not confuse maternal privation with maternal deprivation.

Exam tip

The Rutter studies of Romanian orphans are longitudinal research. In an exam you could show your understanding of research methods by explaining the strengths and limitations of longitudinal research.

Revision activity

'The mother–child relationship acts as a prototype for future attachments.' Referring to the 'internal working model', write a paragraph explaining what this means. Make notes on this theory because in an exam you could be given a hypothetical case study of a child who has been in some way 'institutionalised' and asked to explain the child's behaviour in terms of the development of 'an internal working model'. Make sure you can explain why it is difficult to 'prove' a relationship between a hypothetical internal model and adult behaviour.

Summary

You should be able to:

- define examples of caregiver–infant interactions
- describe and evaluate the learning theory of attachment
- describe and evaluate Bowlby's explanation of attachment
- describe the characteristics of three types of attachment: secure attachment, insecure–avoidant and insecure–resistant
- describe the procedures used in the Strange Situation
- explain how the Strange Situation is used in attachment research

- describe research into cultural variations in attachment
- explain how attachment creates an internal working model
- explain the effects of disruption of attachment and differentiate between disruption of attachment and privation
- describe research into the failure to form attachment (privation)
- describe and evaluate research into the effect of institutional care.

Now test yourself

TESTED

1 (a) Write a definition for the term attachment.
  (b) Define interactional synchrony.
  (c) Suggest how caregiver–infant interaction may influence the development of attachment.
  (d) Outline the stages of attachment.
  (e) Identify the age at which a child develops multiple attachments.
  (f) In Harlow's study of monkeys, describe the difference between the two surrogate mothers.
  (g) Attachment: nature or nurture? What did Harlow conclude?
2 (a) Suggest one difference between imprinting and attachment.
  (b) Give one reason why research with non-human animals is useful.
  (c) Give one reason why research with non-human animals is not useful.
  (d) Outline how behaviourist psychologists explain attachment.
  (e) Outline the procedure used in the Strange Situation.
  (f) Describe four types of behaviour that are observed in the Strange Situation.
  (g) Explain why attachment is adaptive.
  (h) Why is Bowlby's theory of attachment a 'nature' rather than a 'nurture' theory of attachment?
  (i) Outline how the behaviour of a securely attached infant differs from that of one who is insecurely attached.
3 (a) Psychologists have found that several factors influence the development of attachments. Which one of the following factors does not influence the development of attachment?
    (i) the age of the child
    (ii) intelligence of parents
    (iii) the child's temperament.
  (b) In cross-cultural research, Sagi, van Ijzendoorn and Koren-Karie (1991) studied attachment styles of infants in eight countries. Which one of the following countries was not included in this research: Great Britain, Japan, Sweden, France, USA?
  (c) Fill in the blanks:
    (i) Bowlby said infants form _____, rather than multiple, attachments.
    (ii) Harlow said that _____ is essential to an infant's psychological health.
    (iii) Lorenz said through _____ chicks attach to the first moving object they see.

Answers on page 234

Exam practice

1 (a) Discuss the problems faced when researching caregiver–infant interaction. [4]
  (b) Outline and evaluate learning theory as an explanation of attachment formation. [8]
  (c) Compare Bowlby's explanation of attachment with the learning theory of attachment. [4]
  (d) Explain ethical problems associated with an observational study of children. [4]
  (e) Evaluate research into the effects of disruption of attachment. [8]

Answers and quick quizzes 8, 9, 10 and 11 online

ONLINE

Psychopathology

Definitions of abnormality REVISED

Abnormality as behaviour that deviates from the statistical norm

Some psychologists propose that behaviour is normally distributed. If this is true, then people whose behaviour is different (more than two standard deviations above or below the mean) can be defined as 'abnormal'.

Criticism

This accounts for the frequency of behaviour, not its desirability. It does not allow us to distinguish between rare behaviour that is eccentric (elective) and rare behaviour that is psychologically abnormal. Some behaviour, such as **depression**, is psychologically abnormal but is not that rare.

Abnormality as behaviour that deviates from the social norm

Some people behave in socially deviant ways. Because their behaviour does not fit in with social norms or meet social expectations, they are seen as different. For example, a person who has 20 cats in their home may be seen as abnormal.

Criticism

This definition could be used to discriminate against people whom the majority disapprove of and want to remove from society. Whether behaviour is seen as normal depends on its context.

Social norms and attitudes change – homosexuality was believed to be a mental illness until the 1970s. Social norms vary within and between cultures.

Abnormality as failure to function adequately

People who cannot look after themselves or who are perceived to be irrational or out of control are often described as abnormal. The problem with this is that it involves others in making value judgements about what it means to function adequately. The individuals themselves may not think they have a problem and their unusual behaviour may be a way of coping with their difficulties in life.

Abnormality as deviation from ideal mental health

Jahoda (1958) identified six conditions associated with ideal mental health:
1 A positive self-attitude and high self-esteem
2 A drive to realise self-potential (personal growth)
3 The ability to cope with stress
4 Being in control and making your own decisions (personal autonomy)
5 An accurate perception of reality and the ability to feel for others
6 The ability to adapt to changes in one's environment

> **Abnormality:** a psychological condition, or behaviour, that differs from how most people behave and that is harmful, or which causes distress to the individual or those around them.
>
> **Depression:** a mental disorder that causes people to experience a depressed mood.

Criticism

The degree to which a person meets the six criteria may vary over time, so the degree to which any individual can be defined as 'normal' might vary from day to day.

It is a subjective standard – it is difficult to measure self-esteem and self-potential. It is also an ethnocentric standard – it describes normality from a Western individualistic rather than from a collectivist cultural standpoint.

> **Revision activity**
>
> In the exam you could be given a statement or description such as 'Approximately 1% of the population suffer from schizophrenia' and asked to apply the definitions of abnormality. Make sure you understand the difference between the definitions and the strengths and limitations of each definition.

The characteristics of phobias, depression and OCD

REVISED

Phobic disorders

Phobias are a form of anxiety disorder in which the emotional response to an often harmless object (for example, a spider) has become chronic and disabling fear. Phobias consist of irrational fears that are out of proportion to the reality of the threat provided by the fear-provoking stimulus.

> **Phobia:** an anxiety disorder involving an overwhelming and debilitating fear of something.

- **Physical symptoms:** the body's response to stress, such as breathlessness and tightness in the chest, hyperventilation (increased breathing) and palpitations (increased heart rate).
- **Behavioural symptoms:** avoidance behaviour is shown as the individual usually avoids the feared object, which can restrict their everyday behaviour.
- **Emotional symptoms:** anxiety is accompanied by a feeling of dread. The individual is frightened and distressed and may feel they are about to die or lose control of their bodily functions.
- **Cognitive symptoms:** anxiety can decrease concentration and so impair the person's ability to perform complex tasks. Reduced cognitive capacity can inhibit workplace functioning.
- **Social symptoms:** anxiety may reduce the individual's ability to cope with social settings and so inhibit personal and social functioning.

Diagnostic criteria

Those who suffer from a phobia:
- have a persistent fear of a specific object or situation
- find that exposure to the fear-provoking stimulus produces a rapid anxiety response
- recognise that the fear experienced is excessive
- either avoid the phobic stimulus or respond with great anxiety
- find the phobic reactions interfere with their working or social life.

Obsessive compulsive disorder

Obsessive compulsive disorder (OCD) is a severe anxiety disorder thought to affect around 1–3% of the UK population (source: National Institute of Mental Health). OCD affects both men and women equally.

> **OCD:** obsessive compulsive disorder – an anxiety disorder that involves obsessive thoughts and compulsive behaviour.

Exam practice answers and quick quizzes at **www.hoddereducation.co.uk/myrevisionnotes**

- **Physical symptoms:** the body's response to stress, such as breathlessness and tightness in the chest, hyperventilation (increased breathing) and palpitations (increased heart rate).
- **Behavioural symptoms:** compulsive behaviour – the irresistible urge to carry out repetitive behaviour to avoid some form of danger.
- **Emotional symptoms:** anxiety and depression – OCD can last a few years or decades and sufferers can go through intermittent periods of depression.
- **Cognitive symptoms:** obsession is the persistent and recurrent thoughts and images which enter the mind and cannot be removed.

Diagnostic criteria

Those who suffer from OCD:
- acknowledge the problem but are powerless to overcome it
- suffer from severe anxiety (leading to symptoms)
- suffer from severe depression (i.e. a symptom)
- experience onset in their late teens/early 20s
- experience either obsession or compulsion
- find obsessions and/or compulsions in their daily routine are time consuming.

Depression (unipolar)

Depression is a mood disorder in which a negative emotional state colours a person's thoughts and behaviour. Clinical depression occurs when depression lasts a long time and affects a person's ability to function normally. Depressive illness is the cause of more than 25% of all deaths by suicide.
- **Physical symptoms:** aches and pains, lack of energy, loss of weight and appetite.
- **Behavioural symptoms:** sufferers stop socialising, lose interest in sex, may attempt suicide, take longer to complete daily activities.
- **Emotional symptoms:** feelings of sadness and despair, and absence of feeling, little or no interest in everyday activities.
- **Cognitive symptoms:** memory and concentration are affected, sufferers think negatively and may consider committing suicide, also suffer from persistent worrying.

Diagnostic criteria

Diagnosis requires five or more symptoms, including for at least two weeks:
- extreme sadness
- tearfulness
- depressed mood
- loss of interest in, and pleasure in, usual activities as well as social withdrawal.

The behavioural approach to explaining and treating phobias

REVISED

The behavioural approach makes three assumptions. First, it assumes that all behaviour is learned; second, that what has been learned can be unlearned; and third, that abnormal behaviour is learned in the same way as normal behaviour. This model sees the abnormal behaviour as the problem and not a symptom of an underlying cause.

Behaviourists propose that **classical conditioning** can explain phobias. In classical conditioning, an unconditioned stimulus, such as an unexpected loud noise, triggers a natural reflex, for example the startle response and fear. But if another stimulus, such as seeing a spider, occurs at the same time, this may in future elicit the fear response. Watson and Rayner (1920) demonstrated how classical conditioning could explain the way in which fear could be learned.

Behaviourists also propose that abnormal behaviour can be learned by the process of operant conditioning, in which behaviour is learned through the consequences of our actions. If our actions result in rewarding consequences (positive reinforcement), or in something nasty ceasing (negative reinforcement), we will repeat the behaviour, but we will not repeat behaviour that has bad outcomes. Phobias such as fear of heights can be learned in this way. We become anxious at the thought of climbing the ladder, so we employ a window cleaner in order to avoid using a ladder, and this removes the anxiety (negative reinforcement).

> **Classical conditioning:** treatment, based on the behavioural approach, in which an undesirable behaviour can be paired with an unpleasant response (aversion therapy).

Classical conditioning (learning by association)

We learn by associating things together. Pavlov's dogs learned to associate a bell with food so that eventually the sound of the bell alone would cause the dogs to salivate. Little Albert learned to associate a white rat with loud and frightening noises so that after a few days anything white and furry would evoke a fear response.

Operant conditioning (reward and punishment)

If we are rewarded for behaviour we are more likely to repeat it; if we're punished we're less likely to do it again. Abnormal behaviour is therefore caused by people reinforcing inappropriate behaviour, making it more likely to be repeated. For example, a panic attack gets the child's attention, making it likely that the child will repeat the behaviour.

> **Typical mistake**
>
> It is a mistake to suggest that punishment leads to negative reinforcement.

Social learning theory (modelling)

Behaviourists also propose that we acquire behaviour by copying others and that the observer is more likely to copy the behaviour they see if the model is rewarded for their behaviour (Bandura's Bobo doll study). Mineka *et al.* (1994) showed monkeys video footage of other monkeys that were clearly frightened of snakes. When exposed to snakes it was found that the observer monkeys had also developed a fear of snakes.

The two-process model

The learning and maintenance of a phobia involves both classical and operant conditioning – classical conditioning because the fear is first learned by association, operant conditioning because avoiding the fear-provoking stimulus prevents us from unlearning the fear, so operant conditioning explains why a phobia persists. Example: at a young age you are in the garden and a butterfly gets in your hair. Your sister screams and this frightens you. You have learned to associate butterflies with being frightened. To unlearn this fear you need to associate butterflies with something pleasant, but you avoid butterflies, which is reinforcing because it prevents anxiety – as a result you remain frightened of butterflies.

Treatments based on the behaviourist approach

Since the abnormal behaviour has been learned, treatment concentrates on unlearning inappropriate behaviour and replacing it with the learning of new behaviours.

Treatments based on classical conditioning are often used to treat phobias and involve the patient learning to associate their phobic stimulus (for example, a snake) with relaxation.

Systematic desensitisation

This is a type of behaviour therapy where the undesired behaviour, for instance a person's phobia, is broken down into the small stimulus–response units that comprise it. The patient is taught a muscle relaxation technique and breathing exercises. The patient creates a fear hierarchy, starting at stimuli that create the least anxiety and building up in stages to fear-provoking images. The patient works their way up, starting at the least unpleasant and practising their relaxation technique as they go. The role of the therapist is to help the patient recognise the reason for the fear, and whether the fear is rational or not, and to help the patient as the fear is unlearned.

The therapy consists of:
- the construction of a hierarchy of fears
- training in relaxation – the relaxed state is incompatible with anxiety
- graded exposure (in imagination) and relaxation
- homework – practice in real life.

McGrath *et al.* (1990) reported that, following systematic **desensitisation**, 70% of patients showed improvement in symptoms, but few patients were completely free of anxiety.

In flooding (exposure therapy) the patient is confronted with the phobic stimulus. The theory is that the person suffers panic but because the adrenaline (fight-or-flight) response is short lived, the person soon calms due to lack of adrenaline. Exposure therapy seems to be more effective than systematic desensitisation.

> **Desensitisation:** the theory that repeated exposure to violence in the media reduces the emotional impact of the violence because people become 'used to it' so it has less impact on them.
>
> **Systematic desensitisation:** treatment based on the behavioural approach in which a person having a phobia is gradually reintroduced to a feared object or situation.

> **Exam tip**
>
> Make sure you know the difference between classical and operant conditioning.

> **Evaluation**
>
> The behavioural approach is supported by experimental evidence.
>
> It is hopeful as it predicts that people can change their behaviour. However, it is criticised as being dehumanising as people are reduced to programmed stimulus–response units.
>
> The approach cannot explain or cure all psychological disorders.
>
> The approach offers a testable explanation for phobias, but Menzies and Clark (1993) reported that only 2% of children who had hydrophobia had suffered a traumatic event involving water. The approach cannot explain why phobias for some objects are more common than others. Many objects are far more threatening than spiders and snakes, for instance. Seligman believes we have a genetic predisposition to associate fear with some threats based on our more primitive past.

The cognitive approach to explaining and treating depression

REVISED

The cognitive approach to depression assumes that the human mind is like an information processor and that people can control how they select, store and think about information. In the cognitive approach, psychological problems are caused when people make incorrect inferences about themselves or others, and have negative thoughts about themselves and the future. For example, depressive people often believe that they are unloved, that they are failures as parents, and that nothing good will ever happen in the future.

The cognitive approach explains depression in terms of an overly pessimistic outlook on life. Beck (1967), for example, describes the 'cognitive triad' in which a depressed patient has a negative view of themselves, the world and the future (see Figure 1.6). The cognitive approach views the symptoms as the causes of depression.

Negative views about the world
'Everybody hates me because I am worthless'

Negative views about oneself
'I am worthless'

Negative views about the future
'I'll never be good at anything because everybody hates me'

Figure 1.6 Beck's cognitive triad

Ellis's ABC model (1962)

A: activating agent (for example, getting a grade B in an exam).

B: belief (which can be rational) that grade B is good enough or (irrational) that grade B is a disaster.

C: consequence (which can be healthy) – bank grade B and feel relieved or (unhealthy) worry that you will fail the next exam.

The cognitive model has been most successful in explaining and treating depression because of the negative thinking.

Beck's cognitive triad

Beck believes patients get drawn into a negative pattern of viewing themselves, the world and the future. Combined with negative schemas and cognitive biases, this produces an inescapable cycle of negative thoughts. Beck believes that a depressed person has developed a negative set of schemas upon which their expectations about life are based. For example, they may have developed a self-blame schema which makes them feel responsible for all the things that go wrong in their life. Depressed people also overgeneralise, drawing negative conclusions about all situations based on one, perhaps trivial, event. For example, not being invited to a party convinces the person that they have no friends and that no one will ever like them.

Treatment based on the cognitive approach

Cognitive therapies all work in a similar way – first getting the patient to recognise their irrational perceptions, then agreeing on a more realistic approach, and finally putting this into practice in a real-life situation.

> **Revision activity**
>
> Practise until you are sure you can draw and label a diagram showing Beck's cognitive triad from memory.

Cognitive behaviour therapy (CBT)

CBT recognises the importance of changing both behaviour and thinking. The assumptions underlying CBT are:

- it is our interpretation of events rather than the events themselves that is important
- thoughts, behaviours and feelings all influence each other
- the role of the therapist is to help the patient identify their irrational thoughts and to change their interpretations of themselves to get rid of negative biases
- the patient must change both their thinking and their behaviour.

Butler *et al.* (2006) studied the results from more than 10 000 patients and found that CBT was effective in treating depression (more successfully than anti-depressives), anxiety disorder, panic disorder and social phobia.

Evaluation

The cognitive approach focuses on how the individual experiences the world rather than relying on interpretations by other people.

The approach is hopeful as it assumes people have the power to change their behaviour.

The approach may encourage the idea that people are responsible for their own psychological problems and could lead to people being blamed for psychological abnormalities.

There is a possibility that false memories may be created.

The approach is reductionist as it ignores biological causes of psychological abnormality such as genetics and biochemistry.

The biological approach to explaining and treating OCD

REVISED

Biological approaches to psychopathology explore differences caused by genetics, biochemistry and brain anatomy. The biological approach assumes that psychological abnormalities such as OCD are symptoms of underlying physical causes.

Genetic explanation

Research suggests that OCD runs in families. Lenane (1990) reported that 30% of first-degree relatives of those who had OCD also had an OCD.

Neural (biochemical) explanation

OCD may result from a deficiency of **serotonin** (neurotransmitter) or a malfunction of its metabolism such as blocked serotonin receptors. Zohar *et al.* (1996) found that some tricyclic drugs that inhibit the re-uptake of serotonin were beneficial for around 60% of the OCD sufferers.

Drug treatments for OCD

Anti-anxiety (anxiolytic) drugs such as benzodiazepines slow the activity of the central nervous system (CNS), reducing serotonin activity and thus anxiety, and increasing relaxation. **Beta blockers** act on the autonomic nervous system (ANS) to reduce activity in the ANS associated with anxiety – these drugs reduce heart rate, blood pressure and levels of **cortisol**. Antidepressant drugs, such as Prozac, can be used to elevate

Serotonin: low levels of the neurotransmitter serotonin appear to be linked with aggressive behaviour.

Beta blockers: drugs that act on the sympathetic nervous system (SNS) rather than the brain to reduce heart rate and blood pressure and thus lessen the harmful effects of stress.

Cortisol: the stress hormone can cause damage to health because raised cortisol levels lower immune function. Cortisol is released by the adrenal glands in response to fear or stress as part of the fight-or-flight mechanism.

mood. SSRI (selective serotonin reuptake inhibitor) drugs reduce symptoms of OCD and these SSRIs are the main treatment for OCD (for example, Prozac). SSRIs increase levels of the neurotransmitter serotonin and are an effective treatment for anxiety disorders.

Evaluation

Biological therapies act rapidly to reduce the symptoms of OCD.

Drug therapy can be used alongside therapies such as CBT.

Drug treatments are easy to administer and do not involve the patient changing their lifestyle or behaviour.

Biological therapies may give rise to ethical concerns and some drug therapies have unpleasant side effects. Taking drugs may lead to addiction and dependency.

Drugs may simply suppress the symptoms, not cure the disorder.

Revision activity

Make a chart comparing the strengths and limitations of behaviourist, cognitive and biological treatments.

Typical mistake

Reductionism as a concept does not refer to one approach, ignoring other approaches. Reductionism refers to the principle of taking a complex concept or behaviour and reducing it to its simple constituent parts.

Summary

You should be able to:
- describe definitions of abnormality, including deviation from social norms, failure to function adequately and deviation from ideal mental health
- evaluate these definitions of psychological abnormality
- describe and evaluate the behavioural, emotional and cognitive characteristics of

phobias, depression and obsessive compulsive disorders
- describe and evaluate the behavioural approach to explaining and treating phobias
- describe and evaluate the cognitive approach to explaining and treating depression
- describe and evaluate the biological approach to explaining and treating OCD.

Now test yourself

TESTED

1 (a) If 'abnormality is behaviour that deviates from the statistical norm', what does this mean?
  (b) What does 'abnormality is behaviour that deviates from the social norm' mean?
  (c) Identify three of the six conditions that Jahoda associated with ideal mental health.
  (d) What is a phobic disorder?
  (e) Outline the diagnostic criteria for OCD.
  (f) List three diagnostic criteria for unipolar depression.
  (g) Outline two characteristics of obsessive compulsive disorder.
2 (a) Are the statements A–D TRUE or FALSE?
    A   The behavioural explanation of phobia is a 'nurture' explanation.
    B   In classical conditioning we learn by rewards and punishment.
    C   The avoidance of a feared object strengthens the fear by reinforcement.
    D   Systematic desensitisation is a therapy in which a phobia can be unlearned.
  (b) Outline what happens during the behaviourist treatment called 'flooding'.
  (c) Comment on the ethics of 'flooding'.
  (d) Suggest why the behaviourist explanation of phobia is helpful.
  (e) In systematic desensitisation, what is a fear hierarchy?
  (f) Outline the two processes involved in the learning and maintenance of a phobia.
3 (a) Which of A, B, C, D and E are not features of Beck's cognitive triad?
    A   A negative view of the world
    B   A negative view of family
    C   A negative view of self
    D   A negative view of the future
    E   A negative view of politicians

(b) Write a definition for cognitive behavioural therapy.
(c) Suggest why the behavioural explanation of depression can be described as reductionist.
(d) Explain one advantage of cognitive treatment for disorders.
(e) Suggest why it could be argued that CBT may cause an ethical issue.
(f) Explain one disadvantage of cognitive treatment for disorders.
4 (a) How are the processes of classical and operant conditioning involved in learning a phobia?
(b) Briefly describe how systematic desensitisation may be used to treat phobia.
(c) List one difference between classical and operant conditioning.
(d) Outline one advantage of the behavioural explanation for psychological illness.
(e) Outline the assumptions of the behavioural approach to abnormality.
(f) How does Beck's cognitive triad explain depression?
(g) Outline the neural explanation for depression.
(h) List one strength and one limitation of biological treatments for psychological illness.

Answers on page 235

Exam practice

1 (a) Outline one difference between depression and phobia. [1]
(b) How do behavioural psychologists explain depression? [4]
(c) Outline what physiological research might suggest about depression. [2]
(d) Briefly outline one advantage of the behavioural explanation of depression. [2]
(e) Outline the behavioural symptoms of a person suffering from a phobia. [2]

2 Read the item and then answer the questions:

Patient Y has been seeing a behavioural therapist who has treated him by systematic desensitisation for his phobia of spiders. So far he has received 15 weekly one-hour sessions and at the end of each session his fear was measured on a score of 1–20 where 20 means extreme fear. The therapist has analysed the data to see whether the therapy is effective. The results are shown in Figure 1.7.

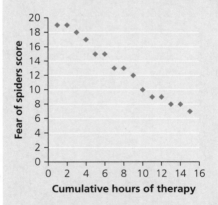

Figure 1.7 The relationship between hours of therapy received and fear of spiders

(a) Outline what the scattergraph suggests about the relationship between the therapy and patient Y's spider phobia. [2]
(b) Identify an appropriate inferential test that could be used to analyse the data. [1]
(c) Suggest whether or not Patient Y should be encouraged to continue with the therapy. [2]
(d) List one ethical issue that should be dealt with before the patient starts the therapy. [2]
(e) Explain whether or not the outcome of the therapy can be applied to other phobic patients. [2]
(f) Identify the level of measurement of the weekly fear score. [1]
(g) Identify whether the fear scores are primary or secondary data. [1]

Answers and quick quizzes 12, 13, 14 and 15 online

ONLINE

Approaches in psychology

Origins of psychology

REVISED

Wilhelm Wundt opened the Institute for Experimental Psychology in Germany in 1879 and this was the beginning of modern psychology. Wundt wanted to study the structure of the human mind and he concentrated on three areas of mental functioning: thoughts, images and feelings. Wundt believed in **reductionism**, that consciousness could be broken down (or reduced) to its basic elements without sacrificing any of the properties of the whole. Wundt argued that conscious mental states could be scientifically studied using introspection, the examination of one's conscious thoughts and feelings.

> **Reductionism:** the principle of breaking behaviour into simple constituents or the use of simple principles.

Learning approaches

REVISED

The behaviourist approach

As discussed earlier, the behaviourist approach makes three assumptions. First, it assumes that all behaviour is learned; second, that what has been learned can be unlearned; and third, that abnormal behaviour is learned in the same way as normal behaviour.

Behaviourists propose that classical conditioning can explain phobias. In classical conditioning, an unconditioned stimulus, such as an unexpected loud noise, triggers a natural reflex, for example the startle response and fear. But if another stimulus, such as seeing a spider, occurs at the same time, this may elicit the fear response in future. Watson and Rayner (1920) demonstrated how classical conditioning could explain the way in which fear could be learned.

Behaviourists also propose that behaviour can be learned by the process of operant conditioning, in which behaviour is learned through the consequences of our actions. Behaviourists believe that we are a product of our environment, that at birth we are a *tabula rasa*, or blank slate. Our genetic make-up is largely ignored and our personality, IQ, achievements and behaviour are shaped by the environment in which we are reared. Behaviourism is at the extreme end of nurture in the nature–nurture debate.

Classical conditioning

Classical conditioning is the association of two events that occur together – for example, bell and food, rat and loud noise – which then results in a response being transferred from one to the other – bell elicits salivation. In classical conditioning, the behavioural response is one we are not able to control: reflex behaviour.

Research: Pavlov's dogs

Russian physiologist Ivan Pavlov was looking at salivation in dogs in response to being fed when he noticed that his dogs would begin to salivate whenever he entered the room, even when he was not bringing them food. At first this was something of a nuisance (not to mention messy!).

Pavlovian conditioning

Pavlov (1902) started from the idea that there are some things that a dog does not need to learn. For example, dogs don't learn to salivate whenever they see food. This reflex is 'hard wired' into the dog, it is an unconditioned response (i.e. a stimulus–response connection that requires no learning). Pavlov showed the existence of the unconditioned response by presenting a dog with a bowl of food and then measuring its salivary secretions. When Pavlov discovered that any object or event which the dogs learned to associate with food (such as the lab assistant) would trigger the same response, he realised that somehow the dogs had learned to associate food with his lab assistant. This must have been learned, because at one point the dogs did not do it, and there came a point where they started, so their behaviour had changed.

In behaviourist terms, the lab assistant was originally a neutral stimulus (neutral because it produces no response). What had happened was that the neutral stimulus (the lab assistant) had become associated with an unconditioned stimulus (food). In his experiment, Pavlov used a bell as his neutral stimulus. Whenever he gave food to his dogs, he also rang a bell. After repeating this procedure a number of times, he tried the bell on its own and the bell on its own now caused an increase in salivation. So the dogs had learned an association between the bell and the food, and a new behaviour had been learned.

Because this response was learned (or conditioned), it is called a conditioned response. The neutral stimulus has become a conditioned stimulus.

Before conditioning – the neutral stimulus (BELL) does not cause a response.

During conditioning – the neutral stimulus (BELL) is paired with the unconditioned stimulus (FOOD), which produces an unconditioned response (SALIVATION).

After conditioning – the neutral stimulus (BELL) causes the conditioned response (SALIVATION).

Case study: research involving classical conditioning

Little Albert: Watson and Rayner (1920)

Aims: Could fear of an animal be conditioned by simultaneously presenting the animal and banging a steel bar so that the loud noise would frighten the child?

Participant: 'Albert B' aged nine months who was not afraid of white rats.

Procedure: Albert was placed on a table in the middle of a room and he played with a white rat. As he played, Watson and Rayner struck a steel bar with a hammer behind Albert's back and he cried with fear. After seven pairings of the two stimuli (loud noise and rat), Albert was presented with only the rat and became very distressed as the rat appeared. Seventeen days after the original pairing of the stimuli, Watson took a non-white rabbit into the room and Albert became distressed.

Conclusions: Watson and Rayner concluded that they had succeeded in conditioning in an infant fear of an animal the child would not ordinarily be frightened of.

Operant conditioning

Operant conditioning suggests that consequences of behaviour – punishment or reward – determine whether that behaviour will be repeated – 'operant' since the animal/person operates on the environment and then faces the consequences, positive or negative.

B. F. Skinner: operant conditioning

Skinner (1938) believed that classical conditioning was too simplistic to be a complete explanation of complex human behaviour. He believed that the best way to understand behaviour is to look at the causes of an action and its consequences. He called this approach operant conditioning.

Operant conditioning deals with operants – intentional actions that have an effect on the surrounding environment. Skinner set out to identify the processes which made certain operant behaviours more or less likely to occur. He identified three types of responses or operants that can follow behaviour:

Figure 2.1 **A rat in a Skinner box**

- **Neutral operants:** responses from the environment that neither increase nor decrease the probability of a behaviour being repeated.
- **Reinforcers:** responses from the environment that increase the probability of a behaviour being repeated. Reinforcers can be either positive or negative.
- **Punishers:** responses from the environment that decrease the likelihood of a behaviour being repeated. Punishment weakens behaviour.

For example, if you tidy your room and your parent gives you a treat, you have been positively reinforced (i.e. rewarded) and are likely to repeat the behaviour.

Skinner showed how positive reinforcement worked by placing a hungry rat in his 'Skinner box' (see Figure 2.1). The box contained a lever on the side and as the rat moved about the box it would accidentally knock the lever. Immediately

it did so a food pellet would drop into a container next to the lever.

After a few times of being put in the box the rats quickly learned to go straight to the lever. The consequence of receiving food if they pressed the lever ensured that they would repeat the action again and again. Positive reinforcement strengthens a behaviour by providing a consequence an individual finds rewarding.

Skinner found that some types of reinforcement schedules are more effective than others. The type of reinforcement which causes people to go on repeating the behaviour for the longest time without reinforcement is variable-ratio reinforcement. The type of reinforcement which has the quickest rate of extinction (i.e. the disappearance of a previously learned behaviour when the behaviour is not reinforced) is continuous reinforcement.

Continuous reinforcement

An animal/human is positively reinforced every time a specific behaviour occurs, for example every time a lever is pressed a pellet is delivered and then food delivery is shut off.
- Response rate is SLOW.
- Extinction rate is FAST.

Fixed ratio reinforcement

Behaviour is reinforced only after the behaviour has occurred for a specified number of times. For example, reinforcement is given after every nth correct response, such as a dog receiving a treat for every third time it sits on command.
- Response rate is FAST.
- Extinction rate is MEDIUM.

Fixed interval reinforcement

Behaviour is reinforced after a fixed time interval providing at least one correct response has been made. Another example would be if every 15 minutes a reward is delivered (providing at least one lever press has been made) then food delivery is shut off.

- Response rate is MEDIUM.
- Extinction rate is MEDIUM.

Variable ratio reinforcement

Behaviour is reinforced after an unpredictable number of times, for example fruit machine gambling.

- Response rate is FAST.
- Extinction rate is SLOW.

Social learning theory

In **social learning theory** Albert Bandura (1977) states behaviour is learned from the environment through the process of observational learning.

Bandura proposed that humans are active information processors who think about the relationship between their behaviour and its consequences. Observational learning could not occur unless cognitive processes were at work. Children observe the people around them and the people who are observed are called models. These models provide examples of behaviour to observe and imitate, for example pro- and anti-social behaviour. Children pay attention to some of these models and at a later date they may imitate the behaviour they have observed. The child is more likely to attend to and imitate models it perceives as similar to itself and thus is more likely to imitate behaviour modelled by people of the same sex. Bandura also found that a child will take into account what happens to 'the model' when deciding whether or not to copy someone's actions. This is known as vicarious reinforcement.

> **Social learning theory:** the theory that behaviour is learned from the environment through the process of observational learning and that children learn aggression by observing role models whom they then imitate.

Bandura, Ross and Ross (1961)

The study aimed to find out whether aggression can be learned through imitation. The participants were 72 children from a university nursery, 36 boys and 36 girls with an average age of about four and a half years. To ensure that each group contained equally aggressive children, the children were observed beforehand and rated, using a five-point scale, in terms of their physical aggression, verbal aggression, aggression towards inanimate objects and 'aggressive inhibition'. The marks were added together to give an aggression score for the child.

Phase 1: Each child was taken to a room and in one corner there was a 5 ft inflatable Bobo doll and a mallet. The experimenter invited the 'model' and the child to play and then left the room. There were three conditions (with 24 children in each):

- **Non-aggressive condition:** the model played with the toys in a quiet manner.
- **Aggressive condition:** the model spent the first minute playing quietly but then spent the rest of the time being aggressive towards the Bobo doll, for example sitting on it and repeatedly punching it on the nose, picking up the doll and striking it on the head with the mallet, throwing the doll in the air and kicking it about the room accompanied by various comments such as 'POW' and 'He sure is a tough fellow'.
- **Control:** No exposure to a role model.

Phase 2: The child was taken to another room to 'mildly' provoke him/her to behave aggressively by showing a room of attractive toys and then saying they couldn't play with them.

Phase 3: The child was moved to another room which contained some aggressive toys (such as a mallet and a dart gun), some non-aggressive toys (for instance, dolls and farm animals) and a 3 ft Bobo doll. The experimenter stayed with the child while he/she played for 20 minutes, during which time the child was observed through a one-way mirror. The observers recorded what the child was doing every five seconds, using the following measures:

- **Imitation of physical aggression:** any specific acts which were imitated.
- **Imitative verbal aggression:** any phrases which were imitated, such as 'POW'.
- **Imitative non-aggressive verbal responses:** such as 'He keeps coming back for more'.
- **Non-imitative physical and verbal aggression:** aggressive acts directed at toys other than the Bobo doll, for example saying things not said by the model, or playing with the gun.

The children imitated the models they saw both in terms of specific acts and in general levels of their behaviour.

- **Imitation:** children in the aggressive condition imitated many of the models' physical and verbal behaviours, both aggressive and non-aggressive.
- **Non-imitative aggression:** the aggressive group displayed much more non-imitative aggression than did the non-aggressive group.
- **Non-aggressive behaviour:** children in the non-aggressive condition spent more time playing non-aggressively and also spent more time just sitting and playing with nothing.
- **Gender:** boys imitated more physical aggression than girls but not verbal aggression. There was some evidence of a 'same-sex effect' between model and children, in other words boys were more aggressive if they watched a male rather than a female model and girls were more affected by a female model.

Conclusion: Bandura concluded that learning can take place in the absence of either classical or operant conditioning.

Evaluation

The behaviourist approach proposes a simple testable explanation that is supported by experimental evidence.

The behaviourist approach is hopeful as it predicts that people can change (re-learn) their behaviour.

Learning theories cannot explain all psychological disorders.

Learning theories are reductionist as they ignore biological causes of behaviour.

Learning theories are deterministic as they assume people do not consciously choose how to behave.

Exam tip

Nature or nurture? When you revise this topic make sure you can explain why learning theories support the nurture side of the nature–nurture debate.

The cognitive approach

REVISED

Cognitive psychologists believe that to understand human behaviour we must understand the internal processes of the human mind. They believe that the human mind is like an information processor and that people have the free will to control how they think and behave.

The **cognitive approach** uses computer analogies to explain the workings of the human mind and adopts an information processing approach: sensory input, some sort of process and behavioural output. Cognitive psychologists study internal processes, including perception, attention, memory and thinking, and usually use laboratory experiments to study behaviour because the cognitive approach is scientific.

Cognitive approach: an approach that proposes that to be normal is to be able to use cognitive processes to monitor and control our behaviour.

The computer model

The development of computers allowed psychologists to try to understand the complexities of human cognition by comparing it with something simpler and better understood – an artificial system such as a computer. Essentially, the computer model proposes that, like a computer, the mind codes information, stores information, uses information and produces an output.

Theoretical models

Cognitive psychologists propose theoretical models that can then be tested by experimental research. Examples of theoretical models are the working memory model and the multi-store model of memory, and the theory that memories are always reconstructions, tested in the research by Loftus and Palmer (1974).

Schemas

Schemas are internal mental representations that allow us to organise thoughts, categorise events and predict outcomes. Our schemas start in early life and new experiences either fit with existing schema (in which case we assimilate) or entirely new schemas are developed (in which case we accommodate). Schemas are our subjective interpretation of events and are prone to distortion.

> **Exam tip**
>
> **Free will or determinism?** Make sure you can explain why the cognitive approach supports free will.

Loftus and Palmer (1974)

The reliability of eyewitness memory

- **Aim:** to find out whether leading questions distort (change) an eyewitness memory of an event.
- **Method and design:** two laboratory experiments; both have independent design.
- **IV and DV:** IV in experiment 1: the strength of the verb – *contacted, bumped, collided, hit, smashed*. IV in experiment 2: whether the leading question included the verb *hit* or *smashed*.
- **Participants:** Experiment 1: an opportunity sample of 45 participants, all university students, randomly allocated to five groups of 9; Experiment 2: an opportunity sample of 150 participants, all university students, randomly allocated to three groups of 50.

Procedure

- **Experiment 1:** 45 participants watched a video of a car accident. Afterwards participants were asked to write an account of what they had seen and were then given a questionnaire which included the *critical leading question*. The participants were divided into five groups and each group received a different version of the critical question, containing the verb *smashed, collided, bumped, hit* or *contacted*.
- **Experiment 2:** 150 participants, in three groups of 50, were shown a film of a car accident

and were given a questionnaire. Group 1 were asked the leading question containing the word 'hit', Group 2 were asked it with the word 'smashed' and Group 3 (the control group) were not asked a leading question. A week later the participants returned and were asked further questions, including the critical question '*Did you see any broken glass?*' (there was no broken glass in the film).

- **Controls:** all watched the same film in the same environment, all wrote a description of what they had seen before they were questioned. In experiment 2 there was a control group to establish a baseline for the erroneous reporting of seeing broken glass.

Findings

- **Experiment 1**: the *smashed* group estimated the speed of the crash at 9 mph faster than the *contacted* group.
- **Experiment 2**: The *smashed* group were significantly more likely to report seeing broken glass than the control group. There was no difference in reports of seeing broken glass between the *hit* group and the control group.

Conclusion: the meaning of the verb used in the leading question (the semantics) had become integrated with the memory of the event, thus changing the memory and causing a false memory to be constructed.

Cognitive neuroscience

Cognitive neuroscience integrates the theories of cognitive science with approaches in experimental psychology, neuropsychology and neuroscience. Cognitive neuroscience uses new technologies to 'measure the brain', including transcranial magnetic stimulation (TMS), EEG and advanced brain imaging methods such as MRI and PET scans. Advances in neuroimaging and associated data analysis methods have made it possible to research the relationship between thought processes and brain activity. The research by Maguire (2000) analysed MRI scans to show how the structure of the hippocampi changed in response to environmental demand.

Maguire (2000)

Navigation-related structural change in the hippocampi of London taxi drivers

- **Aim:** to find out whether changes in the brain could be detected in those with extensive navigation experience.
- **The hypothesis:** that the hippocampi in London taxi drivers will be structurally different to the hippocampi in non-taxi drivers.
- **Method: natural experiment** – independent design: participants: two groups. Group 1: 16 right-handed male taxi drivers, average age 44, all licensed more than 18 months, average time as taxi driver 14.3 years. Group 2: 16 right-handed male, age-matched, non-taxi drivers. IV: London taxi driver (brain) or non-taxi driver (brain). DV: structure and volume of hippocampi.

Procedure

- **Stage 1**: MRI scans of brains of 50 healthy, right-handed, male non-taxi drivers aged 33–61 were analysed to establish a comparison database of 'average hippocampi' (analysis by voxel-based morphometry (VBM)).
- **Stage 2:** MRI scans of brains of 16 taxi drivers and of 16 matched controls were analysed by VBM and compared to this database.
- **Control:** the expert conducting the analysis did not know whether MRI scan was of taxi driver brain or not.

Findings

Increased volume of grey matter was found in both the right and left hippocampi in taxi driver brains, especially the right posteria hippocampus. Correlational analysis found that the volume of the right posteria hippocampus increased as the length of time as taxi driver increased. Taxi drivers had greater volume in the posteria hippocampus but non-taxi drivers had greater volume in the anterior hippocampus, indicating a redistribution of the grey matter in the hippocampus.

Conclusion:

- That the structure of the brain changes in response to environmental demand.
- That the mental map of the city of London is stored in the posteria hippocampi in taxi drivers.
- That normal activity can induce changes in the structure of the brain and that this has many implications for rehabilitation after brain injury.

Evaluation

The cognitive approach focuses on how people experience the world rather than relying on interpretations by other people.

The approach is hopeful as it assumes people have the power to change their behaviour.

The approach could lead to people being blamed for psychological abnormalities.

The approach is reductionist, as it ignores biological causes of psychological abnormality such as genetics and biochemistry.

Exam tip

Make sure you can explain the problems that arise when measuring mental processes.

The biological approach

The **biological approach** assumes that there is a direct relationship between biology and behaviour and explores how behaviour is influenced by genetics, biochemistry and brain anatomy. The biological model is deterministic and takes the 'nature' stance in the nature–nurture debate.

Biological psychologists use scientific research methods because they allow for tight control of variables, testable hypotheses and cause and effect relationships to be established. Other research methods used by biological psychologists are as follows:

- **Twin and family studies:** in twin studies comparisons of MZ and DZ twins are used and if concordance rates for MZ are significantly higher than for DZ, a genetic component is assumed.
- **Brain scans:** these allow us to see which areas of the brain are active when we carry out certain activities. Methods include PET scans (positron emission tomography), CAT scans (computer-aided topography) and MRI scans (magnetic resonance imaging).
- **Chemical manipulation:** drugs may be administered to see how they influence behaviour – for example, the use of SSRI drugs in the treatment of depression.
- **Genes:** the biological approach emphasises the importance of genetic inheritance, for example geneticists assume that IQ is partially genetically determined. Heritability refers to the proportion of the characteristic that is seen as being genetic and some disorders, such as **schizophrenia**, run in families, suggesting an underlying genetic cause. However, even if we inherit a gene, the environment may influence the genetic effect. The genotype refers to the sum total of genes transmitted from parent to offspring. The phenotype refers to the observable physical characteristics of an organism as determined by both genetic make-up and environmental influence.

> **Biological approach:** an approach that assumes that psychological abnormalities are symptoms of underlying physical causes.

> **Schizophrenia:** a complex psychotic disorder which often involves perceptual disturbances, such as hallucinations, or thought disorders, such as delusions.

Biological structures

There are two opposing theories:

- **Localisation of function:** the theory that functions such as memory, language, perception, attention, etc., are located in specific brain areas. For example, Broca's area is where speech production 'is done' and the hippocampus is somewhere that memory 'happens'.
- **Mass action:** that functions such as memory are distributed throughout the brain and if one area is damaged another area can take over, and in any given behaviour, many parts of the brain all work together.

Neurochemistry (neurotransmitters)

Neurotransmitters are biochemical substances that carry the signals between brain cells. Too much or too little of a neurotransmitter may result in psychological disorders. For example, too much dopamine is thought to lead to schizophrenia. Some examples of neurotransmitter substances are:

- **adrenaline:** increases our levels of arousal, prepares us for a fast response
- **serotonin:** the 'feel-good' neurotransmitter that improves our mood
- **dopamine:** involved in muscle movement, memory, emotion and schizophrenia
- **endorphins:** hormones (such as beta-endorphin) which are involved in pleasure and pain and which are released at times of pain and during exercise.

> **Revision activity**
>
> Make a wall chart showing examples of behaviour that has been found to have a biological cause and what the biological cause is.

> **Exam tip**
>
> **Nature or nurture?** When you revise this topic make sure you can explain why the biological approach supports the nature side of the nature–nurture debate.

The biological approach does not blame people for their dysfunctional or abnormal behaviour.

The scientific status and association with the medical profession means that this approach enjoys credibility.

Objective evidence shows that biological causes can be linked to psychological symptoms.

Even if we know which part of the brain is active and how much activity there is, we can't know whether the brain activity causes the behaviour or the behaviour causes the brain activity.

The approach gives a reductionist explanation for human behaviour and ignores social and cognitive factors known to influence behaviour.

The psychodynamic approach

REVISED

The **psychodynamic approach** assumes that behaviour is motivated by unconscious forces, that the human personality comprises the id, the ego and the superego, and that the development of the personality progresses in five psychosexual stages (the oral, anal, phallic, latent and genital stages).

Psychodynamic approach: the assumption that behaviour is motivated by unconscious forces.

The psychosexual stages of development

Freud believed that as we develop our sexual or life energy (libido), we focus on different parts of the body. Each stage has an optimal level of satisfaction – too much or too little satisfaction in each stage leads to fixations that shape later personality.

- **Oral (0–2ish):** the child is born into this stage and satisfaction centres on the mouth, eating and sucking.
- **Anal (2–4ish):** pleasure is now centred on the anus, particularly defecation. The ego develops in order to resolve conflict between the id (which wants instant pleasure and pooing at will) and parents who require restraint.
- **Phallic (4–6ish):** pleasure is now centred on the penis (boys) and the child starts to develop desires for the opposite-sex parent. The boy's desire for the mother results in him wanting to take the place of the father (Oedipus complex). This causes anxiety since he believes that if the father discovers his desire, the father will castrate him. In the phallic stage the girl desires the father, but realising that she does not have a penis develops penis envy and the wish to be a boy. The girl blames her mother for her castrated state and this creates great tension (Electra complex), so the girl represses her feelings and identifies with the mother to take on the female gender role.
- **Latency (6ish–puberty):** this is an almost dormant period during which time the child learns appropriate social and gender-specific rules and patterns of behaviour.
- **Genital (puberty onwards):** Libido is now directed towards the genitals and sexual maturity begins.

The unconscious mind

Freud's theory was that psychic energy motivates us and creates conflicts. He separated the mind into two parts: the conscious mind of which we are aware, and the unconscious mind that is unknown to us and which forms the larger part beneath the surface of conscious awareness.

The structure of the personality

The id (instincts and drives) motivates you to seek pleasure while avoiding pain and to do so at whatever cost to others – it is selfish. The id operates on the Pleasure Principle, is present at birth and is driven by two instinctive drives: Eros or life instinct, motivating us to behave in life-preserving ways and life-enhancing ways, and Thanatos or death instinct. The id drives us to seek instant gratification and is happy for us to destroy anything that gets in our way.

The ego develops during the anal stage of development. The ego represents what the conscious mind believes is the real 'us'. Operating on the reality principle, the ego is logical and seeks to maintain balance in a real world.

The superego develops during the phallic stage as a resolution to the Oedipus complex or the Electra conflict. The superego operates on the morality principle and motivates us to behave in a socially responsible manner. Freud believed that a strong ego was essential to psychological health and that our well-being depends on minimising conflict and satisfying the needs of the different parts of personality.

Ego defence mechanisms

Ego defence mechanisms are operations of the unconscious mind. The real reasons underlying behaviour cannot be known. Examples of ego defence mechanisms are as follows:

- **Repression:** thoughts or desires that are upsetting are locked away in the unconscious mind.
- **Displacement:** usually involves anger which is displaced/redirected towards a substitute. Freud suggested that displacement could be an explanation of depression – where anger is redirected against the self.
- **Projection:** projecting unconscious unacceptable characteristics on to others – for example, according to Freud, Little Hans projected his unconscious wish that his mother drown his sister onto a fear that his mother would drown him in the bath.
- **Denial:** the person simply denies the existence of the problem.
- **Sublimation:** unacceptable desires are channelled into positive behaviour, for example aggression into sport.
- **Regression:** when stressed, the person reverts to an earlier, usually childhood, stage of development.

> **Typical mistake**
>
> It is a mistake to suggest that the case study of Little Hans was unethical because Hans was not asked for his consent.

Case study: Freud (1909)

Analysis of a phobia in a five-year-old boy

In a longitudinal case study, Hans' father wrote letters to Freud, who analysed the information and wrote back. Freud met Hans only once.

Hans' father wrote to Freud when the boy was five years old, describing the main problem: 'He is afraid a horse will bite him in the street, and this fear seems somehow connected with his having been frightened by a large penis.' Hans had an interest in that part of his body he called his 'widdler'. When his mother found him playing with his widdler she threatened that she would arrange for it to be cut off. Hans' father told him that women have no widdlers and Freud reasoned that this would lead Hans to think: 'Mother had a widdler before and now she hasn't. It must have been cut off. She said mine might be cut off if I touched it.' This would serve to confirm his fears of castration.

Hans told his father about a dream involving two giraffes, a big one and a crumpled one. Hans took away the crumpled one and this made the big one cry out. Hans sat down on the crumpled one. Hans' father thought that this was a representation of what happened in the mornings between Hans and his parents. Hans liked to get into his parents' bed but his father (the big giraffe) often objected. Hans took away his mother (the crumpled one), which caused his father to cry out. Hans sat on top of his mother to claim her for himself. Freud wondered if the giraffe's long neck represented the large adult penis.

Freud suggested that Hans' fear of horses was actually a projection of his unconscious fear of his father. The black around the horses' mouths and the blinkers in front of their eyes were symbols for his father's moustache and glasses.

Hans developed two final fantasies which showed that he had now resolved his feelings about his father. 'The plumber came and first he took away my behind with a pair of pincers, and then he gave me another, and then the same with my widdler.' This was taken to mean that Hans was given a bigger backside and widdler, like Daddy's. Freud felt that the case study of Hans provided support for his ideas about infant sexuality.

Evaluation

The psychodynamic approach identifies the importance of traumatic childhood experience in adult problems.

Freud's theories changed people's attitudes to mental illness. Psychosomatic illnesses demonstrate the link between mind and body.

The approach is not scientific: Freud's theories are not falsifiable (his hypotheses are not testable).

The approach over-emphasises experience, suggesting that past experience motivates current behaviour.

Exam tip

In a discussion of the psychodynamic approach, if you suggest that the approach is unscientific you need to explain why.

Humanistic psychology

Humanistic psychologists, such as Rogers and Maslow in the 1950s, recognise the existence of **free will**, suggest that individuals have a need for self-actualisation and that the potential for personal growth depends on circumstances. Another assumption is that if children receive unconditional positive regard they will develop satisfactorily, but if they experience conditional regard, they are prevented from realising their potential.

Humanistic psychologists rely on **self-report methods**, as they believe that psychologists should treat as 'evidence' how the individual reports their own conscious experiences. Abraham Maslow believed that people have an inborn desire to be self-actualised, to be all they can be. He proposed a hierarchy of needs, shown in Figure 2.2, and that people are motivated to fulfil basic needs before they can move on to more advanced needs.

The lowest levels of the hierarchy of needs pyramid are made up of the most basic needs, while the more complex needs are located at the top of the pyramid. Needs at the bottom of the pyramid are basic physical

Free will: the assumption that people have the free will to select and decide their own behaviour.

Self-report methods: a way of finding out about people's behaviour by interviewing them or by asking them to fill out questionnaires.

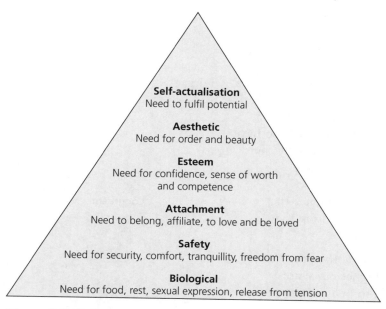

Figure 2.2 Hierarchy of needs

requirements, including the need for food, sleep and warmth. As people progress up the pyramid, needs become increasingly psychological and social, such as the need for love, friendship and intimacy. Further up the pyramid, the need for personal esteem and feelings of accomplishment take priority. Maslow emphasised the importance of self-actualisation, which is a process of growing and developing as a person in order to achieve individual potential.

Revision activity

Draw a sketch of the pyramid showing the hierarchy of human needs. Make a list of people whom you judge to have achieved self-actualisation.

Personality development

Central to Rogers' personality theory is the notion of self or self-concept. According to Rogers, the self is influenced by the experiences a person has in their life, two primary sources being childhood experiences and evaluation by others. According to Rogers (1959), we want to feel and behave in ways that are consistent with our self-image and which reflect what we would like to be like: our ideal self.

Self-concept has three components:
- Self-worth (self-esteem): what we think about ourselves. Feelings of self-worth are developed in early childhood and are formed from the interaction of the child with the mother and father.
- Self-image: how we see ourselves, which is important to good psychological health. Self-image includes the influence of our body image on personality.
- Ideal self: the person we would like to be. It consists of our goals and ambitions in life, and is forever developing.

Self-worth and positive regard

Rogers (1951) viewed the child as having two basic needs: positive regard from other people and self-worth. Our feelings of self-worth are of fundamental importance both to psychological health and to the likelihood that we can achieve self-actualisation. A person who has high self-worth — that is, has confidence and positive feelings about themselves — faces challenges in life, accepts failure and is open with people. A person with low self-worth may avoid challenges in life, not accept that life can be unhappy at times, and will be defensive and guarded with other people. Rogers believed feelings of self-worth developed in early childhood and were formed from the interaction of the child with the parents. Unconditional positive regard is where parents accept and love the person for what they are. Positive regard is not withdrawn if the person does something wrong or makes a mistake. People who are able to self-actualise are more likely to have received unconditional positive regard from others, especially their parents, in childhood. Conditional positive regard is where positive regard, praise and approval depend upon the child behaving in ways that the parents think are correct. Hence the child is not loved for the person they are but on condition that they behave only in ways approved by the parents.

The closer our self-image and ideal self are to each other, the more consistent or congruent we are and the higher our sense of self-worth – see Figure 2.3. A person is said to be in a state of incongruence if some of their experience is unacceptable to them and is denied or distorted in the self-image. Incongruence is 'a discrepancy between the actual experience of the person and the self-picture of the individual insofar as it represents that experience'.

Rogers suggested that we prefer to see ourselves in ways that are consistent with our self-image and may use defence mechanisms such as denial in order to feel less threatened by some of what we consider to be our undesirable feelings. A person whose self-concept is incongruent with their real feelings and experiences will use defence mechanisms because the truth hurts.

Hence, a difference may exist between a person's ideal self and actual experience. Where a person's ideal self and actual experience are consistent or very similar, a state of congruence exists. Rarely, if ever, does a total state of congruence exist; all people experience a certain amount of incongruence. The development of congruence is dependent on unconditional positive regard. Rogers believed that for a person to achieve self-actualisation they must be in a state of congruence.

The influence on counselling

Therapy aims to uncover distortions and denials so the individual can gain insight into their true self. Client-centred therapy is based on the therapist giving the client unconditional positive regard, being genuine and honest and showing empathy. **Humanistic** theory has been incorporated into many differing views on psychotherapy and many argue now that humanistic counselling provides a foundation for individual change.

Congruent

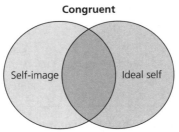

The self-image is similar to the ideal self.
There is more overlap.
This person can self-actualise.

Incongruent

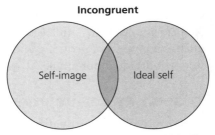

The self-image is different to the ideal self.
There is only a little overlap.
Here self-actualisation will be difficult.

Figure 2.3 Congruence vs incongruence

Exam tip

The humanistic approach sits on the side of nurture rather than nature. Make sure you can explain why.

Humanistic approach: humanistic psychology assumes that a healthy psychological attitude is dependent on taking personal responsibility and striving towards personal growth.

Exam tip

In the exam you could be given a hypothetical example of a person and asked to explain their behaviour from the humanistic approach.

The humanistic approach empowers individuals by emphasising free will and the ability to change.

It formed the basis for client-centred therapy, which is an effective treatment for some disorders.

The approach is not scientific and it is criticised as being culturally biased as it seems relevant only to people who live in Western cultures where the emphasis is on individualism.

The approach overemphasises past experience, suggesting that parenting causes psychological problems.

Revision activity

Write your own definitions of the humanistic terminology: hierarchy of needs, unconditional positive regard, congruence, incongruence.

Comparison of approaches

REVISED

Approach	Origin of behaviour	Limitation	Comment
Biological Behaviour is a symptom of an underlying biological cause.	Inside the person: ● genetic ● brain damage ● neurotransmission.	Deterministic. Reductionist. No free will. Can't explain why talking cures or conditioning are effective.	Ignores psychosocial factors but is scientific. Does not 'blame' the individual. Useful because effective treatment = drugs.
Behavioural Behaviour is learned and can be unlearned.	Behaviour is learned in interaction with the environment: ● classical conditioning ● operant conditioning ● social learning theory.	Deterministic because the past predicts current behaviour. No free will. Can't explain why drugs or talking cures work.	Ignores biological factors. Does not 'blame' the individual. Useful because effective treatment based on conditioning (learning).
Psychodynamic Behaviour is a symptom of an unconscious cause and of conflict between the id, ego and superego.	Inside the person + early experience: ● Oedipus complex ● ego defences ● repression and regression.	Deterministic because the past predicts current behaviour. No free will. Can't explain why drug treatment is effective. Not based on scientific evidence.	Ignores biological factors. Does not 'blame' the individual. Useful because effective treatment – a talking cure, psychoanalysis.
Cognitive Behaviour is the result of conscious mental processes.	Inside the person. Rational and irrational thoughts: ● attention ● memory ● language ● decision making.	May 'blame' the individual: 'If you didn't think irrationally you wouldn't have a problem.' Can't explain why drug treatment is effective.	Ignores biological and social factors. Useful because effective treatment – talking cure, CBT.
Humanistic Behaviour is the result of the drive to reach self-actualisation.	Inside the person. Self-esteem, accepting (or not) the 'self' as it is.	Self-orientated – encourages selfishness. Culturally biased to individualistic cultures. Not based on scientific evidence.	Ignores biological factors. Useful because effective treatment – talking cure, client-centred therapy.

Summary

You should be able to:
- describe the origins of psychology and understand what is meant by introspection
- describe and evaluate the assumptions of learning approaches and explain the behaviourist theories of learning
- describe and evaluate the assumptions of the cognitive approach and explain what is meant by mental schema
- describe and evaluate the assumptions of the biological approach and distinguish between genotype and phenotype

- describe and evaluate the assumptions of the psychodynamic approach, including the structure of personality, defence mechanisms and the psychosexual stages of development
- describe and evaluate the assumptions of humanistic psychologists, the role of free will, self-actualisation and Maslow's hierarchy of needs
- compare and contrast the different approaches to explaining human behaviour.

Now test yourself

1 (a) Which approach suggests that behaviour is learned by observing role models?
  (b) Which approach suggests that behaviour is caused by genetic inheritance?
  (c) What do cognitive psychologists assume are the causes of behaviour?
  (d) Why can the humanistic approach be criticised as unscientific?
  (e) Identify the three parts of the human personality proposed by the psychodynamic approach.
  (f) What do we do when we 'introspect'?
  (g) Wundt relied on participants self-reporting their mental processes. Did he collect objective or subjective data?
  (h) Explain why the biological approach is deterministic.
  (i) Explain why the psychodynamic approach is unscientific.
2 TRUE or FALSE?
  (a) Wundt believed that consciousness could be broken down to its basic elements.
  (b) Watson and Rayner (1920) demonstrated how operant conditioning could explain how a phobia is learned.
  (c) Behaviourism supports the nurture debate.
  (d) A reinforcer increases the probability that behaviour will be repeated.
  (e) Bandura proposes that cognitive processes are involved when children learn by observation.
  (f) Cognitive psychologists do not believe people have the free will to choose their behaviour.
  (g) Maguire (2000) suggests that the way we behave can change the structure of the brain.
  (h) Neurotransmitters are biochemical substances that carry signals between brain cells.
  (i) Freud collected quantitative data in the case study of Little Hans.
  (j) Maslow believed that humans were born with a desire for self-actualisation.
  (k) Congruence is measured by the extent to which our self-image and ideal self match each other.
3 (a) Why does the Maguire (2000) research belong in the biological approach?
  (b) Why does the Loftus and Palmer study of eyewitness memory belong in the cognitive approach?
  (c) Why does the Watson and Rayner study of Little Albert belong in the behaviourist approach?
  (d) Why is the Bandura Bobo doll study a study of learning?
  (e) Suggest one difference between the biological and the behaviourist approach.
  (f) Suggest one similarity between the biological and the behaviourist approach.
  (g) Suggest one similarity between the humanistic and psychodynamic approaches.
  (h) Explain one strength of the biological approach.
  (i) Explain one strength of the cognitive approach.
  (j) Explain a limitation of the behaviourist approach.
  (k) Suggest why ethical issues may arise from taking a humanistic approach.

Answers on page 236

Exam practice

1 Outline one problem that arises when cognitive psychologists study internal mental processes such as memory or attention. [2]

2 Pinky and Perky are identical twins who both like strawberries and both dislike broccoli. How might a biological psychologist explain this? [2]

3 Samira is terrified of beetles and is afraid to go into the garden. How would a behaviourist psychologist explain Samira's phobia? [2]

4 Which TWO of the following statements are FALSE? [2]
  A Repression means that people can't access unpleasant memories.
  B Repression involves people deciding to forget unpleasant memories.
  C Repression involves unpleasant memories being kept from conscious awareness.
  D The id is responsible for pleasure-seeking behaviour.
  E The superego is responsible for good behaviour.
  F The superego is responsible for guilty feelings.

5 In Experiment 2 in the study of eyewitness memory, Loftus and Palmer inferred that the leading question had created a false memory for seeing broken glass. In relation to this study, explain what is meant by inference and explain why studies in the cognitive approach often involve inference. [4]

6 Pandora lacks confidence. She is unhappy and worries that she is not very clever and she hates the way she looks. She goes to see a counselling therapist who suggests that she lacks congruence. Outline what humanistic psychologists mean by congruence. [2]

7 To what extent have biological psychologists increased the understanding of human behaviour? [16]

Answers and quick quizzes 16, 17 and 18 online

ONLINE

Biopsychology

The divisions of the nervous system

REVISED

The nervous system is broken down into two major systems: the central nervous system and the **peripheral nervous system**.

The central nervous system consists of the brain and the spinal cord. The brain is divided into two symmetrical **hemispheres:** left (language, the 'rational' half of the brain, associated with analytical thinking and logical abilities) and right (more involved with musical and artistic abilities).

The brain is divided into four lobes, shown in Figure 2.4:
- frontal (motor cortex)
- parietal (somatosensory cortex)
- occipital (visual cortex)
- temporal (auditory cortex)

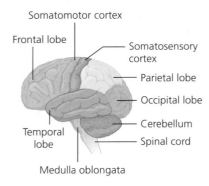

Figure 2.4 The four lobes of the human brain

The brain and spinal cord act together. The brainstem is involved in life-sustaining functions and damage to the brainstem is often fatal. The brainstem includes the medulla oblongata, which controls heartbeat, breathing, blood pressure, digestion, the reticular activating system, involved in arousal and attention and sleep, and the cerebellum, involved in balance, smooth movement and posture.

The peripheral nervous system is divided into two sub-systems – the somatic nervous system, whose primary function is to regulate the actions of the skeletal muscles, and the autonomic nervous system (ANS), which regulates involuntary activity such as heart rate, breathing, blood pressure and digestion. This system is further broken down into two complementary systems: sympathetic and parasympathetic nervous systems.

The sympathetic nervous system controls what has been called the 'fight-or-flight' phenomenon because of its control over the bodily changes needed when we are faced with danger and/or need to defend ourselves or escape. In a fight-or-flight situation the sympathetic nervous system prepares the body: heart rate quickens to get more blood to the muscles, breathing becomes faster and deeper to increase oxygen, blood flow is diverted from the organs so digestion is reduced and pupils dilate for better vision. In an instant, your body is prepared to either defend or escape.

Peripheral nervous system: the peripheral nervous system is divided into two sub-systems – the **Somatic Nervous System**, whose function is to regulate the actions of the skeletal muscles, and the **Autonomic Nervous System**, which regulates involuntary activity such as heart rate, breathing, blood pressure, and digestion.

Hemispheres: The brain has two hemispheres. The left hemisphere controls the right side of the body, and the right hemisphere controls the left side of the body.

Revision activity

Which bit of the central nervous system controls what? Write yourself a quiz so you can check your knowledge. For example: Where is the medulla oblongata? Is visual processing undertaken in the occipital or the temporal lobe of the brain? Does the somatic or the autonomic nervous system control heart rate?

Typical mistake

Make sure you do not confuse the sympathetic nervous system, the parasympathetic nervous system and the peripheral nervous system.

If the situation was not dangerous, the body adjusts but the parasympathetic nervous system takes several minutes to return the body to the state before the fright.

The structure and function of sensory, relay and motor neurons

A neuron is a specialised nerve cell that receives, processes and transmits information to other cells in the body.

Relay and motor neurons

Neurons are capable of carrying a message in one direction only. **Sensory neurons** are afferent neurons, meaning they relay information to the brain only. **Motor neurons** are efferent neurons, meaning they carry information from the brain to the target. **Relay neurons**, or interneurons, relay information from sensory neurons to motor neurons, bypassing the brain. For example, if you touched a hot stove, if the signal went all the way to your brain and back, your hand would be much more burned than from the instant jerk away from the stove.

Sometimes a very quick response is needed, one that does not need the brain's involvement. This is a reflex action. Reflex actions are rapid and happen without us thinking. The process is as follows:
- Receptor detects a stimulus – such as a hot stove.
- Sensory neuron sends signal to relay neuron.
- Motor neuron sends signal to effector.
- Effector produces a response.

Information comes to the neuron through the **dendrites** from other neurons and then continues to the cell body (soma), which is the main part of the neuron, containing the nucleus and maintaining the life-sustaining functions of the neuron – see Figure 2.5. The soma processes information and then passes it along the axon. At the end of the axon are bulb-like structures called terminal buttons, which pass on the information to glands, muscles or other neurons.

> **Sensory neurons:** afferent neurons which send messages from the body to the brain.
>
> **Motor neurons:** efferent neurons which send messages from the brain to the body.
>
> **Relay neurons:** these relay information from sensory neurons to motor neurons bypassing the brain.
>
> **Dendrites:** neurons have dendrites and information is passed through the dendrites to other neurons.

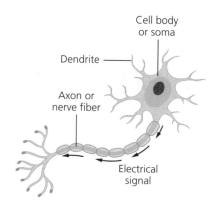

Figure 2.5 The process of a reflex action

Synaptic transmission

Information is carried by biochemical substances called neurotransmitters. The terminal buttons and the dendrites of other neurons do not touch, but instead pass the information containing neurotransmitters through a **synapse**. Once the neurotransmitter leaves the axon and passes through the synapse, it is caught on the dendrite by receptor sites.

> **Exam tip**
>
> You may need to be able to describe the difference between a relay and a motor neuron.

> **Synapse:** The gap between the terminal buttons of one neuron and the next.

Neurotransmitters play a role in the way we behave, learn, feel and sleep. Some play a role in mental illnesses:

- Dopamine – correlated with movement, attention and learning. Too much dopamine has been associated with schizophrenia.
- Norepinephrine – too little norepinephrine has been associated with depression, while an excess has been associated with schizophrenia.
- Serotonin – plays a role in mood and aggressive behaviour. Too little serotonin is associated with depression and OCD.
- Endorphins – are involved in pain relief and feelings of pleasure.

Neurotransmission: excitation and inhibition

Some neurons in the CNS release neurotransmitters that excite other neurons and some inhibit (prevent) neuronal activity.

Excitatory neurotransmitters

These are the neurons that conduct the action potential (AP) to release a neurotransmitter and they affect the postsynaptic neurons. What always causes a neuron to release any neurotransmitter (whether it is excitatory or inhibitory) is an action potential. All **excitatory neurotransmitters** cause sodium ions to flow in and the cell becomes less negative on the inside. These excitatory neurotransmitters create a local increase of permeability of sodium ion channels, which leads to a local depolarisation that is known as an **excitatory postsynaptic potential (EPSP)** because we are exciting the post-synaptic cell.

> **Excitatory neurotransmitters:** these excite (activate) other neurons.

> **Revision activity**
>
> Draw and label a diagram of the synapse showing the process of neurotransmission.

Inhibitory neurotransmitters

If an AP goes down the synaptic knob of another neuron and releases an inhibitory neurotransmitter, it is going to be activating different receptor sites on the cell membrane of the postsynaptic cell. When an inhibitory neurotransmitter causes an opening of potassium ion channels, this leads to an inhibitory postsynaptic potential (IPSP) because it is going to be *less* likely to generate an AP. Whether a neuron generates an AP or not depends on the overall sum of EPSPs and IPSPs occurring in the neuron at any moment in time.

> **Typical mistake**
>
> Do not confuse afferent sensory neurons that relay information to the brain with efferent motor neurons that carry information from the brain.

The function of the endocrine system

REVISED

The **endocrine system consists** of a set of glands that releases chemical products into the bloodstream. Glands are organs in the body that produce chemicals that control many of our bodily functions. The endocrine glands consist of the pituitary gland, the thyroid and parathyroid glands, the adrenal glands, the pancreas, the ovaries in women and the testes in men. The chemical messengers produced by these glands are called hormones. The bloodstream carries hormones to all parts of the body and the membrane of every cell has receptors for one or more hormones.

> **Endocrine system:** a set of glands that release chemicals such as hormones into the bloodstream.

- The pituitary gland is a pea-sized gland that controls growth and regulates other glands. The pituitary gland is controlled by the hypothalamus.
- The adrenal glands regulate moods, energy level and the ability to cope with stress. Each adrenal gland secretes adrenaline and noradrenaline, which act quickly. Adrenaline helps a person get ready for an emergency and arouses the sympathetic nervous system. Noradrenaline also alerts the individual to emergency situations by interacting

with the pituitary gland and the liver. Noradrenaline functions as a neurotransmitter when it is released by neurons, but in the adrenal glands is released as a hormone. The activation of the adrenal glands has an important role to play in the fight-or-flight response.

- The **pancreas**, located under the stomach, is a dual-purpose gland that performs both digestive and endocrine functions. The part of the pancreas that serves endocrine functions produces a number of hormones, including insulin – the essential hormone that controls glucose (blood sugar) levels in the body – and is related to metabolism and body weight.
- The ovaries in women and testes in men are the sex-related endocrine glands that produce hormones related to sexual development and reproduction.

> **Pancreas:** this gland performs both digestive and endocrine functions.

The nervous system and the endocrine system are intricately interconnected. The brain's hypothalamus connects the two systems, which work together to control the body's activities. The endocrine system differs from the nervous system – the parts of the endocrine system are not all connected in the way that the parts of the nervous system are and the endocrine system works more slowly than the nervous system because hormones are transported in our blood through the circulatory system.

The fight-or-flight response

REVISED

The fight-or-flight response is a chain of rapidly occurring physiological reactions that mobilises the body's resources to deal with threatening circumstances. It originates in the hypothalamus and includes the pituitary and adrenal glands. This hypothalamic–pituitary–adrenal axis is responsible for arousing the ANS in response to a threat. The sympathetic branch of the nervous system stimulates the adrenal gland to release adrenaline, noradrenaline and corticosteroids into the bloodstream. The increase in adrenaline produces the physiological reactions, such as increased heart rate and blood pressure and a dry mouth, known as the fight-or-flight response. After the threat is gone, it takes 20–60 minutes for the body to return to its pre-arousal levels.

> **Exam tip**
>
> In an exam you could be given a hypothetical situation and asked to describe the resulting physiological changes. For example, '... rushing towards Daniel, growling, snarling and drooling, was a huge black dog'. Outline the physiological changes that may occur in Daniel's body.

> **Revision activity**
>
> Make some SNAP cards so you can play revision snap. For each pair of cards, one card should show the gland name and its pair card should show the function of the gland, for example PANCREAS and DIGESTION, ADRENAL GLAND and MOOD. You could extend this game by adding neurotransmitter substances, such as SEROTONIN and MOOD, and parts of the brain, for instance TEMPORAL LOBE and HEARING, etc.

Localisation of function in the brain

REVISED

Hemispheric lateralisation

The brain has two hemispheres which are connected by, and which communicate with each other via, the corpus callosum.

Lateralisation is the theory that the left and right hemispheres are specialised to do different things. In general:
- the left hemisphere controls the right side of the body, is specialised for language and receives input from the RIGHT visual field
- the right hemisphere controls the left side of the body, is specialised for spatial tasks and receives input from the LEFT visual field.

> **Lateralisation:** the theory that the left and right hemispheres of the brain are specialised to do different things.

Split-brain research: Sperry (1968)

Sperry used split-brain patients to find out what happens when the two hemispheres cannot communicate with each other. The split-brain procedure involves cutting the corpus callosum which connects the two hemispheres. The operation is called a commissurotomy. The participants were 11 individuals who suffered from severe epileptic seizures that could not be controlled by drugs. A commissurotomy was performed to help their epilepsy.

Pictures were presented to the left or right visual field. The participant covered one eye and was instructed to look at a fixed point in the centre of a screen. Slides were projected to the right or left of the screen at a very high speed, one picture every 0.1 seconds or faster. Below the screen there was a gap so that the participant could reach objects but not see their hands.

- If a picture was first shown to the left visual field, the participant did not recognise it when the same picture appeared in the right visual field.
- If visual material appeared in the right visual field, the patient could describe it in speech and writing.

- If visual material appeared to the left visual field, the patient could identify the same object with their right hand but not their left hand.
- If visual material was presented to the left visual field, the participant reported seeing nothing or just a flash of light to their left. However, the participant could point to a matching picture or object with their right hand. This confirms that the right hemisphere cannot speak or write (called aphasia and agraphia).
- Sperry flashed two different pictures to right and left visual fields: $ to the left and ? to the right. Participants would draw a dollar sign with their left hand. All participants would *say* that they saw the question mark but if a patient was asked what he just drew he would say the question mark (which was the wrong answer).
- The right hemisphere was more responsive to emotion. If a nude figure was shown in among a series of geometric shapes, the participant typically denied seeing anything but at the same time the participant might blush or grin (controlled by the right hemisphere).

Sperry suggested that one hemisphere does not know what the other hemisphere is doing.

The specialised functions of the brain

The parietal lobe receives and processes all somatosensory input from the body (touch, pain). Fibres from the spinal cord are distributed by the thalamus to various parts of the parietal lobe. The rear of the parietal lobe has a section called Wernicke's area (see Figure 2.6), which is important for understanding the sensory (auditory and visual) information associated with language.

The frontal lobe is involved in motor skills (including speech) and cognitive functions. The motor centre of the brain, the pre-central gyrus, is located in the rear of the frontal lobe, receives connections from the somatosensory portion in the parietal lobe, and processes and initiates motor functions. Located within the temporal lobe, the basal ganglia work with the cerebellum to coordinate fine motions, such as fingertip movements.

Language centres in the brain

An area on the left side of the frontal lobe, called Broca's area, processes language by controlling the muscles of the mouth, lips and larynx that control sound. If Broca's area is damaged, the result is motor aphasia, in which patients can understand language but cannot produce meaningful or appropriate sounds.

> **Revision activity**
>
> Draw and label a diagram of the two hemispheres of the brain showing which hand is controlled by which hemisphere and the functions of the left and right hemispheres.

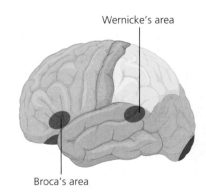

Wernicke's area

Broca's area

Figure 2.6 Language centres in the brain

Broca's area and Wernicke's area are connected by a bundle of nerve fibres called the arcuate fasciculus. Damage to the arcuate fasciculus causes a disorder called conduction aphasia. People with conduction aphasia can understand language but their speech does not make sense and they cannot repeat words.

The occipital lobe receives and processes visual information from the eyes and relates this information to the parietal lobe (Wernicke's area) and motor cortex (frontal lobe). The temporal lobe processes auditory information from the ears and relates it to Wernicke's area of the parietal lobe and the motor cortex of the frontal lobe.

Brain plasticity

REVISED

Brain plasticity refers to changes in neural pathways and synapses caused by changes in behaviour, environment and neural processes. Neuroplasticity has replaced the formerly held position that the brain is a physiologically static organ. Neuroplasticity occurs on a variety of levels, ranging from cellular changes due to learning to large-scale changes involved in cortical remapping in response to injury. The role of neuroplasticity is widely recognised in healthy development, learning, memory and recovery from brain damage. During most of the twentieth century, the general consensus among neuroscientists was that brain structure is relatively unchangeable after early childhood. However, research indicates that experience can actually change both the brain's physical structure and its functional organisation (refer to the study by Maguire on page 42). In a study in 2005, medical students' brains were imaged during the period when they were studying for their exams. In a matter of months, the students' grey matter increased significantly in the posterior and lateral parietal cortex.

Brain plasticity: the changes in neural pathways and synapses caused by changes in behaviour, environment and neural processes.

Functional recovery of the brain after trauma

Brain activity associated with a given function can also move to a different location in the brain in the process of recovery from brain injury and research suggests that brain plasticity can be taken advantage of to counteract the effects of aging.

Merzenich (1996) developed a series of plasticity-based computer programs known as Fast ForWord®. FastForWord® offers seven brain exercises to help with language and learning deficits. In a recent study, adults were given experimental training to see whether it would help to counteract the negative plasticity that results from age-related cognitive decline. The training included six exercises designed to reverse the dysfunctions caused by decline in cognition, memory and motor control. After using the program for 8–10 weeks, there was a significant increase in the participants' task-specific performance. The data collected from the study indicated that a neuroplasticity-based program could improve cognitive function.

Ways of studying the brain

REVISED

Post-mortem studies

Post-mortem researchers often conduct a study of the brain of an individual who has some sort of affliction (for instance, cannot speak, trouble moving left side of body, Alzheimer's, etc.). Researchers look at lesions in the brain that could have an influence on cognitive functions.

Post-mortem studies: a way of studying the brain after a person has died.

The irregularities or damage observed in the brain are studied in relation to the individual's illness, lifestyle and environment. Post-mortem studies provide a unique opportunity for researchers to study the brain in ways that would be impossible on a living person and allow them to develop hypotheses to associate the location in the brain with specific behaviour.

A benefit of post-mortem studies is that they enable researchers to make a wide range of discoveries because of the many different techniques used to obtain tissue samples. A disadvantage of post-mortem studies is that if changes are found in the brain, we cannot know whether those changes caused or resulted from behaviour. Also, post-mortem brain samples are limited because it is extremely difficult for a researcher to get hold of an individual's brain due to consent issues.

Electroencephalogram

Electroencephalography (EEG) records the electrical activity along the scalp and measures voltage fluctuations resulting from ionic current flows within the neurons of the brain. EEG is often used to diagnose sleep disorders and brain death. EEG used to be a first-line method of diagnosis for tumours and other focal brain disorders but this use has decreased with the advent of techniques such as fMRI and CT scans. EEG techniques include measuring evoked potentials (EP), which involves averaging the EEG activity in response to the presentation of a stimulus of some sort (visual, somatosensory or auditory). Event-related potentials (ERPs) refer to averaged EEG responses to complex stimuli. An ERP is the measured brain response that is the direct result of a specific sensory, cognitive or motor event.

The advantage of using EEG is that it provides a non-invasive means of evaluating brain functioning in patients with cognitive diseases.

Functional magnetic resonance imaging

Magnetic resonance imaging (MRI) is a non-invasive medical test that helps physicians diagnose and treat medical conditions. **Functional magnetic resonance imaging** (fMRI) is a relatively new procedure that uses MR imaging to measure the tiny metabolic changes that take place in an active part of the brain. This technique is becoming the diagnostic method of choice for learning how a normal, diseased or injured brain is working, as well as for assessing the potential risks of surgery or other invasive treatments of the brain. Physicians perform fMRI to examine the anatomy of the brain and to determine which part of the brain is handling critical functions such as thought, speech, movement and sensation (brain mapping). fMRI is also used to assess the effects of stroke, trauma or degenerative disease on brain function and to monitor the growth and function of brain tumours.

The advantage of using fMRI is that it provides a non-invasive means of finding out which parts of the brain are active and the level of activity.

> **Functional magnetic resonance imaging (fMRI):** used to examine the anatomy of the brain and to determine which part of the brain is active and the level of brain activity.

> **Exam tip**
>
> You could be given a hypothetical scenario and asked to (a) suggest how you would measure the brain activity, and (b) explain why you would choose the method you described.

Biological rhythms

REVISED

Circadian rhythms

The word '**circadian**' stems from the Latin *circa* (meaning 'about') and *diem* (meaning 'day'). There are some cycles that we are consciously aware of – the sleep/wake cycle being an obvious one – but others we are not, such as our body temperature fluctuating over a 24-hour period.

> **Circadian rhythms:** cycles of behaviour occurring every 24 hours (daily).

The biological basis of circadian rhythms: in non-human species, the pineal gland appears to be the brain structure responsible for regulating the circadian sleep/wake cycle. In humans, the suprachiasmatic nuclei (SCN) appears to control the sleep/wake cycle. The SCN is situated in the hypothalamus just behind the eyes and receives sensory input about light levels through the optic nerve.

Internal (endogenous) pacemakers: to study **endogenous pacemakers** it is necessary to isolate people from external cues for many months. French geologist Michel Siffre regularly spent extended periods of time in caves around the world and was studied during the process. In episodes in 1972 and 1999 his body clock extended from the usual 24 to around 24.5 hours, which appears to suggest:

- there is internal control (endogenous) of the circadian rhythm because even in the absence of external cues we are able to maintain a regular daily cycle
- there must usually be some external cue that keeps this cycle to 24 hours because when this is removed we adopt a 24.5- or 25-hour cycle.

External pacemakers (exogenous zeitgebers): light appears to be crucial in maintaining the 24-hour circadian rhythm, but Luce and Segal (1966) found that on the Arctic Circle people maintain a reasonably constant sleep pattern, averaging seven hours a night, despite six months of darkness in the winter months followed by six months of light in the summer. In these conditions it appears to be social factors rather than light levels that act to reset endogenous rhythms.

Infradian rhythms

Infradian rhythms occur over a period of time greater than 24 hours, for example in non-human animals, migration, mating patterns and hibernation. In humans, the best example of an infradian rhythm is the menstrual cycle, which lasts about one month. The cycle is under the internal (endogenous) control of hormones, particularly oestrogen and progesterone, secreted by the ovaries, but also can be influenced by external factors (zeitgebers), most notably living with other women.

Ultradian rhythms

Ultradian rhythms occur more than once in a 24-hour cycle and most are confined to either day or night, for example the stages of sleep. Sleep is an example of an ultradian rhythm as the cycle of sleep typically lasts about 90 minutes and during a typical night's sleep we will repeat this cycle four or five times. The stages of sleep can be monitored using EEG.

The stages of sleep

Awake: The brain is active and shows what is called desynchronised beta activity.

Stage 1 sleep (15 minutes): This occurs at the start of a night's sleep and lasts a matter of minutes. Brain waves are slower and are called 'theta'.

Stage 2 sleep (20 minutes): This stage is characterised by bursts of high-frequency waves called sleep spindles and at this stage we are still easily woken.

Stage 3 sleep (15 minutes): The brain waves start to slow and become higher in wavelength. These 'delta waves' are associated with deep sleep and we are now more difficult to wake.

> **Endogenous pacemakers:** internal (biological) pacemakers that regulate circadian or other rhythms.
>
> **Exogenous zeitgebers:** external pacemakers such as light and dark that regulate circadian rhythms such as the sleep wake cycle.

> **Typical mistake**
>
> It is a mistake to describe an exogenous zeitgeber as an endogenous pacemaker.

> **Infradian rhythms:** cycles of behaviour occurring over a period of time greater than 24 hours, for example, in women the menstrual cycle.
>
> **Ultradian rhythms:** a cycle of behaviour that repeats itself over a period of less than 24 hours.

Stage 4 sleep (30 minutes): Delta waves constitute most of the brain activity and we are now at our most relaxed and are very difficult to wake up. Heart rate and blood pressure fall, muscles are relaxed and temperature is at its lowest.

REM (rapid eye movement) sleep: The brain becomes very active, almost like a waking brain. Heart rate and blood pressure increase and the eyes move rapidly, giving this stage its name. Our first **REM sleep** lasts for about ten minutes and then we start our journey back down to stage 2, stage 3 and stage 4 sleep; this cycle repeats throughout the night. There are large individual differences between people; those who have been sleep deprived will spend longer in stage 4 and REM sleep.

> **REM sleep:** the stage of sleep in which desynchronised brain activity and rapid eye movements occur.

Summary

You should be able to identify, describe, give examples of and explain:
- the divisions of the nervous system
- the structure and function of sensory, relay and motor neurons, the process of synaptic transmission and the role of neurotransmitters
- the function of the endocrine system – glands and hormones and the role of adrenaline in the fight-or-flight response
- localisation of function in the brain and hemispheric lateralisation
- the visual, auditory and language centres (Broca's and Wernicke's areas) and split-brain research

- plasticity and functional recovery of the brain after trauma
- ways of studying the brain: scanning techniques, including functional magnetic resonance imaging (fMRI), electroencephalogram (EEG) and event-related potentials (ERPs), post-mortem examinations
- biological rhythms: circadian, infradian and ultradian and the difference between these rhythms; the effect of endogenous pacemakers and exogenous zeitgebers on the sleep/wake cycle.

Now test yourself

TESTED ☐

1 (a) Which of these is NOT a part of the brain?
   A The frontal lobe
   B The corpus callosum
   C The memory
   D The occipital lobe
   E Broca's area
  (b) Complete these sentences:
   (i)   The central nervous system consists of the _____.
   (ii) The somatic nervous system and the autonomic nervous system are the two parts of the _____.
   (iii) The biology of the fight-or-flight response is controlled by the _____.
   (iv) Information is carried between brain neurons by _____.
   (v) Relay neurons relay information from _____.
   (vi) Too little serotonin is thought to be the cause of _____.
2 (a) Which two of A, B, C or D were found in the Sperry split-brain research?
   A When an image was displayed on the left of the screen, the participant could not describe what was shown.
   B When an image was displayed on the left of the screen, the participant could find a matching object with their left hand.
   C When an image was displayed on the right of the screen, the participant could describe what was shown.
   D When an image was displayed on the right of the screen, the participant could not find a matching object with their right hand.

3 Complete these sentences:
   (a) The set of glands that releases hormones into the bloodstream is called _____.
   (b) Just beneath the hypothalamus sits a pea-sized gland called _____.
   (c) Adrenaline is a hormone that acts quickly to prepare the body to _____.
   (d) The brain has two hemispheres connected by the _____.
   (e) There are two language centres in the brain called _____.
   (f) A person suffering from _____ can understand language but cannot produce meaningful language.
4 (a) Name two of the lobes of the human brain.
   (b) What is the central nervous system made up of?
   (c) What does the autonomic nervous system control?
   (d) What does the hypothalamus control?
   (e) What prepares the body for fight or flight?
   (f) What are sensory neurons and what do they do?
   (g) What is the difference between a relay and a motor neuron?
   (h) Identify two neurotransmitter substances and their respective influences.
   (i) Name two glands in the endocrine system.
   (j) Explain what the findings from the split-brain studies suggest about the function of the left-brain hemisphere.
   (k) Outline one way to measure brain activity.
   (l) What is an ultradian rhythm?
   (m) What is an exogenous pacemaker?

Answers on page 237

Exam practice

1 During the fight-or-flight response, which of the following is true? [1]
   A   There is a decrease in the release of adrenaline.
   B   There is an extra flow of blood to the surface of the skin.
   C   The sympathetic division is in control.
   D   There is a reduction in the rate of respiration.
2 Briefly explain one function of the pancreas. [2]
3 Pinky and Perky are identical twins who were separated at birth, but Pinky is an introvert and Perky is an extrovert. Explain this difference in their personalities. [2]
4 Outline the role of adrenaline during the fight-or-fight response. [2]
5 Outline how split-brain studies investigated the effect of disconnecting the two hemispheres of the brain. [4]
6 Outline the structures and processes involved in neurotransmission. [6]
7 The postman ran as fast as he could from the snarling dog. Describe how the fight-or-flight response helped the postman escape unharmed. [6]
8 Outline two ethical issues that may arise when studying biological processes. [4]

Answers and quick quizzes 19, 20, 21 and 22 online

ONLINE

Research methods

Psychologists use many methods to conduct research. Quantitative research measures amounts of behaviour, usually by assigning a numeric value to what is being measured (the quantity). Qualitative research measures what behaviour is like (the quality) and usually results in descriptive data. **Quantitative data** are collected as numbers, while **qualitative data** are collected as descriptions.

Experimental methods

REVISED

Laboratory experiments

A laboratory experiment is a method of conducting research in which researchers try to control all the variables except the one that is changed between the experimental conditions. The variable that is changed is called the **independent variable (IV)** and the effect it may have is called the **dependent variable (DV)**. So the IV is manipulated and its effect (the DV) is measured. Laboratory experiments are conducted in controlled and often artificial settings.

> **Quantitative data:** objective, precise, usually numerical data that can be statistically analysed.
>
> **Qualitative data:** rich and detailed data collected in real-life settings, for example people's subjective opinions.
>
> **Independent variable (IV):** the variable that is manipulated (changed) between experimental conditions.
>
> **Dependent variable (DV):** the effect of the IV, or what is measured, in an experiment.

> **Evaluation**
>
> **Strengths**
> - High levels of control in a laboratory experiment allow extraneous variables that might affect the IV or the DV to be minimised. The researcher can be sure that any changes in the DV are the result of changes in the IV.
> - High levels of control make it possible to measure the effect of one variable on another. Statements about cause and effect can be made.
> - Laboratory experiments can be replicated to check the findings with either the same or a different group of participants.
>
> **Weaknesses**
> - Laboratory experiments may not measure how people behave outside in their everyday lives.
> - Aspects of the experiment may act as cues and cause the participants (and the experimenter) to change the way they behave (demand characteristics). This can mean that it is not the effect of the IV that is measured, leading to invalid results.

> **Typical mistake**
>
> In the exam students often confuse the IV with the DV – make sure you can define both and know which is which.

Field experiments

A field experiment is a way of conducting research in an everyday environment (such as a school or hospital), where one or more IVs are manipulated by the experimenter and the effect on the DV is measured. One difference between laboratory and field experiments is an increase in the naturalness of the setting and a decrease in the level of control that the experimenter is able to achieve. The key difference is the extent to which participants know they are being studied. Participants are aware of being studied in some field experiments, but this is not true of most, which is why participants' behaviour is more natural.

Evaluation

Strengths
- Field experiments allow psychologists to measure how people behave in their everyday lives.
- Manipulation of the IV and some level of control make it possible to measure the effect of one variable on another.
- If participants do not know they are participating in a study, they will be unaware that they are being watched and this reduces the probability that their behaviour results from demand characteristics.

Weaknesses
- It is not always possible to control for extraneous variables that might affect the IV or the DV so the researcher cannot always be sure that any changes in the DV are the result of changes in the IV.
- Field experiments can be difficult to replicate and thus it may not be possible to check the **reliability** of the findings.
- It may not be possible to ask participants for their informed consent, and participants may be deceived and not be debriefed, all of which are breaches of British Psychological Society ethical guidelines.

Reliability: reliability of results means consistency. In other words, if something is measured more than once, the same effect should result.

Natural (quasi) experiments

A natural experiment is one in which, rather than being manipulated by the researcher, the IV to be studied is naturally occurring. Some examples of naturally occurring variables are gender, age, ethnicity, occupation and being a smoker or non-smoker. When the IV is naturally occurring, participants cannot be randomly allocated between conditions. Just to complicate matters, a natural experiment may take place in a laboratory or in a field experimental setting.

Evaluation

Strengths
- Natural experiments allow psychologists to study the effects of IVs that could be unethical to manipulate.
- When participants are unaware of the experiment and the task is not contrived, research may have high internal validity.

Weaknesses
- Since participants cannot be allocated randomly between conditions it is possible that random variables (individual differences other than the IV) can also affect the DV. This may lead to low internal validity.
- Natural experiments can be difficult to replicate with a different group of participants. It may not be possible to check the reliability of the findings.

Observational techniques

REVISED

When psychologists conduct an observation, they usually watch people's behaviour but remain inconspicuous and do nothing to change or interfere with it.

Types of observation

The following types of observations can be carried out:
- **Naturalistic observation:** people or animals are observed in their natural environment, without any sort of intervention or manipulation of variables and without their knowledge.

- **Controlled observation:** the researcher may manipulate the behaviour of the observers or the observed, for example the Milgram study can be described as a controlled observation. These types of studies allow for greater control of confounding variables, meaning it is easier to establish cause and effect relationships.
- **Overt observation:** participants know they are being observed. This reduces ethical issues of consent and privacy but reduces validity due to increased demand characteristics.
- **Covert observation:** participants are unaware of the observation. This raises ethical issues (privacy and consent) but increases validity by reducing demand characteristics. Sometimes one-way mirrors might be used to discretely observe people, for example shopping behaviour in a supermarket.
- **Participant observation:** here the researchers get involved with the group of participants they are observing.
- **Non-participant observation:** participants are observed from a distance rather than the researchers infiltrating the group.

> **Typical mistake**
>
> It is wrong to tell the examiner that all covert observations are unethical.

Evaluation

Strengths

- Behaviour can be observed in its usual setting and there are generally no problems with demand characteristics unless the situation in which the participants are being observed has been specially contrived.
- Useful when researching children or animals.
- A useful way to gather data for a pilot study.

Weaknesses

- No explanation for the observed behaviour is gained because the observer counts instances of behaviour but does not ask participants to explain why they acted as they did.
- Observers may 'see what they expect to see' (observer bias) or may miss, or misinterpret, behaviour.
- Observational studies are difficult to replicate.

Self-report techniques

REVISED

Interviews and questionnaires

One way to find out about people's behaviour is to ask them, and psychologists often do this. However, what we say about our behaviour and how we actually behave may be different.

Structured interviews

All participants are asked the same questions in the same order. **Structured interviews** can be replicated and can be used to compare people's responses. However, they can be time consuming and require skilled researchers. People's responses can be affected by **social desirability bias**. This is a research term that describes the tendency of survey respondents to answer questions in a manner that will be viewed favourably by others. It can take the form of over-reporting of good behaviour or under-reporting of undesirable behaviour.

> **Structured interviews:** participants are asked the same questions in the same order.
>
> **Social desirability bias:** when people try to show themselves in the best possible way, so that when answering questions in interviews or questionnaires they give answers that are socially acceptable but are not truthful.
>
> **Unstructured interviews:** participants can discuss anything freely and the interviewer devises new questions on the basis of answers previously given.

Unstructured interviews

Participants can discuss anything freely and the interviewer can devise new questions on the basis of answers given previously. **Unstructured interviews** provide rich and detailed information, but they are not replicable and people's responses cannot be compared. They can be time consuming and people's responses can be affected by social desirability bias.

Questionnaires

Questionnaires are usually written but can be conducted face to face, or completed over the telephone, or on the internet. Participants complete printed questionnaires which are similar to structured interviews in that all participants are asked the same questions in the same order. Questionnaires are a practical way to collect a large amount of information quickly and they can be replicated. Problems can arise if the questions are unclear or if they suggest a 'desirable' response, as responses can be affected by social desirability bias.

Evaluation

Strengths
- Questionnaires can be used with large samples of participants.
- Structured interviews and questionnaires allow research to be replicated to test reliability.
- Interviews allow rich, detailed information to be gathered 'first hand' directly from the participants.

Weaknesses
- Self-report techniques cannot assume that participants will tell the truth; bias such as social desirability bias may lead to invalid results.
- Questionnaires or interviews may include leading questions that cause response bias.
- When closed questions are used, participants cannot explain their answers.

Correlation

REVISED

Correlation is a statistical technique used to quantify the strength of relationship between two variables. Studies that use correlational analysis cannot draw conclusions about cause and effect. For example, if a relationship is found between behaving aggressively and playing violent video games, individual differences in personality could be a factor that causes both of these. Just because two events occur together does not mean that one necessarily *causes* the other.

Correlation: a statistical technique used to calculate the correlation coefficient in order to quantify the strength of relationship between two variables.

Analysis of variables between co-variables

The correlation coefficient is a mathematical measure of the degree of relatedness between sets of data. Once calculated, a correlation coefficient will have a value between −1 and +1. Correlational data can be plotted as points on a scatter diagram. A line of best fit is then drawn through the points to show the trend of the data.
- If both variables increase together, this is a positive correlation.
- If one variable increases as the other decreases, this is a negative correlation.
- If no line of best fit can be drawn, there is no correlation.

Revision activity

Sketch three scatter diagrams, one showing a positive correlation, one showing a negative correlation and one showing no correlation.

REVISED

Evaluation

Strengths

- Correlational analysis allows researchers to calculate the strength of a relationship between variables as a quantitative measure. A co-efficient of +0.9 indicates a strong positive correlation; a coefficient of −0.3 may indicate a weak negative correlation.
- Where a correlation is found, it is possible to make predictions about one variable from the other.

Weaknesses

- Researchers cannot assume that one variable causes the other.
- Correlation between variables may be misleading and can be misinterpreted.
- A lack of correlation may not mean there is no relationship because the relationship could be non-linear.

Case studies

A case study is a detailed study into the life and background of one person (or a small group of people). Case studies involve looking at past records and asking other people about the participant's past and present behaviour. They are often focused on people who have unusual abilities or difficulties.

> **Exam tip**
>
> Remember, a case study is an ideographic research method.

Evaluation

Strengths

- They give a detailed picture of an individual and help to discover how a person's past may be related to their present behaviour.
- They can form a basis for future research.
- By studying the unusual we can learn more about the usual.

Weaknesses

- They can tell you about one person only, so findings can never be generalised.
- The interviewer may be biased and/or the interviewee may not tell the truth.
- Retrospective studies may rely on memory, which may be inaccurate or distorted, and past records may be incomplete.

Content analysis

A content analysis is a technique for systematically describing written, spoken or visual communication. It provides a quantitative (numerical) description. Content analyses may involve newspapers, magazines, television, video, movies or the internet. Content analysis studies human behaviour indirectly by looking at sources such as newspaper articles, television programmes and magazines. It is useful because an analysis of the sources we produce can inform us about the beliefs, prejudices and values of a society.

> **Typical mistake**
>
> It is a mistake to suggest that content analysis collects qualitative data only.

Manstead and McCulloch (1981)

Manstead and McCulloch (1981) watched 170 television advertisements in a week and scored them on a whole range of factors, such as the gender of the product user, the gender of the person in authority, the gender of the person providing the technical information and the type of product being advertised. They found that women were more likely to be portrayed as product users, to be cast in dependent roles and to be situated at home, but that men were more likely to be portrayed as product experts and as authority figures.

Evaluation

Strengths
- Can produce lots of detailed and easily analysed material about a particular aspect of society.
- Replication is possible if details of the sources (the content) and how the analysis was conducted are published.

Weaknesses
- Observers carrying out the analysis may be biased; to avoid bias, more than one observer should be used, with inter-rater reliability being established.
- The choice of content to be analysed can introduce a source of bias.

Now test yourself

TESTED

1 (a) Describe the main difference between a laboratory and a field experiment.
  (b) What is the defining characteristic of a natural (quasi) experiment?
  (c) Outline ONE advantage of using an experimental method in psychological research.
  (d) Outline ONE disadvantage of using an experimental method in psychological research.
  (e) Describe ONE disadvantage of naturalistic observations.
  (f) What is meant by inter-observer reliability?
  (g) When using the interview method, researchers may choose to ask open or closed questions. How do these differ?
  (h) Outline one advantage of using questionnaires to collect information.
  (i) Outline one disadvantage of using questionnaires to collect information.
  (j) What is the independent variable (IV) in a psychological experiment?
  (k) What is the dependent variable (DV) in a psychological experiment?
  (l) What is one advantage of using the observational method?
  (m) What is one disadvantage of using the observational method?
  (n) Why can't the findings from a case study be generalised to a wider population?
  (o) Identify one disadvantage of content analysis.

Answers on page 237 and quick quizzes 23 and 24 online

Scientific processes

You must be able to describe and explain the scientific processes involved in research.

Ethical research

REVISED

The British Psychological Society (BPS) has issued a set of **ethical guidelines** for research involving human participants. The following guidelines are adapted from 'Ethical principles for conducting research with human participants'. The complete text is available on the BPS website (www.bps.org.uk).

> **Ethical guidelines:** the British Psychological Society's ethical guidelines are designed to protect the well-being and dignity of research participants.

Ethical guidelines

- **Introduction:** good psychological research is possible only if there is mutual respect and confidence between investigators and participants. Ethical guidelines are necessary to clarify the conditions under which psychological research is acceptable.
- **General:** it is essential that the investigation should be considered from the standpoint of all participants; and foreseeable threats to their psychological well-being, health, values or dignity should be eliminated.
- **Consent:** whenever possible, the investigator should inform all participants of the objectives of the investigation. The investigator should inform the participants of all aspects of the research or intervention that might reasonably be expected to influence willingness to participate. Where research involves any persons under 16 years of age, consent should be obtained from parents or from those *in loco parentis*.
- **Deception:** the misleading of participants is unacceptable if the participants are typically likely to object or show unease once debriefed. Where this is in any doubt, appropriate consultation must precede the investigation. Intentional deception of the participants over the purpose and general nature of the investigation should be avoided whenever possible.
- **Debriefing:** where the participants are aware that they have taken part in an investigation, when the data have been collected the investigator should provide the participants with any necessary information to complete their understanding of the nature of the research.
- **Withdrawal from the investigation:** at the onset of the investigation, investigators should make plain to participants their right to withdraw from the research at any time, irrespective of whether or not payment or other inducement has been offered. The participant has the right to withdraw retrospectively any consent given, and to require that their own data, including recordings, be destroyed.
- **Confidentiality:** subject to the requirements of legislation, including the Data Protection Act, information obtained about a participant during an investigation is confidential unless otherwise agreed in advance. Participants in psychological research have a right to expect that information they provide will be treated confidentially and, if published, will not be identifiable as theirs.
- **Protection of participants:** investigators have a responsibility to protect participants from physical and mental harm during the investigation. Normally, the risk of harm must be no greater than in

ordinary life, i.e. participants should not be exposed to risks greater than or additional to those encountered in their normal lifestyles. Participants must be protected from stress by all appropriate measures, including the assurance that answers to personal questions need not be given.

- **Observational research:** studies based upon observation must respect the privacy and psychological well-being of the individuals studied. Unless those observed give their consent to being observed, observational research is acceptable only in situations where those observed would expect to be observed by strangers.
- **Giving advice:** if, in the normal course of psychological research, a participant solicits advice concerning educational, personality, behavioural or health issues, caution should be exercised. If the issue is serious and the investigator is not qualified to offer assistance, the appropriate source of professional advice should be recommended.

The dilemma of deception and informed consent

It can be argued that if participants are not deceived about the true aims of a study they will show the effects of demand characteristics. The dilemma for researchers is to design research that accurately portrays human behaviour while at the same time ensuring that they do not breach the ethical guidelines. Researchers may solve this dilemma by undertaking a cost–benefit analysis of the research before they commence. However, trying to balance potential benefits against potential costs raises problems because it is almost impossible to calculate the costs and benefits before a study, as the researchers cannot predict events accurately.

In some situations where deception may be used and it is not possible to obtain fully informed consent from the participants, psychologists propose the following alternatives.

Presumptive consent

When presumptive consent is gained, people who are members of the population to be studied are informed of the details of the study and asked whether, *if they were to participate*, they would consider the research acceptable.

Prior general consent

This involves asking questions of people who have volunteered to participate before they are selected to take part. For example:
- Would you mind being involved in a study in which you were deceived?
- Would you mind taking part in a study if you were not informed of its true objectives?
- Would you mind taking part in a study that might cause you some stress?

Participants who say they 'would not mind' may later be selected to participate and it is assumed they have agreed in principle to the conditions of the study.

Research methods and ethical issues

Each research method raises different ethical issues.

Laboratory experiment: even when told they have the right to withdraw, participants may feel reluctant to do so and may feel they should do things they would not normally do.

Field experiment: it may be difficult to obtain informed consent and participants may not be able to withdraw. It may be difficult to debrief the participants.

> **Typical mistake**
>
> Make sure you know that debriefing a participant takes place *after* they have participated, not before.

> **Typical mistake**
>
> Failing to gain informed consent is *not* the same as deception. Make sure you understand the difference.

Natural experiment: confidentiality may be a problem, as the sample studied may be identifiable. Where naturally occurring social variables are studied (such as family income, ethnicity), ethical issues may arise when drawing conclusions and publishing the findings.

Correlational studies: ethical issues can arise when researching relationships between socially sensitive variables because published results can be misinterpreted as suggesting 'cause and effect'.

Naturalistic observations: if informed consent is not gained, people should be observed in public places only and where they would not be distressed to find they were being observed. If the location in which behaviour was observed is identifiable, an ethical issue may arise in terms of protecting confidentiality.

Interviews and questionnaires: participants should not be asked embarrassing questions and should be reminded that they do not have to answer any questions if they do not wish to. Protecting confidentiality is important.

> **Naturalistic observations:** a research method in which psychologists watch people's behaviour but remain inconspicuous and do nothing to change or interfere with it.

Aims and hypotheses

REVISED

The **research aim** is a general statement of the purpose of the study and should make clear what the study intends to investigate. The aim states the purpose of the study but is not precise enough to test.

A hypothesis states precisely what the researcher believes to be true about the target population. It is often generated from a theory and is a testable statement.

> **Research aim:** a general statement of the purpose of the study. It should make clear what the study intends to investigate.

Experimental and alternative hypotheses

The term 'experimental hypothesis' is used when experimental research is being conducted (laboratory, field or natural experiments); otherwise the term 'alternative hypothesis' is used. The experimental hypothesis states that some difference (or effect) will occur; that the IV will have a significant effect on the DV.

The Null hypothesis

The **Null hypothesis** is a statement of no difference (or of no correlation); in effect it says the IV does not affect the DV. If data analysis forces researchers to reject the Null hypothesis because a significant effect is found, they then accept the experimental hypothesis.

> **Null hypothesis:** a statement of no difference or of no correlation — the IV does not affect the DV. It is tested by the inferential statistical test.

Directional and non-directional hypotheses

A directional hypothesis is termed a 'one-tailed hypothesis' because it predicts the direction in which the results are expected to go. Directional hypotheses are used when previous research evidence suggests that it is possible to make a clear prediction about the way in which the IV will affect the DV.

A non-directional hypothesis is termed a 'two-tailed hypothesis' because, although researchers expect that the IV will affect the DV, they are not sure how.

> **Revision activity**
>
> Bandura predicted that the children would imitate the behaviour of role models. Write an operationalised Null hypothesis for the Bandura study.

> **Revision activity**
>
> Write a fully operationalised directional hypothesis for the Bandura study.

> **Typical mistake**
>
> Do not confuse the alternative hypothesis with the Null hypothesis, and directional and non-directional hypotheses.

Sampling techniques

In some research the target population might be as broad as all humans, all males, all females, but in other types of research the target population might be a smaller group such as teenagers, pre-school children or people who donate to charity. It is more or less impossible to study every single person in a target population, so psychologists select a sample of the population that is likely to be representative of the target population they are interested in.

When researchers conduct research, the target population is the group of people to whom they wish to generalise their findings. The sample of participants is the group of people who take part in the study, and a representative sample is a sample of people who are representative of the target population. There are several ways in which researchers select a sample.

Random sampling

This involves having the names of the target population and giving everyone an equal chance of being selected. A random sample can be selected by a computer or, in a small population, by selecting names from a hat.
- **Strength:** a true random sample avoids bias, as every member of the target population has an equal chance of being selected.
- **Weakness:** it is almost impossible to obtain a truly random sample because not all the names of the target population may be known.

Opportunity sampling

This involves asking whoever is available and willing to participate. An **opportunity sample** is not likely to be representative of any target population because it will probably comprise friends of the researcher, or students, or people in a specific workplace. The people approached will be those who are local and available.
- **Strength:** the researchers can quickly and inexpensively acquire a sample, and face-to-face ethical briefings and debriefings can be undertaken.
- **Weakness:** opportunity samples are almost always biased samples, as who participates is dependent on who is asked and who happens to be available at the time.

> **Opportunity sampling:** asking whoever is available and willing to participate.

> **Typical mistake**
>
> An opportunity sample of people who are approached in a street is not a random sample.

Volunteer sampling

Volunteer samples are exactly that: people who volunteer to participate. A volunteer sample may not be representative of the target population because there may be differences between the sorts of people who volunteer and those who do not.
- **Strength:** the participants should have given their informed consent, will be interested in the research and may be less likely to withdraw.
- **Weakness:** a volunteer sample may be a biased sample that is not representative of the target population because volunteers may be different in some way from non-volunteers. For example, they may be more helpful (or more curious) than non-volunteers.

> **Volunteer sampling:** participants volunteer to participate, for example by responding to advertisements.

> **Systematic sample:** participants are selected in a systematic way from the target population, for example every tenth participant on a list of names.

Systematic sampling

A **systematic sample** selects participants in a systematic way from the target population, for example every tenth participant on a list of names.

To take a systematic sample you list all the members of the population and then decide on a sample size. By dividing the number of people in the population by the number of people you want in your sample, you get a number and then you take every nth to get a systematic sample.

- **Strength:** this method should provide a representative sample.
- **Weakness:** is possible only if you can identify all members of the population to be studied.

Stratified sampling

In **stratified sampling** the researcher identifies the different types of people that make up the target population and works out the proportions needed for the sample to be representative.

A list is made of each variable of interest, such as gender, age group, occupation, which might have an effect on the research. For example, if we are interested in why some people donate to a charity and some don't, gender, age and income may be important, so we work out the relative percentage of each group in our population of interest. The sample must then contain all these groups in the same proportion as in the target population.

- **Strength:** the sample should be highly representative of the target population and therefore we can generalise from the results obtained.
- **Weakness:** gathering such a sample would be time consuming and difficult to do, so this method is rarely used.

> **Stratified sample:** the sample is made in proportion to the types of people in the population.

Sample representativeness

The sample of participants should be a true representation of diversity in the target population. Students are often used as participants, but an all-student sample is representative only of a target population of students. Likewise, an all-male sample may be representative only of an all-male target population. If the sample is not representative, the research findings cannot be generalised to the target population.

Researchers also need to decide how many participants are needed, which depends on several factors:

- The sample must be large enough to be representative of the target population.
- Too many participants make research expensive and time consuming.
- If the research has important implications, the sample size should be larger than it would be in a less important study. In small samples, the individual differences between participants will have a greater effect.
- If the effect being studied is likely to be small, a larger sample will be required.

Pilot studies

REVISED

A **pilot study** is an initial run-through of the procedures to be used in the research and usually involves selecting a few people and trying out the study on them. Pilot studies save time, and in some cases money, by identifying any flaws in the procedures. A pilot study can help the researcher spot any unusual things or confusion in the information given to participants or problems with the task devised. For example, the procedure (task) may be too difficult and the researcher may get a floor effect because none of the participants can complete the task, or the task may be too easy so that all participants achieve high scores and

> **Pilot study:** a trial run of research with a small number of participants allow researchers to make necessary adjustments and to save wasting valuable resources.

thus a ceiling effect occurs. The ceiling effect usually happens when the task is too easy so that all participants score very highly, while the floor effect occurs when the task is too difficult so that all scores are very low. A pilot study is very useful when a questionnaire is to be used, as the study can help identify any potential misunderstanding of the questions.

Experimental designs

REVISED

Independent groups

Different participants are used in each of the conditions.
- **Strengths:** no participants are 'lost' between trials. Participants can be randomly allocated between the conditions to distribute individual differences evenly. There are no practice effects.
- **Weaknesses:** needs more participants and there may be important differences between the groups to start with that are not removed by the random allocation of participants between conditions.

Repeated measures

The same group of participants is used in each of the conditions.
- **Strengths:** requires fewer participants and controls for individual differences between participants as, in effect, the participants are compared against themselves.
- **Weaknesses:** cannot be used in studies in which participation in one condition will affect responses in another (for example, where participants learn tasks). Cannot be used in studies where an order effect would create a problem (see below).

Order effects and counterbalancing

When a **repeated measures design** is used, problems may arise from participants doing the same task twice. The second time they carry out the task, they may be better than the first time because they have had practice, or worse than the first time because they have lost interest or are tired. If this happens, then an order effect is occurring.

One way that researchers control for **order effects** is to use a **counterbalancing** technique. The group of participants is split and half the group complete condition A followed by condition B; the other half completes condition B followed by condition A. In this way, any order effects are balanced out.

Matched pairs (matched participants) design

Separate groups of participants are used and are matched on a one-to-one basis on characteristics such as age or sex, to control for the possible effect of individual differences.
- **Strengths:** matching participants controls for some individual differences. It can be used when a repeated measures design is not appropriate (for example, when performing the task twice would result in a practice effect).
- **Weaknesses:** a large number of prospective participants are needed from which to select matched pairs. It is difficult to match on some characteristics (such as personality).

> **Repeated measures design:** the same group of participants is used in each of the conditions.
>
> **Order effects:** in a repeated measures design, order effects arise from participants doing the same task twice because the second time they may be better than the first time as they have had practice or worse than the first time because they have lost interest or are tired.
>
> **Counterbalancing:** a way of controlling for order effects by having half the participants complete condition A followed by condition B; the other participants complete condition B followed by condition A.

Observational design

When designing an observation the researcher must decide how different behaviour should be categorised in order to measure causes and effects. Some types of behaviour are relatively easy to categorise – for instance, 'walk', 'run', 'sleep', 'smoke' – but others are more subtle. Unless behaviour is clearly categorised, different observers may interpret the same behaviour in different ways, resulting in low **inter-observer reliability**. When planning an observational study, the formulation of the hypothesis and decisions about how best to categorise the behaviour should be undertaken by carrying out preliminary observations of a small sample of participants. When the behavioural categories have been decided, researchers also decide who is going to be observed, how and when, and how the categories of behaviour are collected.

> **Inter-observer reliability:** whether, in an observational study, if several observers are coding behaviour, their codings or ratings agree with each other.

Focal sampling records the behaviour of one individual at a time. One disadvantage of this method is that your focal 'person' may not engage in any of the behaviour categories of interest. Also, the person you are observing may become aware of your interest.

Event sampling consists of observing a group and recording each time a specific behaviour (the event) occurs. This allows observation of a large number of individuals, but has the disadvantage that certain individuals or behaviour may be more conspicuous than others, leading to biased recording.

Time sampling divides the observation period into sample intervals, for example every two minutes. A watch can be used to indicate each sample interval. The observer makes a note of the behaviour occurring at each time interval on a pre-prepared tally chart. The study by Bandura (the Bobo doll study) used a time sampling technique.

Questionnaire construction

Questionnaires provide a relatively cheap, quick and efficient way of obtaining large amounts of information from a large sample of people. Often a questionnaire uses both open and closed questions to collect data, which means that both quantitative and qualitative data can be obtained. The questions should address the aims of the research. The longer the questionnaire is, the less likely people are to complete it. A pilot study can be used to ensure people understand the questions. On the questionnaire, easier questions should be first, followed by more difficult questions, and technical jargon should be avoided.

Closed questions

Closed questions allow only answers which fit into categories that the researcher has decided in advance. Closed questions can also be rating scales and this often involves the participant choosing which option on the scale best reflects their attitude.

- **Strengths:** the data can be quickly obtained as closed questions are easy to answer. The questions are standardised – all respondents are asked the same questions in the same order – which means the questionnaire can be replicated to check for reliability.
- **Weaknesses:** the answers lack detail – they tell the researcher 'what' but not 'why'.

Open questions

Open questions enable respondents to answer in as much detail as they like and provide qualitative information. However, they are harder to analyse and make comparisons from.

- **Strengths:** rich, qualitative data are obtained as open questions allow the respondent to elaborate and explain their answer.
- **Weaknesses:** it takes longer for the researcher to analyse qualitative information as they have to read the answers and try to put them into categories by coding, which is often subjective and difficult. Open questions may be problematic as they require writing skills and/or an ability to express feelings verbally.

Design of interviews

Interviews involve social interaction. The language the interviewer uses should be appropriate to the group of people being studied and interviews may not be the best method to use for researching socially sensitive topics. The researcher must decide whether to use a structured or non-structured interview and must consider who the interviewer will be because the interviewer's gender, ethnicity and age can have a big effect on respondents' answers.

Structured interview

The questions are asked in a fixed and standardised order and the interviewer will not deviate from the interview schedule.

- **Strengths:** structured interviews are easy to replicate as a fixed set of closed questions is used, which means it is easy to test for reliability. Structured interviews are fairly quick to conduct, which means that many interviews can take place within a short amount of time.
- **Weaknesses:** structured interviews are not flexible, so new questions cannot be asked during the interview.

Unstructured interview

These are sometimes referred to as discovery interviews and they will contain open-ended questions that can be asked in any order.

- **Strengths:** the questions can be changed depending on the respondents' answers. They generate qualitative data through the use of open questions, which allow the respondents to talk in depth. They have increased validity because the interviewer has the opportunity to ask for clarification.
- **Weaknesses:** can be time consuming to conduct and to analyse the qualitative data. Training interviewers is expensive and the interviewer may need skills, for example the ability to establish a rapport with the respondent.

> **Exam tip**
>
> Be prepared to answer an exam question on the difference between a structured and an unstructured interview.

Research variables

REVISED

Independent variable: the variable we *manipulate* in experimental research.

Dependent variable: the variable we *measure* in experimental research.

Operationalisation of variables: being able to define variables in order to manipulate the IV and measure the DV. However, some variables are easier to operationalise than others – for example, performance on a memory test might be operationalised as 'the number of words remembered', but it is more difficult to operationalise 'attention'. Both

> **Operationalisation of variables:** being able to define variables in order to manipulate the IV and measure the DV, for example performance on a memory test might be operationalised as 'the number of words remembered from a list of words'.

the IV and the DV need to be precisely operationalised, otherwise the research cannot be replicated because another researcher would not be able to set up a study to repeat the same measurements.

Control of extraneous variables: any variables that change between the conditions, other than the IV, are difficult to control (for example, how tired the participants are). Environmental variables that may affect participants' performance, such as the time of day or location, also need to be controlled.

Controls

Extraneous or confounding variables: are there any variables that have not been controlled and that may also have an effect on the IV or on the DV (which reduces the experimental validity of the study)? Confounding variables may be environmental variables that may affect participants' performance, such as the time of day or location, and also need to be controlled.

Controls and standardisation: controls should be used to try to avoid variables other than the IV from affecting the DV. Controls can include random allocation of participants to experimental conditions to distribute individual differences within the sample equally between conditions. Controls can also include counterbalancing (see Repeated measures on page 73) and the use of standardised instructions and procedures by which all participants are told what to do in exactly the same way and are treated in exactly the same way.

Demand characteristics and investigator effects

As soon as people know their behaviour is of interest, it is likely to change. There are various ways in which participation in research can affect behaviour:

- **Hawthorne effect:** if people are aware that they are being studied, they are likely to try harder on tasks and pay more attention. This may mean that any findings, such as response times, are artificially high, which may lead to invalid conclusions.
- **Demand characteristics:** sometimes, features of the research situation may give cues to participants as to how they are expected to behave. This may lead to response bias, in which participants try to please the experimenter (or deliberately do the opposite), in which case conclusions drawn from the findings may be invalid. Demand characteristics may be reduced if a single-blind procedure is used. Here, participants do not know which condition they are participating in, or are given a false account of the experiment. If a single-blind procedure is used, ethical issues arise because fully informed consent cannot be gained.
- **Social desirability bias:** people usually try to show themselves in the best possible way. So, when answering questions in interviews or questionnaires, they may give answers that are socially acceptable but not truthful. For example, people tend to under-report anti-social behaviour, such as alcohol consumption and smoking, and over-report pro-social behaviour, such as giving to charity.

> **Hawthorne effect:** when people are aware that they are being studied, it is likely that they will try harder on tasks and will pay more attention.

> **Typical mistake**
>
> It is a mistake to suggest that a demand characteristic is something that the participant does.

Investigator effects

Researchers may unwittingly affect the results of their research in several ways:

- **Investigator expectancy:** the researcher's expectations can affect how they design their research and bias how and what they decide to measure, and how the findings are analysed.
- **Experimenter bias:** the experimenter can affect the way participants behave. One way to reduce experimenter effects is to use a double-blind procedure in which neither the experimenter nor the participants know what the research hypothesis is.
- **Interviewer effects:** the interviewer's expectations may lead them to ask leading questions, or they may focus only on answers that match their expectations.
- **Observer bias:** when observing behaviour, observers may make biased interpretations of the meaning of behaviour.

Reliability and validity

REVISED

Reliability

Reliability of results means consistency. In other words, if something is measured more than once, the same effect should result. If my tape measure tells me I am 152 cm tall one day but 182 cm tall the next, the tape measure I am using is not reliable.

> **Typical mistake**
>
> Make sure you do not make a point about reliability supported by evidence relating to validity.

Internal reliability refers to how consistently a method measures within itself. For example, my tape measure should measure the same distance between 0 cm and 10 cm as it does between 10 cm and 20 cm. To test for internal reliability, researchers may use the split-half technique in which half of the scores are compared with the other half to see how similar they are.

External reliability refers to the consistency of measures over time (i.e. if repeated). For example, personality tests should not give different results if the same person is tested more than once. External reliability can be tested by the test–re-test method. For example, the same participants can be tested on more than one occasion to see whether their results remain similar.

Inter-observer reliability assesses whether, in an observational study, if several observers are coding behaviour, their coding or rating agrees with that of the others. To improve reliability, all observers must have clear and operationalised categories of behaviour and must be trained in how to use the system. Inter-observer reliability can be measured using correlational analysis, in which a high positive correlation among ratings indicates that high inter-observer reliability has been established.

Validity

Internal validity refers to the extent to which a technique measures what it is supposed to measure, whether the IV really caused the effect on the DV or whether some other factor was responsible. One aspect of internal validity is mundane realism, i.e. do the measures used generalise to real life? For example, does a measure of long-term memory based on remembering lists of words generalise to how people really remember past events?

External validity refers to the validity of a study outside the research situation and provides some idea of the extent to which the findings can

> **Internal validity:** the extent to which a technique measures what it is supposed to measure, whether the IV really caused the effect on the DV or whether some other factor was responsible.
>
> **External validity:** the validity of a study outside the research situation and the extent to which the findings can be generalised.

be generalised. To assess the external validity of research, three factors should be considered:

- How representative is the sample of participants of the population to which the results are to be generalised (population validity)?
- Do the research setting and situation generalise to a realistic real-life setting or situation (ecological validity)?
- Do the findings generalise to the past and to the future (ecological and historical validity)? For example, 50 years ago in the UK people were more conformist and obedient than they are today.

Face validity is simply whether the test appears, at face value, to measure what it claims to.

Construct validity refers to the extent to which a test captures a specific construct or trait, and it overlaps with some of the other aspects of validity. To test for construct validity it must be demonstrated that the phenomenon being measured actually exists. So, the construct validity of a test for intelligence is dependent on a model or theory of intelligence.

Concurrent validity is the degree to which a test corresponds to an external criterion that is known concurrently (i.e. occurring at the same time). If the new test is validated by a comparison with a currently existing criterion, we have concurrent validity.

Temporal validity refers to the extent to which the findings and conclusions of study are valid when we consider the differences and progressions that come with time. Studies that are temporally valid will either be recent studies or will be studies that consider something which has not changed since the study was completed, but a study into social influence in the 1950s may be low in temporal validity today.

Improving validity

Internal validity can be improved by controlling extraneous variables, using standardised instructions, counterbalancing, and eliminating demand characteristics and investigator effects. External validity can be improved by setting experiments in an everyday, non-artificial setting and by carrying out covert rather than overt observations, and using **random sampling** techniques to select participants.

> **Typical mistake**
>
> Do not confuse research reliability and research validity.

> **Random sampling:** having the names of the target population and giving everyone an equal chance of being selected.

Features of science

REVISED

The empirical approach (all knowledge comes through our senses) is the scientific approach. The nature of scientific enquiry may be thought of as to do with theory and the foundation of hypotheses and with empirical methods of enquiry (that is, experiments, observations). The most empirical method of enquiry in science is the experiment. The important features of the experiment are control over variables (independent, dependent and extraneous), careful objective measurement and establishing cause and effect relationships.

Key features include the following:
- **Empirical evidence:** data being collected through direct observation or experiment; empirical evidence does not rely on opinion or belief. Experiments and observations are carried out and reported in detail so that other investigators can repeat and attempt to verify the work.
- **Objectivity:** researchers remain unbiased in their investigations and all sources of bias such as personal or subjective ideas are eliminated.

- **Control:** extraneous variables need to be controlled in order to be able to establish cause (IV) and effect (DV).
- **Predictability:** scientists should aim to be able to predict behaviour from the findings of research.
- **Hypothesis testing:** a hypothesis serves as a prediction and is derived from a theory. Hypotheses are stated in a form that can be tested (i.e. operationalised).
- **Replication:** can a particular method and finding be repeated with different/the same people and/or on different occasions to see whether the results are the same? If a discovery is reported but it cannot be replicated by other scientists, it will not be accepted. Replicability of research is vital in establishing a scientific theory.
- **Falsifiability:** the scientific process is based on the hypothetico-deductive model as proposed by Karl Popper (1935). Popper suggested that theories should come first and these should be used to generate hypotheses which can be falsified by observations and experiment. According to Popper, falsification is the only way to be certain because 'no amount of observations of white swans can allow us to conclude that all swans are white, but the observation of a single black swan is sufficient to falsify that conclusion'.

Is psychology a science?

Thomas Kuhn argued that scientific disciplines have one predominant paradigm that almost all scientists subscribe to and that anything with several paradigms (e.g. more than one model or theory) is not a science until the multiple theories are unified. Because psychologists do not have any universal laws of human behaviour, and with many paradigms (approaches) within psychology, Kuhn would argue that psychology is not a science.

According to Kuhn, a paradigm shift is a change in the basic assumptions, or paradigms, within the ruling theory of a science. Kuhn believed that 'a student in the humanities (e.g. psychology) has constantly before him a number of competing solutions to problems' (think of the different approaches to explaining behaviour as being the competing explanations). Kuhn argued that once a paradigm shift is complete, a scientist such as a physicist or chemist cannot reject the new theory (paradigm), but in psychology researchers can choose to adopt an array of stances, such as cognitive, behaviourist, biological and psychodynamic explanations for human behaviour.

Peer review

REVISED

Peers are professionals in the same field as the psychologist whose research is being reviewed. The most common way of validating new knowledge is peer review. Peer reviews occur before a study is published and serve three main purposes:

- **Allocation of research funding:** the peer reviews help to determine where research funding should go.
- **Publication in scientific journals:** peer reviews help decide whether research is good enough to be published and positive peer reviews can catch the eye of journal editors.
- **Research rating of a university department:** a positive peer review can improve the research rating and credibility of a university/ department.

> **Exam tip**
>
> If you answer a question on peer review, make it clear that this occurs before research is published.

- **The internet and peer review:** more research is being published in internet-based journals and the nature of peer review is changing. Usually, peers are experts in the research field, but when published on the internet, any reader can review research.

Reporting psychological investigations

Psychological reports are always presented in the same research report structure.

Sections of a scientific report

Title page: this indicates what the study is about – the research question.

Abstract: this allows the reader to find out the essentials of the research before they read the detail. The abstract gives brief details of the topic of the study, the participants – who, when, where, how many – the method, design, experimental task, major findings and the conclusion drawn from them, and implications for further research.

Introduction: this explains the background to the research hypothesis and outlines specific and relevant background research. The introduction includes the aim of the research and the hypotheses to be tested.

Method: this is written in detail so that research can be replicated. It includes details on:
- **experimental design:** (if appropriate) independent and dependent variables, what participants had to do, what was controlled and how
- **participants:** the target population, how the sample was obtained, why this sample was chosen, and details such as age range and gender of the sample
- **materials:** for example, pictures, word lists, instructions, debrief, etc. – examples of the actual materials are included in the appendix to the report
- **procedure:** the precise procedure followed, including detail on the brief, standardised instructions and debriefing.

Results: this is a summary of the findings, including statistics, tables and/or charts and, if appropriate, the inferential statistical tests used and why these tests were chosen, the observed and critical values of the tests and the research conclusion in terms of the hypothesis.

Discussion: this compares the results to background materials from the introduction section and whether/why similarities/differences have been found. It also contains a critique of the research and ideas for further research.

References: all the books and materials referred to in the course of the research are cited here. In psychological reports, references are always set out in APA referencing format (APA referencing guidelines are laid out in the sixth edition of the *Publication Manual of the American Psychological Association*). References are listed in alphabetical order by surname.

> **Revision activity**
>
> Practise writing references in the APA format because in the exam you may be given an example of a wrongly written reference and asked to correct it.

Economic implications of psychological research

Memory

Research into eyewitness testimony could have implications for the economy because improving eye witness testimony can lead to more accurate eye witnesses, thus saving time and money on police resources.

If the cognitive interview is more effective than the standard police interview, then time and therefore money could be saved by conducting more effective interviews.

Social influence

Understanding minority influence has implications for the economy because influential minorities can advocate change that will benefit the economy – for example, they can persuade people to recycle, thus saving money and using fewer resources.

Psychopathology

Research into the effectiveness of treatment for mental illness could lead to the NHS saving money. Also, if treatments are effective, people will be able to return to work and will contribute to the economy rather than being unable to work and claiming benefits.

Treatments that have a long-term effect, such as CBT, could save money on treating people in the future.

Attachment

Bowlby's view that children need their mothers may lead to women feeling pressure to stay at home and be 'a good mother', which means they would not be working and paying taxes.

Research shows that the harmful effects of deprivation/privation have implications for the economy. A child who has secure childhood attachments goes on to become a productive member of society who contributes to the economy, but children who grow up in disrupted families or who experience deprivation or privation may require the government to help or support them in later life.

Biopsychology and cognitive psychology

Having machines that can recognise faces, and translate text from one language to another, saves time and money. The application of biopsychology and cognitive psychology has contributed to the development of such machines. Facial recognition systems can identify a person from a digital image, or from a video source, by comparing selected facial features from the image to a facial database. Used in security systems, facial recognition systems can reduce crime and prevent identity fraud. In casinos, guests entering the gambling area are photographed and their faces are compared with the database of known cheaters and suspicious people or to identify favoured guests so that employees can give them special treatment. Future applications may include ATM and cheque-cashing security so that there will be no need for a picture ID, bank card or personal identification number (PIN) to verify a customer's identity.

The application of cognitive psychology has contributed to the development of machines that can translate text from one language to another and real-time translation is being developed to translate conference calls while they are in progress. Cognitive psychologists have also contributed to the development of speech-recognition software and modern smartphones have voice-activated features that handle tasks such as finding a location, dialling a phone number and dictating email.

Now test yourself

1 (a) A student investigating bullying in secondary schools designed a questionnaire to be circulated to all students. Identify one ethical issue the researcher would need to consider.
  (b) List two ways that Milgram broke today's ethical guidelines.
  (c) List one way that Bandura broke today's ethical guidelines.
  (d) Students who revise for two hours a day for three weeks before the exam will attain higher grades in their maths exam than students who do not revise.
    (i) Is this a Null hypothesis or an alternative hypothesis?
    (ii) Is this a one-tailed or a two-tailed hypothesis?
    (iii) Is this a directional or a non-directional hypothesis?

2 (a) There are 53 students studying psychology. Explain how I could obtain a random sample of 20 psychology students.
  (b) Why is an opportunity sample almost always a biased sample?
  (c) If you want a systematic sample of 20, from a list of 100 names which will you pick?
  (d) I am testing a new drug. Would it be better if I selected a large sample or a small sample?
  (e) Suggest one reason why a pilot study is useful.
  (f) Explain the difference between an independent design and a repeated measures design.

3 (a) Why are fewer participants needed in a repeated measures design?
  (b) Suggest when it would be better to use an independent design.
  (c) Why did the Bandura Bobo doll study use a matched participants design?
  (d) Complete these sentences:
    (i) Focal sampling records the behaviour of _____
    (ii) In an event sampled observation _____
    (iii) In a time sampled observation _____
  (e) TRUE or FALSE?
    (i) Closed questions can be used to collect frequency data.
    (ii) Closed questions collect quantitative data.
    (iii) The answers to open questions lack detail.
    (iv) Qualitative data is often subjective.
    (v) In a structured interview, questions are asked in a fixed order.
    (vi) Open questions collect qualitative data.

4 What does 'operationalisation of variables' mean?

5 You are going to conduct an observation of pro-social behaviour on the high street. Suggest two categories of behaviour you might observe.

6 A researcher used a questionnaire to find out whether people were interested in space research. The questionnaire had eight questions. The critical question, rated on a scale of 0–10, where 0 is boring and 10 is extremely interesting, was: how interesting do you find news about space research? The questionnaire was handed out to an opportunity sample of 100 people.
  (a) Comment on the reliability of this research.
  (b) Comment on the validity of this research.

7 List three features we expect to see in a scientific research project.

8 Suggest one of the purposes of peer review.

9 Where in the report of a psychological study would you find the information 'The 20 volunteer male participants were aged between 18 and 30 and all lived in South London'?

Answers on page 238 and quick quizzes 25, 26, 27 and 28 online

Data handling and analysis

Primary and secondary data
REVISED

Primary data are data that are collected by different methods, including observation, surveys, interviews, experiments and case studies. Primary data are more reliable than secondary data because the researcher knows their sources.

Secondary data are data collected from external sources, for example radio, the internet, magazines, newspapers, reviews and research articles. However, with secondary data, issues such as validity and reliability occur as the researcher can be less sure of the accuracy of the source.

A meta-analysis is a statistical technique that involves combining and analysing the results of different individual studies on a specific topic. This technique allows researchers to identify any trends and relationships that might exist. Because a meta-analysis combines multiple smaller samples into a much larger pool of data, researchers can sometimes identify trends that would not be seen in smaller-scale studies.

Quantitative and qualitative data
REVISED

Experimental research, observations, interviews and questionnaires can result in quantitative and/or qualitative data.

Quantitative data are scientific and objective. Numeric measures are used and data can be statistically analysed. Data are high in reliability. However, quantitative data may lack detail and are often collected in contrived settings.

Qualitative data are rich and detailed and often collected in real-life settings. They can provide information on people's attitudes, opinions and beliefs. However, qualitative data may be subjective and an imprecise measure and may be low in reliability.

> **Revision activity**
>
> Make a list of the research you know that collects qualitative data, for example the Strange Situation.

Levels of measurement
REVISED

Nominal-level data (frequencies of occurrence)

Example: How many cars are red, black or blue? In a box of fruit, how many are peaches, pears or plums?

Use the mode as the measure of central tendency – it makes no sense to calculate the mean because you cannot have an average of five red cars and two yellow cars, or six peaches and four plums.

Ordinal-level data (can be ranked in order: first, second, third, etc.)

Example: Six students' ratings (out of 10) of how hard they are revising = 3, 6, 7, 8, 9, 10.

Use the median as the measure of central tendency (middle score) because the mean can be affected by 'extreme' scores.

Interval-level data (measured on a fixed scale, for example height in inches)

Example: Temperature in degrees = 13.1, 15.2, 16.2, 17.2, 18.2, 19.5.

Use the mean as the measure of central tendency (mathematical midpoint) because this gives a precise measure of the central tendency – but beware, in small samples the mean can be affected by 'extreme' scores.

Descriptive statistics

Measures of central tendency and dispersion are used to summarise large amounts of data into typical or average values and to provide information on the variability or spread of the scores.

Measures of central tendency

There are three ways to calculate the average of a set of scores: the mean, the median and the mode.

The mean

To calculate the mean, all the scores are added up and the total is divided by the number of scores. For example, take the following set of scores: 2, 3, 5, 7, 8, 9, 13, 17. The mean of this set of scores is 64 divided by 8 = 8.

The advantage of the mean is that it takes into account all the values from the raw scores. However, if there are unusual (extremely high or low) scores in the dataset, the mean can be distorted, and if used inappropriately it may have a 'weird' decimal point that was not in the original scores (for example, 2.4 dogs).

The median

The median is the central score in a list of rank-ordered scores. In an odd number of scores, the median is the middle number. In an even-numbered set of scores, the median is the midpoint between the two middle scores. For example, take the following set of scores: 2, 3, 5, 7, 8, 9, 12, 17, 18. The median of this set of scores is 8. The mean of this set of scores is 9 (81 divided by 9).

The median is useful when the scores can be ranked (put in order) and the advantage of the median is that it is not affected by extreme scores. However, the median does not take account of the values of all of the scores and it can be misleading if used in small sets of scores.

The mode

The mode is the score that occurs most frequently in a set of scores. For example, take the following set of scores: 4, 4, 4, 5, 5, 6, 10, 12, 13, 14.

The mode of this set is 4 because it occurs three times (the most frequently). The median of this set of scores is (5 + 6)/2 = 5.5. The mean is 7.7 (77 divided by 10).

This example shows that each of the measures of central tendency may describe the midpoint of a set of scores differently.

The mode is useful when nominal data are collected and is not affected by extreme scores.

However, the mode tells us nothing about the value of the other scores and there may be more than one mode in a set of data.

Measures of dispersion

Measures of dispersion tell us about the spread of the data. The main measures of dispersion are the range and the standard deviation.

Range

To calculate the range of a set of scores, subtract the lowest score from the highest score. For example, the range of 4, 4, 4, 5, 5, 6, 10, 12, 13, 14 is 14 minus 4 = 10. NB: The range can also be calculated as highest score minus lowest score +1.

The range is a useful measure because if our research has more than one condition, we can compare the range of the scores in each condition. A low range indicates consistency in participant scores and thus low levels of individual differences. A high range indicates variation in participant scores and thus high levels of participant differences. (Note that 'low' or 'high' is relative to the maximum possible range of scores.)

The advantage of the range is that it is easy and quick to work out. However, the range can be misleading when there are extremely high or low scores in a dataset.

Percentages (%)

You need to be able to calculate percentages. For example, if you are carrying out observational research you will probably want to know what percentage of the behaviours you observed fell into specific categories, or if you are doing a survey, handing questionnaires to an opportunity sample, you may want to calculate what percentage of participants were male or female. If you have studied Milgram's research into obedience, you will know that 26/40 $\left(\frac{26}{40}\right)$ participants administered a 450 V electric shock and this can also be shown as 65%.

When you say 'per cent' you are really saying 'per 100'. One per cent (1%) means 1 per 100, 4% means 4 per 100, 50% means 50 per hundred, etc. If a bank offers a rate of 4% per year on a savings bond, it means that for every £100 saved it will pay £4 interest.

Examples

(a) A sample of 150 people were asked whether they disliked bananas and 55 people said they did. What percentage of the sample disliked bananas?
 ● Step 1: 55 disliked bananas, divided by the total sample of 150 = 0.36666....
 ● Step 2: multiply 0.36666 by 100 = 36.666
 ● Step 3: round up to two decimal places, so the answer is 36.67%

(b) A sample of 200 students were asked whether they studied French at GCSE and 45 said yes. What percentage of the sample of students said they studied French?
 ● Step 1: 45 said yes, divided by the total sample of 200 = 0.225
 ● Step 2: multiply 0.225 by 100 = 22.5%

Standard deviation

REVISED

Standard deviation is used to measure how the scores are distributed around the central point (the mean). The greater the standard deviation, the larger the spread of the scores.

Standard deviation is useful because we know when scores are normally distributed, about 68% of the scores will lie within one standard deviation above or below the mean. (See Normal distribution on page 89.)

Standard deviation allows for an interpretation of any individual score in a set and is particularly useful in large sets of scores. Also it is a sensitive measure of dispersion because all the scores are used in its calculation. However, standard deviation is quite complicated to calculate and is not useful when data are not normally distributed.

Analysis of correlation

REVISED

Correlation is a statistical technique used to calculate the correlation coefficient in order to quantify the strength of relationship between two variables. An example is whether there is a relationship between aggressive behaviour and playing violent video games. However, studies that use correlational analysis cannot draw conclusions about cause and effect. If a relationship is found between behaving aggressively and playing violent video games, individual differences in personality variables could be one factor that causes both of these. Just because two events (or behaviours) occur together does not mean that one necessarily causes the other.

The correlation coefficient is a mathematical measure of the degree of relatedness between sets of data. Once calculated, a correlation coefficient will have a value between −1 and +1.

A perfect positive correlation, indicated by +1, is where as variable X increases, variable Y increases. A perfect negative correlation, indicated by −1, is where as variable X decreases, variable Y decreases. The relationship between two variables can be shown as a scattergram (see page 88).

Presentation of quantitative data

REVISED

When information is provided in graphs and charts, it makes it easier for others to understand the findings of research.

Line graphs

A line graph can be used to represent data in list form.

Example: A class of students was asked to memorise a list of 14 words and then given 1 minute to write down as many of the words as they could remember. The teacher recorded how many times each word was remembered and the position of the word in the list. The results are shown in the line graph in Figure 2.7.

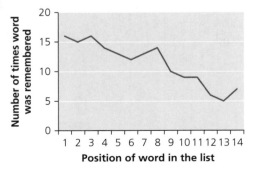

Figure 2.7 Line graph indicating the number of times each word was remembered

Bar charts

Bar charts are used when scores are in categories, when there is no fixed order for the items on the x-axis, or to show a comparison of means for continuous data. The bar chart in Figure 2.8 shows the results of a survey of pet ownership percentage. (It doesn't add up to 100% because some families reported owning dogs, cats, rabbits and fish.) The bars in bar charts should be the same width but should not touch. The space between the bars illustrates that the variable on the y-axis consists of discrete data.

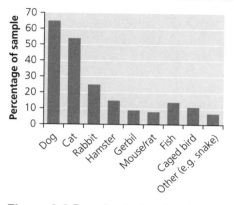

Figure 2.8 Bar chart showing pet ownership

Pie charts

A pie chart is a circle divided into sectors to illustrate numerical proportion. The arc length of each sector is proportional to the quantity it represents. It is difficult to compare different sections of a given pie chart, or to compare data across different pie charts. Pie charts can be replaced in most cases by other diagrams such as the bar chart. Figure 2.9 shows a pie chart representing the school exam results in the table.

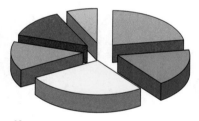

A grades	20%
B grades	19%
C grades	25%
D grades	12%
E grades	15%
U grades	9%

Key
- ▨ A grades   ▧ B grades
- ☐ C grades   ▨ D grades
- ▪ E grades   ▨ U grades

Figure 2.9 Pie chart representing school exam results

> **Revision activity**
>
> Draw a pie chart – remember we need to represent each part of the data as a proportion of 360, because there are 360 degrees in a circle.
>
> For example, if 25% of the 100 exam grades are C grades, we will represent this on the circle as a segment with an angle of $\left(\frac{25}{100}\right) \times 360 = 90$ degrees.

Frequency tables

A frequency table shows the values of one or more variables. The data collected during an observation are often collected on a frequency table. The 'tally chart' example is a frequency table from an observation of car colours in a car park.

Colour of car	Tally	Frequency
red	⊮ИТ ⊮ИТ I	11
green	⊮ИТ III	8
silver	⊮ИТ ⊮ИТ ⊮ИТ I	16
blue	⊮ИТ I	6
black	III	3
white	⊮ИТ ⊮ИТ II	12
other	IIII	4
total		60

Histograms

Histograms show frequencies of scores (how the scores are distributed) using columns. They should be used to display frequency distributions of continuous data and there should be no gaps between the bars. The example in Figure 2.10 shows the exam results (marks) for a class of 30 students in a mock exam, marked out of a maximum of 100. The scores have been grouped into ranges of 10 marks.

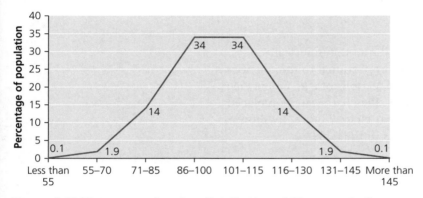

Figure 2.10 **Histogram showing distribution of IQ scores in the population**

Reminder: discrete data are counted, continuous data are measured.

Discrete data can take only certain values, for example the number of students in a class is discrete data (you can't have half a student), or the results of rolling two dice can have discrete values only (you can't throw 5½). The number of children in a family is discrete data as you can't have half a child. Continuous data can take any value (within a range) – for example, a person's height (could be any value, within the range of human heights, not just certain fixed heights), the time taken to run a race, and IQ scores (which are assumed to be normally distributed in the population).

Scatter diagrams

Scatter diagrams, like the ones shown in Figure 2.11, are used to depict the result of correlational analysis. A scatter diagram shows at a glance whether there appears to be a positive or a negative correlation, or no correlation.

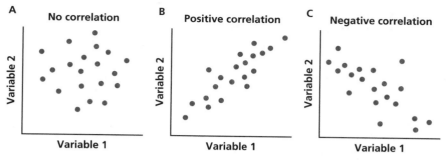

Figure 2.11 **No correlation, positive correlation and negative correlation**

Typical mistake

If you are asked to sketch a diagram in an exam, do not forget to label the *y* axis.

Tables

Psychologists present the findings of research, for example measures of central tendency and dispersions, in tables to make it easy for others to see and interpret the results at a glance.

Example:

Correct answers in a French test	Condition A male	Condition B female
Mean	12.11	15.23
Median	11	14
Range	6	4
Standard deviation	2.25	3.5

Normal and skewed distribution

REVISED

Normal distribution

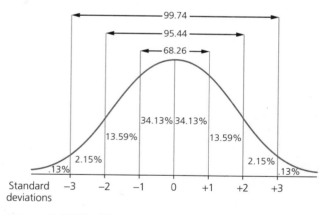

Figure 2.12 **The U-shaped curve of normal distribution**

In a normally distributed set of scores:

- 68.26% of the scores lie +1 or −1 standard deviations above or below the mean
- 95.44% of the scores lie +2 or −2 standard deviations above or below the mean
- 99.74% of scores lie +3 or −3 standard deviations above or below the mean.

Thus in a normally distributed set of scores, only 4.56% of the scores will lie more than +2 or −2 standard deviations above or below the mean.

However, sometimes the sample size may be so small that it is difficult to know whether the data are normally distributed – if not, this is a skewed distribution (see Figure 2.13).

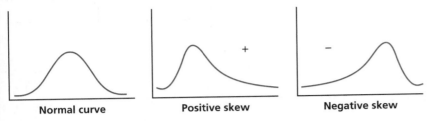

Normal curve   +   **Positive skew**   −   **Negative skew**

Figure 2.13 Normal and skewed distributions

Content analysis and coding

REVISED

Content analysis involves the coding and analysis of qualitative data. Review page 83.

Analysing and presenting qualitative data

In interviews and observations, qualitative data might result from video or audio recordings or written notes. Likewise, qualitative data can result when open questions are asked in interviews or questionnaires, or when participants are invited to explain why they behave in a certain way.

It is important when analysing qualitative data that researchers avoid subjective or biased misinterpretations. Misinterpretation can be avoided by:

- using accurate language to operationalise the variables to be measured – for example, if observing play-fighting in children, an operationalised definition might be 'hitting while smiling'
- using a team of observers who have verified that they have achieved inter-observer reliability converting qualitative data into quantitative data; one way to do this is by coding the data.

When a sample of qualitative data has been collected – for example from a survey or from magazines or newspapers, or from interview notes – coding units are identified in order to categorise the data. A coding unit could be specific words or phrases that are looked for (the operationalised definitions). The coding units may then be counted to see how frequently they occur. The resulting frequency is a form of quantitative data.

Thematic analysis

Thematic analysis is a form of analysis used in qualitative research. It emphasises identifying, examining and recording patterns (or themes) within data. Themes are patterns across datasets that are associated with a specific research question. The themes become the categories for analysis. Thematic analysis is performed through the process of coding in six phases to create established, meaningful patterns. These phases are: (1) familiarisation with data, (2) generating initial codes, (3) searching for themes among codes, (4) reviewing themes, (5) defining and naming themes, and (6) producing the final report.

Summary

You should be able to:
- describe and evaluate experimental research methods, including laboratory, field and natural experiments
- describe and evaluate non-experimental research methods, including correlational analysis, observational techniques, self-report techniques including questionnaires and interviews, and case studies.

You should be confident you can identify and describe features of investigation design:
- aims
- hypotheses, including directional and non-directional
- experimental design (independent groups, repeated measures and matched pairs)
- design of naturalistic observations, including the development and use of behavioural categories
- design of questionnaires and interviews
- operationalisation of variables, including independent and dependent variables
- pilot studies and control of extraneous variables.

You should be able to:
- define reliability and validity and differentiate between these

- describe the British Psychological Society (BPS) Code of Ethics and recognise ethical issues and the ways in which psychologists deal with them
- describe and evaluate sampling techniques, including random, opportunity and volunteer sampling
- define demand characteristics and explain ways by which an investigator may affect research
- define quantitative and qualitative data and differentiate between these
- present quantitative data in visual diagrams, including graphs, scatter diagrams and tables
- calculate measures of central tendency, including median, mean and mode, and know when to use these
- calculate measures of dispersion, including ranges and standard deviation, and be able to explain why dispersions are useful
- analyse and interpretet correlational data and differentiate between positive and negative correlations
- describe ways of analysing qualitative data and the processes involved in content analysis.

Quick quizzes 28, 30 and 31 online

Inferential testing

Introduction and the sign test

You need to understand how and why inferential tests are used. **A statistically significant result** is one which is unlikely to have occurred by chance. In this case researchers will reject the Null hypothesis and retain the alternative hypothesis. Using inferential statistical tests allows psychologists to find out whether their findings are significant. Many inferential statistical tests require that data are normally distributed. If not (skewed distribution) then it is necessary to use a non-parametric inferential statistical test.

The sign test

The sign test is a non-parametric inferential test of difference that is suitable for use with repeated measures design where data were collected at nominal level (for a reminder see page 83). The sign test examines the direction of difference between pairs of scores.

Example: A psychologist wanted to find out whether watching a documentary about landfill waste influenced student attitudes towards recycling. A sample of students was used and a baseline measure of attitudes towards recycling was taken using a rating scale question where 0 = unfavourable and 10 = very favourable. The students then watched a 20-minute documentary about landfill waste, after which they were asked the same attitude question. A table of results was constructed.

Participant	Attitude	Direction of difference
1	More favourable	+
2	More favourable	+
3	No change	Omitted
4	Less favourable	−
5	More favourable	+
6	More favourable	+

Four of the six participants reported more favourable attitudes; however, as an inferential test the sign test is not very powerful as it takes into consideration only the direction of the differences rather than the value of any differences.

Which inferential test to use

The Mann–Whitney U test is a non-parametric test of the significance of the difference between two conditions suitable for use when an independent design has been used and the level of data collected is 'at least' ordinal (can be placed in rank order).

An unrelated T test is a parametric test of the significance of the difference between two conditions, suitable for use when an independent design has been used and the level of data collected is 'at least' ordinal and the data are normally distributed.

The Wilcoxon matched pairs signed ranks test is a non-parametric test of the significance of the difference between two conditions when a repeated measures design has been used and the level of data collected is 'at least' ordinal.

The related T test is a parametric test of the significance of the difference between two conditions when a repeated measures design has been used and the level of data collected is 'at least' ordinal and the data are normally distributed.

The Spearman's Rho (RANK ORDER) correlation co-efficient is used when a correlation between two independent variables is being analysed. Spearman's is a non-parametric test which calculates the correlation co-efficient between ranked scores when both sets of scores are 'at least' ordinal data.

Pearson's R correlation coefficient is used when a correlation between two independent variables is being analysed. Pearson's is a parametric test which calculates the correlation co-efficient between actual scores which must be at least ordinal.

The Chi-square test is a test of significance of association which is used when nominal-level data (frequency data) have been collected.

Probability (p) and statistical significance

REVISED

When psychologists test an alternate hypothesis, for example 'group A will remember more words than group B', even if the results show there is a difference, as scientists they must be confident that the difference is caused by the IV rather than being a 'chance' event. The probability that the result of research (for example, a difference between two conditions) 'happened by chance' can be calculated and a minimum threshold of statistical significance can be set.

The statistical significance (the probability value or p-value) of a result indicates the degree to which the result is 'true' in terms of being representative of the population. In other words, statistical significance refers to whether any differences observed between groups being studied (or relationships between variables) are 'real' or whether they are simply due to chance.

Researchers select the level of significance before conducting statistical analysis. In psychology, usually, either the 0.05 level (the 5% level of chance or 95% level of confidence) or the 0.01 level (1% level of chance or 99% level of confidence) is used.

If the probability of a chance result is less than or equal to the significance level (for example, $p \leq 0.05$), the Null hypothesis is rejected and the result is said to be statistically significant.

A probability of $p \leq 0.01$ means that the probability is equal to or less than 1 in 100 (1%) that the results could have occurred *if the Null hypothesis is true*. Therefore, the Null hypothesis is rejected and the alternative (experimental) hypothesis is retained.

A probability of $p \leq 0.05$ means that the probability is equal to or less than 5 in 100 (5%) that the results could have occurred if the Null hypothesis is true.

> **Exam tip**
>
> In an exam you may be given a hypothetical research study and asked to explain a choice of statistical test. If you selected a Mann-Whitney test, an appropriate explanation would be: 'I wanted to find out whether the difference between the two experimental groups is significant and for an independent design with ordinal-level data the Mann-Whitney U test is appropriate.'

Levels of significance

Level	Probability	Significance	When used
1% level	$p \leq 0.01$	Highly significant	Where the researcher needs to be confident a Null hypothesis is false. For example, given the Null hypothesis 'Drug X has no effect on cancer', before prescribing Drug X a researcher should be 99% confident that this Null hypothesis is false
5% level	$p \leq 0.05$	Significant	The conventional level for psychology research
10% level	$p \leq 0.10$	Marginal	When the researcher is not concerned about making a mistake

Use of statistical tables and Type I and Type II errors

REVISED

For all of the different inferential tests, clever mathematicians have calculated the critical values for significance. When the inferential test has calculated the statistical result we compare the result against a table of critical values.

Type I and Type II errors

When psychologists decide whether to reject or retain the Null hypothesis they look at the results of the statistical test. However, there is always the possibility that they may make an error.

A Type I error is deciding to reject the Null hypothesis, concluding that the IV did have a significant effect on the DV when actually the result was due to chance or some other factor.

A Type II error is deciding to retain the Null hypothesis, concluding that the IV had no significant effect on the DV when actually the result was caused by the IV.

The level of significance selected affects whether researchers are likely to make a Type I or a Type II error. If researchers set the level of significance low at $p \leq 0.10$ they are more likely to make a Type I error. However, if researchers set the level of significance high, e.g. at $p \leq 0.001$ they are more likely to make a Type II error.

> **Revision activity**
>
> Practise looking up critical values. For example, if the result of a correlational study for eight pairs of scores was +0.84, is this significant at $p \leq 0.05$?

> **A Type I error**: rejecting the Null hypothesis, concluding that the IV did have a significant effect on the DV when actually the result was due to chance or some other factor.
>
> **A Type II error**: retaining the Null hypothesis when the change in the DV was caused by the IV.

Summary

You must be able to:
- explain what an inferential test is used for
- identify when to use 'which' inferential statistical test
- explain why a specific test is appropriate
- respond to questions on probability and significance
- look up a critical value in a significance table
- explain what is meant by Type I and Type II errors.

Now test yourself

TESTED

1 Fill in the blanks:
   (a) When I make a _____ I decide to reject the _____ hypothesis, concluding that the IV did have a significant effect on the DV when actually the result was due to chance or some other factor.
   (b) A _____ is deciding to retain the _____ hypothesis, concluding that the IV had no significant effect on the DV when actually the result was caused by the IV.

(c) A researcher sets a level of significance at $p < 0.001$. Why is she likely to make a Type II error?

(d) In a normally distributed set of scores, what percentage of scores will be found within one standard deviation above the mean?

(e) If there are 50 scores in a dataset and these scores are normally distributed, how many scores will lie within one standard deviation below the mean?

(f) Ten participants were asked, on a scale of 0–10, where 0 means not at all likely and 10 means definitely: how likely are you to try to reduce the amount of sugar you eat? Then they were shown a 30-minute documentary on the health problems associated with sugar, after which they were asked the same question about their sugar intake. Suggest one inferential statistical test that could be used to analyse the data and justify your choice of test.

(g) A researcher carried out a laboratory experiment having an independent design. There were 20 participants in each of the two conditions. The resulting ordinal data were found not to be normally distributed. Which inferential test should the researcher use to analyse the data? Justify your choice.

(h) A researcher carried out a laboratory experiment having a repeated measures design. There were 20 participants in both conditions. The resulting interval-level data were normally distributed. Which inferential test should the researcher use to analyse the data? Justify your choice.

(i) A researcher carried out a study looking for a relationship between age and memory. Twenty participants aged 40–75 completed a short memory task on which they could score between 0 and 15. The data were found not to be normally distributed. Which inferential test should the researcher use to analyse the correlation? Justify your choice.

(j) A researcher carried out a study looking for an association between cheerfulness and self-esteem. One hundred students completed questionnaires in which they categorised their self-esteem as high or low and their cheerfulness as very cheerful or not cheerful. Why is Chi-square the appropriate statistical test to use?

(k) If a psychologist finds the results are significant at $p < 0.01$, what does this mean?

(l) If a psychologist finds the results are significant at $p < 0.001$, what does this mean?

(m) If a psychologist finds the results are significant at $p < 0.10$, what does this mean?

2 Psychologists wanted to find out whether reading influences spelling ability. They put up posters in a local university asking for ten volunteers who read at least one book every week and ten volunteers who never read books. Each participant was asked to spell 30 words, such as address, accommodation, embarrassing, and each correctly spelled word was scored 1 point – high scores indicated better spelling ability. The scores are shown in the table.

Does read at least one book each week Number of correct spellings	Never reads a book Number of correct spellings
30	26
25	11
24	15
15	14
23	22
25	21
24	17
25	20
23	12
10	9
Mean 22.4	Mean 16.1
Range 20	Range 17

For a top band mark, the context of the research must always be referred to.

(a) Identify the experimental design used in this study and outline one advantage of this design.

(b) Describe one other experimental design that researchers use in psychology.

(c) Are the data collected in this study primary data or secondary data?

(d) Outline an advantage of collecting quantitative data in this study.

(e) Suggest one way in which the psychologist might have controlled for the effects of extraneous variables in this study.

(f) Write a directional hypothesis for this study.

(g) Explain what the calculated measure of dispersion suggests.

(h) Which measure of central tendency is calculated in this study and what is the advantage of using this measure of central tendency?

(i) Name an alternative measure of central tendency that could be used in this study.

(j) What conclusion might be drawn from the results of this study?

(k) Which of the following type of graph should be used to present the data in this study: scatter diagram OR pie chart OR bar chart?

(l) At the end of the study the psychologist debriefed each participant. Write a debriefing that the psychologist could read out to all the participants.

(m) Explain how using the standard deviation rather than the range would improve the study.

Answers on page 239

Exam practice

1 A psychologist who was studying biorhythms wanted to test whether the time of day affects running speed. She put up a poster in a university asking for student volunteers. Eventually a sample of 20 students was collected and these students were randomly allocated to two conditions, 'early' and 'late'. In the 'early' condition, ten students were asked to run 100 metres at 10 a.m. In the 'late' condition, ten students ran the same 100 metres at 10 p.m. The time to run the 100 metres was recorded in seconds. The results were as follows:

	Early condition – ran 100 m at 10 am	Late condition – ran 100 m at 10 pm
Mean	13.2	18.5
Std deviation	3.9	5.5

(a) Identify the experimental design used in this study. [1]

(b) Write an appropriate Null hypothesis for this study. [3]

(c) Explain what the measure of central tendency seems to suggest about this study. [2]

(d) Explain why the standard deviation is called a 'measure of dispersion'. [3]

(e) What does the standard deviation suggest about the effect of time of day on the ability to run 100 meters [3]

(f) The running time of one of the students in the late condition was an anomalous score because it was more than three standard deviations below the mean. What percentage of the scores in the late condition were more than three standard deviations below the mean? Show your working. [2]

(g) In a normal distribution, how many times will fall more than three standard deviations from the mean? [1]

(h) The researcher was deciding which inferential test to use to analyse the results of the early and late running speed. Which of these tests would you use and why? [3]

(i) The result of the inferential test was significant at $p \leq 0.05$. Explain whether the researcher should retain or reject the Null hypothesis. [3]

(j) Based on the results of this research (in (i) above), write a recommendation for students at university who are planning to run a marathon for charity. [2]

(k) Suggest whether this research is reliable. [2]

(l) Suggest two factors other than time of day that could have affected the time it took for students to run 100 meters. [2]

(m) Comment on the validity of the result of this study. [3]

2 (a) You have been asked to design a study to investigate the effect of time of day on concentration. You design a test in which participants are given 20 seconds to draw a circle (O) in as many of the boxes in a 10 × 10 grid as they can (similar to the one shown). The maximum score is 100.

Some participants will be tested at 10 am and some at 10 pm. Discuss the following aspects of this investigation:
- How you would obtain suitable participants for this study?
- How you would ensure that the task is standardised for every participant?
- What factors would you try to control?
- How you would make sure your study is ethical? [9]

3 A psychologist wanted to find out whether drinking a popular 'energy' drink influenced sports performance. To test this he put up a poster in a local sports club asking people aged between 18 and 30 who were interested in testing the benefits of energy drinks to contact him by email on greatpsychologist@youknowwhere.com. He set up individual meetings in the sports club with each of the first 20 respondents. When they met he asked them to run 100 metres as fast as possible on a running track. He recorded their time in seconds. After the run, participants were asked to rest for 15 minutes and then given a carton of the energy drink. After the drink they were asked to run 100 metres on the running track as fast as they could. The time of the second run was recorded in seconds. When 20 participants had taken part, the psychologist analysed the results, which were as follows:

	Time taken to run 100 metres before energy drink (seconds)	Time taken to run 100 metres after energy drink (seconds)
Mean score	15.2	14.5
Range	3	6

(a) Identify the independent variable and the dependent variable in this study. [2]
(b) Write a suitable Null hypothesis for this study. [3]
(c) Identify the sampling technique used in this study and explain one disadvantage of using this technique. [4]
(d) Name an appropriate statistical test that could be used to analyse the significance of the findings and explain why the test you chose would be a suitable test for this research. [4]
(e) The difference in the running speed before and after the energy drink was found not to be significant at $p \leq 0.05$. Explain what is meant by not significant at $p \leq 0.05$. [2]
(f) The psychologist decided to submit the research to peer review. Explain why it is useful for psychological research to undergo peer review. [3]
(g) When people first contacted the psychologist he set up individual meetings in the sports club. In each meeting he briefed the volunteer participant about the research and what they would be asked to do. Write a briefing that the psychologist could read out to each participant. [6]

Answers and quick quizzes 32 and 33 online

ONLINE

Gender and culture – universality and bias

REVISED

Cultural bias

Culture can be defined as 'the beliefs, attitudes, social and child-rearing practices, etc.' that people of a group share and that distinguishes one group from other groups.

Ethnocentrism is the effect that your own cultural perspective has on the way you perceive other cultures and people from other cultures. Most research is carried out by Western (European and US) organisations and it is often assumed that what is true of our culture is also true of other cultures. For example, the concept of 'self' evolved in the English language at the time of the Industrial Revolution and is associated with a view of a person as an individual. However, many cultures view the person within their social or family context and the self-concept is less distinctive. Many studies of personality in non-Western cultures have been assessed using translated personality tests rather than new, culture-relevant tests.

Emic or etic

Emic constructs are traits that are specific to a certain culture (such as monogamy in Western culture). **Etic constructs** are universal traits that can be found across cultures (for example, family). Berry (1969) suggested that in the history of psychology, emic (culturally specific) constructs have been assumed to be etic. For example, in Western culture, intelligence has been defined as problem solving, reasoning and memory and these constructs have been used to measure intelligence in other cultures. However, these measures might not be relevant in other cultures. For example, the skill of hunting, which was essential for survival in pre-literate society, may not be relevant to intelligent behaviour today. Other emic constructs could be research into conformity, relationships and diagnosing psychological disorders.

Cultures differ as to whether they are **individualistic** or **collectivist**. In individualistic cultures, one's identity is defined by personal characteristics and achievements, independence and self-identity. In collectivist cultures, identity is defined by collective achievements and interdependence.

Cultural relativism

Cultural relativism is the view that the beliefs, customs and ethics are relative to the individual within their own social context. In other words, what is considered moral in one society may be considered immoral in another, and since no universal standard of morality exists, no one has the right to judge and all cultures are of equal value.

Bias in psychological research

Temporal bias

All cultures change over time – for example, in the 1950s British culture was very different to the way it is today and homosexuality was seen as a mental illness.

Exam tip

If you make links between research and an issue and/or debate (what you may have been taught to call an IDA point) in an exam answer, make sure you fully explain the point you are making – because rote-learned IDA comments gain few, if any, marks.

Culture: the beliefs, attitudes, social and child-rearing practices, etc. that people of a group share and that distinguish one group from other groups.

Emic constructs: traits that are specific to a certain culture.

Etic constructs: universal traits that can be found across cultures.

Individualistic culture: one's identity is defined by personal characteristics and achievements, independence and self-identity.

Collectivist culture: identity is defined by collective achievements and interdependence.

Cultural relativism: the view that the beliefs, customs and ethics are relative to the individual within their own social context. Cultural relativists believe that all cultures are of equal value.

Sample bias: occurs when participants are drawn from one group (for example students) and then the results are generalised to explain behaviour from different cultures.

Research and sample bias

Problems may arise because of translation and also because, although in cross-cultural research samples may be taken from similar groups (for example, students), the social backgrounds and life experiences of the participants from different cultures may be very different.

Alpha and beta bias

When **alpha bias** occurs, research tends to emphasise and over-exaggerate differences between cultures (or between genders). When **beta bias** occurs, research tends to minimise or ignore differences between cultures (and genders). Examples of beta bias are evolutionary theories of behaviour where men are portrayed as hunting and women as looking after children.

The effect of **ethnocentrism**, alpha and/or beta bias is to create and perpetuate stereotypes and to make cultures (and genders) seem more different (or more similar) than they are.

Gender bias – androcentrism

Androcentrism occurs when male views and behaviour are viewed as 'the norm' and used to explain both male and female behaviour. Androcentrism also occurs where female behaviour is different and is construed as abnormal or inferior. Examples of androcentric psychology are Bowlby's research into attachment, which suggested women should stay at home and care for children, and Freud suggesting that women suffered from 'penis envy'.

Universality in the structure of the human brain

Some psychologists question the universality of neuropsychology and suggest that we cannot rule out the possibility that different brain organisations may emerge as a result of different cultural experiences. Recent neuroscience research that demonstrates the importance of the cultural environment in shaping the organisation of the human nervous system has been supported. For example, research into brain plasticity by Maguire (2000) showed that the ecological demands of our daily lives appear to generate processes of adaptation at both cultural and biological levels.

Free will and determinism

REVISED

Most people feel that they have free will to make choices and that their behaviour is not determined for them but is the product of their own volition. However, this position creates difficulties for scientific research, which assumes causal and deterministic relationships. **Determinism** suggests that individuals cannot be held responsible for their actions. **Hard determinism** is when biological explanations suggest behaviour is caused by genetic factors. Some psychologists see the source of determinism as being outside the individual, a position known as **environmental determinism**. For example, Bandura (1961) showed that children with violent parents will in turn become violent parents through observation and imitation. The term **soft determinism** is often used to describe situations in which people do have a choice but their behaviour is subject to some form of biological or environmental pressure. **Psychic determinism** is the type of determinism that suggests all mental processes

Alpha bias: when alpha bias occurs, research tends to emphasise and over-exaggerate differences between cultures (or between genders).

Beta bias: when beta bias occurs, research tends to minimise or ignore differences between cultures (and genders).

Ethnocentrism: the effect that your own cultural perspective has on the way you perceive other cultures and people from other cultures.

Androcentrism: when male views and behaviour are viewed as 'the norm' and used to explain both male and female behaviour.

Determinism: the assumption that people cannot be held responsible for their actions because their behaviour is determined (caused) by factors outside their control.

Hard (biological) determinism: when biological explanations suggest behaviour is caused by genetic factors.

Environmental determinism: the assumption that behaviour is caused by factors outside the individual, for example classical conditioning.

Soft determinism: the theory that in some situations people do have a choice, but their behaviour is subject to some form of biological or environmental pressure.

Psychic determinism: suggests all mental processes are determined by the unconscious or pre-existing mental complexes.

are determined by the unconscious or pre-existing mental complexes – for example, the assumption made by Freud that childhood experiences during the development of the ego and the superego will shape all future thought processes.

The psychological approaches

Physiological approach (hard determinism)

This usually sees behaviour as being caused by some biological factor and if this is the case then behaviour is determined by biology, thus the individual has no free will to choose to behave differently.

Cognitive approach (free will)

This explains behaviour as being caused by cognitive factors, such as thought processes, attention, decision making, etc. Thus this approach does allow free will to choose behaviour. For example, in cognitive behavioural therapy, it is assumed that the person can choose not to think irrationally. However, some cognitive psychologists explain behaviour as being caused by maturation (ageing), in which case behaviour is determined by biology, thus the individual has no free will to choose to behave differently. For example, Piaget suggested that children's thought processes change at predetermined ages, thus giving a deterministic explanation.

Humanistic approach (free will)

The humanistic approach assumes that people have **free will**. Humanistic psychologists believe that in the exercise of free will people have 'personal agency' and that we can make choices in life, the paths we go down and their consequences.

> **Free will:** the assumption that people have the free will to select and decide their own behaviour.

Social approach (soft determinism)

This approach looks at the behaviour of people in groups and whether the research allows 'free will' may depend on which approach is used. For example, Milgram maintained that although his participants were influenced by the social situation they were in, they had the free will to choose not to continue giving electric shocks.

Learning approaches (environmental determinism)

These usually explain behaviour in terms of stimulus – response learning caused by past experience. If this is the case then the individual does not have the free will to choose to behave differently because behaviour is determined by past experiences.

Psychodynamic approach (psychic determinism)

This explains behaviour in terms of unconscious forces which the individual can neither escape nor explain. In addition, because the unconscious forces are the result of early childhood experience, behaviour is determined by two factors, the past and unconscious motivation, so the individual has no free will to choose their behaviour.

The nature–nurture debate

REVISED

To what extent is any behaviour the result of your genetic code (**nature** – the genes you inherit) or due to your life experiences (**nurture** – your parents, your upbringing, your experiences generally). This is an ongoing debate, especially in the areas of language, aggression, gender and dysfunctional behaviour. Some research explains behaviour as being caused by nature. For example, Piaget suggested that children's thought processes change at predetermined ages. Other research, for example Bandura, demonstrates that behaviour is not innate and that children who observe adult role models behaving aggressively imitate aggressive actions. Of course, nature and nurture interact and much research sees nature as 'potential' which is modified by nurture.

> **Nature:** the extent to which behaviour is the result of genes, biology, hormones, age, gender etc.
>
> **Nurture:** the extent to which behaviour is due to life experiences such as parents or upbringing or culture.

The psychological approaches

Physiological approach

Some research suggests that behaviour is caused by biological factors and if this is the case then behaviour is caused by nature. However, the research by Maguire found that the hippocampus in the brains of taxi drivers changed as a result of their environment, which suggests an interaction between nature and nurture.

Cognitive approach

An example of the nature–nurture debate in cognitive psychology is the question of how children acquire the ability to use human language. On the nature side of the argument is Noam Chomsky, who proposed that we are born with an innate, biological language-acquisition device which facilitates, during a critical period, the development of language. On the nurture side of the argument are the behaviourists, who propose that we learn to use human language by imitation and reinforcement – but many attempts to teach non-human primates to communicate using human language have not given a definite answer to this question.

Social approach

Much social research takes the nurture side of the debate, showing that behaviour is influenced by the social environment. For example, research by Piliavin *et al.* demonstrated that it was not the dispositional characteristics of the passengers, for instance their kind nature, but the situation of the victim, lame or drunk, which influenced whether help was given.

Learning approaches

These approaches explain behaviour in terms of nurture. From the perspective of behaviourists, when we are born we are a 'blank slate' and from the moment of birth we learn our behaviour.

Psychodynamic approach

This perspective recognises the influence of both nature and nurture. According to Freud, the id is the innate (nature) part of the human personality driving us to seek pleasure and avoid pain, but the ego and the superego are developed as a result of early experiences (nurture).

The interactionist approach

This approach combines both nature and nurture and is illustrated by the genetic disorder phenylketonuria. The inheritance of two recessive genes from each parent results in the prevention of the synthesis of an enzyme to metabolise phenylalanine, causing mental retardation. However, if the child is diagnosed early and placed on a low-protein diet through childhood, this averts a lifelong disorder. Thus nature (the genes) are not expressed because of nurture (the diet).

Holism and reductionism

Levels of explanation for behaviour

Behaviour can be explained in terms of biological processes, basic psychological processes, the attributes of the person enacting the behaviour, and sociocultural processes. The four levels are as follows:

- The biological level of explanation focuses on the biological and chemical processes underlying behaviour. For example, a biological level of explanation for aggression might focus on the role played by genes or hormones or activity in specific brain areas.
- The basic processes level of explanation focuses on the psychological (e.g. cognitive) processes that are universal across humans. For example, a basic processes level of explanation for aggression might focus on the thoughts and emotions that precede it.
- The person level of explanation focuses on individual differences in behaviour. For example, a person level explanation for aggression might focus on personality differences in people.
- The sociocultural level of explanation focuses on the influence of other people on behaviour by studying behaviour in social and cultural contexts. For example, a sociocultural level of explanation for aggression might focus on how being in a crowd influences aggressive behaviour.

> **Levels of explanation for behaviour:** psychologists use four levels of explanation for behaviour (a) biological processes, (b) basic psychological processes, (c) the attributes of the person and (d) sociocultural processes.

Reductionism

Reductionism is the principle of analysing complex things into simple constituents, for example explaining complex human behaviour in terms of simplistic single-factor causes, such as inherited genes. One of the basic goals of science is to reduce all phenomena to separate simple parts to understand how they work, so reductionism may be a necessary part of understanding what causes human behaviour. Reductionist hypotheses are easier to test and the fact that they can be 'proven' (or not) makes them more believable. However, reductionist explanations distract psychologists because simplistic explanations for behaviour may prevent further attempts to find more complex but less clear-cut explanations.

Holism

Holism is the principle that complex phenomena cannot be understood through an analysis of the constituent parts alone because the behaviour of the 'whole system' cannot be explained in terms of the 'sum' of the behaviour of all the different parts. Reductionism is a goal of science, but although simple explanations are appropriate in some situations, simple explanations rarely explain the richness of human experience and prevent the search for more complex answers.

> **Holism:** the principle that complex phenomena cannot be understood through an analysis of the constituent parts alone.

The psychological approaches

The physiological approach

Physiological (biological) reductionism explains behaviour in terms of biological factors, especially when explaining behaviour in terms of genes, as in some explanations of dysfunctional behaviour.

The cognitive approach

This can be described as reductionist when it proposes a computer-like information-processing approach as a means to describe and explain behaviour.

Learning approaches

These approaches use a very reductionist vocabulary: stimulus, response, reinforcement and punishment. This is called environmental reductionism because behaviourists reduce the concept of the mind to behavioural components, i.e. stimulus–response links.

The psychodynamic approach

This is reductionist because it relies on the interaction between three components – the id, the ego and the superego – to explain complex behaviour.

Ideographic and nomothetic approaches

REVISED

The term 'nomothetic' comes from the Greek word 'nomo', meaning 'law'. Psychologists who take a **nomothetic** approach to psychological investigation study groups to make generalisations about behaviour. The term idiographic comes from the Greek word 'idios', meaning 'own'. Psychologists who take an ideographic approach to psychological investigation want to discover what makes each of us unique.

Experimental and other quantitative methods are favoured from a nomothetic point of view. Case studies and other qualitative methods are idiographic. Nomothetic, experimental research enables the development of general laws of behaviour. **Ideographic**, qualitative research provides a more complete (holistic) understanding of an individual's behaviour. Behaviourist, cognitive and biological approaches tend to take a nomothetic approach and focus on establishing generalisations. Humanistic approaches are interested in the individual and are thus ideographic. The psychodynamic approach is ideographic because although Freud suggested that the structure of the unconscious mind is common to everyone, each patient's individual problems arise from unique childhood experience.

> **Nomothetic:** psychologists who take a nomothetic approach to psychological investigation study groups to make generalisations about behaviour.
>
> **Idiographic:** psychologists who take an ideographic approach to psychological investigation want to discover what makes each of us unique.

> **Revision activity**
>
> Draw up a chart showing the psychological approaches and where they 'generally' stand on each of the issues and debates.

Ethical implications of research

REVISED

Ethics in research

Ethical issues may arise because of a conflict of interest between the researcher and the researched. The researcher may wish to collect in-depth, high-quality data and may be tempted to consider unethical research practice in order to try to obtain data.

Ethical risks and responsibilities

Researchers need to consider the potential physical or psychological risks to participants and are responsible for ensuring that the level of risk is minimised and that participants are fully aware of any risk before they agree to participate. The risks may be physical or psychological arising from discussion of sensitive topics, stirring painful memories or disclosure of personal information. Ethical issues relate especially to interview methods, where participants may be encouraged to disclose personal information, but ethical issues arise in all research involving human participants.

(To revise the basic principles of ethical research refer to the notes on the BPS ethical guidelines on pages 68–9.)

Research with vulnerable groups

Care is needed in research with young children, and with people who are ill, or recently bereaved, or others who may be vulnerable.

Socially sensitive research

There is increasing research interest in 'sensitive' social issues such as sexuality and child abuse. Any topic could potentially be seen to be sensitive and ethical issues may arise when in-depth interviews/questionnaires are used that may unleash painful emotions and memories in participants.

Revision activity

As you work through your three 'applied options', make a list of some socially sensitive research questions.

Summary

You should be able to demonstrate knowledge and understanding of:
- gender bias, including androcentrism and alpha and beta bias; cultural bias, including ethnocentrism and cultural relativism
- free will and determinism: hard determinism and soft determinism; biological, environmental and psychic determinism; the scientific emphasis on causal explanations
- the nature–nurture debate: the relative importance of heredity and environment in determining behaviour; the interactionist approach
- holism and reductionism: levels of explanation in psychology; biological reductionism and environmental reductionism
- idiographic and nomothetic approaches to psychological investigation
- ethical implications of research studies and theory, including issues related to socially sensitive research.

Now test yourself

TESTED ☐

1 (a) What do psychologists mean when they describe research as ethnocentric?
   (b) What is the difference between an emic and an etic construct?
   (c) What is the difference between alpha bias and beta bias?
   (d) Give an example of research which involved an androcentric sample.
   (e) Why may the Asch study of conformity involve temporal bias?
2 (a) TRUE or FALSE?
      (i) The physiological approach is not reductionist.
      (ii) The behaviourist approach is deterministic.
      (iii) The psychodynamic approach suggests people have free will.
      (iv) The cognitive approach is not deterministic.
      (v) The behaviourist approach gives a nature explanation.
      (vi) The physiological approach gives a nature explanation.
   (b) What word is used to describe psychologists who study people as individuals rather than as groups?
   (c) List one nomothetic example and one ideographic example in psychological research or theory.
   (d) Explain the difference between biological determinism and environmental determinism.
   (e) Which of the four levels of explanation is used by the humanistic approach?
   (f) Which of the four levels of explanation is used by the physiological approach?
   (g) Outline what is meant by reductionism.
   (h) Explain whether research into social influence is nomothetic or ideographic.

Answers on page 240

Exam practice

1 (a) Which of the following approaches is most likely to be described as environmental determinism? Write A, B, C or D in the space provided. One mark is awarded for the correct answer. [1]

    A Biological approach
    B Behaviourist approach
    C Psychodynamic approach
    D Social approach

  (b) A psychologist researching friendship patterns recruited 50 female participants and asked them to complete a questionnaire. Which of the following biases is demonstrated by this research? [1]

    A Gender bias
    B Androcentric bias
    C Cultural bias

  (c) Name two types of reductionism in psychology. [2]

  (d) In psychological research, what is the difference between alpha bias and beta bias? [2]

  (e) Outline what psychologists mean by determinism. [2]

  (f) Discuss whether reductionist explanations in psychology are useful. [6]

  (g) In a study of eating behaviour, researchers went to Anon secondary school and interviewed 50 girls aged 12–14. They asked them questions about their eating habits, diet and family life. They then classified each girl according to the risk of developing an eating disorder. Explain what is meant by 'socially sensitive research' and suggest why this research can be seen as socially sensitive. [6]

Answers and quick quiz 34 online

ONLINE

Relationships

Evolutionary explanations REVISED

Research into interpersonal attraction looks at what makes us attracted to others. Evolutionary psychologists propose that mate choice is unconsciously guided by cues that indicate some survival advantage for offspring and that because **parental investment** in reproduction is different for males and females, mate choice cues are different for males and females.

Sexual selection and human reproductive behaviour

Parental investment

A baby spends nine months in the womb and is helpless, dependent upon the mother at birth, and requires intensive rearing. As a result, in her lifetime a female has relatively few offspring and requires a mate who is willing and able to provide resources and support for her and the offspring.

From the evolutionary perspective women should be attracted to males who have social and economic advantages, who possess valuable resources and who appear willing to share those resources. From the male perspective, parental investment may be low and reproductive capacity is limited only by the number of females who are willing to reproduce with him, thus males may be more inclined to seek a quantity of fertile mates. Also, males will want to make sure they are not tricked into raising the offspring of another male. From the evolutionary perspective men should be attracted to females who show signs of good reproductive potential, indicated by physical characteristics such as smooth skin, white teeth, glossy hair, youth and healthiness, and should also seek sexual faithfulness.

Both males and females will be interested in good genetic quality in order that their offspring survive. Some signs of 'good genes' are youth, a healthy complexion and symmetry, which may explain why symmetry has been found to be important in perceived attractiveness.

> **Parental investment:** an evolutionary theory suggesting that because a female has relatively few offspring she will require a mate who is able to provide resources and thus women are attracted to males who have social and economic advantages. However, because male reproductive capacity is limited only by the number of females who are willing to reproduce with him, males will be attracted to females who show physical characteristics of good reproductive potential.

Research: attractiveness

Waynforth and Dunbar (1995) analysed personal adverts in US newspapers and found that compared with 25% females, 42% males wanted younger partners. Also 44% males advertised for physically attractive partners but only 22% females did. Females advertised their attractiveness but males advertised their economic resources.

Cunningham (1986) conducted a cross-cultural study in which men were asked to rate photographs of women. Large eyes, small nose and chin, prominent cheek bones, high eyebrows and a big smile were the characteristics most associated with female beauty. Buss (1986) proposed that humans have evolved a preference for these facial characteristics to ensure we care for our young and that men all over the world share the same ideal of beauty.

Exam practice answers and quick quizzes at **www.hoddereducation.co.uk/myrevisionnotes**

Although Darwin proposed that human mate choices would be guided by the same cues that motivate animal mate choices, human behaviour may be very different from animal behaviour because it is motivated more by cultural and cognitive factors. Also, evolutionary explanations offer an 'after the fact' explanation for behaviours that are continuously observed.

Factors affecting attraction

REVISED

Self-disclosure is the act of revealing ourselves to another person. It comprises everything an individual chooses to tell the other person about themselves. According to Altman and Taylor (1973), there are two dimensions to self-disclosure, breadth and depth, and both are important in developing a fully intimate relationship. The range of topics discussed by two individuals is the breadth of disclosure and the degree to which the information revealed is private or personal is the depth of that disclosure. It is easier for breadth to be expanded first in a relationship because it consists of outer layers of personality and everyday lives. Depth in disclosure is more difficult because it may include painful memories and traits that we prefer to hide. This is why we reveal ourselves most thoroughly to our spouses and close family.

Figure 3.1 **What makes us attracted to others?**

Self-disclosure is an important building block for intimacy and intimacy cannot be achieved without it. Most self-disclosure occurs early in the development of a relationship, but more intimate self-disclosure occurs later. Sexual self-disclosure is the act of revealing one's sexual preferences to one's sexual partner and this fosters understanding and intimacy. Laurenceau (2005) used a method that involved writing daily diary entries and found that relationship satisfaction correlated with sexual disclosure, and for men, high levels of sexual self-disclosure predicted greater relationship satisfaction, though this was not true for women.

Self-disclosure in marriage: self-disclosure is a method of relationship maintenance; partners learn a shared communication system and disclosures are a large part of building that system. Research suggests that wives' perceptions of their husbands' self-disclosures are a strong predictor of how long a couple will stay together. Those who think their husbands are not sharing enough are likely to break up sooner, and those husbands and wives who reported the highest ratings of marital satisfaction showed the highest ratings in intimacy.

Physical attractiveness

Usually, the first thing we notice about others is what they look like. **Physical attractiveness** may be one of the most important factors in interpersonal attraction. Feingold (1992) found that if a person is physically attractive we attribute other positive characteristics, such as sociability, to them as well. This is called the halo effect (see Figure 3.2) and in the early stages of relationship formation physical attractiveness is an important factor.

However, not everyone is equally beautiful. Walster *et al.* (1966) in the **matching hypothesis** suggested that we are attracted to people whom we perceive to be similarly attractive to ourselves so that we are not rejected by potential partners who are more attractive than us. Physical attractiveness may be an important factor from an evolutionary perspective because characteristics, such as good skin and glossy hair, indicate breeding success.

Physical attractiveness: may be an important factor in interpersonal attraction because if a person is physically attractive we attribute other positive characteristics to them as well.

Matching hypothesis: the suggestion that we are attracted to people we regard as similarly attractive to ourselves to avoid being rejected by more attractive potential partners.

Walster *et al.* (1966)

The matching hypothesis

A total of 664 students were invited to attend a 'computer' dance. They were told they would be 'matched' to a partner by a computer. Before the dance, each student completed a series of questionnaires, supposedly so that the computer could complete the 'matching'. In reality the students, who had been rated for physical attractiveness by the experimenters, were randomly allocated to pairs in which the only control was that the male was taller than the female.

After the dance the students were asked to complete questionnaires on which they rated how much they liked their partner, whether they wanted to see their partner again, how attractive they found their partner and how attractive they thought their partner found them.

There was a significant positive correlation between the experimenters' rating of the physical attractiveness of both the male and female students and how much they were liked by their partner. There was also a significant positive correlation between how attractive the students rated their partner to be and how much they liked them.

Is physical attraction associated with positive characteristics?

Wheeler and Kim (1997) investigated the **halo effect** and found that American, Canadian and Korean students rated physically attractive people as friendly, extrovert, happy and sociable.

Landy and Siegall (1974) asked male participants to evaluate an essay to which was attached a picture of either an attractive or an unattractive female (the supposed author). Half the participants were given the good essay and half the poor one. The essays (good and poor) were rated as better if they were thought to be written by the attractive author.

Figure 3.2 **The halo effect**

Evaluation

In the computer dance study, a correlational design was used, and it could be that the students rated their partner as more attractive because they liked them rather than rating their liking based on how attractive they perceived their partner to be.

Attractiveness may be important only in the early stages of a relationship. Murstein and Christie (1976) found a correlation between husbands' ratings of how satisfied they were with their marriage and how attractive they thought their wife was and thought them to be. They found no correlation between the wives' satisfaction with their marriage and their perception of their husbands' attractiveness or how attractive their husbands found them.

Much research into attractiveness is based on biased samples of students, and young people may value physical attractiveness more than older people do.

Halo effect: if a person is physically attractive we attribute other positive characteristics to them as well.

Exam tip

Link to issues and debates: Can you explain why the Walster *et al.* 'computer dance' study gives a reductionist explanation for interpersonal attraction?

Filter theory

Kerckoff and Davis (1962) proposed a relationship formation theory known as the filter model. They proposed that three filters are important before we enter a relationship and at different times in a relationship. We start with a field of those who are free for relationships – the availables –

Exam practice answers and quick quizzes at **www.hoddereducation.co.uk/myrevisionnotes**

and gradually narrow them down to a field of those we would consider as potential partners – the desirables.

The first filter stage is the social and demographic variables where we tend to pick people with similar educational and economic backgrounds to us. The second filter stage is the similarity of attitudes and values, where people with different values, attitudes and interests from us are filtered out. The third filter stage is the complementarity of emotional needs, where we decide how well as two people we fit together as a couple.

In support of **filter theory**, Kandal (1978) asked secondary school students who was their best friend among a group of students and found that the best friends tended to be of the same age, religion, sex, social class and ethnic background.

Kerckoff and Davis (1962) tested the filter theory using student couples who had been together for either more than or less than 18 months. Over a period of seven months, the couples completed several questionnaires which gathered data on attitude similarity and personality traits. They found that attitude similarity was the most important factor up to about 18 months into a relationship, but after this psychological and emotional compatibility were more important.

> **Filter theory:** the theory that three filters are important before, and at different times in, a relationship. The three filters are social and demographic variables, similarity of attitudes and values, and complementarity of emotional needs.
>
> **Temporal bias:** assuming that findings from previous research done many years in the past can be applied to explain behaviour today.
>
> **Social exchange theory:** the theory that relationships are based on 'exchanges' in which each person seeks to maximise their rewards and minimise their costs and thus make a profit.

Evaluation

The filter model is a useful way to think about the importance of demographic factors and similarity of attitudes and values in relationships. However, the theory was written in 1962, which means that there is low historical validity (**temporal bias**) as the research was conducted at a time when Western ideals were dominant. Also, the theory ignores important differences in relationships (imposed etic), for example between cultures or in same-sex couples.

Much research into filter theory is based on biased samples. For example, both Kerckoff and Davis and Kandal used all student participants, thus their research cannot be generalised to explain factors causing attraction in mature adult relationships.

Social exchange theory

REVISED

Psychological theories suggest that we form and maintain our relationships mainly because of self-interest. The **social exchange theory** by Thibaut and Kelley (1959) focuses on the interactive nature of relationships and assumes that relationships are based on 'exchanges' in which each person seeks to maximise their rewards and minimise their costs and thus make a profit. Rewards may include being looked after, companionship and even sex. Costs may include time and effort and financial investment. The model proposes that people stay in relationships when they are 'in profit' but that relationships may fail when either partner's costs exceed their rewards.

This theory proposes four stages in the development of a relationship:
- **The sampling stage** in which the potential costs and rewards of a new relationship are considered and compared with other known relationships.

Figure 3.3 Social exchange theory

- **The bargaining stage** in which partners receive and give rewards to test whether a deeper relationship is worthwhile.
- **The commitment stage** in which relationship predictability increases, and because each partner knows how to 'get rewards' from the other, costs are reduced.
- **The institutionalisation stage** in which norms are developed and patterns of rewards and costs are established for each partner.

The theory also proposes a comparison level by which people judge all their relationships. Our personal comparison level is the accumulation of all our relationship experiences. If we judge that the profit from a potential new relationship is greater than our comparison level, the partner will be viewed positively and a new relationship will be formed.

Rusbult and Martz (1995) proposed that women stay in abusive relationships because their investment is high (children and somewhere to live) but the cost of leaving is higher (nowhere to live and no money). Thus the woman is still 'in relationship profit' and she will remain in the relationship.

Aronson and Linder (1965) researched four conditions to test the effects of profit and loss on how much a confederate was liked when he evaluated participants: (1) Positive – all positive evaluations given; (2) Negative – all negative evaluations given; (3) Overall profit – negative evaluations followed by positive evaluations; (4) Overall cost – positive evaluations followed by negative evaluations. Participants in the overall profit condition liked the confederate more than those in the positive condition, and participants in the overall cost condition disliked the confederate more than those in the negative condition.

Hatfield *et al.* (1979) asked newly married couples and found that under-benefited partners were the least satisfied, over-benefited the next, and those who perceived their relationship to be equitable were most satisfied.

Evaluation

This theory can be applied to different kinds of relationships (such as friendships, colleagues, lovers) and, because people will perceive rewards, costs and their comparison level differently, can be used to explain individual differences – what is acceptable for one person may be unacceptable for another.

The theory proposes that the basis for the formation of human relationships is self-interest and that relationships are based on selfish concerns. Even if it is true, perhaps the model explains the formation of relationships in individualistic cultures only.

The theory is based on subjective judgement of what constitutes a reward, cost or profit, and thus can be used to justify almost any behaviour in terms of a calculated profit outcome.

The theory focuses on the perspective of the 'individual in the relationship' and ignores the social world (social context) in which their relationship exists. Families, children, friends, neighbours and shared social events can also be important factors in the formation of relationships.

Equity theory

Walster *et al.* (1978)

Equity does not mean equality, it means fairness. The **equity theory** of relationships assumes that people try to ensure that their relationships are fair and that people become distressed, and may leave the relationship, if they perceive unfairness.

This theory proposes that people who give a great deal in their relationship but who receive little in return may perceive inequity and become dissatisfied. People who receive a great deal b-ut who give little in return may also perceive inequity and become dissatisfied. This theory predicts that the greater the inequity, the greater the dissatisfaction and the less likely it is that the relationship will continue.

What is considered to be fair is each partner's subjective judgement of their respective inputs and outputs; deciding whether a relationship is equitable may involve complicated calculations. The theory proposes that an equitable relationship is one in which one partner's benefits divided by their costs are equal to the other partner's benefits divided by their costs. If the result of this calculation results in perceived inequity (unfairness), we may try to restore fairness in one or more of the following ways:

- change the amount we put into the relationship
- change the amount we receive from the relationship
- change our subjective evaluation of relative inputs and outputs to restore the appearance of equity
- compare the relationship with our comparison level for other relationships
- be persuaded by the partner that our subjective perception of relative inputs and outputs is wrong.

Figure 3.4 Equity theory of relationships

Equity theory: assumes that people try to ensure that their relationships are fair and may leave a relationship if they perceive unfairness.

Clark (1984)

Equity in short-term relationships

Male participants were introduced to 'Paula', who was described as:

(a) a married woman visiting briefly

(b) a newcomer to the area and single, wanting to make friends.

They were asked to locate a sequence of numbers in a matrix with Paula who had 'already circled some numbers'. Each participant was told he and Paula would receive a joint payment based on their performance and that they had to decide how much each was to receive.

To measure equity, pen colour was used. If participants chose the same pen colour it would indicate working with Paula and not being concerned about equity. If they chose a different pen colour it would suggest their input would be distinct and suggest seeking equity.

- 90% of the participants who thought Paula was married chose a different colour pen.
- 90% of the participants who thought Paula was single chose the same colour pen.

These findings suggest that equity is sought in short-term relationships.

Evaluation

Equity theory takes a 'rational economist' approach to explaining human relationships, but in relationships people may be influenced by emotion rather than by rational thought. Perhaps such explanations apply only to short-term relationships in young people in Western culture. Clark and Mills (1979) proposed that in long-term relationships, there is less concern for equity because partners believe things will balance out over time.

It is difficult to see how romantic relationships can be studied in the laboratory and research studies are low in mundane realism. It is also difficult to gain a valid measure of a person's subjective assessment of their inputs to, and benefits from, their relationships as their judgement of these may vary from day to day.

Rusbult's investment model

REVISED

Commitment is an important factor in maintaining relationships. Rusbult (1980) defined commitment as 'a person's intention to maintain the relationship and to remain psychologically attached to it'.

Rusbult's investment model of commitment consists of three processes that are positively associated with commitment: satisfaction level, quality of alternatives and investment size.

Satisfaction level refers to the positive versus the negative emotions experienced in a relationship. A person whose needs are met by their partner will enjoy a higher level of satisfaction.

The quality of alternatives is defined as the attractiveness of the best obtainable alternative to a relationship. For example, if someone's need for intimacy could be met elsewhere, their quality of alternatives would be high.

Investment size is how much an individual has already invested in the relationship, where investment can be financial (a house) or emotional (such as in the welfare of the children). A person may stay in a relationship because they have already invested significantly in it.

Rusbult also proposed two other factors linked to commitment. The first factor, equity, is the ability to be fair. Rusbult suggested that fairness in a relationship is very important because unfairness causes distress, and a partner in an inequitable relationship will be less committed and may want to end the relationship. The second factor is social support, such as family and friends. If family and friends approve of and support the relationship, this produces a positive influence on commitment, causing the couple to stay together longer.

Rusbult studied students' relationships and found that satisfaction and investment were key predictors for staying in the relationship, with availability of alternatives as a trigger for ending the relationship.

Sprecher (1988) carried out a study which supports Rusbult's theory. The aim was to study the extent to which different factors explained commitment to relationships. Data were collected from 197 couples. Relationship commitment was predicted to positively correlate with satisfaction, investment and social support, and correlate negatively with alternative quality and inequity. Results showed that the variables, except investment, were related (as predicted) to relationship commitment and the two most important predictors of relationship commitment were satisfaction and alternatives.

> **Evaluation**
>
> As with equity theory, it is difficult to see how human romantic relationships can be studied in the laboratory, and many research studies rely on self-report.
>
> Since qualitative factors, such as satisfaction with a relationship, may vary from week to week, it is difficult to gain a reliable measure of a person's subjective assessment of their investment in their relationship. Also, when findings are correlations between factors, researchers cannot make statements about cause and effect.
>
> Much research into relationships is based on the self-report of student samples, and the relationships of young people are usually more volatile than those of older people.

> **Revision activity**
>
> Make a list of the similarities and differences between social exchange theory, equity theory and the investment model of relationships.

Duck's model of relationship breakdown

REVISED

Duck (1999) proposed three factors to explain why relationships break down.

- **Lack of social skills:** some people lack social and interpersonal skills, which leads others to perceive them as uninteresting and disinterested in 'relating to them'.
- **Lack of stimulation:** people expect their relationships to develop. According to social exchange theory, stimulation is rewarding and lack of it leads to boredom and/or disinterest.
- **Maintenance difficulties:** As proposed by equity theory, relationships require a lot of input by both partners and if partners are separated and daily contact is decreased, it may be difficult for the relationship to survive.

The four-stage model of relationship breakdown (Duck 1999)

Stage 1: Intrapsychic phase. There may be little outward show of dissatisfaction with the relationship but one partner may be inwardly re-evaluating the relationship in terms of the costs and benefits. There may be an attempt to put things right, but if this fails, eventually the dissatisfied partner will communicate their feelings.

Stage 2: Dyadic phase. The person who is dissatisfied tells the other partner. This phase is characterised by arguments as to who is responsible for the relationship problem. There may be discussion as to how the relationship can be repaired, but both partners are aware that the relationship may end.

Stage 3: Social phase. Partners have informed friends and family about the problems in the relationship and these others may try to help or may take sides. Friends and family may speed up the eventual ending of the relationship, perhaps by interfering, and may provide social support when the relationship does end.

Stage 4: Grave dressing phase. Both partners try to justify leaving the relationship and their actions and construct a representation of the failed relationship that does not present them in unfavourable terms. This

> **Intrapsychic phase:** the first stage in relationship breakdown in which one partner may be inwardly re-evaluating the relationship in terms of the costs and benefits.
>
> **Dyadic phase:** the second stage in relationship breakdown in which the person who is dissatisfied tells the other partner and both partners are aware that the relationship may end.
>
> **Social phase:** the third stage in relationship breakdown in which partners inform friends and family about the problems in the relationship and others may try to help or may take sides.
>
> **Grave dressing phase:** the fourth and final stage in relationship breakdown in which both partners try to justify leaving the relationship and construct a representation of the failed relationship that presents them in favourable terms.

process is important because each partner must present themselves to other possible 'future' partners as trustworthy and loyal.

Evaluation

The Duck model shows the processes that take place when a relationship fails. This is useful because relationship counsellors can use this model to help repair failing relationships. For example, if the relationship is in the dyadic phase, partners can be helped to focus on taking positive steps to repair the relationship rather than focusing on the past and arguing about 'who is to blame'.

The model does not explain why relationships break down, it only describes relationship breakdown. The model focuses on what people do rather than how they feel. Emotional satisfaction or dissatisfaction is an important factor when trying to understand why romantic relationships break down.

Virtual relationships in social media

REVISED

Electronically mediated interaction alters the way we communicate with and meet others and also changes the way in which relationships develop and are maintained. Physical attraction and eye contact are absent and thus what is written (the text) increases in importance. Electronically mediated communication is seen as inferior to face-to-face communication because it offers potential partners reduced information to go on when developing a relationship. This reduction in cues leads to a form of **deindividuation** in which partners who are more or less anonymous may behave in an uninhibited manner and may breach social norms. However, non-face-to-face communication is not new – people have been conducting, and maintaining, relationships by letter and telephone for decades.

Deindividuation: the diminishing of one's sense of individuality and sense of responsibility that occurs when an individual becomes anonymous in a large crowd and with behaviour disjointed from personal or social standards of conduct.

Advantages and disadvantages of virtual relationships

Electronic relationships have advantages. Duck (1999) reported that those who lack social skills, who live in rural areas, or who have physical handicaps may benefit. Internet chat rooms allow people to make a range of friends they would otherwise not get the opportunity to meet in 'real life'.

Young (1999) proposed the Anonymity, Convenience and Escape (ACE) model of computer-mediated communication. The Social Identity model of Deindividuation (SIDE) (Lea and Spears 1991) suggests that in computer-mediated communication, awareness of individual identity is replaced by awareness of group identity and that being anonymous leads to strong social relationships in groups that meet on the internet.

Perhaps the main disadvantage of electronic relationships is the possibility of deception. Van Gelder (1985) described a case in which a male psychiatrist who wanted to experience what it was like to be a woman pretended to be a psychologist, 'Joan', who had supposedly been injured in a road accident. 'Joan' set up an online support group for other disabled women and over two years deceived many women by forming intense friendships and romances with them.

Virtual relationships: self-disclosure

The development of a relationship is related to an increase in **self-disclosure** (hint: revise self-disclosure in relationships on page 107). Being able to disclose the characteristics of one's true self can create bonds of understanding between people and heighten the intimacy of a **virtual relationship**.

The ability to be anonymous in a virtual relationship is important because when anonymous, the costs and risks of social sanctions for what is said or done are reduced. In a face-to-face relationship there is often a cost to disclosing negative aspects of oneself. These barriers are usually not present in virtual relationships and while anonymity can bring out the worst in an individual, it can also allow for the expression of one's true feelings. Research suggests that in virtual relationships people will often reveal themselves far more intimately than they would do in face-to-face relationships.

> **Self-disclosure:** the act of revealing ourselves, consciously or otherwise, to another person. There are two dimensions to self-disclosure: breadth and depth.
>
> **Virtual relationship:** electronically mediated relationship in which physical attraction and eye contact are absent; when partners are more or less anonymous they may behave in a deindividuated and uninhibited manner.

Research: virtual relationships

Parks and Floyd (1996) studied the relationships formed by internet users. They found that people reported disclosing significantly more in their virtual relationships compared with their real-life relationships.

In a series of studies reported by Joinson (2001a) self-disclosure was significantly higher in discussions based on computer-mediated communication (CMC) compared with face-to-face (FtF) discussion.

A second study compared the level of self-disclosure in FtF discussion, CMC discussion and CMC with video link discussion. In the CMC plus video link, the levels of self-disclosure were similar to those in the FtF discussion, but in the CMC with no video link there were significantly higher levels of self-disclosure.

These findings suggest that anonymity, especially being visually anonymous, leads to higher levels of self-disclosure.

Virtual relationships: the absence of gating

Bargh *et al.* (2002) looked at how and why relationships that start over the internet are more intimate than those which start in a face-to-face physical communication. They found that there are aspects of online virtual communication compared with face-to-face communications that enable a deep level of intimacy to form quickly. For example, when you are talking to someone online, you are able to be your true self without the usual physical **gating features** present in face-to-face encounters. Physical appearance, age, clothing, race and class distinctions all function as distractions to the expression of one's true self. In virtual relationships, such gating features do not exist.

> **Gating features:** the physical barriers that arise between people when they interact in person such as physical appearance, age, clothing and race.

> **Revision activity**
>
> Make a list of the differences between 'normal' relationships and virtual relationships.

Parasocial relationships

REVISED

Parasocial relationships are one-sided relationships, where one person extends emotional energy, interest and time, and the other party, the persona, is completely unaware of the other's existence. Parasocial relationships are most common with celebrities, organisations (such as sports teams) and television stars.

Parasocial relationships expand the social network in a way that negates the chance of rejection. For some, the one-sided nature of the relationship is a relief from strained relationships in their real life.

> **Parasocial relationship:** a one-sided relationship where one person extends emotional energy, interest and time, and the other party, the persona, is completely unaware of the other's existence.

Reality television allows viewers to share the intimate and personal lives of television personas, and celebrities openly share their opinions and activities through various social media outlets such as Twitter and Facebook.

There are similarities between parasocial relationships and more traditional social relationships. Just as relational maintenance is important in sustaining a relationship with our real-life friends and family, relational maintenance also occurs in parasocial relationships through events such as weekly viewings, blogs and the use of social media sites. Parasocial relationships are popular within these online communities and this may be due to the increased sense of 'knowing' the personas, or the perception of parasocial interactions as having a high reward and no chance of rejection.

Parasocial relationships:
- may help fight loneliness as the parasocial relationship expands individuals' social networks
- can help teach important lessons because people are more likely to listen to the 'role model' in a parasocial relationship
- are advantageous because of the support that the person gains from the relationship.

Although some parasocial relationships are pathological and a symptom of loneliness and social anxiety, some psychologists believe that they can broaden one's social network.

Levels of parasocial relationships

Giles and Maltby (2006) said parasocial relationships can occur and progress on three levels:
- **Entertainment–social:** fans are attracted to celebrities because it provides entertainment.
- **Intense–personal:** fans sense a connection with the celebrity, for example feeling as though they are 'soul mates'.
- **Borderline pathological:** fans in this category have uncontrollable behaviours and fantasies about their celebrity, which are completely unconnected to reality. The addiction felt by certain fans can eventually become borderline pathological, which can lead to behaviours such as stalking and obsession.

The absorption–addiction model

McCutcheon *et al.* (2002) suggested the **absorption–addiction model**, which applies to individuals with a weak sense of identity and consists of two stages:
- **Stage 1: Absorption:** the person's attention is entirely focused on the celebrity and they find out everything they can about that person.
- **Stage 2: Addiction:** the individual craves greater and greater closeness to the chosen celebrity and becomes increasingly delusional in thinking and behaviour.

This model suggests that people seek parasocial relationships to fill the dissatisfaction they feel in their own lives. This theory predicts a correlation between poor psychological health and the strength of parasocial relationships. In support of this theory, Maltby *et al.* (2004) concluded that intense personal celebrity worship was associated with poorer mental health, and particularly with depression, anxiety, social dysfunction, stress and low life satisfaction.

> **Absorption–addiction model:** this model of parasocial relationships suggests that people with a weak sense of self-identity seek parasocial relationships to fill the dissatisfaction they feel in their lives.

Attachment theory

Keinlen (1998) and McCann (2001) suggested that parasocial relationships with celebrities are most likely to happen with people who are 'insecurely attached' because parasocial relationships do not come with the threat of disappointment and break-up. The **attachment theory of parasocial relationships** is a psychodynamic explanation as it argues that the tendency to form parasocial relationships originates in the early childhood relationships between the child and the primary caregiver. This theory argues that those with insecure attachments are more likely to become strongly attached to celebrities and that those with anxious–ambivalent attachment style are likely to be needy and clingy in their real face-to-face relationships, which makes parasocial relationships very attractive to them.

Leets (1999) studied whether attachment styles influenced the extent to which individuals engage in parasocial interaction. A sample of 115 students completed the parasocial scale and two attachment-style questionnaires. Results provided evidence that attachment styles are related to parasocial behaviour. Those with anxious–ambivalent attachment styles were the most likely to form parasocial relationships, those with secure attachment styles were in the middle and insecure–avoidants were least likely to develop such relationships.

> **Attachment theory of parasocial relationships:** a psychodynamic explanation proposing that the need for parasocial relationships originates in early childhood and that those with insecure attachments are more likely to develop parasocial relationships because these relationships do not come with the threat of disappointment and break-up.

> **Revision activity**
>
> It might be a good idea to revise what you learned about the psychodynamic approach and attachment theory.

> **Typical mistake**
>
> When evaluating research into relationships, do not write generic points about ecological validity or generalisability without relating the points to the aim of the research or to the context of the exam question.

Summary

You should be able to demonstrate knowledge and understanding of:
- evolutionary explanations for partner preferences, including the relationship between sexual selection and human reproductive behaviour
- factors affecting attraction in romantic relationships, including self-disclosure, physical attractiveness, including the matching hypothesis, and filter theory
- theories of romantic relationships, including social exchange theory, equity theory and

Rusbult's investment model of commitment, as well as Duck's phase model of relationship breakdown
- virtual relationships in social media, self-disclosure in virtual relationships and the effects of absence of gating on the nature of virtual relationships
- parasocial relationships, levels of parasocial relationships, the absorption–addiction model and the attachment theory explanation.

Now test yourself

TESTED

1 Fill in the blanks:
  (a) Evolutionary psychologists propose that mate choice is unconsciously guided by cues that indicate some _____ for offspring.
  (b) Evolutionary psychologists suggest that women should be attracted to males who possess, and will share, _____.
  (c) Self-disclosure is the act of _____ to another person.
  (d) The halo effect means that we attribute _____ to attractive people.
  (e) The _____ proposes that we are attracted to people whom we perceive to be similarly attractive to ourselves.

(f) In the filter theory of relationship formation there are three stages of filter – first the social and demographic variables, second _____ and finally the complementarity of emotional needs.

(g) In social exchange theory, which one of the following sequences shows the order of the stages in the development of a relationship?
- A Commitment, bargaining, institutionalisation, sampling
- B Sampling, bargaining, commitment, institutionalisation
- C Bargaining, sampling, commitment, partnership
- D Bargaining, sampling, commitment, marriage

(h) Equity theory proposes that an _____ is one in which one partner's benefits divided by their costs is equal to the other partner's benefits divided by their costs.

(i) Rusbult's investment model consists of three processes that are positively associated with commitment, satisfaction level, _____ and investment size.

(j) Which one of the following sequences shows the correct order of Duck's phases of relationship breakdown?
- A Dyadic, intrapsychic, social, grave dressing
- B Intrapsychic, dyadic, social, grave dressing
- C Intrapsychic, social, dyadic, grave dressing
- D Social, dyadic, intrapsychic, grave dressing

(k) Which of the features listed below is NOT a feature of the investment model of relationships?
- A Investment
- B Satisfaction
- C Joint bank account
- D Commitment

(l) In parasocial relationships, gating features (the physical or material barriers that may arise between people when they interact in person) are missing, such as _____, race or class.

(m) In the addiction stage of the absorption–addiction model of parasocial relationships, the individual craves _____ to the chosen celebrity and becomes _____ in thinking and behaviour.

(n) The attachment theory of parasocial relationships proposes that those with _____ are more likely to become strongly attached to celebrities.

Answers on page 240

Exam practice

1 One theory of relationship formation is known as filter theory. Three stages of filter are proposed. The first filter stage is the social and demographic variables where we tend to pick people with similar educational and economic background to us. The second filter stage is the similarity of attitudes and values, where people with different values, attitudes and interests to us are filtered out. Outline the missing third filter stage. [1]

2 Social exchange theory assumes that relationships are based on 'exchanges' in which each person seeks to maximise their rewards and minimise their costs. Outline any two of the four stages in the development of a relationship. One mark awarded for each correct outline. [2]

3 Psychologists suggest that relationships that start over the internet are more intimate than those which start in a face-to-face physical communication because you are able to be your true self without the physical gating features present in face-to-face encounters.
List three features that may act as gating features in face-to-face relationships. [3]

4 From the evolutionary perspective, explain why physical attractiveness may be an important factor in interpersonal attraction. [4]

5 Suggest two problems that arise during research into relationship formation and breakdown. [4]

6 Discuss the extent to which psychologists can explain the breakdown of relationships. [16]

For a top band answer, knowledge of the psychology of relationship breakdown is accurate and generally well detailed. Discussion is thorough and effective. The answer is clear, coherent and focused. Specialist terminology is used effectively. Minor detail and/or expansion of argument may sometimes be missing.

Answers and quick quizzes 35, 36 and 37 online

ONLINE

Gender

Sex and gender

REVISED

Sex is a biological term. Across time and culture, this is defined in terms of reproduction and other biological aspects such as anatomy, brain chemistry and hormones. All societies make the same distinction. **Gender** is a psychological term. It refers to the ideas we hold about the behaviour, personality and attitudes of males and females within a given society. Discussions about gender include terms such as masculinity, femininity and androgyny. Gender identity is the classification of oneself as male or female. Children work out early on whether they are girls or boys and then look for behaviour characteristic of their gender in others.

Sex-role stereotypes

Historically, societies have had strong ideas about gender roles and expectations for gendered behaviour. **Sex-role stereotypes** are widely shared assumptions about the personalities, attitudes and behaviour of a particular gender group. They have tended to be social and cultural norms that we hold about male and female behaviours that may be exclusive to that gender – for example, females are stereotyped to be nurturing and males aggressive. Any behaviour not consistent with stereotypes is said to be deviant, such as aggressive behaviour in females.

Androgyny and measuring androgyny

Androgyny is a psychological phenomenon where the individual has high levels of both male and female stereotypical characteristics. Androgyny is not related to biology or sexual orientation; it is purely related to attitudes, beliefs and behaviours. Bem's theory in the 1970s suggested that individuals who had high levels of both male and female characteristics were more resilient and less likely to suffer from mental health issues.

One test for measuring androgyny is the Bem Sex Role Inventory (BSRI). The personality test includes 60 items: 20 stereotypically male-related characteristics (including aggressive and ambitious), 20 stereotypically female-related (such as compassionate and gentle) and 20 neutral (such as truthful). Participants would rate each item on a scale of 1–7 and would be classified as masculine, feminine, androgynous or undifferentiated. High levels of androgyny would be the result of a high score for both male- and female-related characteristics. Masculinity is a high level of male traits seen as being desirable and a rejection of female-perceived characteristics, and femininity is a high level of female traits seen as desirable and a rejection of male-perceived characteristics.

> **Revision activity**
>
> Read through the Approaches section from Component 2 to remind yourself of the main concepts of biological, cognitive and learning approaches and make a list of the key features.

> **Gender:** a psychological term that refers to the ideas we hold about the behaviour, personality and attitudes of males and females within a given society.
>
> **Sex-role stereotypes:** the shared assumptions about the personalities, attitudes and behaviour of a particular gender group whose members are perceived as sharing the same characteristics.
>
> **Androgyny:** the combination of masculine and feminine characteristics.

Theories of androgyny can explain how individuals can be different depending on the context, for example Olympic athlete Jessica Ennis-Hill can be competitive in the heptathlon and nurturing of her son Reggie.

It could be argued that research into sex-role stereotyping is alpha biased, which highlights the differences between males and females.

The BSRI is easy to complete and has high levels of test–retest reliability.

The BSRI can be criticised for being culturally biased and lacks temporal validity as it was developed in the USA in the 1970s.

Revision activity

Write a glossary of the key terms for gender.

The role of chromosomes and hormones in gender development

REVISED

During prenatal development, individuals have sex glands (gonads) which are identical and have the ability to turn into either testes or ovaries. If a Y **chromosome** is present it produces a protein which causes the gonads to become testes, which will eventually produce testosterone and lead to the development of male sex organs. Without the Y chromosome this does not occur and therefore female sex organs develop. The chromosome pattern for a male is XY and for a female is XX.

Hormones such as **testosterone** affect gender development in the womb, with males being exposed to more testosterone, which may explain the differences found between male and female brains. Testosterone affects the areas of the brain concerned with risk-taking behaviour, which can explain why males are found to be more willing to engage in risky behaviour than females. **Oestrogen** is a hormone produced by the ovaries linked to the female reproductive cycle and is found in higher levels in females from puberty, although males will have oestrogen in lower levels. **Oxytocin** is a neuropeptide as it acts as a hormone and neurotransmitter and is produced in the hypothalamus in the brain and secreted by the pituitary gland. It is mainly produced during labour to encourage uterine contraction and is secreted during breastfeeding. It is also believed to have psychological effects that encourage bonding behaviour between the mother and the child. It is produced in males and females when kissing, leading to positive emotions.

Chromosomes: humans have 46 chromosomes in each cell, arranged in pairs, of which one is the sex-linked X or Y.

Testosterone: a sex hormone which is more present in males than females and affects development and behaviour both before and after birth.

Oestrogen: a hormone produced by the ovaries linked to the female reproductive cycle.

Oxytocin: a neuropeptide produced in the hypothalamus in the brain and secreted by the pituitary gland during labour.

Research: biology and gender

Twisk and Stacey (2007) found that in serious head-on collisions, where one driver was going too fast or overtaking inappropriately, statistics showed that the driver was more likely to be male. This suggests that hormonal differences may account for the difference in brain structure and risk-taking behaviour.

Beeman (1947) castrated male mice and found that aggressiveness reduced. He later injected the mice with testosterone which re-established their aggressiveness, which is arguably a male trait.

Bryden and Saxby (1985) found that when males perform spatial tasks, there is greater electrical activity in the right hemisphere whereas females seem to use both hemispheres.

There is support for the theory that hormones affect male and female behaviour differently. An example is Money (1975), in which Bruce was brought up as a girl but behaved in a very boyish way and reverted to male gender by choice.

The difference in the male and female brains can be studied using scans (Bellis *et al.*, 2001); this is an objective way of testing gender differences.

However, hormonal influences on behaviour are hard to establish, partly because behaviour is affected by social and other influences after birth.

It does not take into account social factors such as the influence of reinforcements of appropriate behaviour and unconscious factors such as the Oedipus complex.

Atypical sex chromosome patterns

Klinefelter's syndrome is a genetic disorder found in males where they have an extra X chromosome. This is where the genetic material in either the egg or the sperm splits unevenly. This will lead to increased female characteristics such as wider hips and higher voice and reduced male characteristics such as smaller testicles and penis. People who have this syndrome may have trouble using language to express themselves; they may be shy and have trouble fitting in.

Turner syndrome is a chromosome abnormality affecting only females, caused by the complete or partial deletion of the X chromosome (X0). Turner syndrome affects the typical developmental changes during puberty where the girl will not have the normal growth spurt and in most cases fail to produce the sex hormones oestrogen and progesterone.

Exam tip

When answering a question on the role of chromosomes and hormones, ensure you emphasise the impact on gender, it is very easy just to describe the biology.

Revision activity

Make a mind map to show the role of hormones and chromosomes in gender.

Cognitive explanations of gender development

REVISED

Kohlberg's theory

The work of Kohlberg is based on Piagetian ideas that as the brain develops over childhood so does the ability of the child to think in complex and abstract ways. Kohlberg (1966) puts forward a stage theory of gender development, whereby the child's understanding of gender is constrained by their cognitive ability and cognition that causes the behaviour. At each successive stage, the child thinks in qualitatively different ways about gender and their understanding becomes more complex and abstract.

- The first stage is **gender identity**, which is usually reached by the age of two years. At this stage the child is able to correctly label themselves as a boy or a girl.
- The second stage is **gender stability**, which is usually reached by the age of four years, when the child realises that gender remains the same across time. For example, 'I am a boy and when I grow up I will be a man.'
- The third stage is **gender constancy**, which is usually reached by seven years when the child starts to understand that gender is independent of external features.

Gender identity: the classification of oneself as male or female, boy or girl. Young children work out whether they are girls or boys and then look for behaviour characteristic of their gendered sense of identity.

Gender stability: usually reached by the age of four years when the child realises that his/her gender remains the same across time.

Gender constancy: a child's emerging sense of the permanence of being a boy or a girl.

Kohlberg put forward the view that it was not until the final stage that the child is motivated to adopt behaviours appropriate to their gender. At this stage children will actively seek out activities associated with their gender and to behave in a way that is consistent with their gender.

Research: cognition and development

Slaby and Frey (1975) interviewed 55 children aged 2–5 years to measure each of Kohlberg's stages: 'Are you a boy or a girl?' (gender identity); 'When you grow up will you be a mummy or a daddy?' (gender stability); 'Could you be a boy or a girl if you wanted?' (gender constancy). Based on their responses they were then labelled 'high gender constancy' (HGC) or 'low gender constancy' (LGC). A few weeks later they were shown a film with a male and a female performing the same activity on opposite sides of the screen. The HGC children spent more time observing the same-gender adult compared with the LGC group. This shows that cognitive ability does influence gender-related behaviour.

Munroe et al. (1984) found the sequence of gender development was consistent across other cultures (Kenya, Nepal, Belize and Samoa). This suggests that the development on gender is universal and therefore further supports Kohlberg's theory of gender development.

Martin and Halverson (1983) found that when pre-schoolers are asked whether they themselves would change gender if they wore gender-inappropriate dress, almost all of them realised that they would remain the same. This goes against Kohlberg's theory as it would predict that the children were too young to be able to know this. Thompson (1975) also found that children as young as two years could categorise items as belonging to either male or female, thus showing an understanding of gender long before they achieved constancy at the age of seven.

Evaluation

The theory suggests gender develops as the child actively engages with their social world rather than passively observing as suggested by social learning theory (SLT).

Research suggests that Kohlberg may have underestimated the age at which children are aware of gender-appropriate behaviour and it could be as early as 18 months (Serbin, 2001).

Kohlberg's theory is purely a cognitive explanation for gender development, ignoring the role of socialisation as presented in SLT, and that children may be passive recipients of behaviour. The theory ignores impact of parents, culture and peers and overemphasises the role of the individual child's cognition.

Bussey and Bandura (1992) found that when four year olds played with gender-appropriate toys this led to the children feeling comfortable and when playing with gender-inappropriate toys to the children feeling uncomfortable. Kohlberg argued that this would not happen until children were seven.

Gender schema theory

Gender **schema** theory suggests that children play a more active role in their own gender development from an earlier age. A gender schema contains ideas about what is appropriate behaviour for males and females and this will influence their behaviour. Schemas will include toys, clothes, activities and behaviours. Unlike Kohlberg's theory, gender

Schema: this is a mental concept that informs a person about what to expect from a variety of experiences and situations. Schemas are developed based on information provided by life experiences and are then stored in memory.

schema theory says that once gender identity is gained, the child is motivated to seek gender-specific toys and same-sex peers.

- About the age of 2–3 years children develop schemas for physical differences between the sexes, leading to the child developing schemas for gender-specific characteristics and gender awareness.
- Around five years **gender roles** become more rigid and the child identifies activities and objects associated with their own gender and starts to ignore or reject those that do not fit in with this schema.
- By the age of seven years their view of what is gender-appropriate behaviour is more flexible. For example, a boy may view ballet as a male activity because they are a boy and like ballet.

Children at this age will pay attention to same-sex role models and this is an important step towards establishing self-identity. Part of the development of social identity is to make social comparisons with members of their own gender group (in-group) and the opposite gender (out-group). Children will evaluate their in-group and their associated behaviour and activities in a positive light and members of the out-group and their related behaviour as negative.

> **Gender roles:** attitudes and behaviour considered appropriate and typical for people who are classified as male or female.

Research: gender schema theory

Bauer (1993) set out to study the way in which children call upon gender schemas when processing information. Children observed the experimenter carry out short sequences of stereotypically female, male and gender-neutral activities (changing a nappy, shaving a teddy bear or treasure hunts). Results showed that boys more than girls tend to make use of gender schemas by the age of 25 months.

Campbell *et al.* (2000) studied three groups of babies – aged 3 months, 9 months and 18 months – using a visual preference technique. The three-month-old babies showed a slight preference towards watching same-sex babies, more so in males than females. Nine-month male babies preferred to look at boys'

toys. The effect continued to 18 months. This suggests that babies develop gender schemas before they can even talk. The boys have a stronger drive to tune into their group (in-group).

Campbell (2004) carried out a longitudinal study of 56 children at 27 and 39 months. The children were asked to point to: girl or boy; girls' or boys' toy; boys' or girls' activity. The findings show that 53% of two year olds could carry out the gender-labelling task and by the age of three, 94% could. At the age of two, 20% could stereotype toys and by three, 51% of children could stereotype. Campbell concluded that gender schemas develop rapidly between the ages of two and three years but not for everything.

Evaluation

One strength is that the schema theory suggests that children are active in the development of gender rather than passive recipients as suggested by social learning theory.

A weakness is that Campbell *et al.* (2002) found no evidence of greater preference for gender-consistent toys in two-year-old boys and girls who showed more gender knowledge.

Both Kohlberg and schema theory focus on the first seven years and ignore puberty when gender identity is most vulnerable. It could be argued that this is due to hormonal influences rather than cognition.

One advantage of gender schema theory over Kohlberg's theory is the inclusion of social and cultural influences on the development of gender. This increases the validity of the theory.

Revision activity

Make a mind map for Kohlberg's stage theory and schema theory of gender development.

Exam tip

When evaluating either Kohlberg or gender schema theory, using the other theory to compare will make your answer more effective. However, you need to find a point of comparison and not just describe one theory and then the other.

Psychodynamic explanations for gender development

REVISED

The psychodynamic theory of gender development suggests that gender identity and role are acquired during the third stage of psychosexual development, the phallic stage. As the child enters the phallic stage, the focus of its libido moves to the genitals and the development of girls and boys differs. The key concepts here are the identification with the same-sex parent to reduce anxiety, internalisation of their moral standards and development of a superego.

Male gender development

Boys enter the Oedipus complex. They start to sexually desire their mother and realise that their father stands in the way of the satisfaction of their desire. This frustration of the id results in aggressive feelings being directed towards the father. At the same time, the boy realises that his father is more powerful than he is and starts to fear that if the father finds out about the boy's desire for his mother, he will castrate him (**castration anxiety**). The boy deals with the conflict this causes by starting to identify with the father and wanting to be like him. Eventually he internalises his father into his own psyche. This becomes his superego and, in taking on his father as part of himself, the boy takes on the male gender identity.

Female gender development

Girls enter the Electra complex, which starts with the realisation that they have no penis. This leads them to believe that they have been castrated, something for which they blame their mother. Because she has no penis the girl sees herself as powerless and wishes that she had one (**penis envy**). She starts to desire her father because he has one and becomes jealous and hostile towards her mother, mirroring the Oedipus complex in boys. Eventually, she starts to identify with and to internalise her mother, developing a superego and a female gender identity. At this point she represses her desire for a penis and substitutes it with the desire for a baby.

Psychodynamic psychologists base their theories on case studies of people who were undergoing treatment for psychological problems. (Review the psychodynamic approach on page 44 in Component 2.)

> **Castration anxiety:** a psychoanalytical term which is used to refer to the anxiety experienced by the young boy as a result of the rivalry with his father for the affections of the mother.
>
> **Penis envy:** a stage in Freud's psychodynamic theory in female psychosexual development, in which females experience anxiety upon realisation that they do not have a penis.

Evaluation

One strength of the psychodynamic theory is that it is supported by clinical case studies such as Little Hans and his phobia of horses, from which Freud developed the Oedipus complex where the child identifies with the same-sex parent. Case studies like this one which included subjective interviews of Hans helped develop this idea.

According to cognitive theories of gender development children start to show gender-based preferences for toys as early as the age of one and usually have clear ideas about their own gender identity by the age of two. This is counter to the psychodynamic theory which suggests gender identity does not occur until the child is three and is not complete until five years.

Psychodynamic explanations for gender development lack temporal validity as they reflect the stereotypical gender roles in the early 1900s that women are inferior to men, which is not an idea that is widely considered acceptable today.

Revision activity

Make a list of all the key terms from the psychodynamic approach. Use the key words to describe Freud's theory of gender in 100 words, then 50 words.

Examination tip

Freud's theory is complex and you need to just relate to gender development, you do not need to describe all of the stages here.

Social learning theory as applied to gender development

According to the social learning theory most behaviours are learned through a process of observation and imitation. Like traditional behaviourist psychologists, social learning theorists argue that reinforcement places a central role in whether people choose to imitate others or not. Studies show that we are more likely to imitate people if the imitative behaviour is rewarded – this can be direct or vicariously through a role model. We therefore take into account what happens to other people when deciding whether or not to copy someone's actions. These people or characters are known as models and the imitation behaviour is referred to as modelling.

Additionally, Bandura suggested four cognitive processes central to learning:
- **Attention:** the child is selective in who they pay attention to – they are most likely to pay attention to a same-sex model.
- **Retention:** the child has to have the ability to form a mental representation of the observed behaviour so they can recall it later.
- **Reproduction:** the child takes the mental representation and puts it into practice.
- **Motivation:** the child needs to be motivated to model the behaviour – they may know what 'playing like a boy' looks like and they make the decision as to whether to copy it.

Research: gender and social learning

Fagot and Leinbach (1989) in a longitudinal study of gender development found a tendency for parents to encourage gender-stereotypical behaviour in their children. This tendency was strongest among parents who held strongly gender-stereotyped attitudes.

Fagot et al. (1992) measured the effects of parenting style and children's later gender roles. They compared 27 egalitarian families (shared parenting) with 42 traditional families. They interviewed the parents when their child was 18 months old and they observed them play with the toddler at 28 and 48 months. When children reached four years old, they were given a variety of gender-labelling tasks to examine their own gender schemas. Findings were that the children in traditional families tended to use gender labels earlier and showed more gender-role stereotyping. This suggests that parents are important role models for children's acquisition of gender roles.

Evaluation

Social learning theory has difficulty explaining how children's understanding of gender changes over time.

Cognitive processes play a greater role in the learning of gender than social learning theory allows for. However, Bandura did add the process of modelling, making it more of a socio-cognitive theory.

There is also the issue that some aspects of gender role behaviour appear to be universal to all cultures. For example, men are consistently found to be more aggressive than women, regardless of culture.

Similarly, there are cross-cultural similarities in the features women and men find desirable in potential reproductive partners (Buss et al., 1990). These universal features suggest that some aspects of gender roles are the result of innate, genetic influences that social learning theory does not take account of.

Revision activity

Draw a flow diagram or a comic strip to show the process of vicarious learning including modelling.

The influence of culture on gender roles

The importance of culture on gender roles is to show that behaviour is not universal as suggested by biological theories. Cultural research is carried out to show similarities between gender roles in different cultures, and differences between cultures in stereotypical behaviours. Cross-cultural studies help us to decide whether it is biology or socialisation that determines our gender roles. In terms of gender there are two different types of cultures: traditional cultures, where there are clear differences in male and female roles and power, and egalitarian cultures, where gender roles are more flexible and equal. The fact that women want providers may be less to do with biology and more to do with the fact that women earn less in society, a social issue rather than a biological issue. Anthropological research shows that men are generally similar in all cultures: more aggressive, violent, competitive and dominant, less empathic and less sensitive than women. However, the way in which their behaviour is expressed is influenced by cultural factors.

Examination tip

When answering a question on social learning theory as applied to gender development, make sure that you specifically shape your answer to gender. The best way to do this is to give specific examples as you outline or describe the process of modelling.

Research: gender roles and culture

Buss (1989) explored what males and females looked for in a marriage partner. The study involved over 10,000 people from 37 different cultures, including a wide diversity of ethnic, religious, political and economic groups. It was found that women desired mates who had good financial prospects whereas men placed more importance on physical attractiveness. Men generally wanted mates who were younger than them. Both sexes wanted mates who were intelligent, kind and dependable.

Mead (1935) studied three New Guinea tribes and found that in the Arapesh tribe, gender roles of men and women were similar, both being unaggressive and sensitive and of a peaceful temperament. In the Mundugumor tribe, both men and women were uncooperative, aggressive, insensitive and war-like. In the Tchambuli tribe, women were dominant, with economic and political influences; men stayed at home and were more submissive.

However, when Mead reanalysed her data she realised that although both sexes of the Arapesh were non-aggressive and both sexes of the Mundugumor were aggressive, in all three societies the men were more aggressive than the women. This suggests that some behaviours are innate and universal but the degree to which these behaviours are expressed is relative to the particular culture.

Evaluation

Cultural bias is an issue because even though the research is looking into cultural differences, most of the researchers were Western.

Measures used to carry out the research were developed by Western psychology and are an imposed etic as the result would be meaningless in a culture other than the one in which the tests were developed.

Research suggests there are cultural differences in gender roles which shows the effect of social factors as being equally important to biological effects (nurture as well as nature).

The influence of media on gender roles

The effect of the media on behaviour is connected to the principle of social learning through the concept of vicarious conditioning. It emphasises the importance of modelling and role models. The

Exam practice answers and quick quizzes at **www.hoddereducation.co.uk/myrevisionnotes**

media offers the ideal opportunity to present positive and negative role models for children to imitate as well as gender behaviours for children to observe and imitate. All types of media, such as television programmes, adverts, magazines, newspapers and films, present gender stereotypes on a daily basis. As well as identifying with family and peers to model behaviour, young children may well identify with television and film characters and imitate them. Mediating cognitive factors will determine who potential role models are, for example whether they are attractive or similar in personality, and personal characteristics such as age, gender and ethnicity. Children are now subject to the influence of video gaming and social media such as Facebook and Twitter.

Media influence on gender roles

Matthews, J.L. (2007) found gender role differences in advertisements where males were portrayed in adverts for cars and technical items compared with females who were portrayed in adverts for beauty and cleaning products.

Williams (1986) compared two towns. One town had television and the other had no television at the time of the original study in the 1970s. Children in the town with television were more gender stereotyped than those without, although when TV came to the second town, the children soon caught up.

Hopper (2005) found that teenage girls were more likely to read magazines than teenage boys, which may explain why a higher proportion of magazines are seemingly directed towards girls.

Pierce (1993) used content analysis to research gender stereotypes in popular US teenage magazine stories. Results showed that 63% of female characters looked to others for social support, suggesting dependency.

Evaluation

Media influences are backed up with research evidence which suggests that the media can have a positive effect on gender role stereotypes, for example televising the women's football world cup can encourage more females to play sports. This increases the validity of the explanation of the effects the media has on real life.

Research into media effects on gender roles is mainly correlational – their cause and effect cannot be established.

Revision activity

Plan two points to compare the social and biological explanations for gender development.

Atypical gender development: gender identity disorder

REVISED

Gender identity disorder is a feeling of mismatch between anatomy and gender identity which manifests itself as a sense of inappropriateness in gender role matching and a refusal to participate in activities specific to their sex. **Gender dysphoria** is anxiety, uncertainty or persistently uncomfortable feelings about one's assigned gender (based on one's anatomical sex). Dysphoria is the major symptom of gender identity disorder (GID), which is the term used by official psychiatric classifications of mental disorders.

Gender dysphoria: the term commonly used (DSM-V) for gender identity disorder. It is defined by strong, persistent feelings of identification with the opposite gender and discomfort with one's own assigned sex, which results in significant distress.

If the four diagnostic criteria in the (DSM-IV-TR) are met, a diagnosis of GID can be made:

- Longstanding and strong identification with another gender.
- Longstanding disquiet about the sex assigned or a sense of incongruity in the gender-assigned role of that sex.
- Significant clinical discomfort or impairment at work, in social situations or in other important life areas.
- Strong preference for playmates of the other sex.

The experience of gender dysphoria has to be present for at least two years, along with the person's insistence that they are of the opposite sex. According to NHS Direct, 1 in 4,000 people in the UK are receiving treatment for the disorder and the prevalence is five times higher in males than in females.

Biological explanations for gender identity disorder

Biological explanations for **gender identity disorder** have found differences in the brain associated with sexual behaviour. For example, a research has found that part of the hypothalamus (bed nucleus of the stria terminals, BST) in typical males is larger than in males with GID, which is more in line with that of typical females (Zhou *et al.*, 1995). During early stages of foetal development, males rely on the production of the hormone androgen. Problems can arise when either androgen is not produced or the cell receptors do not respond to the androgen (Zucker and Green, 1992). Chung *et al.* (2002) argued that prenatal hormonal influences might remain dormant until adulthood and then trigger a change. This may account for the higher proportion of males diagnosed with GID than females.

> **Gender identity disorder:** a feeling of mismatch between anatomy and gender identity which manifests itself as anxiety about one's assigned gender and a refusal to participate in activities specific to one's sex.

There may also be a genetic prevalence to GID. Coolidge *et al.* (2002) examined the concordance rates for 157 pairs of twins aged 4–17 years (96 MZ and 61 DZ). The parents completed a six-item questionnaire based on the DSM-IV. The prevalence of clinically significant symptoms in the sample was estimated to be 2.3%; further analysis of the data showed that 62% of the variance accounted for the genetic variance supporting a strong heritable component to GID.

Biological bases for gender dysphoria

Bennett (2006) cited one of the few studies of the genetic processes involved in GID, which found that 2% of the sample of more than 300 monozygotic (MZ) and dizygotic (DZ) twins showed some evidence of GID based on self-report measures.

Pool *et al.* (2000) pointed out that males have around twice as many somatostatin neurons than women. They found that in both male-to-female transsexuals and female-to-male transsexuals, the number of these neurons corresponded to their gender of choice, not to their biological sex. They concluded that this clearly points to a neurobiological basis for gender dysphoria.

Zho *et al.* (1995) studied an area in the hypothalamus known as the BSTc. This is thought to be fully developed after five years and influences sexual behaviour. In post-mortems of six male-to-female transsexuals who had received feminising hormones, it was found to be the same size as in heterosexual women. Also, the number of neurons in the BSTc showed a similar pattern to that in heterosexual women.

One of the problems for any explanation is research that shows that cross-gender behaviour starts very early, for example in toddlers and pre-school children. In children with GID the pattern of opposite-sex behaviour is so distinct that parents would need to be actively and consistently promoting it, not just tolerant of it. This suggests a strong social/cultural link, not just a biological one.

Another problem is that males seem to be five times more prone to GID than females. Could this be due to the greater biological vulnerability in the womb of male foetuses, leading to the incomplete development of a 'male brain'? This suggests stronger support for biological explanations than for social explanations.

Social explanations for gender identity disorder

Social explanations centre on maladaptive learning experiences, maladaptive cognitive processes and psychodynamic fixations in childhood. The psychodynamic view is that problems can result from difficulties establishing gender identity during the phallic stage of personality development. It could also be related to attachment between the mother and the child. It is a severe form of separation anxiety found in males, who remain psychologically attached to their mother and develop a gender identity to replace the mother (Coates and Person, 1985). To reduce the anxiety created the child imitates the mother by cross-gender behaviour. Another social explanation could be due to parents having a strong desire for a child of the opposite sex and, not necessarily deliberately, reinforcing gender-inappropriate behaviour (di Ceglie, 2000). In this case mothers may praise young boys for wearing girls' clothing.

Rekers (1986) linked GID in boys to an absence of a father figure either physically or psychologically. He conducted research on 36 GID boys. In the group of most dysphoric boys, 75% had no father figure. In the group of least dysphoric boys, 21% had no father figure. In the cases where there was a father figure, he was often described as psychologically absent.

The most convincing evidence comes from Rekers (1986), who associated father absence with gender disturbance in boys. Although he acknowledged that these correlational studies did not necessarily imply that the absence of a male role model in early life causes GID, he believed that this was not an unreasonable conclusion to draw. Nevertheless, it is important to note the research supporting the biological explanation can be used as a criticism of this view.

Gender identity disorder is a socially sensitive area of research and it could be argued that social explanations place blame on the families.

Psychodynamic explanations are subjective and cannot be tested scientifically, which weakens it as an explanation of GID.

It could be argued that GID is influenced by both biological and social factors. GID is intensified during puberty when hormonal changes, alongside social and emotional changes, are taking place.

Make a table to show the comparisons between the biological and social explanations for gender identity disorder. Include research evidence and how the evidence supports/challenges the explanation.

Summary

You must be able to demonstrate knowledge and understanding of:

- sex and gender, sex-role stereotypes, androgyny and measuring androgyny, including the Bem Sex Role Inventory
- the role of chromosomes and hormones (testosterone, oestrogen and oxytocin) in sex and gender
- atypical sex chromosome patterns: Klinefelter's syndrome and Turner syndrome
- cognitive explanations of gender development, Kohlberg's theory, gender identity, gender stability and gender constancy, gender schema theory
- the psychodynamic explanation of gender development, Freud's psychoanalytic theory, the Oedipus complex and the Electra complex, identification and internalisation
- social learning theory as applied to gender development and the influence of culture and media on gender roles
- atypical gender development: gender identity disorder, and biological and social explanations for gender identity disorder.

Now test yourself

TESTED

1 (a) Which of these sex chromosome structures is found in females?
   A XXY
   B XO
   C XX
   D XY

(b) Which of the following is not one of Kohlberg's stages of development?
   A Gender constancy
   B Gender flexibility
   C Gender identity
   D Gender stability

(c) Which of the following is not a key term from Freud's psychodynamic theory of gender?
   A Castration anxiety
   B Vicarious reinforcement
   C Internalisation
   D Id impulses

(d) Which is the correct name for a measure of androgyny?
   A Bun Sex Role Inventory
   B Bem Sex Role Inventory
   C Bem Sex Route Inventory
   D Bem Social Role Inventory

(e) According to NHS Direct, what is the prevalence of gender identity disorder?
   A 1/1000
   B 1/40,000
   C 1/10,000
   D 1/4000

(f) In which of the stages in Freud's theory does the Oedipus conflict take place?
   A Latency
   B Phallic
   C Oral
   D Genital

(g) Mead looked at cultural differences in gender roles. Which of the following tribes did Mead not research?
   A Arapesh
   B Mundugumor
   C Kolufo
   D Tchambuli

2 Fill in the blanks in the following sentences to outline the key features of social learning theory.
   (a) A child is most likely to pay _____ to a _____ sex model.
   (b) A child is more likely to imitate people if the imitative behaviour is _____.
   (c) The child needs to have the ability to form a _____ _____ of the observed behaviour so they can recall it later.
   (d) Children need to have the _____ to perform the observed action in order to _____ it.
3 (a) Outline the difference between one social and one biological explanation for gender identity disorder.
   (b) List two symptoms of gender identity disorder.
4 Outline evidence to support the role of hormones in gender development.
5 For each of the following 'evidence' write an opposing argument.
   (a) Hopper (2005) found that teenage girls were more likely to read magazines than teenage boys, which shows a higher proportion of magazines are directed towards girls. However, ...
   (b) It is proposed that hormones have a significant effect on the development of gender. However, ...
6 Define the following terms:
   (a) Sex.
   (b) Gender.
   (c) Sex-role stereotypes.
7 Briefly outline Turner syndrome of atypical sex chromosome patterns.
8 Outline one strength of the media's influence on gender roles.
9 Evaluate gender schema theory.

Answers on page 241

Exam practice

1 Which one of the following statements about Kohlberg's cognitive theory of gender development is false? [1]
   A The theory is based on Piagetian ideas that cognition causes behaviour.
   B Kohlberg puts forward a stage theory of gender development.
   C By the age of two a child is able to correctly label themselves as a boy or a girl.
   D The theory includes the influence of social and culture on the development of gender.
   E Only when children have gender constancy do they actively seek out activities associated with their gender.
2 Which of the following is one of the cognitive processes involved in the social learning theory of gender role development? [1]
   A Constancy
   B Perception
   C Attention
   D Intelligence
   E Synaesthesia
3 (a) Outline the role of testosterone in gender development. [4]
   (b) Evaluate the role of hormones in gender development. [6]
4 Gender identity disorder is a feeling of mismatch between anatomy and gender identity which manifests itself as a sense of inappropriateness in gender-role matching and a refusal to participate in activities specific to their sex.
   (a) Briefly outline one social explanation for gender identity disorder. [2]
   (b) Explain one strength and one limitation of the social explanation of gender identity disorder. [6]
5 Outline and evaluate the psychodynamic explanations for gender development. [8]

6 Androgyny is a psychological phenomenon where the individual has high levels of both male and female stereotypical characteristics. Androgyny is not related to biology or sexual orientation, it is purely related to attitudes, beliefs and behaviours. Bem's theory in the 1970s suggested that individuals who had high levels of both male and female characteristics were more resilient and less likely to suffer from metal health issues.

   (a) Briefly outline the BSRI as a measure of androgyny. [2]

   (b) Explain one limitation of measuring androgyny. [2]

7 Which of these sex chromosome structures is found in Klinefelters syndrome? [1]

   A XXY

   B XO

   C XX

   D XY

8 Discuss gender schema theory as an explanation of gender development. [16]

Answers and quick quizzes 62, 63, 64 and 65 online

ONLINE

Cognition and development

Piaget's theory of cognitive development

Piaget believed that the way children learn and develop proceeds as a set of age-related (maturational) stages common to all.

- **Schemas:** according to Piaget, children are born with certain schemas, including those for sucking and grasping. In the first year of life other simple schemata develop, and later the schemas become more complex and include schemas for abstract concepts. Schemas are being updated and added to throughout life. Currently you are building a schema for Piaget.
- **Equilibrium and disequilibrium:** if a new experience does not match existing schema then a state of disequilibrium is produced. The child needs to accommodate to restore the balance, i.e. alter their perception of how things work. According to Piaget, disequilibrium is essential for learning; however, there appears to be little or no empirical evidence to support this.
- **Assimilation:** new information or experiences can be fitted into the child's existing schema or current understanding of the world. A child sees a kitten and is able to fit this into the same schema as the schema for cat.
- **Accommodation:** new information or experiences cannot be fitted into the child's current understanding so they either have to alter existing schema or create a whole new schema – for example, kitten does not fit in with schema for cow so a new schema needs to be constructed, bringing about a structural change.
- **Operations:** these are mental transformations or manipulations that occur in the mind. In other words, a child that has operational thought can do things in their head, for example count. In pre-operational thinking the child needs something 'concrete' to manipulate – for example, they will use their fingers to count.

Stages of intellectual development

Figure 3.5 shows Piaget's stages of intellectual development.

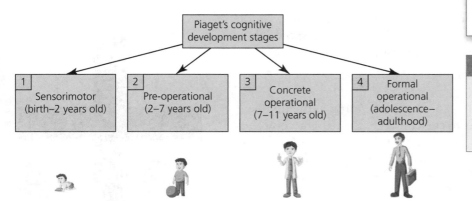

Figure 3.5 Piaget's stages of cognitive development

Schemas: mental structures that are being added to and changed throughout life.

Equilibrium and disequilibrium: (Piagetian) equilibrium is when all experiences fit existing schemas but if a new experience does not match existing schemas then a state of disequilibrium is produced. According to Piaget, disequilibrium is essential for learning.

Assimilation: (Piagetian) new information or experiences can be fitted into the child's existing schema or current understanding of the world.

Accommodation: (Piagetian) new information or experiences cannot be fitted into the child's current understanding so either an existing schema is changed or a new schema is created.

Operations: (Piagetian) mental transformations that occur in the mind. In other words, a child who has operational thought can reason things in their mind.

Revision activity

As you revise Piaget's theory, make your own glossary of Piagetian terminology.

Stage 1: Sensorimotor stage (0–2 years)

A child's understanding of the world comes directly through their senses from moment to moment. The child thinks only about objects and/or people they can sense and/or manipulate, hence the term 'sensorimotor'. When an object is out of view it is no longer considered and therefore the child lacks **object permanence**.

> **Object permanence:** when a child has not developed object permanence they assume that an object no longer exists if it cannot be seen.

Research evidence

Piaget carried out research on his own children and found that if they were shown an attractive object that was then hidden from view, up to the age of eight months they did not bother to look for the object, assuming it no longer existed, but after eight months they would continue to search for it.

Evidence against

Bower and Wishart (1972) showed objects to children between the ages of one and four months. Lights were switched off so that the objects were no longer visible but the child was seen (by infrared camera) continuing to search for the object.

Stage 2: Pre-operational stage (2–7 years)

The child is still dominated by the external world but is now able to create some simple internal representations of the world (schemas) through an increasing ability to use language. This stage is called 'pre-operational' since the child is unable to perform 'mental' operations. This stage can be subdivided into pre-conceptual (2–4 years) and intuitive (4–7 years).

Animism

In the pre-conceptual stage children may attribute feelings to inanimate objects (known as **animism**), so the child may think toys have feelings. Other inabilities include not being able to **decentre** or to place things in logical order (seriation).

> **Animism:** (Piagetian) attributing feelings to inanimate objects.
>
> **Decentre:** this is the ability to consider multiple aspects of a situation.

Egocentrism

The child is unable to see things from other people's perspectives. For example, a two year old may believe that if they cannot see you, you will not be able to see them. Piaget demonstrated this with the three mountains task. In the task children look at a model and are asked to choose a photo that shows the perspective view as seen by someone else – say, person X or person Y (see Figure 3.6). According to Piaget, children below the age of seven years tend to choose the photo that shows 'their' view of the mountains so they pick a photo of their own perspective.

Figure 3.6 The three mountains task

Research evidence

Hughes (1975) repeated the three mountains task using a situation he thought would be more familiar to the child, i.e. the naughty boy hiding from the policeman (see Figure 3.7). There were three dolls (two policemen and a boy). The child was asked to position the boy so the policemen could not see him. This was done for four arrangements – 22 out of 30 children were successful on all four tasks and 90% of children aged 3–5 years could complete the task successfully, suggesting that it was lack of understanding rather than egocentrism that caused the problems for Piaget's participants.

Figure 3.7 The naughty boy hiding from the policemen

Conservation

To conserve something is to preserve it or keep it the same, to *maintain the same quantity*. In terms of thought processes, a child can conserve when they understand that quantity does not change even if it *looks* different. For example, if you pour water from a wide glass into a narrow glass, the quantity looks as if it has increased. Young children are influenced by what they see (concrete information) and if the appearance changes they will say that there is more water in the narrow glass.

Piaget suggested that seven years is a watershed and that children above this age have developed their ability to conserve. Evidence to support this was gathered using **conservation** tasks in which Piaget used quantities such as a row of counters (number conservation) and a ball of Plasticine (conservation of mass). His procedure was to show the child two equal quantities, for example two rows of counters equally spaced out. He asked the child, 'Do the rows have the same number of counters?', to which the child answered, 'Yes'. Piaget then transformed one display, for example spreading out one row of counters so that it looked longer. Piaget asked the child again, 'Do the rows both have the same number of counters?' Some children said 'Yes' (they were the ones who could conserve), some children said 'No' (they could not conserve). See Figures 3.9 and 3.10 below.

The ability to conserve is the realisation that the appearance of an object can change but the underlying quality can remain the same. Piaget believed the inability to conserve was due to two factors:

- **Centration:** the child is only considering the appearance – so, for example, in conservation of volume they focus on the height of the liquid and ignore the width.
- **Reversibility:** the child is unable to perform the mental operation of 'visualising the task being carried out in reverse', for example the liquid being poured back into the original container.

According to Piaget, the child who changes their answer has not developed the ability to conserve. Children have developed the ability to conserve when they understand that quantity does not change when appearance changes.

Conservation of **mass** involves two rolls of Plasticine, where before the transformation they look the same and after the transformation they look different.

Conservation of **volume** involves liquid being poured from a short, fat glass into a tall, thin one (see Figure 3.11), where before the transformation the liquid looks the same and after the transformation (in the tall glass) it looks different.

Exam tip

Remember what the ability to conserve means – think about why you pay more for strawberry conserve than you do for strawberry jam. In strawberry conserve only the appearance of the strawberries has changed – the quality and taste of the berries remain the same (have been conserved).

Figure 3.8 Strawberry conserve: only the appearance of the berries has changed

Conservation: (Piagetian) understanding that the quantity of an object does not change when appearance changes.

Figure 3.11 Conservation of volume

Figure 3.9 Question 1: Are there the same number of counters in each row?

Figure 3.10 Question 2: Are there the same number of counters in each row?

Research: the ability to conserve

Samuel, J. and Bryant, P. (1984) argued that the reason young children get these tasks wrong was not because they cannot conserve but because being asked the same question twice confuses them. The child may think that the reason the experimenter asks the same question again is because he wants a different answer. They tested the theory that 'asking the same question twice' is the reason why children fail to conserve from the ages of five to eight and a half years. The children were divided into four age groups, whose mean ages were five years three months, six years three months, seven years three months and eight years three months. Each group was further subdivided into three subgroups, each with the same mean age. The following tasks were carried out:

- Standard: traditional Piagetian conservation task, where the child is asked two questions about the size of the object before and after it was changed.
- One judgement: only one question asked, about the size of the object after it was changed.
- Fixed array control: child saw only one display, the post-transformation one.

The reason for having a control group was to be able to explain the performance of the other two groups in terms of the information they had from the pre-transformation display. If the control group could not cope with the task, then failure might be due to problems understanding just the one question. The children were given 12 separate trials, consisting of two equal and two unequal quantities for each of the three kinds of material shown below.

	Pre-transformation		Post-transformation
	Equal quantities	**Unequal quantities**	
1 Mass	Two equal Plasticine cylinders.	Two unequal Plasticine cylinders, one longer than the other.	One cylinder is squashed so it looks like a sausage.
2 Number	Two rows of six counters each, arranged identically.	One row of six counters and one of five arranged to look equal in length.	One row was either spread out or bunched up so the two rows were not of equal length.
3 Volume	Two identical glasses, with the *same* amounts of liquid.	Two identical glasses, with *different* amounts of liquid.	The liquid from one glass is poured into a narrower or wider one.

Findings: there were no differences found in the equal and unequal conditions and therefore the results for these were combined. The table below shows the mean number of errors for each child (rounded to the nearest whole number). An error is a failure to conserve.

Age	Standard	One question	Control
5	8	7	9
6	6	4	6
7	3	3	5
8	2	1	3

Conclusions: asking the same question twice may cause some children to fail to conserve, but the results also provide support for Piaget's theory because as the age of the children increased, the children made fewer errors of conservation, regardless of which condition they were tested in.

More research

Siegal (1991) carried out an ingenious study to show the effects of demand characteristics in Piaget's conservation procedures. Children of three and four years were tested on the procedure, being asked the same question twice. They then watched as other children repeated the procedure and were asked to explain what they had seen. Often when the children got the task wrong the observing participants explained that they had done so only to please the adults. Many of the children who themselves had got the answer wrong were able to explain why others were also getting it wrong.

McGarrigle and Donaldson (1974) repeated Piaget's conservation experiment on six year olds. The child was shown two rows of equal numbers of counters. The child agreed that the two rows were the same. When a naughty teddy bear messed up the row of counters, 62% of children in this age group were able to conserve. This shows that children are better able to conserve than Piaget proposed. In the teddy condition there is a reason for the counters to be messed up (naughty teddy), so the situation has meaning.

Class inclusion

Another method Piaget used to test conservation was class inclusion. He used a selection of different coloured wooden beads – they were mostly brown wooden ones but with a few white ones, as in Figure 3.12. When asked 'Are there more brown beads or more white beads?', children usually got the answer right. However, if they were asked 'Are there more brown beads or more beads?', they generally said 'More brown beads', even though all were beads. Piaget explained this in terms of the child's inability to distinguish between superordinate groups (beads) and a subclass or subordinate group, brown beads.

Donaldson (1978), however, believed that the nature of the question confuses the child. She presented children with four toy cows laid on their side (as if asleep). Three of the cows were brown and one was white. When asked 'Are there more brown cows or white cows?', children got it right. But when asked 'Are there more brown cows or more cows?', only 25% answered correctly, pretty much as Piaget would have predicted. However, when asked 'Are there more brown cows or more sleeping cows?', this percentage doubled. You are now comparing two subordinate groups, brown cows and sleeping cows, and the task becomes easier.

Figure 3.12 Beads used to test class inclusion

Stage 3: Concrete operational stage (7–approximately 11 years)

The child is now able to conserve and can perform quite complex operations, but only if 'real' objects are 'at hand'. The child cannot perform mental operations (transformations). For example, if asked 'If Betty is taller than Jenny and shorter than Jean, who is the tallest?', without real figures to manipulate the child cannot answer.

Stage 4: Formal operational stage (aged 11+)

The child can now perform logical operations and abstract reasoning – but according to Piaget only 30% of people ever achieve the stage of formal operations.

Evaluation

Piaget's research has generated further research.

Piaget often underestimated the age at which children could perform activities.

Variations in an experimental procedure can produce very different findings.

Piaget's original studies used questions not well suited to the age range of the children he was studying. Instructions may have been confusing or the tasks themselves too complex – for example, the three mountains task that was reworked by Hughes in a more familiar format.

The word 'more' is also a possible source of confusion. Adults use the word to mean a greater number whereas children use it to mean larger or taking up more space.

Revision activity

Make a poster showing the main characteristics of each of Piaget's stages of cognitive development. Collect some counters or Plasticine and role play the conservation tasks.

Exam tip

When you evaluate Piaget's theory, remember that in this theory age is the motivating factor in cognitive development, so this is a maturational theory, suggesting nature (age) rather than nurture (experience) is what drives change in cognitive development.

Vygotsky's theory of cognitive development

Lev Vygotsky (1896–1934) was a Soviet psychologist who proposed a theory of the development of higher cognitive functions in children that saw reasoning as emerging through practical activity in a social environment. In the 1930s Vygotsky's ideas were introduced in the West and in the 1970s they became a central component of the development of new paradigms in developmental and educational psychology. Vygotsky was not published in England until 1962.

According to Vygotsky (1934), 'The ability to think and reason is the result of social interaction ... and **cognitive development is the result of the active internalisation of problem-solving processes that occur in interaction between children and those with whom they have contact**'. For Piaget, the child is a scientist who is focused on discovering things, whereas for Vygotsky, the child is an apprentice who is learning with others. Vygotsky suggested that 'any function in the child's cultural development appears twice, first on the social plane, then on the psychological plane'. For example, pointing can be seen as originally unsuccessful grasping, but if the mother interprets and provides support, the baby learns to deliberately 'point' and the gesture now has social meaning.

The Zone of Proximal Development

According to Vygotsky, each child has a zone of ability and a **Zone of Proximal Development (ZOPD)**, which is 'potential ability' if the child is guided (scaffolded) by a more able adult or peer. The ZOPD has been defined as 'the distance between the actual developmental level as determined by independent problem solving and the level of potential development as determined through problem solving under adult guidance, or in collaboration with more capable peers'.

Vygotsky recommended peer tutoring as an effective way of teaching to foster cooperative and interactive relationships between learner and teacher. The role of the teacher is to 'help the child's disorganised informal concepts become the systematic and organised understanding of the adult' and to 'actively challenge the child to move on from the level of their present understanding to the ZOPD'.

Scaffolding

Wood *et al.* (1976) define **scaffolding** as 'support with the elements of the task that are initially beyond the learner's capacity, thus permitting him/her to concentrate on and complete the parts of the task that are within his/her range of competence'. Vygotsky never used the term 'scaffolding' as this term was introduced by Wood *et al.* in 1976. Once the child, with the benefit of scaffolding, can complete the task, the scaffolding can be removed and the child will be able to complete the task again on their own. Scaffolding helps the child move into the ZOPD.

Vygotsky's theory of ZOPD and scaffolding has been applied to education. In the classroom, scaffolding can be performed with just about any task. Silver (2011) suggested these guidelines:

- Assess the learner's current knowledge and experience for the academic content.
- Relate content to what students already understand or can do.
- Break a task into small, manageable tasks with opportunities for intermittent feedback.
- Use verbal cues and prompts to assist students.

Zone of Proximal Development (ZOPD): the distance between independent ability level and potential ability level when problem solving in collaboration with more capable adults or peers.

Scaffolding: giving support with the elements of a task that is initially beyond the learner's capacity, thus helping the child move into the Zone of Proximal Development.

Revision activity

Think of some tasks that a young child could learn and some ways that scaffolding could help them learn. For example, think of using stabilisers while learning to ride a bike as 'scaffolding'.

Research: Wood and Middleton (1975)

Scaffolding

Four year olds were given a set of blocks and pegs to build a 3D model shown in a picture, but the task proved too difficult for them to complete alone. Wood and Middleton observed how mothers interacted with their children to build the 3D model. The type of support given by mothers included:

- general encouragement, for example 'Now you have a go'
- specific instructions, for example 'Get four big blocks'
- direct demonstration, for example showing the child how to place one block on another.

No single strategy was best for helping the child to progress. Mothers whose assistance was most effective were those who varied their strategy according to how the child was doing. When the child was doing well, they became less specific in their help. When the child started to struggle, they gave increasingly specific instructions until the child started to make progress again.

Wood concluded that scaffolding (i.e. assistance) is most effective when the support is matched to the needs of the learner. Wood identified the processes that aid effective scaffolding as:

- Gain and maintain the learner's interest in the task.
- Make the task simple.
- Emphasise the aspects that will help with the solution.
- Control the child's level of frustration.
- Demonstrate the task.

Benefits in education

There are various educational benefits resulting from this theory:

- It provides individualised instruction.
- Through the structure provided by scaffolding, students spend more time on learning and discovering, resulting in quicker learning.
- It engages the learner and motivates them to learn.
- It minimises the level of frustration for the learner.

Evaluation

Vygotsky's theory of cognitive development sounds a bit like common sense.

Potential for misjudging the ZOPD and success hinges on identifying the area that is just beyond but not too far beyond students' ability.

The full benefits are not seen unless teachers are trained.

The theory requires the teacher to give up control.

Exam tip

Make a list of similarities and differences between Piaget and Vygotsky. For example, remember that Vygotsky proposes that cognitive development is the result of the internalisation of problem-solving processes that occurs in interaction between children and others. In this theory social interaction is the motivating factor in cognitive development, suggesting nurture rather than nature is what drives change in cognitive development.

Baillargeon's explanation of early infant abilities

REVISED

Baillargeon's research focuses on early infant reasoning in four domains:

- **Physical reasoning** – for example, what expectations do infants possess about simple physical events?
- **Psychological reasoning** – for example, how do infants predict and interpret the actions of people and under what conditions do infants take into account the beliefs of people to predict their actions?
- **Biological reasoning** – for example, do infants just view animals as self-propelled agents?
- **Socio-moral reasoning** – for example, what principles guide infants' expectations about how people should act toward others?

Knowledge of the physical world and violation of expectation research

Piaget's experiments on the development of object permanence in infants required the children to manually search for the hidden object. Baillargeon argues that Piaget's finding that babies do not develop object permanence until 8–12 months old was rooted in their lack of motor ability and not in their inadequate cognitive development.

Baillargeon used a technique that has come to be known as the **violation of expectation (VoE)** paradigm. It exploits the fact that babies tend to look for longer at things they have not seen before. In a VoE experiment, a baby is introduced to a novel situation and is repeatedly shown this stimulus until they indicate, by looking away, that it is no longer new to them. The baby is then shown two new stimuli – one is physically possible and the other could not physically happen in the way it appears to.

In one study, Baillargeon (1987) habituated three-month-old babies to a truck rolling down a track and behind a screen. The screen was removed. A box was introduced and placed either (a) beside the track where the truck would roll past it, or (b) on the track where it should block the truck's path. The screen was then replaced and the truck sent down the track. In both events the truck passed behind the screen unimpeded. This would be impossible in the situation in which the box had been placed so that it blocked the track. Baillargeon found that the infants looked significantly longer at this impossible event and concluded that they knew that the box still existed despite being behind the screen in the 'impossible event'. This research seems to indicate that three-month-old babies have an understanding of the physical world that Piaget said does not develop until 9–12 months.

> **Violation of expectation (VoE):** research presenting a child with a visual situation that 'in the real world' could not 'physically happen'.

Research: Baillargeon and DeVos (1991)

Object permanence in infants

Aim: to obtain evidence of object permanence in young infants.

Procedures: experiments were conducted with babies aged three and a half months, five and a half months and six and a half months. In one experiment, three and a half-month-old babies watched a short or a tall carrot slide along a track (see Figure 3.13). The track's centre was hidden by a screen with a large window in its upper half. The short carrot was shorter than the window's lower edge and so did not appear in the window when passing behind the screen, but the tall carrot

Figure 3.13 Tall carrot travels along the track ... it should appear in the window!

was taller than the window's lower edge and hence should have appeared in the window but did not.

Findings: the babies looked for longer at the tall carrot than the short carrot event, suggesting that they expected the tall carrot to appear in the screen window and were surprised that it did not.

In another experiment, four-month-old babies saw a toy car roll along a track that was partly hidden by a screen. A large toy mouse was placed behind the screen, either on top of or behind the track. The babies looked for longer when the mouse stood on top as opposed to at the back of the track, suggesting that they could make a mental representation of the trajectory of the car and the location of the mouse behind the screen and were surprised to see the car reappear from behind the screen when the mouse stood in its path.

This research suggests that babies from the age of three and a half months are able to form mental representations of objects and to reason about hidden objects.

Because many factors affect how long an infant looks at an object, including colour, the people present, novelty and shape, the limitation of using the VoE method is that results rely on the interpretation of the researcher.

Haith (1998) argued that it is overly deterministic to suggest that increased looking time provides evidence that infants have innate knowledge of how the physical world behaves.

Is it valid to conclude that 'looking time' is an indicator of infants' understanding of objects and object permanence?

Is it valid to infer that babies have an innate understanding of object permanence because they look longer at the VoE event?

Is it possible to design a valid experiment to measure what infants know about objects?

The development of social cognition

REVISED

Social cognition, sometimes called emotional intelligence, plays a major role in children's social and emotional development. It is therefore important to understand what it is and how a child's environment can affect the development of this skill.

Selman's levels of perspective-taking

Very young children do not understand that other people have different feelings from their own, but as they grow older they develop the ability to analyse the perspectives of other people involved in a situation from the viewpoint of an objective bystander, and they can even imagine how different cultural or social values would influence the perceptions of the bystander.

Robert Selman, a psychoanalyst, devised a five-stage model to describe the development of **perspective-taking**. The development of this five-stage model was based on analysis of children's responses to stories like the following.

> Holly is an eight-year-old girl who likes to climb trees. She is the best tree climber in the neighbourhood. One day while climbing a tree she falls off the bottom branch but does not hurt herself. Her father sees her fall and is upset. He asks her to promise not to climb trees any more, and Holly promises. Later that day, Holly and her friends meet Sean. Sean's kitten is caught up in a tree and cannot get down. Something has to be done right away or the kitten may fall. Holly is the only one who climbs trees well enough to reach the kitten and get it down, but she remembers her promise to her father.

Perspective-taking: the ability to see the world through the 'eyes' of another person.

Children of different ages are presented with the situation in the story (see Figure 3.14) and are asked:
● If Holly climbs the tree, should she be punished?
● Will her father understand if she climbs the tree?
● Will Sean understand why Holly has trouble deciding what to do?

Figure 3.14 The cat up the tree poses a moral dilemma

According to Selman, children's answers will depend on their age group.

- **Undifferentiated perspective-taking:** age 3–6.
  - **Description:** children recognise that the self and others can have different thoughts and feelings, but they frequently confuse the two.
  - **Response:** the child predicts that Holly will save the kitten because she does not want it to get hurt and believes that Holly's father will feel just as she does about her climbing the tree.
- **Social-informational perspective-taking:** age 5–9.
  - **Description:** children understand that different perspectives may result because people have access to different information.
  - **Response:** when asked how Holly's father will react when he finds out that she climbed the tree, the child responds, 'If he didn't know anything about the kitten, he would be angry, but if Holly shows him the kitten, he might change his mind.'
- **Self-reflective perspective-taking:** age 7–12.
  - **Description:** children can view their own thoughts, feelings and behaviour from the other person's perspective. They also recognise that others can do the same.
  - **Response:** when asked whether Holly thinks she will be punished, the child says, 'No, Holly knows her father will understand why she climbed the tree.' This response assumes that Holly's point of view is influenced by her father being able to see from her point of view and understand why she climbed the tree to save the kitten.
- **Third-party perspective-taking:** age 10–15.
  - **Description:** children can step outside a two-person situation and imagine how the self and other are viewed from the point of view of a third, impartial party.
  - **Response:** when asked whether Holly should be punished, the child says, 'No, because Holly thought it was important to save the kitten but also knows that her father told her not to climb the tree, so she'd only think she would be punished if she couldn't get her father to understand why she had to climb the tree.' This response views both Holly's and her father's perspectives simultaneously.
- **Societal perspective-taking:** age 15–adult.
  - **Description:** individuals understand that third-party perspective-taking can be influenced by one or more systems of larger societal values.
  - **Response:** when asked whether Holly should be punished, the individual responds, 'No, because the value of humane treatment of animals justifies Holly's action and her father's appreciation of this value will lead him not to punish her.'

Exam tip

In the exam you could be given a hypothetical situation (like Holly and the kitten) and be asked to apply Selman's theory to suggest how a child would reason and make decisions. Learn the age-related stages of Selman's theory and remember that, as with Piaget, for Selman age (nature) is the motivating factor in the development of perspective-taking.

Selman's perspective taking is useful because it has shown that a child's increasing ability to take into consideration the perspective of other people is important in their social development.

The poor perspective-taking abilities of maltreated children may help to explain why they lack social skills.

Individual differences: cognitive factors are important, but some children with the ability to take into account the perspective of another person are not very good at social interaction because they lack motivation to use the ability.

The theory does not explain how children move from one stage to the next or identify the factors which cause them to develop the skills to move to the next stage. As with Kohlberg's theory of moral development, Selman's theory is descriptive but not explanatory.

Theory of mind as an explanation for autism

Theory of mind (ToM) is the ability to attribute mental states such as beliefs, intentions, desires, pretending and knowing to oneself and to others, and to understand that others have beliefs, desires, intentions and perspectives that are different from one's own. A child's ability to get along with others and to see things from the perspective of another person is crucial and relies on the development of ToM.

Development of ToM occurs around four years of age when children realise that thoughts in the mind may not be true. For example, if children are allowed to discover that a chocolate box contains pencils and are then asked what their friend will think is in the box, three year olds assume that the friend will know it has pencils inside, just as they do, but four year olds recognise that the friend will be tricked, just as they were.

Autism and the theory of mind

Autism is a mental disorder which first becomes apparent in early childhood. The main characteristics of an autistic child are that they avoid social contact, their use of language is abnormal, and they often engage in so-called 'stereotypic' or bizarre behaviours. An example of stereotypic behaviours would be incessant rocking or an obsessive routine.

Various explanations for autism have been suggested and one of these is related to ToM. Each of us has a ToM, which is our understanding that other people have separate mental states and they see the world from their point of view which differs from our own. Young children do not have this ToM and cannot imagine that someone else is experiencing different feelings or thoughts to theirs. By the age of four, however, children have begun to develop a ToM, but this is possibly not true of autistic children.

The Sally–Anne study

The **Sally–Anne** (false belief) test is a first-order theory of mind test. Read the case study on page 144 for a description of the test.

The Sally–Anne task is a 'false belief task' because older children and adults will give the correct answer, 'In her basket', which is a false belief. It is not actually right but it is what Sally should believe. Young children and possibly autistic children give an incorrect answer. They say, 'It's in Anne's box'. They cannot suppose what is in someone else's mind (in this case Sally's mind) and can only give the answer in their own mind (they have seen that the marble is in the box).

> **Theory of mind (ToM):** the ability to attribute mental states to oneself and to others. This includes beliefs, intentions and desires. It is also the ability to understand that others have beliefs and intentions that are different from one's own.

> **Autism:** a mental disorder which becomes apparent in early childhood.

> **Revision activity**
>
> Role play the 'Sally–Anne test' with a friend. You will need a large marble (or a small ball), two dolls (one is Sally and the other is Anne), a small basket and a small box.

> **Sally–Anne task:** a 'false belief' task which is used to find out whether young children have developed theory of mind.

Research: Baron-Cohen *et al.* (1985)

Baron-Cohen, S., Leslie, A.M. and Frith, U. (1985) Does the autistic child have a 'theory of mind'? *Cognition*, 21, 37–46.

Participants: 20 autistic children, 14 Down's syndrome children and 27 normal children.

The table gives details of the children's **chronological** and **mental ages**. Mental age was measured using a non-verbal and a verbal test. Verbal tests assess intelligence through the use of language.

	Number (*N*)	Mean CA (chronological age)	Mean MA (mental age) non-verbal	Mean MA (mental age) verbal
Autistic	20	11 years 11 months	9 years 3 months	5 years 5 months
Down's syndrome	14	10 years 11 months	5 years 11 months	2 years 11 months
Normal	27	4 years 5 months	not tested	not tested

The Down's syndrome children were included to control for the possibility that poor performance by the autistic children might be due to their mental retardation (low intelligence). Down's syndrome is an inherited condition in which children have an extra gene that causes mental retardation as well as clearly identifiable facial features. All children were tested individually and were tested using the false belief task or the 'Sally–Anne test'. In this test, children are introduced to two dolls: Sally and Anne.

- Sally puts a marble in her basket.
- Sally leaves the room.
- Anne puts the marble in her own box.
- When Sally returns, the experimenter asks the child, 'Where will Sally look for her marble?'

If the child says (or points to) 'the basket' they demonstrate that they have a theory of mind because they can perceive that Sally, who was out of the room, still believes the marble is in the basket. If the child indicates the box, then they have not got a ToM because they are assuming that Sally is thinking what they are thinking.

The child is unable to accommodate Sally's false (wrong) belief.

The children were also asked two control questions: 'Where is the marble now?' and 'Where was the marble at the beginning?' Finally, the experiment was repeated twice for each child, moving the marble to the experimenter's pocket instead of the box.

Results: all children answered the control questions correctly and all children gave consistent responses to the other questions. In other words, they either always answered the false belief question correctly or they always answered incorrectly. There was just one exception – a Down's syndrome participant. The results are shown in the table below.

Experimental group	Number of correct responders	Percentage (%)
Autistic	4/20	20%
Down's syndrome	12/14	86%
Normal	23/27	85%

Revision activity

Read the Sally–Anne study and as you make notes, write answers to these questions: (a) In terms of chronological age, which group was the youngest? (b) In terms of mental age, which group do you think was the youngest? (c) How do you think the differences in mental age might affect the results? (d) Why do you think the autistic children had particularly low scores on the verbal IQ (intelligent quotient) measure? (e) Find out how to calculate IQ: what is the difference between MA and CA?

Chronological age: the calendar age of a person dated from their birth.

Mental age: the mental age of a person as measured by standardised tests.

The theory of mind is supported by evidence. There is now such a wide body of research support for this concept that it has become seen as part of a typical child's cognitive development.

It has increased our understanding of the difficulties involved in autism.

Theory of mind does not account for all problems associated with autism. It is difficult to see how it can account for features such as obsessive behaviours, some language problems and special abilities such as eidetic memory.

Although Baron-Cohen *et al.* emphasise that autistic children do not have theory of mind, it is possible that the autistic child has no motivation to understand other people's intentions.

The role of the mirror neuron system in social cognition

Gallese *et al.* (1996) identified a set of neurons in the pre-motor cortex as the 'mirror neuron system'. **Mirror neurons** are a type of neuron which respond to actions we observe in others and which fire in the same way when we recreate the action of 'another' ourselves. They are thought to be responsible for sophisticated human thought processes. Because the mirror neuron system consists of neurons that are activated when animals perform an action and when they observe another animal perform the same action, the mirror neuron system is believed to be concerned with understanding the behaviour, intentions and emotional states of others and may underlie the development of ToM. Defects in the mirror neuron system are linked to disorders such as autism. Freud (*Inhibitions, Symptoms and Anxiety*, 1926) suggested that 'it was only by empathy that we can know the existence of psychic life in others', but Gallese (2007) reminds us that all we can ever do, when observing behaviour of others, is to 'attribute mental states' or to 'mind read'. Gallese introduces the idea of 'embodied simulation' where we map the actions and emotions of others onto our own motor representations. In humans, brain activity consistent with the presence of mirror neurons has been found in the pre-motor cortex, the supplementary motor area, the primary somatosensory cortex and the inferior parietal cortex.

In sum, unlike other brain cells, mirror neurons 'fire' when you generate an action and also when you see the same action as happening in another person. For example, mirror neurons will fire when you see someone smile and the same ones will fire when you smile.

> **Mirror neuron:** a type of neuron which activates when we observe others and which fires in the same way when we recreate the action of 'another' ourselves.

> **Revision activity**
>
> Watch Vittorio Gallese: 'From mirror neurons to embodied simulation' on YouTube. For a diagram of the location of mirror neurons in the brain, look up www.ncbi.nlm.nih.gov/pmc/articles/PMC3510904/figure/F1/

Research: mirror neurons

Wicker (2003) found that when a participant watched a film in which people wrinkled up their faces as if they had smelled something nasty, fMRI scans showed showed similar activity to a situation in which the participant really did smell something nasty.

Keyssers *et al.* (2004) found that watching a film of someone being touched on the leg generated the same brain activity as actually being touched, suggesting mirror neurons for touch.

Evaluation

Impairments in the mirror neuron system may help to explain the problems associated with autism. This offers insightful hypotheses for further research.

fMRI scans are not sufficiently detailed to identify what is happening at the level of individual neurons.

The mirror neuron system does not take personality into account. When we assess intentions, we take into account known personality characteristics (for example, Mike is smiling because he is friendly). There is no evidence that the mirror neuron system can explain how we do this.

Most information on the role of the mirror neuron system has come from monkeys, so the findings cannot necessarily generalise to humans' brains.

Reducing complex human behaviour of social cognition to the activity of single neurons is a reductionist oversimplification. Whether a child imitates others can be due to a range of factors, such as temperament, attachment and mood.

Some psychologists argue that mirror neurons come from sensorimotor experience and the mirror neuron system is a product, as well as a process, of social interaction. Cecilia Heyes argues that mirror neurons in humans are the product of social interaction and she rejects the theory advanced by V.S. Ramachandran that mirror neurons have been 'the driving force behind the great leap forward in human evolution'.

Exam tip

Be prepared to explain how mirror neurons give rise to a biological explanation for the lack of ToM in autism.

Summary

You must be able to demonstrate knowledge and understanding of:
- Piaget's theory of cognitive development – schemas, assimilation, accommodation, equilibration, stages of intellectual development and the characteristics of these stages, including object permanence, conservation, egocentrism and class inclusion
- Vygotsky's theory of cognitive development, including the Zone of Proximal Development and scaffolding

- Baillargeon's explanation of early infant abilities, including knowledge of the physical world and violation of expectation research
- the development of social cognition, including Selman's levels of perspective-taking, the theory of mind, including theory of mind as an explanation for autism, the Sally–Anne study, and the role of the mirror neuron system in social cognition.

Now test yourself

TESTED

1 Fill in the blanks in the following sentences.
   (a) If a child has a new experience that does not match an existing then a state of _____ is produced.
   (b) _____ allows new information or experiences to be fitted into the child's current understanding of the world.
   (c) Piaget proposes _____ stages of cognitive development.
   (d) In the _____ of cognitive development the child has not developed object permanence.
   (e) _____ is the tendency to attribute feelings to inanimate objects such as dolls and teddy bears.

(f) In the pre-operational stage of development the child is _____ and unable to see things from another person's perspective.

(g) A child has developed the ability to _____ when they understand that the quantity of an object does not change when its appearance does.

(h) The research by Samuel and Bryant supports Piaget's theory because as the _____ increased, the children made fewer errors of conservation.

(i) I bought a bunch of flowers. Six were yellow and eight were red. Are there more red flowers or flowers? According to Piaget, this type of question can be used to test _____.

(j) For Piaget the child is a scientist but for Vygotsky the child is an _____.

(k) According to Vygotsky, each child has a zone of ability and a _____ which is potential ability if the child is guided by a more able adult.

(l) In the picture below, four giraffes are walking past the window. If the tallest giraffe did not 'appear' in the window frame, Baillargeon would call this a _____.

(m) _____ takes place when a child is helped with elements of a task that are beyond their capacity, thus permitting them to complete the parts of the task that are within their range of competence.

(n) Selman has developed a _____-_____ model of the development of perspective-taking.

(o) The Sally–Anne test is a _____ task.

(p) _____ is our understanding that we, and others, have mental states and that other people have mental states that differ from our own.

(q) The biological theory that mirror neurons are responsible for social cognition can be criticised as _____.

Answers on page 242

Exam practice

1 In Piaget's theory, which one of the following sequences shows the order of the stages of cognitive development? [1]
   A   Sensorimotor, concrete operational, pre-operational, formal operations
   B   Sensorimotor, pre-operational, concrete operational, formal operations
   C   Pre-operational, sensorimotor, concrete operational, formal operations
   D   Concrete operational, sensorimotor, pre-operational, formal operations

2 Which one of the following statements describes a child who has not developed object permanence? [1]
   A   The inability to understand abstract and hypothetical ideas
   B   The inability to understand that people still exist when out of sight
   C   The inability to understand things are the same even if they look different
   D   The inability to understand things from different points of view

3 In Selman's theory, which one of the following sequences shows the order of the stages of perspective-taking? [1]
   A   Self-reflective; third-party undifferentiated; social-informational; societal
   B   Undifferentiated; social-informational; self-reflective; third-party; societal
   C   Social-informational; self-reflective; third-party; societal; undifferentiated
   D   Third-party; undifferentiated; social-informational; self-reflective; societal

4 Briefly outline theory of mind as an explanation for autism. [2]

5 Evaluate theory of mind as an explanation for autism. [6]

6 Read the item and answer the question that follows.

Two primary school teachers set up their maths classes very differently. In Mr Smith's class children usually work alone and have to solve problems by trial and error. In Mr Jones' class, after he has demonstrated how to do the task, children are allowed to work in pairs of differing ability and are encouraged to talk through each stage to help each other.

Discuss Piaget's and Vygotsky's theories of cognitive development. Refer to the item above in your answer. [16]

7 Which one of the following statements describes a feature of Piaget's concrete operational stage? [1]

   A   Unable to see the world from another person's point of view

   B   Unable to understand that people still exist when out of sight

   C   Does not understand that the quality of an object remains the same if its appearance changes

   D   Without a real object to manipulate is unable to perform mental transformations

8 Outline what Vygotsky meant by Zone of Proximal Development. [2]

9 Explain one strength and one limitation of Vygotsky's theory of cognitive development. [6]

10 Read the item and then answer the questions that follow.

Possible event

A psychologist investigating object permanence studied 50 babies aged four months. She habituated each baby to a scene in which a tall giraffe and a short giraffe walked behind a screen with a cut-out window.

In the possible event the short giraffe was not seen until it emerged from behind the screen. In the impossible event the tall giraffe was not shown in the cut-out section of the screen so was not seen until it emerged from behind the screen. In both the possible and impossible events the psychologist measured how long the baby gazed at the screen and calculated mean gaze times. She found the babies gazed at the impossible event for longer.

Impossible event

  (a) Explain one limitation of carrying out research with four-month-old babies. [2]

  (b) Baillargeon studied early infant abilities by conducting violation of expectation studies. What is meant by 'violation of expectation'? [2]

  (c) Discuss violation of expectation research by Baillargeon *et al*. [8]

Answers and quick quizzes 54, 55, 56 and 57

ONLINE

Schizophrenia

Classification of schizophrenia

Schizophrenia is a complex illness affecting a person's thoughts, perceptions, behaviour and ability to communicate. It is a severe and disabling condition. Worldwide, schizophrenia affects around 1 in 100 people. Schizophrenia typically begins in late adolescence or early adulthood. It affects men and women equally, but the age of onset is typically earlier in men than in women. A distinction is often made between Type I, which is acute onset with mostly positive symptoms, and Type II, which is slow onset and mostly negative symptoms. A psychotic episode may last for any length of time and many patients suffer repeated bouts of the illness throughout their lives.

Positive symptoms

The main **positive symptoms** are **hallucinations**, **delusions** and disordered thinking.

Hallucinations are perceptual disturbances that can be very frightening. A typical symptom is auditory hallucination, such as hearing internal voices. The internal voices may talk about the person, warn of dangers or give out orders.

Delusions are disturbances of thought involving false beliefs. There are several types of delusions:

- **Paranoid delusions:** where the sufferer believes that they are being persecuted or conspired against.
- **Delusions of grandeur:** where the person believes that they are a famous person.
- **Delusions of control:** where the person believes that their thoughts are controlled in some way.

With disordered thinking and speech, the sufferer may be unable to concentrate or to sort thoughts into logical sequences and communication may be difficult because they may believe that other people hear their thoughts.

Negative symptoms

The negative symptoms are as follows:

- **Affective (emotional):** there is a reduction in the range and intensity of emotional expression (flattening of emotion). Unexpected emotions may be displayed, such as laughing at the 'wrong time'.
- **Poverty of speech:** there is a reduction in speech fluency and in willingness to talk to others.
- **Avolition:** this is a psychological term meaning a severe lack of initiative or motivation or the will to become engaged in goal-oriented behaviour. Because of this the sufferer may spend whole days doing nothing and may appear to lose interest in life.
- **Catatonia:** the patient's movements are disturbed, so they may remain motionless for hours, exhibit waxy flexibility, or move frantically and purposelessly.

Schizophrenia: a complex psychotic disorder which often involves perceptual disturbances such as hallucinations or thought disorders such as delusions.

Revision activity

Read through the topics on psychopathology in Component 1.

Positive symptoms: hallucinations, delusions and disordered thinking. They can be thought of as positive because they are 'added' to a person.

Hallucinations: perceptual disturbances such as hearing internal voices.

Delusions: disturbances of thought usually involving false beliefs.

Avolition: a psychological term meaning a severe lack of initiative or motivation.

Subtypes (not in the DSM 5)

Because the symptoms of schizophrenia are so varied and patients show different mixtures of symptoms, several subtypes of schizophrenia have been proposed, including:

- **paranoid** – dominated by delusions, especially of persecution
- **disorganised/hebephrenic** – thought disorder and disorganised behaviour are the most prominent symptoms
- **catatonic** – characterised by disturbed movements.

Reliability and validity in diagnosis and classification

Reliability refers to the extent to which different psychiatrists agree on patients' diagnoses (inter-observer reliability).

Validity refers to the extent to which a classification system measures what it claims to measure.

Three kinds of validity are relevant:

- **Aetiological validity:** the extent to which the cause of the disorder is the same for each sufferer.
- **Descriptive validity:** the extent to which individuals diagnosed with the same disorder are similar.
- **Predictive validity:** the extent to which the diagnostic categories predict the outcome of treatment.

The medical model of mental illness states that mental illnesses are discrete disorders which can be identified by groups of symptoms. There are two major systems in use for classification and diagnosis:

- The *International Classification of Diseases* (*ICD*) is published by the World Health Organization and is used throughout the world. ICD-10 is the current version.
- The *Diagnostic and Statistical Manual* (*DSM*) is primarily used in the USA. DSM 5 is the current version.

There are differences between the ICD and the DSM in the diagnostic criteria. For example, the DSM requires symptoms to be present for six months but the ICD requires one month, the DSM emphasises the functional impairment but the ICD focuses more on the symptoms which are rarely found in other disorders, and the ICD-10 recognises subtypes of schizophrenia while the DSM 5 has removed all subtypes.

Evaluation

The existence of different manuals causes problems for reliability of diagnosis. For example, when a patient changes to a new care team, they may disagree with the initial diagnosis, leading to confusion about the appropriate treatment. The DSM has links to insurance and pharmaceutical companies in the USA, and critics have accused it of medicalising normal mental states to boost the profits of US health insurers.

Revision activity

Read the Rosenhan (1973) study, 'On being sane in insane places' which showed how easy it was to acquire a diagnosis of schizophrenia. The study also showed how being labelled as 'schizophrenic' influenced how a person's normal behaviour was viewed by medical professionals.

Is diagnosis reliable?

Although using the ICD-10 and the DSM should improve inter-rater reliability, doctors may interpret the patient's symptoms differently and patients may report their symptoms differently.

For a diagnosis to be reliable, all doctors who see the patient should agree on the diagnosis.

Copeland (1971) conducted a study in which 134 US and UK psychiatrists were given a description of a patient. It was found that 69% of US psychiatrists diagnosed schizophrenia compared with only 2% of UK psychiatrists. This suggests that the diagnosis is unreliable (and influenced by culture).

Symptom overlap

There is a **symptom overlap** between schizophrenia and other mental disorders. For example, psychosis occurs in bipolar disorder and depression. Schizoaffective disorder is defined as a separate illness in the DSM, where the patient experiences bipolar mania and/or depression as well as symptoms of schizophrenia. These mixed-diagnostic categories reduce the reliability and validity of classification.

Comorbidity

In medicine, **comorbidity** is the presence of one or more additional disorders co-occurring with a primary disorder. Psychiatric comorbidities are common among patients with schizophrenia. Anxiety and depressive symptoms are also very common throughout the course of schizophrenia, with an estimated prevalence of 15% for panic disorder, 29% for post-traumatic stress disorder and 23% for obsessive compulsive disorder. It is estimated that comorbid depression occurs in 50% of patients, and many patients have a lifetime diagnosis of comorbid substance abuse. Comorbidity and symptom overlap reduces the validity and reliability of diagnosis.

The validity of diagnosis (aetiological validity)

People who are diagnosed with schizophrenia can show very different symptoms – for example, one patient has delusions and hallucinations but another patient does not, which brings into question the validity of classification and diagnosis. If the diagnosis is not valid, this has implications for treatment and many critics are becoming increasingly concerned about the over-prescription of antipsychotic medication.

> **Symptom overlap:** the extent to which a symptom appears in more than one mental disorder. Reduces the reliability and validity of classification and diagnosis.
>
> **Comorbidity:** the presence of one or more additional disorders co-occurring with a primary disorder.

Research: cultural differences in schizophrenia

Luhrmann *et al.* (2014) interviewed 20 schizophrenics in cities in California and in India and Ghana who were experiencing voices in their heads. Most of the patients were in their thirties or forties and had been ill for years.

There were several cultural differences in how patients experienced their symptoms. In California, patients reported the most negative feelings about their voices, only a few said they had personal relationships and/or they could never figure out who was speaking to them. In Ghana and India, patients' experiences were, relatively, more positive. They were more likely to report having constructive relationships with the voices in their heads and most heard voices they attributed to gods or disembodied spirits.

The researchers concluded that social expectations about minds influence and shape the voice-hearing experience. The difference seemed to be that patients in India or Ghana were more comfortable interpreting their voices as relationships and not as a sign of a violated mind. It was suggested that the American cultural emphasis on autonomy shapes 'a general cognitive bias to interpret unusual auditory events as symptoms of illness'.

Gender differences

H. Häfner (2003) gathered data from literature as well as from a sample of 232 people admitted to hospital with their first episode. Data from the study indicated that men and women have an equal lifetime risk for schizophrenia. However, schizophrenia usually occurs in women 3–4 years later than in men. Most men develop schizophrenia between 15 and 25 years of age, but in women the most frequent onset is between the ages of 15 and 30, with a smaller peak between 45 and 50. Women also tend to have milder forms of the disease in their younger years than their male counterparts do. In later years, however, symptoms in men tend to decrease in severity while women often have a renewed onset of psychotic symptoms and a worse course of the disease.

> **Revision activity**
>
> Make a list of at least TWO reasons why diagnosis may not be reliable and TWO reasons why classification may not be valid.

Biological explanations for schizophrenia

REVISED

The biological approach assumes that psychological abnormalities are symptoms of underlying physical causes.

Genes

Genes are sequences of the DNA that code for the proteins that make up our bodies. People have different versions (known as alleles) of the same genes. According to the genetic explanation, people with schizophrenia have inherited alleles that cause, or make them more vulnerable to, schizophrenia. Evidence shows that schizophrenia runs in families. First-degree relatives (offspring, parents and siblings) share about 50% of their genetic variation, while second-degree relatives (uncles, aunts, etc.) share approximately 25%. If a condition is heritable, closer relatives are more likely to share it.

Family studies

These compare rates of schizophrenia in relatives of people with the diagnosis with people in the general population (about 1% risk). It has been found that the risk rises with the degree of relatedness to an affected individual, supporting the genetic explanation of schizophrenia. Kendler *et al.* (1985) found that first-degree relatives of a patient with schizophrenia have an 18-fold increase in risk.

Twin studies

Monozygotic twins share 100% of their DNA. **Dizygotic** twins share on average only 50% of their genes, like other siblings. DZ twins can be different sexes. MZ twin studies are often used to test the genetic heritability of medical and psychological conditions. If a condition is 100% genetically determined, the concordance rate between MZ twins should also be 100% since they share 100% of their DNA.

> **Monozygotic:** as in identical twins – originating from one egg.
>
> **Dizygotic:** as in non-identical twins – originating from two fertilized eggs.

Adoption studies

Studying people who were adopted is another way to assess the heritability of conditions such as schizophrenia, while minimising the effects of shared environments. Outcomes are compared between the affected individual's biological and adoptive families.

Research: risk of developing schizophrenia

Kety *et al.* (1994) looked at a sample of adoptees with chronic schizophrenia and found that the prevalence of the disorder was ten times higher in the biological relatives of the schizophrenic adoptees than in the biological relatives of the control group.

Gottesman (1991) compiled more than 40 studies in order to work out the risks of developing schizophrenia and found that two classes of relatives have especially high risks of developing schizophrenia: the offspring of two schizophrenic parents and an MZ co-twin of a schizophrenic. Gottesman found that those who share the greatest number of genes with schizophrenia sufferers have an increased risk of developing schizophrenia themselves.

Gottesman and Shields (1976 and 1982) reviewed the results of twin studies looking for concordance rates for schizophrenia. It was found that in MZ twins there was a concordance rate of 35–58% compared with DZ twin rates that ranged from 9% to 26%.

Tienari *et al.*, starting in 1969, identified 112 adopted children whose biological mothers had been diagnosed with schizophrenia and compared them with a matched control group of adopted children whose biological mothers had no mental disorder. The children had all been adopted before the age of four years. By 1987, 7% of the biological children of mothers who had been diagnosed with schizophrenia had been diagnosed with schizophrenia compared with 1.5% of the controls. This supports the genetic hypothesis, without the confounding influence of shared environments.

Evaluation

There is a lot of evidence supporting the genetic explanation.

Family studies do not control for shared family environments, meaning that environmental influences from living with a parent with schizophrenia could also be affecting the development of the illness.

Genetic explanations are deterministic – if you have these genes, you are born to have the disorder.

Since the concordance rate among MZ twins is not 100%, there is not a single dominant gene for schizophrenia. The problem is that families, including twins, share the same environment, and since even where people share the same genes there is only a 50% chance of them both developing schizophrenia, the environment must contribute a significant effect.

Revision activity

Re-read the biopsychology section in Component 2.

Neurotransmitters are biochemical substances that carry the signals between brain cells. According to the **dopamine hypothesis** of schizophrenia, people with the disorder have abnormalities in dopamine neurotransmission. Dopamine is a neurotransmitter that is active in the **limbic system**, the part of the brain that deals with emotions and drives, including fear and reward. The dopamine hypothesis suggests excess dopamine activity could cause the positive symptoms of schizophrenia, such as delusions, hallucinations and loss of touch with reality.

Dopamine agonists are drugs that increase the amount of dopamine activity in the brain. Examples include amphetamines and L-DOPA, a treatment for Parkinson's disease. Amphetamines and similar drugs increase levels of dopamine in the brain and can cause symptoms which resemble those present in psychosis, particularly after large doses or prolonged use. Similarly, those treated with dopamine–enhancing drugs for Parkinson's disease can experience psychotic side effects mimicking the symptoms of schizophrenia. A group of drugs called antipsychotics such as **clozapine** has been found to antagonize dopamine binding

Dopamine hypothesis: the suggestion that excess dopamine activity causes the positive symptoms of schizophrenia.

Limbic system: a set of evolutionarily primitive brain structures located on top of the brainstem that is involved in many emotions such as fear, anger and aggression.

Dopamine agonist: a drug that increases the amount of dopamine activity in the brain.

Clozapine: an atypical antipsychotic drug that is a dopamine antagonist.

(particularly at dopamine receptors) and reduce positive psychotic symptoms. The link was strengthened by experiments which suggested that the binding affinity of antipsychotic drugs for D_2 dopamine receptors was inversely related to their therapeutic dose.

Research: dopamine receptors

Wong *et al.* (1986) using positron emission tomography (PET scans) found a two-fold increase in the density of postsynaptic dopamine receptors in a group of schizophrenia patients who had never been treated with drugs.

Post-mortem analysis of the brains of schizophrenia patients show increased dopamine receptor density in parts of the limbic system.

Neural correlates

Research has shown a correlation between differences in brain structure and schizophrenia. Young *et al.* (1990) used MRI scans to investigate the brain structures in schizophrenia patients and found structural differences compared with 'normal brains'. Warner (1994) suggested that early brain trauma, for example viral infection during pregnancy, may relate to structural abnormalities in brains of schizophrenic patients. Also in schizophrenia there is reduced symmetry in the temporal, frontal and occipital lobes, and this reduced symmetry is thought to originate during lateralisation of the brain during foetal life.

Evaluation

A limitation of the post-mortem studies is that the patients were usually receiving dopaminergic drugs in their lifetimes, which may account for changes in receptor density.

Just because drugs that are **dopamine antagonists** 'work' doesn't mean that too much dopamine causes schizophrenia. Paracetamol cures headaches but headaches are not caused by low levels of paracetamol.

Biological explanations are reductionist because in reducing the problem down to the basic units of genes and neurotransmitters, it ignores the experiences of the patient.

If an excess of dopamine is the cause of schizophrenia then reducing the level of dopamine should reduce both positive and negative symptoms, but traditional antipsychotic drugs reduced the positive symptoms only.

Dopamine antagonist: a drug that decreases the amount of dopamine activity in the brain.

Psychological explanations for schizophrenia

REVISED

Family dysfunction

Some psychologists suggest that family relationships with 'abnormal' communication styles may play a part, creating highly stressful environments. McGlashan (1994) suggested that **expressed emotion (EE)** comprises critical or emotionally over-involved attitudes and behaviours displayed by one or more parents to their schizophrenic offspring. Research into EE reveals that family dynamics are an important predictor of relapse of positive symptoms.

Expressed emotion (EE): the theory that dysfunctional family relationships, involving high EE, cause schizophrenia.

Studies by Brown *et al.* (1972) and by Vaughn *et al.* (1976) established the detrimental effects of ineffective medication and high face-to-face contact (more than 35 hours per week) on relapse rates of patients living in high-EE families. More recently, Kavanagh (1992) conducted a meta-analysis and reported a 48% relapse rate in a high-EE environment, versus 21% in a low-EE environment. In cross-cultural research, Leff *et al.* (1987) found that high EE in Indian families is also associated with relapse and concluded that the significantly better outcome for Indian patients compared with a London cohort was due to the substantially lower proportion of high-EE relatives in the Indian study group.

It is arguable as to whether high EE exists as a true cause of relapse in schizophrenia or whether it reflects the stress within the family of living with a patient with chronic mental illness. Smith *et al.* (1993) found that high-EE relatives report higher levels of stress and have more difficulty coping than low-EE relatives. Eva *et al.* (1995) found that relatives who score highly on EE assessments tend to listen less effectively and talk more in family interviews.

> **Evaluation**
>
> The theory that high levels of EE cause schizophrenic relapse led to an effective therapy where high-EE relatives are shown how to reduce their negatively expressed emotion.
>
> Terkelsen *et al.* (1983) suggest that 'blaming the family' creates an atmosphere of adversity and mistrust, with poorer outcomes for the patient.
>
> Mari and Streiner (1994) found that family therapy significantly reduced expressed emotion and hospitalisation and increased medication compliance.

Cognitive explanations

Cognitive psychologists study mental processes such as memory, emotion, perception, attention and language and describe how disruption of these processes may lead to some of the symptoms of schizophrenia. Schizophrenics are prone to magical thinking and odd beliefs and superstitions even when these do not form part of a delusion. O'Farrell (2000) suggests that cognitive impairments accompany schizophrenia in 75% of cases and that affected functions can include memory, attention, motor skills, executive function and intelligence. Cognitive impairments often pre-date the onset of schizophrenia, suggesting that they are not a result of the illness.

One cognitive explanation proposes that a breakdown in normal cognitive processes can result in delusional thinking, that delusional thinking results from an extreme and distorted form of the normal process of belief formation. Usually, when we form a belief we make inferences about the data we perceive. The beliefs can then be tested against reality and/or updated on the basis of new evidence. The mind of the psychotic patient fails to properly reality test and they accept bizarre explanations for their experiences. For example, they might see their neighbours talking and jump to the conclusion that they are being plotted against. According to the cognitive view, schizophrenia symptoms exist on a continuum with ordinary beliefs.

Research: cognitive explanations

Garety and Helmsley (1994) tested the hypothesis that schizophrenic patients are more likely than others to jump to conclusions based on limited evidence. Participants were shown jars with different proportions of coloured beads. Individual beads were then placed in front of them and they were asked to guess which jar the beads came from. Delusional schizophrenic patients made their guesses more quickly and with greater confidence, suggesting that they are prone to jumping to conclusions.

Frith (1979) developed a neuropsychological explanation of schizophrenia, which combined biological and cognitive explanations. He proposed that schizophrenic symptoms are linked to faulty attentional filtering and that information that would normally be suppressed and ignored reaches the patient's consciousness, to be experienced as hallucinations and delusions.

Evaluation

Cognitive explanations focus on how the individual experiences the world and their feelings and beliefs rather than relying on interpretations by other people.

Cognitive explanations may encourage the idea that people are responsible for their own psychological problems, i.e. that they could be 'normal' if they 'wanted to'.

Cognitive explanations are reductionist when they ignore biological causes of schizophrenia.

A limitation of cognitive explanations is that they are 'how' explanations, not 'why' explanations – they don't really explain why the irrational cognitive processes develop.

Drug therapy

REVISED

A patient who is diagnosed with schizophrenia is most likely to be offered drug therapy. Medication is usually administered as a daily dose of tablets, but it can be given as a depot injection which lasts a few weeks. Antipsychotic drugs are the main biological treatment for schizophrenia. Antipsychotic drugs work by blocking dopamine receptors on the postsynaptic neuron so that dopamine transmission in the brain is reduced.

Typical antipsychotic drugs

The first class of antipsychotic drugs are the '**typical' antipsychotics**, such as haloperidol and chlorpromazine. They work by blocking the dopamine type 2 (D_2) receptors in parts of the limbic system of the brain. Their action provides support for the dopamine hypothesis of schizophrenia and it was the way that these drugs work that drove the development of the neurochemical hypothesis. Antipsychotic drugs have proved very successful in reducing the acute, positive symptoms of psychosis. According to Comer (2001), antipsychotic drugs reduce schizophrenic symptoms in the majority of patients but are less successful at treating **negative symptoms** such as flattened **affect**.

Side effects: extrapyramidal symptoms (EPS), which are problems with movements, such as involuntary movements, restlessness and tremors. **Tardive dyskinesia** is involuntary movements, usually of the face and neck, which can manifest as lip smacking and protruding tongue.

Typical antipsychotic drugs: drugs such as haloperidol and chlorpromazine. They work by blocking the dopamine type 2 (D_2) receptors in parts of the limbic system of the brain.

Negative symptoms: a reduction in the range and intensity of emotional expression and a reduction in speech fluency as well as a severe lack of initiative or motivation.

Affect: another way of referring to emotion, for example affective disorders are emotional disorders.

Tardive dyskinesia: a dangerous side effect of antipsychotic drugs involving involuntary movement of the face and neck.

Atypical antipsychotic drugs

Atypical drugs such as olanzapine and clozapine have a slightly different mechanism of action as they have a lesser effect on the dopamine type 2 (D_2) receptors and also target receptors in the serotonin system. **Atypical antipsychotic drugs** offer improvement to more patients and may also be effective for treating negative symptoms. The return of psychotic symptoms is common if a patient stops taking the medication.

Side effects: the new-generation antipsychotics, such as olanzapine, offer an advantage over the older drugs as they do not cause the movement disorder tardive dyskinesia. Clozapine carries a risk of a condition called **agranulocytosis**, a potentially fatal reduction in white blood cells. Although very effective, this drug can be given only under direct supervision by a doctor. Olanzapine is an atypical antipsychotic that causes weight gain.

> **Atypical antipsychotic drugs:** atypical drugs such as olanzapine and clozapine have a lesser effect on D_2 receptors and also target receptors in the serotonin system.
>
> **Agranulocytosis:** a potentially fatal reduction in white blood cells as a side effect of taking clozapine and other antipsychotic drugs.

> **Evaluation**
>
> Typical and atypical antipsychotics have similar effects on positive symptoms, but they have different side effects so may be suitable for different patients.
>
> Compliance is a major problem with the drug treatment of schizophrenia. An estimated 40–50% of people with the disorder will have problems sticking to their prescribed medication.
>
> Antipsychotics are powerful drugs with a wide variety of actions on brain and behaviour other than the intended ones.
>
> Unwanted side effects can be serious, causing distress and/or serious health problems.
>
> Ethical issues arise when people are forced to take drugs.
>
> Drug treatments control the symptoms but do not cure the problem.

Psychological therapies for schizophrenia

REVISED

Antipsychotic medications are the main treatments for schizophrenia, but in conjunction with drugs psychological therapies may be used to help the patient to cope with their disorder. When someone has a psychotic episode they may be hospitalised. This may be voluntary or involuntary and doctors and therapists will try a combination of biological and psychological therapies.

Cognitive behavioural therapy

Schizophrenia is associated with numerous cognitive problems, such az attention, memory and perception, and CBT can be successful at helping patients to deal with the practical and emotional consequences of their illness. In CBT the patient learns to identify irrational and unhelpful behaviours and thought patterns, challenge and eradicate those thought patterns, and practise new ways of coping. Coping strategy enhancement (CSE) is a technique which aims to help schizophrenics find the best strategies to deal with their symptoms. The therapist and client work together to find practical ways of coping with symptoms such as hallucinated voices. A recent form of CBT is avatar therapy in which the patient creates an avatar to represent the voice they hear and the therapist communicates through this. Together, they practise strategies for challenging and overcoming the threats made by negative voices.

Research: cognitive behavioural therapy

A case study by Bradshaw (1998) followed a single patient over four years. Over the period of treatment her symptoms improved dramatically and it is likely that the CBT she received contributed to this.

Sensky *et al.* (2000) reported the use of CBT for symptoms in schizophrenia. A randomised controlled design was used to compare the effectiveness of CBT developed particularly for schizophrenia with that of a non-specific befriending control intervention. Both interventions were delivered by two experienced nurses who received regular supervision. Patients were assessed by blind raters at baseline, after treatment (lasting up to nine months) and at a nine-month follow-up. Patients continued to receive routine care throughout the study. Ninety patients received an average of 19 individual treatment sessions over nine months, with no significant between-group differences in treatment duration. Both interventions resulted in significant reductions in positive and negative symptoms and depression. At the nine-month follow-up evaluation, patients who had received CBT continued to improve, while those in the befriending group did not. It was concluded that CBT is effective in treating negative as well as positive symptoms in schizophrenia resistant to standard antipsychotic drugs, with its efficacy sustained over nine months of follow-up.

Evaluation

CBT has limitations – it is not suitable for acutely psychotic patients who are too ill to engage with the demanding therapy.

CBT is not a replacement for biological therapies.

CBT therapy is unlikely to be appropriate for patients where negative symptoms predominate.

Family therapy

The importance of family, particularly in schizophrenic relapse, has led to the development of numerous family interventions. Schizophrenia is not just hard on the patient – their behaviour may seem incomprehensible or even frightening to others. Family interventions use a variety of therapeutic techniques to educate and inform the patient and their family and develop strategies for managing the illness. This includes information on compliance with drug therapy. One form of family therapy, known as the Optimal Treatment Project, combines training for patients and their families in coping with stress, social skills training and crisis management. This method has been successfully used in more than 20 countries worldwide. Family therapy has been found to have a positive influence on many outcomes, including drug compliance. The National Institute for Health and Care Excellence (NICE) suggests that family intervention should be used for patients who have persistent and relapsing conditions and who have a caregiver.

Research: family therapy

Falloon *et al.* (1985) looked at relapse rates for patients receiving family therapy where 11% were re-hospitalised within one year compared with those receiving only individual therapy where 50% were re-hospitalised within one year.

Pharoah *et al.* (2003) found that relapse rates and hospitalisations were significantly reduced following family interventions.

Family therapy is usually used in conjunction with medication.

Family therapy is expensive and requires highly trained staff, over a long period of time, to administer the treatment.

Schizophrenic patients come from a wide variety of family backgrounds and family intervention will not always be appropriate.

As with CBT, family therapy is usually used in conjunction with medication.

Token economy used to manage schizophrenia

Treatments proposed by behaviourist psychologists assume that dysfunctional behaviour is learned and can be unlearned. The symptoms of dysfunctional behaviour are seen as a 'problem to be cured'.

A **token economy** is a system of behaviour management based on the systematic reinforcement of target behaviour. The reinforcers are rewards (the tokens) that can be exchanged for other reinforcers. Token economies, based on operant conditioning, are often used in hospitals to change the behaviour of patients. Behaviour modification therapies, based on operant conditioning, assume that behaviour that brings about pleasurable consequences is likely to be repeated. Behaviour modification can involve positive or negative reinforcement. Positive reinforcement means that desired behaviour is rewarded by a pleasant consequence because the use of a reward encourages the likelihood of the behaviour being repeated – for example, if you praise someone for good work, you encourage (reinforce) its repetition. Negative reinforcement means that desired behaviour is learned because the consequence of the behaviour is that 'something unpleasant' stops happening (or you escape from an aversive stimulus), thus pleasure is felt. Token economies usually involve schedules of reinforcement and are used by clinical and educational psychologists to modify the behaviour of children, or adults, with challenging behaviour.

> **Revision activity**
>
> Re-read behaviourist learning theories.

> **Token economy:** a system of behaviour management based on the systematic reinforcement of target behaviour. The reinforcers are rewards (the tokens) that can be exchanged for other reinforcers.

Research: behavioural therapy

Paul and Lentz (1977) studied behavioural therapy for psychotic disorders and compared the effectiveness of three types of therapy. Eighty-four chronic (long-term) and hospitalised psychiatric patients, all receiving drug treatment, were randomly assigned to one of three treatment conditions: token economy, milieu therapy and custodial care. Patients were matched for age, gender, socio-economic status, symptoms and length of hospitalisation. The study had a longitudinal design and lasted four and a half years, with an 18-month follow-up. Patients were assessed at six-monthly intervals using structured interviews and observations.

- **Token economy therapy:** acceptable behaviour was modelled and instructed and rewarded by tokens that bought necessities such as meals. Tokens could be saved up to rent better sleeping quarters such as single rooms and to obtain passes to leave the hospital.
- **Milieu therapy:** the hospital became a 'therapeutic community' and patients were treated as adults who were expected to play a responsible role in the community, in decision making and in their own readjustment. Group interaction was encouraged and staff praised patients who 'did well'.
- **Custodial care:** patients were treated with drugs and were alone 95% of the time. Only short periods of occupational therapy, group therapy and recreation were provided.

More than 10% of patients in the token economy group and in the milieu therapy group were able to leave the hospital; the token economy patients were more successful at remaining in the community. No patients in custodial care were released. The number of patients remaining on antipsychotic drugs was reduced in the token economy and the milieu therapy. Token economy was most successful in increasing interpersonal and communication skills. Both token economy and milieu therapy reduced symptoms such as delusions, hallucinations and hostile behaviour. It was concluded that behavioural treatments can help reverse the effects of institutionalisation and can foster the development of social skills.

Evaluation

The behavioural model is hopeful as it predicts that people can change (re-learn) their behaviour.

Token economies involving reinforcers that withhold a basic human right, such as food, clothing or privacy, are unethical and have been ruled illegal in the USA.

These therapies are usually effective only in institutions where they can be applied systematically. Conditioning does not cure schizophrenia.

In the Paul and Lentz study, it could be argued that the poor treatment of patients in the custodial care condition was why they did not improve.

The interactionist approach to schizophrenia

REVISED

No single cause of schizophrenia has been identified and research suggests a complex interplay between factors and that environmental factors play a key role in the development of the illness.

The diathesis–stress model of schizophrenia

This model suggests that some people might have a genetic tendency towards schizophrenia (the diathesis) that is triggered by environmental circumstances such as sociocultural factors, family relationships or stress. People diagnosed with schizophrenia come from all types of social backgrounds, but most are clustered in the lower socio-economic groups and live in the poorest areas of cities. The social causation hypothesis suggests that social conditions create stresses that trigger schizophrenia in some people and research suggests that stressful living conditions are associated with the development of schizophrenia and that the totality of stress experienced by an individual may be associated with an eventual schizophrenic episode.

> **Diathesis–stress model:** the suggestion that some people might have a genetic tendency towards schizophrenia (the diathesis) that is triggered by environmental circumstances.

Research: interactionist approach

Brown and Birley (1968) looked at the life events experienced by schizophrenic patients in the 12 weeks prior to an episode of schizophrenia. They found that about 50% of patients experienced a stressful event in the three weeks prior to an episode, but only 12% of patients reported experiencing a stressful event in the previous nine weeks. This suggests that the stressful experience may have triggered the schizophrenic episode.

Hirsch *et al.* (1996) carried out a longitudinal study looking at the life events experienced by 71 schizophrenic patients over a period of four years and found that the cumulative effect of stressful life events in the 12 months prior to a schizophrenic episode had a significant effect.

Walker and Diforio (1997) proposed specific neurobiological mechanisms through which environmental stress may be a risk factor for those with a genetic predisposition to schizophrenia. They proposed that the diathesis for schizophrenia is an abnormality in dopamine neurotransmission and that the expression of this diathesis depends on neuroendocrine pathways through which stress exposure, specifically cortisol release mediated by the hypothalamic–pituitary–adrenal (HPA) axis, influences dopamine transmission. They also proposed that stress-related increase in cortisol levels exacerbates the abnormality in dopamine neurotransmission that underlies vulnerability to schizophrenia, resulting in the onset of the illness.

Exam tip

When answering a question on treating schizophrenia, a route to good marks is to focus on treatments which are currently used for the illness (antipsychotic drugs and variations of CBT) and to include appropriate reference to treatment outcomes.

Now test yourself

TESTED

1 (a) Which of these types of disorder is schizophrenia?
   A A mood disorder
   B An anxiety disorder
   C A psychotic disorder
   D A behavioural disorder
 (b) If you suffer from schizophrenia you:
   A Realise your behaviour is irrational
   B See ghosts
   C Experience a break with reality
   D Have multiple personalities
 (c) For a diagnosis of schizophrenia, how long must symptoms be present?
   A Two weeks
   B One month
   C Six months
   D Two months
 (d) Which of these is not a symptom of schizophrenia?
   A Delusions
   B Catatonic behaviour
   C Hallucinations
   D Distorted body image
 (e) The prevalence of schizophrenia across the world is about:
   A 1 in 1,000
   B 1 in 500
   C 1 in 200
   D 1 in 100
2 (a) Outline the difference between positive and negative symptoms of schizophrenia.
 (b) List two positive symptoms and two negative symptoms of schizophrenia.
 (c) What is the difference between a hallucination and a delusion?
3 Outline evidence to support the hypothesis that genes play a major role in the transmission of schizophrenia.
4 For each of the following 'evidences' write an opposing argument.
 (a) Genes may play a major role in the transmission of schizophrenia and while the rate of schizophrenia in the general population is about 1%, if one parent has schizophrenia then a child has about 10% chance of developing it. However, ...
 (b) It is proposed that an excess of the neurotransmitter dopamine is the cause of schizophrenia and drugs that reduce the levels of dopamine reduce the positive symptoms of schizophrenia. However, ...
5 Outline evidence that supports the hypothesis that schizophrenia is caused by stressful life events.
6 Briefly outline family dysfunction as an explanation for schizophrenia.
7 Outline the theory that suggests schizophrenia is the result of abnormal cognitive processes.

Answers on page 242

Exam practice

1 Outline the diathesis–stress model of schizophrenia.   [4]
2 Evaluate the theory that stressful life events trigger episodes of schizophrenia.   [4]
3 Discuss the theory that schizophrenia is caused by abnormal cognitive processes.   [8]
4 Explain one limitation of drug treatment for schizophrenia.   [2]
5 Discuss biological explanations of schizophrenia.   [16]
6 Discuss token economies as a method used in the management of schizophrenia.   [8]

Answers and quick quizzes 38, 39 and 40 online

ONLINE

Eating behaviour

Explanations for food preferences

REVISED

The evolutionary explanation for food preferences

Our behaviours reflect the evolutionary history of our species and how we have dealt with adaptive problems such as avoiding predators and finding and eating the right types of food. Most of the evolutionary adaptations occurred due to environmental demands when humans were hunter-gatherers (**EEA**). It was adaptive for our ancestors to prefer energy-dense foods that were free of toxins. According to evolutionary psychologists, eating sweet foods would have been adaptive behaviour as sweet foods such as ripe fruit contain large numbers of calories and would provide an easily accessible source of energy. Additionally, sweet foods are rarely poisonous, so sweet foods would be perceived as safe to eat.

Simmen and Hladik (1998) propose that this asymmetrical difference between sweet and bitter taste discrimination reflects different evolutionary functions for energy requirements (sweet food) and avoiding toxins (bitter food). De Araujo *et al.* (2008) genetically modified mice to remove their ability to taste sweetness. When presented with the option of a solution with sugar or an artificial sweetener, the mice chose the sugar. This shows that calorie density is more important than the sweet taste.

> **The Environment of Evolutionary Adaptedness (EEA):** The EEA is the environment to which a species is adapted. The EEA for any specific organism is the set of reproductive problems faced by members of that species over evolutionary time.

Neophobia

During weaning children are introduced to different foods. **Neophobia** is a fear of new food, which is found in young children as they move on from the food they first experience to the wide range of foods they will eat throughout their lives. Neophobia leads to toddlers refusing to eat and spitting out foods that are new to them in favour of the foods they are used to. Parents are encouraged to persevere with introducing new foods to allow for the child to consume a variety of nutrients. Preferences will change once the child is about seven years old.

> **Neophobia:** a fear of new food found in children during weaning.

Taste aversion

It is argued that humans, along with other animals, have an innate **taste aversion** mechanism to recognise toxins in food. This has adaptive value for our ancestors as foods did not always have sell-by dates and safety labels indicating poisons. Evolutionary explanations for food preferences can also explain why today we have an aversion to bitter foods that is genetically hardwired, which makes us less likely to eat food that has gone off or is otherwise toxic. According to Martin Seligman's (1971) theory of biological preparedness, we acquire certain taste aversions or fears more quickly than others.

> **Taste aversion:** an innate mechanism to recognise toxins in food, leading to avoidance.

Taste aversion – nature not nurture?

Steiner (1987) has shown that newborn babies' facial expressions indicate acceptance of and pleasure over a sweet taste and rejection of and disgust for a bitter taste. Therefore it appears that this preference is innate rather than learned.

Mannella (2008) found a variation of taste gene TAS2R38, which can make children very sensitive to bitter tastes. Among the 900 participants aged 5–50 years who were tested, it was found that children were more sensitive to bitter tastes than adults.

Evaluation

Research supports the view that children have innate dislike of bitter tastes and that as we age our dislike can change through learning and experience. This could help to explain why children dislike some vegetables like broccoli as they have a bitter taste.

Evolutionary explanations suggest that eating behaviour is universal and ignores social and cultural differences in food preferences.

One problem with the evolutionary explanation is that it is a retrospective theory and cannot be tested scientifically.

Exam tip

When describing evolutionary explanations make sure you include why the foods we eat now would be adaptive to our ancestors during the EEA. Include why neophobia and taste aversion are adaptive eating behaviours and link from the past to the modern day.

The role of learning in food preference: social influences

One influence on our food preferences can be explained by social learning theory, which suggests that we learn through observation, imitation and reinforcement. Children learn what to eat by **modelling** their parents and develop eating habits as they grow. In this sense, the parents act as eating role models. Observing parents being rewarded by enjoying eating certain foods, the children learn to imitate those food preferences as they expect to receive similar rewards by doing so. This theory would therefore argue that children should show similar preferences to those of their parents, having learned those preferences from them through a process of vicarious learning.

Modelling: the process of learning through observation and imitation.

Food preference – nature not nurture?

Skinner *et al.* (2002) found that the food preferences of two year olds were similar to the preferences of their mothers and go on to explain preferences in later life.

Duncker (1938) found that when children observed a series of role models, including older children, a friend, their mother, an unknown adult and a fictional hero, making food choices different to their own. The findings showed that all the role models had an impact on the children's subsequent food choices, with the exception of the unknown adult.

Fisher and Birch (2000) found that when girls were given a standard lunch but then allowed to freely snack on calorific foods such as ice cream and chocolate bars afterwards, there was a link between how much parents restricted those foods at home and how much of those foods the child ate during the study. This goes against the SLT as it suggests parents trying to discourage certain foods could actually lead to increased intake rather than the reduced intake.

The role of learning in food preference: cultural influences

Different cultures and subcultures have different practices and attitudes to foods. Food also plays a part in social interaction and eating can be seen as a social event. Many social events involve food, which seems to suggest that social learning can be used to explain the cultural influences on eating behaviour. This means some communities of people show differences in eating attitudes mainly due to environmental reasons (such as availability of food), whereas differences between other groups may be based more on religious beliefs. For example, Muslims and Christians living close to each other for generations with equal access to similar foods differed hugely in their eating behaviour.

Research has looked at the change in attitudes and eating behaviour when people move to another country to show whether the influence is cultural or environmental. This is known as the '**acculturation** effect': the adaptation of diet of different ethnic groups to the diet of the country they are living in.

Cultural influence on food preference

Lawrance *et al.* (2007) A content analysis was used to analyse discussions across the UK to explore factors that might affect the food choices of girls and young women of African and South Asian descent living in the UK. The main finding was that all of the women appeared to have low levels of Western food in their diets. However, they appeared to adopt the less healthy aspects of the Western diet, including fatty snack foods.

Ball and Kenardy (2002) studied over 14,000 women between the ages of 18 and 23 in Australia. Results showed that for all ethnic groups, the longer the time spent in Australia the more the women reported attitudes and eating behaviours similar to women born in Australia.

Neural and hormonal mechanisms involved in the control of eating behaviour

REVISED

The role of the hypothalamus, ghrelin and leptin

The **hypothalamus** regulates homeostasis, receiving information about the body to make compensatory changes, and links the nervous system to the endocrine system. The lateral hypothalamus (LH) contains the feeding centre. The feeding centre initiates eating by responding to a decrease in blood glucose and increase in ghrelin, a hormone released from the stomach when it is empty. The ventromedial hypothalamus (VMH) contains the satiety centre, which responds to an increase in blood glucose and a decrease in ghrelin. **Ghrelin** is a hormone which is secreted by the mucus membrane of an empty stomach and stimulates appetite. The secretion of ghrelin stops when food is eaten.

Leptin is an adipocyte-derived hormone, which is involved predominantly in the long-term regulation of body weight and energy balance by acting as a hunger suppressant signal to the brain.

> **Hypothalamus:** the part of the brain responsible for the control of hormones. It links the nervous system to the endocrine system.
>
> **Ghrelin:** a hormone produced and released in the stomach that stimulates eating through the experience of hunger.
>
> **Leptin:** a hormone produced by the fat cells in the body, it is responsible for signalling to the brain to stop eating.

Biological influences on eating behaviour

Sakurai (1998) showed that eating behaviour is controlled by neural circuits that run throughout the brain and not just by the hypothalamus. Although the LH undoubtedly plays an important role in controlling eating, it is not the brain's only 'feeding centre'.

Hetherington and Ranson (1940) lesioned the ventromedial hypothalamus in rats and found that the rats increased their food intake, due to

their satiety centre not working. This shows the role of the VMH in receiving messages from the digestive system to stop eating.

Licinio *et al.* (2004) conducted research with a family in Turkey who had a genetic deficiency resulting in the lack of leptin production. They found that when leptin supplements were given, the family members' eating behaviour became normal.

Evaluation

Most research within this area has been conducted on non-human animals to extrapolate to humans. A strength of using animals is that we can precisely control the animals' environment, which makes research more objective and reliable. However, we could argue that using animals means we cannot generalise findings to explain human eating behaviour.

The role of hormones such as leptin in controlling eating behaviour can be seen as deterministic, suggesting that individuals have no free will concerning their eating behaviour but are free to make choices on the amount of food they eat when they are no longer hungry.

Revision activity

Draw a flow chart for both the lateral hypothalamus and the ventromedial hypothalamus and their role in controlling eating behaviour, then use the information on the diagram to explain neural and hormonal influences on eating behaviour.

Biological explanations for anorexia nervosa

REVISED

Neural explanations for anorexia nervosa

One explanation for anorexia nervosa (AN) is related to serotonin and anxiety. High levels of serotonin in the brain can lead to high levels of anxiety. Reducing calorific intake decreases the serotonin and can therefore decrease the anxiety. The result would be a calming or sense of regaining control. So, those with high levels of **serotonin** may feel 'driven' towards not eating as they consciously or subconsciously realise it actually makes them feel better emotionally because of a physical response in their brain (the reduction of serotonin and consequently the reduction in anxiety). A further explanation is the role of dopamine in AN. Research has focused on the basal ganglia, a part of the brain which uses dopamine in the interpretation of harm and pleasure. Increased **dopamine** activity in this area also appears to alter the way people interpret rewards.

> **Serotonin:** a neurotransmitter responsible for regulating mood.
>
> **Dopamine:** a neurotransmitter that helps control the brain's reward and pleasure centres and our emotional responses.

Biological influences on anorexia

Bailer *et al.* (2007) compared serotonin activity in women with restricted or purging-type anorexia with healthy controls. They found significantly higher serotonin activity in the women recovering from the purging-type anorexia. They also found the highest levels of serotonin activity in women who showed the most anxiety, suggesting that persistent disruption of serotonin levels may lead to increased anxiety, which may trigger anorexia.

Kaye *et al.* (2005) used a PET scan to compare dopamine activity in the brains of ten women recovering from AN and 12 healthy controls. In the AN women, they found over-activity in dopamine receptors of the basal ganglia, suggesting that this over-activity may cause individuals with AN to have difficulties associating good feelings with the things that most people find pleasurable, such as food.

Evaluation

One strength of neural explanations for anorexia is that there are practical applications as imbalance in neurotransmitters can be treated using drug therapy.

One weakness is that drugs that inhibit serotonin (SSRIs) are not found to be effective in treating anorexia, which does not support increased levels of serotonin as an explanation for anorexia.

One weakness is that neural explanations for anorexia are deterministic. The focus solely on neural mechanisms suggests that anorexia is not related to free will.

Exam tip

When answering a question on neural and hormonal mechanisms you need to be concise and emphasise the impact on eating.

Genetic explanations for anorexia nervosa

Research has been carried out to test the genetic basis for AN i.e. to test the likelihood of the disorder being inherited. Research has focused on identifying a specific gene variant found in patients with AN by comparing DNA samples between patients with AN and control groups. Additionally, research has focused on twin studies to show the genetic link between identical (MZ) and non-identical (DZ) twins. As MZ twins share exactly the same genetic make-up and DZ twins share only 50%, it allows psychologists to make useful comparisons measured using concordance rate as percentages. If one of the MZ twins has AN, there is 100% likelihood that the other twin will also have the disorder; the figure is 50% for DZ twins.

Exam tip

There are many points that can be used to evaluate neural explanations for anorexia and it is tempting to write as many points as you can in an exam response. However, it is important to write effective points that are relevant and you must clearly explain why you have included them as a strength or weakness.

Research: the genetic basis for anorexia

Holland (1984) tested the genetic link for 16 MZ females (twin pairs) and 14 DZ females (twin pairs); one of each was diagnosed with AN. Concordance rates for MZ twins was 55% while for DZ twins concordance was 7%.

Bulik *et al.* (2006) found that the genetic contribution for anorexia is between 50% and 80%.

Grice *et al.* (2002) compared DNA samples between AN patients and family members and found higher susceptibility on Chromosome 1 if other family members also have the disorder.

Scott-Van Zeeland *et al.* (2013) tested the role of EPHX2 gene variants in anorexia with 1,205 patients compared with a control group and found a genetic link.

Evaluation

Anorexia is a rare condition and many studies are based on small numbers of participants.

One weakness of the genetic explanation for anorexia is that it is focused on the nature side of the nature/nurture debate. This is due to the fact that twin studies assume that environmental influences are the same for both types of twin and the only difference is the genetics.

No one gene linked to the disorder has been identified and testing gene combinations is complex.

Revision activity

Be creative. For biological explanations for anorexia change the lyrics to a famous song or draw a cartoon to explain how the disorder occurs.

Psychological explanations for anorexia nervosa

REVISED

Family systems theory, including enmeshment, autonomy and control

The family systems theory focuses on the relationships within families and specifically the inter-relationships, for example mother–daughter or between siblings. Problems arise for the child when family inter-relationships become dysfunctional, for example when they become too involved with each other, which leaves no room for the child to develop their self-identity or relationships with peers. This dysfunction in families is known as **enmeshment**, where family members spend most of their time together and the self-identity of the children becomes merged with the identity of the family. During adolescence the anorexic tries to exert control and **autonomy** but they may be unable to do so as they do not own their bodies. To overcome this they can take excessive control over body shape and size by developing abnormal eating habits, leading to anorexia.

Enmeshment: inter-personal relationships between two or more people where personal boundaries are blurred.

Autonomy: the ability to act independently and make choices according to one's free will.

Research: the family and anorexia

Bruch (1991) argued that the parents of anorexics tend to be domineering, and the disorder represents an attempt to gain a sense of autonomy and control as 'such children experience themselves as not owning their own bodies'.

Geist (1989) proposed that the mother of a child with anorexia allowed identification by their daughter, however then placed demands on the child to express only thoughts and feelings that were identical to theirs.

Social learning theory, including modelling, reinforcement and media

According to social learning theory (Bandura, 1973), many behaviours are learned through imitation, that is, by observing others who serve as models for behaviour. Observational learning is particularly effective if those who model the behaviour are seen to be rewarded. Anorexia nervosa is learned through observation and imitation, which is maintained by positive reinforcement. An important aspect of SLT and anorexia is role models, especially through the media. Anorexics particularly are exposed to this vicarious reinforcement (the rewarding of others) and imitate in order to be rewarded themselves.

- Teenagers pay attention to celebrity role models who are extremely thin.
- They develop a mental representation of the ideal body shape.
- They have the ability to reproduce this body shape through excessive dieting.
- They can see that their role models are famous and rich and this may motivate them to imitate the behaviour.

Research: anorexia as learned behaviour

Goresz *et al.* (2001) support the view that the media portray a slender beauty ideal. Review of 25 studies showed that this ideal causes body dissatisfaction and contributes to the development of eating disorders. The effect is most marked in girls under 19 years.

Forehand (2001) found that women feel undue pressure on their appearance and reported that 27% of girls felt that the media pressured them to strive to have the perfect body. There is a high incidence of AN in ballet dancing and modelling, with great pressure to be thin.

Garner *et al.* (1987) Girls with interests in areas with the most reward for weight loss are the most likely to develop an eating disorder, for example dancers, gymnasts, etc. Garner found that 25% of a group of 11–14-year-old ballet dancers developed anorexia during a two-year course.

Revision activity

Make a mind map to show the different explanations for anorexia.

Cognitive theory, including distortions and irrational beliefs

The cognitive explanation for AN states that the disorder is a result of maladaptive thought processes. Often sufferers have misperceptions about their body and have flawed reasoning behind their eating habits concerning themselves and their body. Patients misperceive their bodies and have unrealistic body ideals. Minor events related to eating activate fear of weight gain, leading to anorexics consistently having a distorted body image and believing they are overweight when they are dangerously thin. Additionally, anorexics may have irrational beliefs about food and their body, for example, 'I must lose more weight, I am not yet thin enough.' Other irrational beliefs may include:

- misperceptions of the body as being overweight when it is in fact underweight
- basing feelings of self-worth on self-appearance
- holding flawed beliefs about eating and dieting behaviour
- errors in thinking, for example 'I used to eat food and it made me fat, so I need to stop eating food.'

Exam tip

In this section you are not required to describe the symptoms and features of anorexia; rather, marks are awarded for your explanations for why the symptoms occur.

Revision activity

Make a table to show the comparisons between the biological and psychological explanations for anorexia nervosa. Include research evidence and how the evidence supports/challenges the explanation.

Irrational thought processes and anorexia

Lovell *et al.* (1997) found that people who had recovered from anorexia nervosa two years earlier still had a distorted body image and odd views about food and other 'adolescent issues'.

MacKenzie *et al.* (1993) interviewed female eating disorder patients, along with a control group, about their body weight, shape and ideals. They were also asked to estimate their size in relation to other women. Results showed that patients tended to overestimate their body weight.

Evaluation

One strength of cognitive explanations for anorexia is that they have practical applications as they have led to the development of cognitive treatments.

One weakness of cognitive explanations for anorexia is cause and effect – it is unclear whether irrational beliefs cause the onset of anorexia, or if anorexia leads to irrational beliefs.

Typical mistake

Including details of clinical characteristics of anorexia nervosa rather than focusing the answer on explanations for how it occurs.

Biological explanations for obesity

REVISED

Genetic explanations for obesity

Research into genetics as with anorexia focuses on how likely it is that obesity runs in families and whether by testing family members we can identify specific variant genes that may explain the disorder. If a parent is classed as obese, this results in a 40% chance of the child being obese. If both parents are obese, this figure rises to 80%. One genetic variation that has been linked to obesity is found in Bardet–Biedl syndrome, an identified condition that is caused by mutations of genes that have a role in cell development. Abnormal weight gain typically begins in early childhood and continues to be a problem throughout life.

Research: genetic explanations for obesity

Stunkard (1990) examined the BMI of 93 identical twins and reported that genetic factors accounted for 66–70% of the variance in their body weight. This suggests a strong genetic component to obesity.

Stunkard et al. (1986) gathered information on 540 adult adoptees, their adoptive parents and biological parents. The results showed a strong relationship between the weight category (thin, medium, overweight or obese) of the adoptee and their biological parents.

Stunkard (1990) controlled for environmental influences on obesity by comparing concordance rates with 311 twins reared apart and 362 reared together. The results showed that there was a stronger genetic than environmental link.

Evaluation

Genetic explanations only take into consideration the nature side of the nature/nurture debate and therefore ignore the effects of the environment. However, twins share the same environment so psychologists use twin studies and adoption studies to address this.

Neural explanations for obesity

One neural explanation for obesity is the role of leptin, an adipocyte-derived hormone, which is involved predominantly in the long-term regulation of body weight and energy balance by acting as a hunger suppressant signal to the brain. This is linked to obesity as it is argued that obese individuals lack the hormone leptin and therefore do not have the control to stop eating when full. This is linked to the identified obesity (ob) gene first found in a strain of mice. Mice that were deficient in the gene were obese and insulin resistant and ate voraciously. Studies on the obese mice show that the obesity gene affects the production of leptin.

Research: neural explanations for obesity

Zhang et al. (1994) discovered that mice which receive two copies of the gene for obesity and therefore tend to overeat also had defective genes for leptin. They showed that injecting those mice with leptin caused them to lose weight dramatically, indicating that their lack of leptin production may have caused their obesity.

Licinio et al. (2004) conducted research on a Turkish family with a genetic deficiency which resulted in family members lacking the ability to produce leptin. The researchers found that leptin supplements caused their weight and eating behaviour to become normal.

Evaluation

A strength of neural explanations for obesity is that there is objective, scientific evidence for biology being involved in obesity.

One weakness of neural explanations for obesity is that they are solely focused on biological explanations and ignore social and cognitive factors.

Revision activity

Make your own glossary for eating behaviour.

Psychological explanations for obesity

Restraint theory

Restraint theory looks specifically at what happens when people limit what they eat and how this can then lead to some individuals binge eating. Rather than decreasing, their body weight actually increases, leading to obesity. This is a cognitive theory of obesity that suggests restrained eating can lead to psychological distress which can result in lowered mood. Restrained eating can lead to eating more due to perceived cravings when a food is no longer permitted. Herman and Mak (1975) suggested that attempting not to eat actually increases the probability of overeating as the focus is on food.

Disinhibition

When inevitably the person eats a food that is forbidden, this can lead to the 'what the hell effect' and binge eating will occur. This is known as the **disinhibition** effect. The levels of eating here are likely to be higher than the normal amounts of food consumed when eating is not constrained. This can explain why some individuals never increase their weight as they have never followed a period of restrained eating, and why others will become obese.

Boundary model

Under normal circumstances mechanisms controlling food intake do not allow our weight to fluctuate very much from this set point. If our weight reduces, feeding is stimulated; if it increases, feeding is inhibited. In restrained eating, or dieting, the person is also setting a cognitive limit on food intake. So restrained eaters have two potential boundaries for food intake – one is physiological and set by body weight and the other is cognitive and set by the person. The unrestrained eater will eat until they reach satiety, which is the physiological boundary determined by their body weight set point. The restrained eater will eat until they reach their cognitive boundary, determined by the diet they have set themselves.

> **Restraint theory:** the theory that limiting food intake can lead to overeating.
>
> **Disinhibition:** lack of restraint and impulsivity around food, leading to overeating.

Research: restraint theory

Adriaanse (2011) studied female students who were trying to cut down on their intake of unhealthy snacks such as chocolate and crisps. They were presented with diet intentions expressed in a negative form (for example, 'When I am sad, I will not eat chocolate'). After the participants were exposed to these statements, they kept a snack diary during the following week. The data showed that they ate unhealthy snacks more often and consumed more calories than a control group.

Wardle and Beales (1988) randomly assigned 27 obese individuals to a diet group (focusing on restrained eating patterns), an exercise group or a non-treatment group for seven weeks and tested them at four and six weeks. At week four, food intake and appetite were assessed before and after a preload (small snack); at week six, food intake was assessed under stressful conditions. The results showed that women in the diet condition ate more than women in the non-treatment and exercise groups.

Explanations for the success and failure of dieting

For this section you have seen how the psychological theories of restraint and disinhibition that explain obesity can also explain the failure of dieting. One other perspective is the theory of ironic processes of cognitive control, an approach applied to dieting (Herman and Polivy, 1993). Under certain conditions, efforts to avoid thinking about a stimulus actually lead to an increase in their salience. It is when the cognitive system is under pressure that ironic processes are most observable. In the context of food and eating, there are circumstances in which trying to distract one from thinking about a particular desired food makes evidence of the existence and appeal of that food more prominent. This irony contributes to the failure of maintaining a diet. For example, restrained eaters tend to become preoccupied with food and thoughts of food or of trying not to think about food.

Wegner *et al.* (1987) asked some participants to not think about a white bear and ring the bell when they did. They also asked other participants to think about the bear. Those who were told to not think about the bear rang their bells more often.

In order to be able to succeed at dieting, the boundary model suggests that the psychological and biological boundaries should be set close to one another, thus reducing the chance of overeating and dieting failure. If this were the case, the dieter would be less likely to go beyond their psychological boundary due to hunger or overeating and the diet would be successful. Goal setting has also been suggested to be important for the success of a diet, to enable the dieter to know exactly what they are aiming for and be able to easily assess whether they have met their targets, providing motivation for continued success. Motivation is an important factor in dieting and several areas have been focused on, including financial incentives and improved social networks.

Research: success and failure of dieting

Thomas and Stern (1995) reported that strategies to improve social networks have focused on teaching spouses or significant others to provide social support during the weight loss process and modest success rates have been achieved. Strategies of drawing up contracts in which groups aim for individual or group weight loss targets have also been successful.

Bartlett (2003) found this is best achieved when goals set are realistic and are objectively defined. A good practice in goal setting is to make initial targets easy so that they will be achieved. This increases confidence and motivation levels to succeed towards the next target.

Exam tip

There is overlap here between the explanations for obesity and success and failure of dieting. Restraint theory and the 'white bear' study can be used in both sections. Ensure you frame your answer to the question.

Evaluation

One weakness of psychological research into the failure of dieting is that restraint theory is deterministic as it assumes diets will always fail and it ignores free will.

One weakness is that the explanations for success and failure of dieting ignore individual differences as many people are successful while others fall into a pattern of perpetual dieting behaviour.

Revision activity

Write a set of multiple choice questions and test your friends.

Summary

You must be able to demonstrate knowledge and understanding of:
- explanations for food preferences: the evolutionary explanation, including reference to neophobia and taste aversion; the role of learning in food preference, including social and cultural influences
- neural and hormonal mechanisms involved in the control of eating behaviour, including the role of the hypothalamus, ghrelin and leptin
- biological explanations for anorexia nervosa, including genetic and neural explanations

- psychological explanations for anorexia nervosa: family systems theory, including enmeshment, autonomy and control; social learning theory, including modelling, reinforcement and media; cognitive theory, including distortions and irrational beliefs
- biological explanations for obesity, including genetic and neural explanations
- psychological explanations for obesity, including restraint theory, disinhibition and the boundary model
- explanations for the success and failure of dieting.

Now test yourself

TESTED

1 Fill in the blanks in the following sentences.
   (a) Eating sweet food is adaptive as ripe fruit contain large numbers of _____ and would provide an easily accessible source of _____.
   (b) _____ is a fear of new food, which is found in young children during weaning.
   (c) Children learn food preference when they _____ and _____ their parents' eating behaviour.
   (d) A change in attitudes and eating behaviour when people move to another country is known as the _____ effect.
   (e) _____ is responsible for energy balance by acting as a hunger suppressant signal to the brain.
   (f) According to family systems explanations for anorexia, problems arise for the child when family _____ become dysfunctional.
   (g) The cognitive explanation for anorexia nervosa states that the disorder is a result of _____.
   (h) Eating food that is forbidden can lead to the 'what the hell effect' and binge eating will occur. This is known as the _____.
   (i) Motivation is an important factor in dieting and several areas have been focused upon, including _____ and improved _____.
   (j) The _____ contains the feeding centre.
2 Outline one explanation for the success and one explanation for the failure of dieting.
3 Outline the difference between one social and one biological explanation for anorexia.

4 Outline evidence to support cognitive explanations for anorexia.
5 For each of the following pieces of 'evidence', write an opposing argument.
  (a) Research into the acculturation effect shows how eating behaviour is culturally specific.
  (b) It is proposed that children should show similar preferences to those of their parents, having learned those preferences through a process of vicarious learning.
6 Explain the following terms:
  (a) Taste aversion.
  (b) Neophobia.
  (c) Evolutionary adaptations.
7 Briefly outline neural explanations for obesity.
8 Outline one strength of the family systems explanation for anorexia.
9 Evaluate the boundary model of eating.

Answers on page 243

Exam practice

1 Research has been carried out to show the genetic explanation for anorexia.

Concordance rates for anorexia (Holland, 1984)

	Monozygotic	Dizygotic
Concordance rates	55%	7%

  (a) With reference to the table, explain the significance of the results for monozygotic and dizygotic twins. [3]
  (b) Explain one strength and one weakness for genetic explanations for anorexia. [4]
2 Which of the following is not a neural explanation for anorexia? [1]
  A High levels of serotonin.
  B High levels of GABA.
  C High levels of dopamine.
  D High levels of anxiety.
3 (a) Outline the role of culture in food preferences. [4]
  (b) Evaluate the role of culture in food preferences. [6]
4 Outline and evaluate evolutionary explanations for food preferences. [8]
5 *'Dieting is the practice of eating food in a regulated and supervised fashion to decrease, maintain, or increase body weight. In other words, it is conscious control or restriction of the diet.'* Many argue that dieting will inevitably lead to failure.
  (a) Briefly outline restraint theory as an explanation for failure of dieting. [2]
  (b) Explain one limitation of restraint theory as an explanation for failure of dieting. [2]
  (c) Briefly outline one explanation for how you could ensure a diet is successful. [2]
6 Discuss biological explanations for obesity. [16]

Answers and quick quizzes 58, 59, 60 and 61 online

ONLINE

Stress

The physiology of stress

The general adaptation syndrome (GAS)

Selye (1956) proposed that **stress** leads to a depletion of the body's resources, leaving the animal vulnerable to illness. He proposed that the body reacts in the same way to all **stressors** and he called this the **general adaptation syndrome**. In the GAS model, there are three stages:

- **Stage 1, alarm:** when we perceive a stressor, the ANS responds. Adrenaline, noradrenaline and corticosteroids (stress hormones) are released into the bloodstream. The physiological reaction is increased arousal levels (increased heart rate raised and blood pressure) in readiness for a physical fight-or-flight response.
- **Stage 2, resistance:** if the stressor continues, the bodily reaction (the fight-or-flight response) ceases but output from the adrenal cortex continues and the adrenal glands may become enlarged.
- **Stage 3, exhaustion:** if the stressor continues for a long time, the body's resources are reduced and alarm signs, such as increased blood pressure, may return. The immune system may be damaged and stress-related diseases such as high blood pressure and **cardiovascular disorders** are more likely to occur.

The hypothalamic–pituitary–adrenal system

The stress response originates in the hypothalamus and includes the pituitary and adrenal glands. This hypothalamic–pituitary–adrenal axis is responsible for arousing the ANS in response to a stressor. Under stress, the sympathetic branch of the nervous system stimulates the adrenal gland to release adrenaline, noradrenaline and corticosteroids into the bloodstream. This produces the physiological reactions, such as increased heart rate and blood pressure and a dry mouth, of the fight-or-flight response.

Sympathomedullary pathway

The sympathomedullary pathway (SAM) is activated by an acute stressor and in acute stress the hypothalamus activates the adrenal medulla. The adrenal medulla is the part of the ANS that secretes the hormone adrenaline and adrenaline prepares the body for the fight-or-flight response. The physiological reaction to increased adrenaline includes increased heart rate, the arousal of the sympathetic nervous system and changes in the body such as decreases in digestion and increases in sweating, pulse rate and blood pressure.

The stress hormone cortisol

The stress hormone **cortisol** can cause damage to health because raised cortisol levels reduce immune function and increase risk for depression and mental illness. Cortisol is released in response to stress by the adrenal glands as part of the fight-or-flight mechanism. Selye defined two types of stress: eustress (good stress) and distress (bad stress). During distress, when cortisol is released your body becomes mobilised and ready for

Stress: a characteristic of the environment, for instance workplace stress, or a situation in which a person perceives they are unable to cope with the demands of what is happening; or the response of the body to a stressful situation.

Stressor: an event that causes a stress reaction in the body. Stressors include life events, such as divorce, and workplace stress.

General adaptation syndrome: the theory that there are three stages in our response to long-term stress: the alarm stage, in which the sympathetic branch of the autonomic nervous system is activated; the resistance stage, in which the body attempts to cope by maintaining the same level of arousal; and the exhaustion stage, in which the body's resources and defence against the stressor become exhausted.

Cardiovascular disorders: disorders of the heart and blood vessels – for instance, physical damage to the blood supply system that may in turn lead to the blocking of a blood vessel or vessels.

Cortisol: this stress hormone can cause damage to health because raised cortisol levels lower immune function. Cortisol is released by the adrenal glands in response to fear or stress as part of the fight-or-flight mechanism.

'fight or flight' and unless there is some physical action (such as you run away from the snarling dog), cortisol levels build up in the blood, which presents risk to health. In comparison, during eustress there is a heightened state of arousal and cortisol levels return to normal upon completion of the task.

Revision activity

Make a wall chart showing the physiological response to a stressful event.

The role of stress in illness

REVISED

Stress and the immune system

The immune system defends the body against bacteria, viruses and cancerous cells. When we are stressed, the ability of the **immune system** to protect us is reduced, leading to an increased likelihood of physical illness. This weakening of the immune system is called the **immunosuppressive effect of stress**. In long-term stress, such as stage 3 of Selye's GAS, increased levels of corticosteroids reduce the production of antibodies (a direct effect).

Immune system: a system of cells within the body that is concerned with fighting viruses and bacteria. White blood cells (leucocytes) identify and kill foreign bodies (antigens).

Research: stress and the immune system

Kiecolt–Glaser *et al.* (1984) looked for evidence of a difference in immune response in high- and low-stress conditions and to see whether factors such as anxiety were associated with immune system functioning. Seventy-five first-year medical students gave blood samples one month before their final exams and again after they had sat two papers on the first day of the exams. In comparison with the first blood sample, natural killer cell activity was significantly reduced in the second sample. It was most reduced in those students who were experiencing other stressful events and in those who reported feeling anxious and depressed. This suggests that stress can be associated with reduced immune system function. However, it is not possible to say how long-lasting the reduced effectiveness of the immune system might be.

Stress and cardiovascular disorders

Cardiovascular disorders are disorders of the heart and blood vessels and these are sometimes associated with stress. People who experience stress may engage in unhealthy activities, such as smoking and drinking alcohol, in an attempt to relieve the stress and so stress may be an indirect cause of illness because these behaviours increase the likelihood that the person may develop a cardiovascular disorder. Long-term stress may also have a direct effect on the cardiovascular system because stress causes increased heart rate and raised blood pressure and can damage blood vessels because adrenaline and noradrenaline contribute to increases in blood cholesterol levels, leading to blockages in blood vessels, causing strokes or heart attacks.

Typical mistake

In an exam, when you state that it is reductionist to suggest that stress causes physical illness, you need to explain what you mean and why it is reductionist to suggest that stress causes physical illness.

Sources of stress

REVISED

Major sources of stress can include life events, such as marriage, that cause us to change the way we live, regular everyday hassles such as being stuck in a traffic jam, and the workplace – the kind of work we do, where we work and our colleagues.

Stress in the workplace

Stress in the workplace can originate in six areas:

1 Interpersonal factors: good relationships with co-workers can reduce stress in the workplace.

2 Workload and pressure: having too much work to do and strict deadlines can cause stress.

3 The physical environment: this may be noisy or too hot/cold or may involve working unsociable hours, such as night shifts.

4 Role stress: worry about job security or responsibility may cause stress.

5 Role conflict: having to express one emotion while feeling another may cause stress.

6 Control: how much **control** people have may be a factor in how stressful a job is perceived to be.

> **Control:** the ability to anticipate events that may happen as well as perceiving that one is able to control the events. The most stressful situations seem to be those in which we feel helpless, believing that nothing we do will change the outcome of events.

Research: stress in the workplace

Margolis and Kroes (1974) investigated role conflict and found that when the job requires workers to express one emotion, for example being calm and cheerful, while really feeling another emotion, such as being unhappy or worried, this causes role conflict. Nurses, teachers and paramedics are likely to suffer stress caused by role conflict.

Marmot *et al.* (1997) investigated whether perceived control is an important factor in work-related stress. In their study of 7,000 civil service employees who worked in London, participants who were less senior and who felt they had less control and less social support were more likely to have cardiovascular disorders. It was concluded that how much control people have at work, and how much social support people receive from colleagues, may be factors in whether they suffer from stress-related illness.

Life changes and the Social Readjustment Rating Scale

Holmes and Rahe (1967) constructed an instrument, the Social Readjustment Rating Scale (SRRS), for measuring stress. Stress was defined as the number of **life changes** people had experienced during a fixed period and Holmes and Rahe found that the cumulative amount of life change is related to psychological and physiological illness. The **SRRS** questionnaire lists 43 types of life events that require readjustment, such as marriage, death of a spouse and change of job. People complete the SRRS by ticking the life events they have experienced in the past 12 months. Holmes and Rahe found that people with high life change scores on the SRRS were likely to experience some physical illness and a person having 300 points over 12 months had an 80% chance of becoming ill.

According to Holmes and Rahe, stress can be objectively measured by the SRRS and stressful life changes cause physical illness.

> **Life changes:** events (divorce, bereavement, change of job) that cause a person to make a significant adjustment to aspects of their life. These types of life change can be seen as significant sources of stress.
>
> **SRRS:** the social readjustment rating scale – a standardised questionnaire used to measure stress caused by life changes.

Evaluation

How each person experiences a life event is different and life events other than the 43 on the SRRS may also cause stress. Most of the events listed on the SRRS are likely to be experienced only by mature adults with families, are infrequent, and the daily small hassles of life may be a more significant cause of stress.

> **Revision activity**
>
> Make a list of the limitations of using the SRRS to measure stress.

Daily hassles and stress

DeLongis *et al.* (1982) created the Hassles Scale, which measures positive events (uplifts) as well as hassles. They found that the Hassles Scale was a better predictor of ill health (in people over the age of 45) than life changes. The frequency and intensity of daily hassles significantly

Exam practice answers and quick quizzes at **www.hoddereducation.co.uk/myrevisionnotes**

correlated to ill health. Kanner *et al.* (1981) found that the Hassles Scale was a better predictor of psychological and physiological symptoms than the SRRS, symptoms of stress were significantly correlated, and uplifts were positively related to reduced symptoms for women but not for men.

> **Revision activity**
>
> Make a set of pairs of cards, one card showing a 'source' of stress and a second card showing 'who researched this'. Shuffle the cards and then sort them into pairs. Keep doing this until you have learned them all. You could write one advantage and one limitation on the reverse side of each card.

Measuring stress

Using self-report measures of stress

Holmes and Rahe (1967): Social Readjustment Rating Scale

When completing the SRRS, people tick the life events they have experienced in the last 12 months, thus giving a quantitative measure of the amount of life change (stress). Using the SRRS, stress can be objectively measured as a life changes score. High scores on the SRRS (high-stress scores) predict physical illness.

Kanner *et al.* (1981): Daily Hassles and Uplifts Scales

Kanner *et al.* investigated whether daily hassles or life events were most stressful. They developed a 117-item Hassles Scale and a 135-item Uplifts Scale to examine the relationship between hassles and health. An opportunity sample of 100 participants, 52 women and 48 men, all white, well educated and middle class, were asked to circle the events on both scales that they had experienced the previous month and rate each according to severity (for the **hassles**) and frequency (for the **uplifts**). Each participant was tested once a month for ten months using the two stress measures together with tests for psychological well-being. They found the Hassles Scale was a more accurate predictor of stress-related problems than the SRRS. Uplifts had a positive effect on the stress levels of women but not men.

> **Hassles:** the annoying events in daily life that cause stress.
>
> **Uplifts:** the pleasurable events in life that reduce stress levels.

Delongis *et al.* (1982) tested the hypothesis that daily hassles are a better predictor of later ill health than life events. One hundred participants over the age of 45 were asked to complete four questionnaires: a Hassles Scale, an Uplifts Scale, a life events questionnaire and a health questionnaire. The results found that hassles were significantly positively correlated with ill health, whereas uplifts and life events were not.

> **Evaluation**
>
> Self-report scales may lack validity as people's feelings of stress will vary from day to day and people may over- or underestimate the degree to which they are experiencing stress.

Using physiological measures of stress

Skin conductance response is also known as galvanic skin response (GSR). Sweat is controlled by the sympathetic nervous system so skin conductance is used to measure physiological arousal. If the sympathetic branch of the autonomic nervous system is highly aroused, sweat gland activity increases, which in turn increases skin conductance. In this way, skin conductance can be used as a measure of emotional and sympathetic responses.

> **Revision activity**
>
> A patient went to his GP saying that he was stressed, but the GP measured his blood pressure and heart rate and told him that was not the case. Can you explain why the patient might be annoyed and might make a complaint?

Research: reducing stress

Geer and Maisel (1972) investigated the effect of control in reducing stress. In a laboratory experiment, 60 student participants were shown photographs of dead car crash victims and their stress levels were measured by GSR and heart rate through ECG monitoring. Participants were randomly assigned to three conditions:

- **Group 1:** given control over how long they looked at the images.
- **Group 2:** had no control but did know what was happening.
- **Group 3:** were not given any control.

Group 1 experienced the least stress, Group 2 experienced higher stress and Group 3 showed the highest stress levels.

Johansson *et al.* (1978) investigated whether **workplace stressors** increase stress-related physiological arousal and illness. Participants were a high-risk group of 14 'finishers' in a Swedish sawmill whose work was machine-paced and repetitive, and whose productivity determined the wage rates for the entire factory. These 'finishers' were compared with a low-risk group of ten cleaners, whose work was more varied and self-paced. Levels of stress-related hormones (adrenaline and noradrenaline) in the urine were measured on work days and rest days. Records were kept of stress-related illness and absenteeism.

The high-risk group of 14 finishers secreted more stress hormones on work days than on rest days and higher levels than the control group. The high-risk group of finishers also showed significantly higher levels of stress-related illness and higher levels of absenteeism than the low-risk group of cleaners. Johansson *et al.* concluded that a combination of work stressors, especially repetitive machine-paced work and high levels of responsibility, lead to long-term physiological arousal, which leads to stress-related illness and absenteeism.

Evaluation

Physiological measurements give scientific and objective data that can be used to make comparisons such as before and after stress treatment but reduce the psychological and subjective experience of stress to simplistic single-factor biological measurements.

Workplace stressor: an aspect of working life, such as work overload or role ambiguity, that we experience as stressful and that causes a stress reaction in our body.

Individual differences in stress

REVISED

Type A and Type B personalities

Friedman and Rosenman (1974) defined two types of behaviour pattern, **Type A** and Type B, and studied their relation to coronary heart disease (CHD).

Type A people move, eat and talk rapidly, are competitive and tend to judge themselves by the number of successes they have rather than the quality of their successes. Type A individuals are hard-driving, impatient and aggressive and tend to be achievement-oriented.

Type B people seldom feel any sense of time urgency or impatience, are not preoccupied with their achievements, seldom become angry or irritable, tend to enjoy their recreation and are free of guilt about relaxing.

Type A personality: characterised by behaviour such as walking, eating and talking rapidly, trying to do two or more things at one time, being competitive, hard driving, impatient and aggressive. In physiology, Type A people have a higher level of cholesterol and fat in their bloodstream and a greater likelihood of clotting within the arteries.

Research: personality types

Friedman and Rosenman (1974) studied 3000 men aged between 39 and 59 who were healthy at the start of the study. After eight and a half years, 257 of the men in the sample were diagnosed as having CHD; 70% of those with CHD had been classified as Type A. The Type A men were also found to have higher levels of adrenaline and cholesterol. Twice as many Type A men had died compared with Type Bs. Type As also had higher blood pressure, higher cholesterol and other symptoms of CHD.

Type C personality

Type C people think analytically and tend to be problem solvers because they focus on details. The Type C personality has difficulty expressing emotion, particularly negative emotions such as anger, and people with Type C personality traits may display pathological niceness and conflict avoidance and compliance. Temoshock (1987) suggested that Type C personalities are 'cancer prone' because they respond to stress with a sense of helplessness.

The hardy personality

Kobasa (1979) proposed that some people are better able to deal with stress (the **hardy personality**) and that all people could learn to behave in this way in order to cope better. The key traits of a hardy personality, known as the three Cs, are having:

- a strong sense of personal control
- a strong sense of purpose or commitment
- the ability to see problems positively, as challenges to be overcome rather than as stressors.

According to Kobasa, hardy individuals are committed to face problems and will not stop until they find resolutions, and view change as a challenge to be overcome. Kobasa researched the link between a hardy personality and stress levels. The stress levels of 800 business executives were measured using Holmes and Rahe's SRRS. Hardiness was also assessed using a 'hardiness' test. One hundred and fifty of the executives had high levels of stress and those with low levels of illness were more likely to have scored high on the hardy personality test.

> **Hardy personality:** personality traits such as taking control of life events, seeing stressors or problems as challenges to be overcome, and being committed to solving problems or 'seeing things through'.

> **Evaluation**
>
> Using psychometric tests to measure personality may raise issues of validity and reliability. Also the link between stress levels and personality types is correlational and thus cannot be said to be causational.

> **Exam tip**
>
> This is a good opportunity to link individual differences in stress to the debate about dispositional or situational causes of behaviour.

Managing and coping with stress

REVISED

Physiological treatment for stress focuses on the reduction of the physical symptoms. Psychological approaches focus on encouraging people to deal with the causes of their stress.

Drug therapy

Drugs aim to reduce the physiological, or bodily, response to stress. **Benzodiazepine** is an anti-anxiety (anxiolytic) drug whose brand names include Librium and Valium. These drugs slow down the activity of the CNS and reduce anxiety by enhancing the activity of a natural

> **Benzodiazepine:** an anti-anxiety drug that slows down the activity of the central nervous system and reduces anxiety by enhancing the activity of a natural biochemical substance, gamma-amino-butyric-acid (GABA), which is the body's natural form of anxiety relief.

biochemical substance, gamma-amino-butyric-acid (GABA). GABA is the body's natural form of anxiety relief and it also reduces serotonin activity. Serotonin is a neurotransmitter and people with anxiety need to reduce their levels of serotonin. **Beta-blockers** act on the sympathetic nervous system (SNS) rather than the brain. They reduce heart rate and blood pressure and thus reduce the harmful effects of stress.

Advantages

- Drugs quickly reduce the physiological effects of stress and people prefer drug therapies because 'taking a pill is easy'.
- Drugs do not require people to change the way they think or behave and can be used in conjunction with psychological methods.

Limitations

- All drugs have side effects.
- Long-term use of drugs can lead to physical and psychological dependency.
- Drugs treat the symptoms of stress but do not address the causes of the problem.

Biofeedback

Biofeedback works because our minds can influence the automatic functions of our bodies. Using a special machine, people can learn to control processes such as heart rate and blood pressure. Biofeedback machines provide information about the systems in the body that are affected by stress. There are four stages in learning biofeedback:

1 The person is attached to a machine that monitors changes in heart rate and blood pressure and gives feedback.
2 The person learns to control the symptoms of stress by deep breathing and muscle relaxation and this slows down their heart rate, making them feel more relaxed.
3 The biofeedback from the machine acts like a reward and encourages the person to repeat the breathing techniques.
4 Through practice, the person learns to repeat the breathing techniques in stressful situations.

Advantages

- There are no side effects.
- It reduces symptoms and gives people a sense of control.
- The learned techniques can be generalised to other stressful situations.

Limitations

- It requires specialist equipment and expert supervision.
- It requires the stressed person to commit time and effort.
- Anxious people may find it difficult to learn biofeedback techniques.

Stress inoculation therapy

Stress inoculation therapy (SIT) is a form of CBT. The aim of SIT is to train people to deal with stress before it becomes a problem.

Stress inoculation (Meichenbaum, 1985): preparing people for stress can be like an inoculation to prevent a disease. Stress 'inoculation' proceeds in three stages:

1 **Conceptualisation:** in this stage the client identifies and expresses their feelings and fears and is educated about stress. The client is encouraged to re-live stressful situations, analysing what was stressful about them and how they attempted to deal with them.

> **Beta blockers:** drugs that act on the sympathetic nervous system (SNS) rather than the brain to reduce heart rate and blood pressure and thus lessen the harmful effects of stress.

> **Typical mistake**
>
> Make sure you know the effect of either anti-anxiety drugs or beta blockers.

> **Biofeedback:** biofeedback machines provide information about the systems in the body that are affected by stress such as muscle tension. Electrodes are placed on the skin and when tension is detected, the machine gives a signal; as the person becomes aware of the biological changes they learn techniques to control tension.

> **Stress inoculation therapy (SIT):** a 'talking therapy' and a form of cognitive behaviour therapy (CBT). The aim of SIT is to prepare people to cope with stress in a similar way to an injection preventing a disease.

Exam practice answers and quick quizzes at **www.hoddereducation.co.uk/myrevisionnotes**

2 **Skill acquisition and rehearsal:** in this stage the client is taught how to relax, how to think differently about stressors and how to express their emotions as well as specific skills such as time management.

3 **Application and follow-through:** in this stage the trainer guides the client through progressively more threatening situations so that the patient can apply their newly acquired skills.

Increasing hardiness (Kobasa 1977)

The aim of increasing hardiness is to encourage people to respond to stressors in a positive manner and to teach people the behavioural, physiological and cognitive skills that enable them to cope with stressors. Hardiness training involves three stages:

1 **Focusing:** patients are taught to recognise the signs of stress, such as muscle tension and tiredness, and to identify the sources of the stress.

2 **Reliving stressful encounters:** patients are asked to re-live stressful situations and to analyse those situations so that they can learn from experience.

3 **Self-improvement:** patients use the insights gained to help them see stressors as challenges that can be coped with, leading to improved self-confidence and an enhanced sense of control.

> **Revision activity**
>
> Draw up a chart comparing the advantages and disadvantages of physiological stress management techniques.

Gender differences and stress

REVISED

Gender may be an important factor in stress:
- Women are biologically more able to cope with stress.
- Women are socialised to cope better with stress.
- Women tend to drink and smoke less and may do less stressful work.

From an evolutionary (biological) perspective, men should respond to situations of danger with the fight-or-flight arousal response, whereas women should respond by looking after young ones and each other. From a social perspective, males and females are socialised in different ways. Women learn to use social networks more and this may reduce their stress. When coping with stress, women tend to use more emotion-focused strategies than men, who use problem-focused coping strategies.

Emotion-focused stress management

Lazarus and Folkman (1984) suggested that there are two types of coping responses: emotion focused and problem focused.

Emotion-focused coping involves trying to reduce the negative emotional responses associated with stress such as anxiety, depression and frustration. This may be the only realistic option when the source of stress is outside the person's control. Emotion-focused strategies include keeping busy to take your mind off the issue, letting off steam to other people, and ignoring the problem in the hope that it will go away.

Problem-focused stress management

Problem-focused coping targets the cause of stress in practical ways which tackle the problem that is causing stress, consequently directly reducing the stress. Problem focused strategies include:
- **taking control:** involves changing the relationship between yourself and the source of stress, for example leaving a stressful job

- **information seeking:** a cognitive response to stress as the individual tries to understand the situation and puts into place cognitive strategies to avoid it in future
- **evaluating:** weighing up the pros and cons of different ways of dealing with the stressor.

Stress management: the different ways in which people try to cope with the negative effects of stress: the physical approach, when we try to change the body's response to stress, or the psychological approach, when we try to change the way we react to a stressful situation.

Revision activity

Suggest ONE stressful life event for which an emotion-focused stress management strategy may be appropriate and ONE stressful life event for which a problem-focused **stress management** strategy may be appropriate. Make sure you can explain your choices.

Social support

Research suggests that social support helps in stressful situations because when people have others to turn to they are more able to handle stressors such as unemployment and the everyday problems of living. Researchers make a distinction between perceived and received support. Perceived support refers to a recipient's subjective judgement that they will be offered effective help during times of need. Received support refers to specific supportive actions offered during times of need.

Esteem support: the type of social support such as empathy, concern, affection, love, trust, acceptance, encouragement or caring that shows the individual that they are valued.

Support can come from many sources, such as family, friends, pets and neighbours. There are four common types of social support:

1. Emotional support (esteem support) is the offering of empathy, affection, love or caring. Providing emotional support can let the individual know that they are valued (**esteem support**).
2. **Instrumental support** is the provision of financial assistance or services, demonstrated in the concrete ways people assist others.
3. Informational support is the provision of advice or useful information to help someone solve a problem.
4. Companionship support is the type of support that gives someone a sense of social belonging.

Instrumental support: the type of social support that is concrete and direct and that offers financial assistance or services to others.

Research: social support

Waxler-Morrison *et al.* (1991) studied 133 women diagnosed as suffering from breast cancer and found that those having a network of social support survived longer. The researchers suggested that social support may be effective because friends provide information and encouragement and also because 'sharing a problem' works as a 'buffer' to guard against and reverse the effects of stress.

Evaluation

Psychological approaches can be combined with other treatment methods to alleviate stress.

Psychological approaches focus on the cause of stress and on ways of coping with it and are effective for both short- and long-term stressors. They lead to increased feelings of 'being in control', which can bring increased self-confidence and self-efficacy. There are no physiological side effects.

Limitations: psychological approaches may be successful only with patients who are already determined to make the time and effort to help themselves.

The research findings are based on biased samples of mainly white, middle-class, well-educated people and thus may not generalise to other populations.

Revision activity

Draw up a chart comparing the advantages and disadvantages of physiological and psychological stress management techniques.

Summary

You should be able to demonstrate knowledge and understanding of:

- the physiology of stress, including general adaptation syndrome, the hypothalamic–pituitary–adrenal system, the sympathomedullary pathway and the role of cortisol
- the role of stress in illness, including the effect of stress on the immune system and on cardiovascular disorders
- sources of stress, such as life changes and daily hassles, and stress in the workplace, including the effects of workload and control
- measuring stress by using self-report scales (Social Readjustment Rating Scale and the Hassles and Uplifts Scales) and by using physiological measures, including skin conductance response
- individual differences in stress, especially personality types A, B and C and associated behaviours, and the Hardy personality with its characteristics of commitment, challenge and control
- managing and coping with stress – treating stress with drug therapy (benzodiazepines, beta blockers) or by stress inoculation therapy and biofeedback
- gender differences in coping with stress
- the role of social support in coping with stress and the types of social support.

Now test yourself

TESTED ☐

1 (a) When talking about stress, what does the acronym GAS stand for?
  (b) Fill in the blank space. The hypothalamic–pituitary–adrenal axis is responsible for arousing the _____ in response to a stressor.
  (c) Fill in the blank space. An acute stressor activates the _____.
  (d) What happens in GAS stage 1, the alarm stage?
  (e) Outline the effects of the stress hormone cortisol.
  (f) When we are in a stressful situation, what causes the 'flight or fight' response symptoms such as increased heart rate and blood pressure and a dry mouth?
  (g) Outline how stress affects the immune system.
  (h) How might stress have an indirect effect on health?
  (i) Suggest why long-term stress may cause physical illness.
  (j) Briefly explain why it is difficult to prove conclusively that long-term stress causes physical illness.

2 (a) Give two examples of life-changing events that are listed on the SRRS.
  (b) What is the difference between a life-changing event and a daily hassle?
  (c) Explain how the SRRS measures the amount of life change an individual has experienced.
  (d) Suggest why the SRRS may only measure the stress of a biased sample.
  (e) Tom works in a call centre where there is always a queue of calls waiting to be answered. His call rate is monitored, he has to put up his hand if he needs to go to the rest room, and he cannot hang up on customers who shout and/or swear at him. What factors related to his job may cause Tom to feel stressed?
  (f) How are workload and lack of control causes of stress-related ill health?
  (g) Suggest one advantage of using self-report to measure stress.
  (h) Suggest one disadvantage of using self-report to measure stress.
  (i) Explain why measuring the amount of cortisol in saliva is a reductionist measurement of stress.
  (j) When measuring stress, suggest how researchers could increase validity.

3 (a) Briefly describe the personality characteristics of the Type A personality.
  (b) Why is a Type B personality less likely to suffer stress-related illness?
  (c) Explain the difference between physiological and psychological methods of managing stress.
  (d) Explain how one drug treatment reduces the physiological symptoms of stress.
  (e) What are the characteristics of the hardy personality?
  (f) Suggest one advantage of using drugs to treat stress.
  (g) Outline the processes involved when biofeedback is used to treat stress.
  (h) Outline how stress inoculation (CBT) can be used to help people manage stress.
  (i) Millicent has been having a stressful time at work. Suggest two types of social support her friends may offer.
  (j) Suggest why it may be difficult to gain a valid measure of how social support reduces stress.
  (k) Explain the difference between emotion-focused and problem-focused ways of coping with stress.

Answers on page 244

Exam practice

1 Kobasa (1979) found that some people deal with stress more effectively (the hardy personality). Outline the key traits of a hardy personality. [2]
2 Explain the difference between instrumental and informational social support. [2]
3 Explain one disadvantage of using hassles and uplifts to SRRS to measure stress. [2]
4 You have been retained by a factory making pet food. The factory employs 300 people and production is ongoing 24 hours a day, 7 days each week. The factory floor is noisy and employees have fixed meal breaks. There is a high level of sickness and absenteeism. Make one recommendation for change in the factory and explain why you think this change may reduce levels of sickness and absence. [4]
5 Discuss the extent to which stress can be said to cause physical illness. [8]
6 Discuss psychological approaches to stress management. [8]
7 Tabitha, who lives alone, has had a year full of stressful life events and she is not coping well. Her GP recommends she joins a local support group which meets once a week to chat over coffee and cake. Suggest how this might help Tabitha. [4]

Answers and quick quizzes 41, 42, 43, 44 and 45 online

ONLINE

Aggression

Aggression can take a variety of forms, including physical, verbal and emotional aggression. Aggressive behaviour can express anger, assert dominance and intimidate others.

Neural and hormonal mechanisms in aggression

The limbic system

The **limbic system** is a set of evolutionarily primitive brain structures located on top of the brainstem and under the cortex. Limbic system structures are involved in many of our emotions and motivations, particularly the 'survival' emotions of fear and anger, and emotions related to sexual behaviour. Structures of the limbic system involved in aggression are the:

- **amygdala:** an almond-shaped mass of nuclei involved in emotional responses, hormonal secretions and memory that has been shown to be an area that causes aggression. Stimulation of the amygdala results in increased aggressive behaviour, while damage to this area reduces aggression.
- hypothalamus: is about the size of a pea and is believed to serve a regulatory role in aggression. The hypothalamus has been shown to cause aggressive behaviour when electrically stimulated.

Serotonin and aggression

Low levels of serotonin appear to be linked with aggressive behaviour. This link is tested through comparing levels of the serotonin metabolite 5-HIAA in a participant's cerebrospinal fluid to a history of aggressive behaviour or actual aggression. If serotonin plays a key role in aggression, researchers would expect to see reduced levels of 5-HIAA in more aggressive people.

> **Aggression:** physical or verbal behaviours that can result in physical and psychological harm to oneself, others or objects in the environment.
>
> **Limbic system:** a set of evolutionarily primitive brain structures located on top of the brainstem that is involved in many emotions such as fear, anger and aggression.
>
> **Amygdala:** an almond-shaped mass of nuclei involved in emotional responses that has been shown to be an area of the brain that causes aggression.

Research: serotonin and aggression

Stanley *et al.* (2000) compared the cerebrospinal fluid concentrations of 5-HIAA in aggressive and non-aggressive psychiatric patients. They found that aggressive participants had lower levels of 5-HIAA than the non-aggressive participants.

Davidson *et al.* (2000) suggested that serotonin provides an inhibitory function – in other words, moderate to high levels of serotonin would prevent high aggression levels. The researchers found that tame domestic pets have much higher levels of serotonin because they do not need to be aggressive.

Testosterone and aggression

Testosterone is a male sex hormone (androgen) which has been heavily implicated in aggressive behaviour. Two models are proposed to explain how testosterone influences aggression:

1 The basal model of testosterone proposes that testosterone causes a change in a person's dominance and that the more testosterone someone has, the more competitive and dominant they will become.

2 The reciprocal model of testosterone suggests that testosterone not only affects behaviour but also responds to it. The act of competing for dominant status affects male testosterone levels in two ways. First, testosterone levels increase in the face of a challenge, as an anticipatory response to impending competition. Second, after the competition, testosterone levels rise in winners and decline in losers. Thus, there is reciprocity between testosterone and dominance behaviour, each affecting the other.

> **Exam tip**
>
> Think about this: can we be sure that when the testosterone levels were measured in the Dabbs study they were the same as the levels of testosterone in the men when they committed their crimes? Explain why or why not.

Research: testosterone and aggression

Wagner *et al.* (1979) conducted correlational research using mice and found that overall levels of aggression in mice that had been castrated tended to reduce, but that giving a castrated mouse testosterone led to aggression. Mazur and Booth (1998) supported the basal model of testosterone. They conducted a meta-analysis of research into testosterone and found that men with higher levels were more likely to divorce, be arrested for major offences, buy/sell stolen property and use weapons in fights.

Dabbs (1987) investigated whether male criminals who had higher levels of testosterone had committed more violent crimes. Eighty-eight inmates aged between 18 and 23 years were studied at a state prison in the USA. Guards rated them on how tough they were and then they were split into four categories:

1 25 bo-hogs (tough inmates)
2 19 scrubs (weak inmates)
3 29 cell block (in between)
4 15 'cutters' (prisoners who self-harm).

The bo-hogs' testosterone level average (at 8.7) was found to be significantly higher than that of the scrubs (average 6.8). Of the 11 inmates with the highest testosterone levels, 10 had committed violent crimes, but of the 11 inmates with the lowest testosterone levels, 9 had committed non-violent crimes. The researchers concluded that there was a positive relationship between testosterone levels and violent crime.

> **Evaluation**
>
> Serotonin and/or testosterone studies show a correlation only between neural and hormonal levels and aggression so it is not possible to say that the level of serotonin or testosterone causes aggressive behaviour. Testosterone is only one of many factors that influence aggression and the effects of environmental stimuli have been found to correlate more strongly.
>
> Giving a biological cause for aggressive behaviour is reductionist as even if low levels of serotonin or high levels of testosterone increase the risk of aggression, aggressive behaviour is usually a response to environmental factors. This also links to the issue of nature or nurture as a cause of behaviour, as well as the question of whether people have the free will to choose to engage in aggressive behaviour.

> **Monoamine oxidase A:** an enzyme (MAO-A) that is encoded by the MAO-A gene. Mutation in the MAO-A gene results in monoamine oxidase deficiency. A version of the MAO-A gene has been called the warrior gene.

Genetic factors in aggression

REVISED

Monoamine oxidase A, also known as MAO-A, is an enzyme that in humans is encoded by the MAO-A gene and that degrades amine neurotransmitters, such as dopamine, norepinephrine and serotonin. Mutation in the MAO-A gene results in monoamine oxidase deficiency. Monoamine oxidases (MAOs) are enzymes that are involved in the

Exam practice answers and quick quizzes at **www.hoddereducation.co.uk/myrevisionnotes**

breakdown of neurotransmitters such as serotonin and dopamine and can influence the feelings and behaviour of individuals. A version of the MAO-A gene has been referred to as the warrior gene. There are several different variations of the gene and a connection between a version of the MAO-A gene (3R) and several types of anti-social behaviour has been found. Research has shown that people with the low-activity MAO-A gene displayed higher levels of aggression than individuals with the high-activity MAO-A gene and that low-activity MAO-A could significantly predict aggressive behaviour in a high-provocation situation. Also, low MAO-A activity in combination with abuse experienced during childhood results in an increased risk of adult aggressive behaviour.

> **Exam tip**
>
> If you answer a question on genetic causes of aggressive behaviour, take the opportunity to explain why it is difficult to separate genetic influences on aggressive behaviour from environmental influences.

Research: genetic factors

Brunner (1993) studied five males from the same family in the Netherlands who had all committed aggressive violent crimes, including impulsive aggression, arson and rape, and who were all affected by borderline retardation and demonstrated abnormal and violent behaviour. Urine samples and blood samples were collected over a 24-hour period for DNA analysis. The findings were disturbed monoamine metabolism and deficit of MAO-A.

Brunner concluded impaired metabolism of serotonin was likely to be involved in mental retardation, which could be linked to aggressive behaviour. The research formed the basis for Brunner syndrome, a rare genetic disorder caused by a mutation in the MAO-A gene. It is characterised by lower than average IQ (typically about 85), problematic impulsive behaviour (such as arson and violence), as well as sleep disorders and mood swings. It was identified in 14 males from one family in 1993 and has since been discovered in additional families. Brunner syndrome is caused by a MAO-A deficiency, which is associated with a behavioural phenotype that includes disturbed regulation of impulsive aggression.

Mednick *et al.* (1987) studied the criminal records of Danish children adopted outside their biological family between 1924 and 1947. Having a criminal biological father increased the risk of criminality, but the highest risk was for those who had a criminal biological father and a criminal adoptive father.

Evaluation

Reductionist: giving a genetic explanation for aggressive behaviour reduces complex behaviour to simple biological facts and ignores psychological evidence that suggests aggressive behaviour can be learned or has social causes.

Deterministic: giving a genetic explanation for aggressive behaviour is an example of biological determinism suggesting that people do not have the free-will to choose not to be aggressive.

Nature or nurture: genes are likely to increase the risk of aggression, but only when combined with environmental factors.

Heritability studies provide limited support for a genetic contribution to aggression because these studies usually study criminality rather than aggression and not all crime is violent or aggressive.

Ethological explanations of aggression

REVISED

Ethology is the study of animals in their natural environment. Ethologists are interested in how animal behaviours increase the animal's chance of survival and the reproduction of the species. Konrad Lorenz (1903–1989) was an Austrian zoologist and the founder of modern ethology, the study of animal behaviour by means of comparative zoological methods. Lorenz (1935) proposed that aggression evolved in all animals (including humans) because it is adaptive, because the most aggressive animals control access to resources such as mates, food and territory. Ethologists propose that much animal behaviour is instinctive, species specific and stereotype, and not learned. For ethologists, instinct means a series of predictable behaviours in **fixed action patterns**. Such behaviours are displayed only when a precise signal, known as an innate releasing mechanism (IRM), is present. An example of an IRM is the gaping-beak movement performed by newly hatched chicks, which stimulates the parent bird to regurgitate to feed the offspring. An IRM is an external 'sign', but fixed action pattern behaviour may also require internal stimulation, for example hunger or the sex drive during mating.

Some psychologists suggest there are innate releasing mechanisms in humans, for example reflex behaviours such as sucking, a baby smiling to elicit play from its mother and a baby crying to attract care from its mother.

Fixed action patterns

Lea (1984) described six characteristics of fixed action patterns:
1 **Stereotyped:** the behaviour always occurs in the same form.
2 **Universal:** the behaviour is found throughout the species.
3 **Independence of experience:** the behaviour is not learned.
4 **Ballistic:** once it starts, the behaviour cannot be stopped.
5 **Singleness of purpose:** the behaviour is used in one context only.
6 **Triggering stimuli:** the behaviour is triggered by specific stimuli.

Aggression in male sticklebacks

As hormone levels rise in the mating season, the male stickleback stakes out his territory in preparation for nest building and turns red. The red colour acts as an IRM, triggering aggressive behaviour in other males. This can be tested by presenting dummy fish painted in different colours. Red males will only attack a model of a red colour. If a 'dummy fish' has a brighter red underside than a real invading male, the territorial male stickleback fights the 'dummy' more violently than the real invading male.

Mating and aggression

Animals fight for the right to reproduce and for social supremacy. An example of fighting for social and sexual supremacy is the so-called pecking order among chickens. Every time a group of chickens live together they establish a pecking order in which one chicken dominates the others and can peck others without being pecked. While the pecking order is being established, frequent and violent fights can break out, but once established it is broken only when other individuals enter the group.

> **Ethology:** the study of animals in their natural environment. Ethologists are interested in how animal behaviours increase the animal's chance of survival and the reproduction of the species.

> **Fixed action pattern behaviour:** instinctive and stereotyped behaviour that occurs in every member of a species in response to a specific stimulus called an innate releasing mechanism.

Figure 3.15 Innate releasing mechanism triggers aggressive behaviour in male sticklebacks

---

Evaluation

If human behaviour was made of fixed action patterns it would be rigid and inefficient, reducing the probability of survival, so the ability to change behaviour based on experience is important. Also, if human aggression comprises a wide range of emotional, verbal and physically aggressive behaviours, it is difficult to argue that human aggression is fixed action pattern behaviour.

Evolutionary explanations of human aggression

REVISED

Evolutionary psychologists argue that the reproductive challenges faced by our ancestors can explain aggressive behaviour. For example, a man can never be certain that he is the biological father of his children unless he prevents his female partner having relationships with other men. This might explain why male sexual jealousy is often cited as a cause of aggression and domestic violence.

Research: aggression and infidelity and jealousy

Daly and Wilson (1988) proposed that men have evolved different strategies to deter their partners from committing adultery, ranging from vigilance, for example watching their every move, to violence, and that these strategies are the result of male jealousy and paternal uncertainty.

If a man's female partner has a relationship with another man, he runs the risk of cuckoldry – that he may unwittingly invest resources in rearing children that are not his own. Male sexual jealousy may therefore have evolved to prevent infidelity by women and reduce the risk of cuckoldry. Buss (1988) argued that males have developed strategies for mate retention. These include direct guarding, that is restricting the movements of the female partner, and negative inducements, such as threats of violence to prevent the female partner from 'straying'.

Wilson et al. (1995) found support for the link between sexual jealousy, mate retention and violence. In a questionnaire, women who reported that their partners were jealous were twice as likely to have experienced violence from their partners.

Shackleton et al. (2005) demonstrated the link between mate retention, jealousy and violence. They surveyed 461 men and 560 women who were all in heterosexual relationships. The men answered questions about their use of mate-retention techniques, and the women were asked about their partners' use of mate-retention techniques and how violent their male partners were. There was a positive correlation between men who used mate-retention techniques of direct guarding and negative inducements and their use of violence. Men also tended to use emotional manipulation as a mate-retention technique. There was a positive correlation (in women) between those who had jealous partners and being the victims of violence.

Aggression and social status

In our evolutionary past, loss of status could be harmful for survival and reproduction. Men kill men to defend their status in a peer group and even though status is largely irrelevant for survival nowadays, it is an evolved behaviour that may be passed on genetically.

Harris et al. (2011) studied gang violence and found that status and respect seemed to be an important need for most gang members and that the gang peer system was seen as a context in which participants could earn respect. This was particularly likely to be the case when participants lived in an environment characterised by competition and conflict between gangs representing different territories.

Revision activity

Make a list of the psychologists who would argue that human aggressive behaviour is caused by nurture not by nature.

Evaluation

Application: research into sexual jealousy and violence suggests that mate-retention techniques such as direct guarding and negative inducement can be the early signs of a violent man. This is useful because educating people in these danger signs can reduce the likelihood of women becoming victims of violence.

Methodological issues: surveys are a self-report method and therefore may not collect reliable and valid data. If a man is asked to complete a questionnaire asking how violent he is towards his partner, it is most likely that he will distort the truth due to social desirability bias. Similarly, a woman may be less likely to accurately report her partner as abusive if she fears recriminations from him, or because acknowledging it could mean the end of her relationship with him.

Gender bias: research into domestic violence and infidelity is gender biased – the evolutionary argument for infidelity states that it is something a man must prevent a woman from doing and does not really acknowledge the fact that men may be just as unfaithful as women.

Nature–nurture debate: evolutionary explanations argue that aggressive behaviour has evolved through gene selection and is therefore biological. If jealousy and murder are evolved genetic responses to female infidelity then we would expect all men to behave violently to women, but clearly they do not. There must be an alternative explanation for why many men do not behave violently yet others do.

Anthropomorphism: this is the attribution of human characteristics to non-human creatures such as animals and depicting them as creatures with human motivation. Evolutionary theories of aggression tend to use human behaviour, such as jealousy, to explain the animal behaviour.

Biological determinism: evolutionary theories suggest that aggressive behaviour is innate (instinctive) and is 'in our nature'.

The frustration–aggression hypothesis

REVISED

The **frustration–aggression hypothesis** is a theory of aggression proposed by Dollard and Miller *et al.* in 1939 (the Yale group). The theory proposes that aggressive behaviour occurs when a person's efforts to attain a goal are frustrated. There were two hypotheses:
1 Frustration leads to some form of aggression.
2 Aggression is always the result of frustration.

The revised frustration–aggression hypothesis (Berkowitz 1989) suggests that frustration creates a readiness to respond in an aggressive manner but that aggression will happen only if **environmental cues** that indicate an aggressive response is appropriate are present. This theory suggests that certain environmental cues (such as guns) have become strongly associated with aggressive behaviour and that if a person becomes frustrated in the presence of these cues, they will behave more aggressively.

Frustration–aggression hypothesis: the theory proposed by Dollard and Miller *et al.* in 1939 that aggressive behaviour occurs when a person's efforts to attain a goal are frustrated.

Environmental cue to aggression: the theory that environmental cues (such as guns) have become strongly associated with aggression and aggressive behaviour and that if a person becomes frustrated in the presence of these cues, they will behave more aggressively.

Research: aggressive cues hypothesis

Berkowitz (1967) studied the aggressive cues hypothesis.

Version 1: participants were either angered or praised.

- **No anger and frustration:** the participants' work was evaluated positively by a confederate.
- **Anger and frustration:** the participants' work was criticised by a confederate and they received mild electric shocks and were thus both angered and frustrated.

The participants were then given the opportunity to deliver electric shocks to the confederate who had criticised their work and the angered subjects gave more shocks.

Version 2: anger and frustration were caused by the participants' work being criticised by a confederate and them being given mild electric shocks.

- **Condition 1:** cues to aggression are present – a shotgun and a revolver were present and the experimenter said, 'These must belong to someone else doing an experiment in here.'
- **Condition 2:** no cues to aggression are present – a tennis racket was present.

The rate of electric shocks was higher in the aggressive cues (guns) condition.

Dill and Anderson (1995) tested Berkowitz's reformulation of the frustration–aggression hypothesis, looking at the effects of justified and unjustified frustration on aggression. Three groups of subjects all performed a timed origami (folding paper) task. The participants' success at the origami task was:

- blocked in an unjustified manner
- blocked in a justified manner
- not blocked at all.

In each condition the experimenter stated that they would give the instructions only once and then start the timer. At a predetermined 'fold' in the origami task, a confederate interrupted the experimenter and asked them to slow down.

- In the unjustified group, the experimenter responds, 'I cannot slow down – my girlfriend/boyfriend is picking me up after this and I do not want to make them wait.'
- In the justified condition the experimenter responds, 'I cannot slow down – my supervisor booked this room for another project afterwards and we must continue.'
- In the control condition the experimenter responds, 'Oh, okay, I did not realise I was going too quickly, I will slow down.'

Afterwards the participants were asked to complete questionnaires on their levels of aggression and about the ability and likeability of the research staff. The participants in the unjustified frustration group rated the research staff as having least ability and as least likeable. The justified frustration group rated the staff as less likeable and having less ability than the control group.

Evaluation

Useful because it suggests that if, in society, we can prevent or reduce levels of frustration we can also prevent or reduce aggressive behaviour.

Much of the evidence from laboratory experiments has low mundane realism, for example students being invited to give electric shocks, neither the sample nor the task are representative of day to day hassles.

Ignores differences between people – not everyone who is 'frustrated' will behave aggressively, and the same person may respond differently from one day to the next.

Reductionist (environmental reductionism) as it suggests that aggression is simply an unthinking response to a stimulus such as a gun or knife.

Revision activity

Remind yourself of the difference between biological reductionism and environmental reductionism.

Social learning theory and deindividuation

In **social learning theory**, Bandura (1977) stated that behaviour is learned from the environment through the process of observational learning. Bandura proposed that humans are active information processors, and that children learn aggression by observing role models, whom they then imitate. Children also learn about the consequences of aggression and observe whether there is positive reinforcement (through the model achieving what they wanted) or whether aggression is punished. This is known as direct or **vicarious reinforcement**. According to Bandura, the characteristics of the model and the learner play a role in whether social learning is successful.

- **Attention:** if the model or the behaviour is interesting or 'stands out', the child is more likely to pay attention and learn the behaviour.
- **Retention:** the child needs to be able to remember and recall the information about the behaviour observed.
- **Reproduction:** the child needs to be capable of reproducing the behaviour.
- **Motivation:** the child needs to be motivated to imitate the observed behaviour, and reinforcement and punishment play an important role.

Bandura also found that children are more likely to attend to and imitate models they perceive as similar to themselves and thus are more likely to imitate behaviour modelled by people of the same sex. If a child imitates a model's behaviour and the consequences are rewarding, the child is likely to continue performing the behaviour. Bandura also proposed that children will imitate 'role models' with whom they identify. These may be people they know, such as parents or siblings, or fantasy characters or people in the media. The child identifies with the model who has a quality the child would like to possess and so adopts the observed behaviours, values, beliefs and attitudes of the model.

Review the study on page 39 by Bandura, Ross and Ross (1961) showing that aggressive behaviour could be learned.

> **Social learning theory:** the theory that behaviour is learned through the process of observational learning and that children learn aggression by observing role models whom they then imitate.
>
> **Vicarious reinforcement:** the tendency to imitate behaviour when one observes that others engaging in that behaviour are rewarded.

Research: parental modelling

Brown and Ogden (2003) looked at the influence of parental modelling and control on children's eating attitudes and behaviour. Children aged between 9 and 13 were recruited from two junior schools and one secondary school in England. Children were approached by either the researcher or a teacher at the school and asked to give a consent form to their parents. Questionnaires were then given to 137 parents and children and 112 pairs of completed questionnaires were analysed.

The results indicated that:
- both parents' and children's diets consisted of many unhealthy snack foods such as crisps and biscuits

- there was a strong association between a parent's and their child's snack food intake for all snacks in general, and for unhealthy snacks eaten the previous day
- there were associations between parents' and their children's body dissatisfaction, suggesting that modelling may have a role in the transmission of eating-related attitudes.

The research provides support for the modelling theory and indicates that children's diets are affected by the types of food eaten by their parents. The researchers suggested that modelling appears to have a consistent impact and that a positive parental role model may be a better method for improving a child's diet than attempts at dietary control.

Useful because social learning theory suggests that if, in society, we reduce the amount of modelled aggressive behaviour we can also prevent or reduce aggressive behaviour.

Much of the evidence from laboratory experiments has low mundane realism, for example the children exposed to adults 'bashing Bobo' were put into a situation very different from everyday life. It is not clear that the children thought the 'aggression towards Bobo' was wrong and they may have thought the 'small Bobo' was a new toy.

Social learning theory is environmental reductionism as it ignores all biological causes of aggressive behaviour.

Social learning theory can be criticised as 'soft determinism' as it suggests that children do not have the free will to make 'moral judgements' and that if the conditions are right, any modelled behaviour will be learned.

Deindividuation

Deindividuation refers to a diminishing of one's sense of individuality that co-occurs with behaviour disjointed from personal or social standards of conduct. For example, someone who is an anonymous member of a mob will be more likely to act violently towards a police officer than a person who is identifiable because they feel free to behave aggressively without fearing the consequences.

Le Bon (1895) suggested that in a crowd, individual personalities become dominated by the collective mindset of the crowd. Le Bon proposed that deindividuation occurs when the individual becomes an anonymous member of a crowd and that as a result of deindividuation the individual will behave in an anti-social manner and will fail to take responsibility for their actions. In sum, deindividuation is the loss of one's sense of identity, usually brought on by being an anonymous member of a group, or by hiding behind a uniform or a mask. This theory suggests that the loss of one's identity leads to a lack of inhibitions and therefore to a change in normal standards of behaviour.

> **Deindividuation:** the diminishing of one's sense of individuality and sense of responsibility that occurs when an individual becomes anonymous in a large crowd and is associated with behaviour disjointed from personal or social standards of conduct.

> **Exam tip**
>
> If in an exam you are given a hypothetical situation in which deindividuation could occur, make sure you can explain how this 'situation' may lead to deindividuation and the types of behaviour that may arise.

Research: deindividuation

Rehm *et al.* (1987) assigned either an orange uniform or no uniform to German school children who then played a football match together. Results found that the children who wore the orange uniform consistently played more aggressively than those who wore their normal clothes.

Diener *et al.* (1976) conducted an experiment in which a woman placed a bowl of sweets in her living room for trick-or-treaters. An observer was placed out of sight in order to record the behaviours of the child trick-or-treaters. The observer recorded whether children came individually or in a group.

In one condition, the woman asked the children identification questions such as what their name was, etc. In the other condition, children were completely anonymous. In each condition, the woman invited the children in and said she had to leave the room to look at something in the kitchen, but that each child should take only one piece of candy.

- In the anonymous group condition, children were more likely to take more than one piece of candy. In 60% of cases, the anonymous group children took more than one piece, sometimes even the entire bowl of candy.
- The anonymous individual and the identified group condition took more than one piece of candy 20% of the time.
- In the identified individual condition, children took more than one piece of candy only in 10% of cases.

This suggests that being an anonymous member of a group does lead to anti-social behaviour.

Dodd (1985) evaluated the association between deindividuation and anonymity. Participants were asked what they would do, within the realm of reality, if their identity were kept anonymous and they would receive no repercussions. The responses were grouped into four categories: pro-social, anti-social, non-normative and neutral. The most frequent responses were criminal acts and 36% of the responses were anti-social, 19% non-normative, 36% neutral and only 9% pro-social. This study suggests that anonymity is an important factor in deindividuation and that in some situations behaviour changes from what would otherwise be the norm for a person.

Institutional aggression in the context of prisons

Institutional aggression can be defined as the violent behaviour that arises in institutions such as schools or prisons. In England and Wales in 2006, there were 11,476 violent incidents between prisoners. Two major models (theories) have been proposed in an attempt to understand why violence occurs frequently in prisons – the dispositional explanation (the importation model) and the **situational explanation** (the deprivation model).

The dispositional explanation – the importation model

The **dispositional explanation** suggests that offenders enter prison with particular characteristics, such as personality traits, values and attitudes, and that these characteristics (dispositional factors) predict they are more likely to engage in interpersonal aggression. According to the dispositional theory, aggression is not a product of the institution but is caused by the characteristics of the individual.

> **Situational explanation of aggression:** the explanation that suggests situational (environmental) factors in institutions such as prison cause inmates stress and frustration, which leads to aggression and violence.
>
> **Dispositional explanation of aggression:** the explanation that suggests that offenders enter prison with particular characteristics that predict they are more likely to engage in interpersonal aggression.

Research: dispositional explanation

Keller and Wang (2005) found that prison violence is more likely to occur in facilities that hold troublesome inmates. For example, prisons holding maximum-security inmates had higher levels of violence.

Harer and Steffensmeier (1996) analysed data from 58 male US prisons and found that black inmates displayed higher levels of violent behaviour compared with white inmates. They concluded that the black offenders often entered prison from impoverished communities with higher levels of violent crimes and so they bring into the prison the cultural norms which condone violence.

Poole and Regoli (1983) studied juvenile offenders in four different institutions and found that pre-institutional violence was the best predictor of inmate aggression.

The importation model is not useful because it does not provide suggestions for how to reduce aggression in institutions.

A limitation of the dispositional explanation is the suggestion that aggression is caused by nature rather than nurture. It ignores the environmental situation of the inmates and is thus a reductionist explanation.

A limitation of research into institutional aggression within prisons is that there is a gender bias as only the behaviour of men is analysed and therefore researchers take an androcentric (male-based) view of aggression.

The situational explanation – the deprivation model

The situational explanation (the deprivation model) suggests that it is the situational factors of the prison that cause aggression and that the experience of imprisonment causes inmates stress and frustration, which leads to aggressive behaviour. For example, overcrowding in prisons forces inmates to share cells, which is linked to an increase in aggressive behaviour and self-harm. The situational explanation suggests that inmates' aggressive behaviour is a response to the problems and frustrations of adjusting to loss of freedom and to the isolation, boredom and loneliness of being in prison.

Review the study by Zimbardo (1971), the Stanford Prison Experiment, on page 3.

Research: situational explanation

Bandura *et al.* (1975) studied participants who were told they were working on a task with students from another school. In one condition, participants overheard an assistant refer to the students 'from the other school' as 'animals', while in another condition they were referred to as 'nice'. When the participants were asked to deliver what they believed to be real electric shocks, higher shocks were delivered in the 'animals' condition and this provides support for Zimbardo's belief in the effect of dehumanising labels.

Evaluation

Zimbardo's explanation of institutional aggression is useful as it has real-life relevance. Zimbardo (2007) claimed that the same social psychological processes found in the Stanford Prison Experiment were also apparent during the abuse of Iraqi prisoners at Abu Ghraib prison in Iraq. These included deindividuation and dehumanisation, which led to a lack of accountability for the brutal actions towards the 'prisoners'.

However, McCorkle *et al.* (1995) suggested that the levels of stress associated with imprisonment are constant, whereas outbreaks of violence are not. They claimed violence is due to the management of prisons. They studied 371 state prisons in the US and found little evidence to support the connection between violence and environmental factors such as overcrowding and living conditions.

Research by both Zimbardo and Bandura is unethical and because all participants were students, the samples are not representative and cannot be generalised to the population of offenders in prisons.

Revision activity

Thinking about the interaction of nature and nurture, write an argument outlining why it is difficult to 'prove' whether the dispositional explanation explains aggressive behaviour in prisons.

Media influences on aggression

Research has demonstrated an association between TV viewing and subsequent aggression.

Research: media influence

Paik and Comstick (1994) conducted a meta-analysis of 217 studies that were carried out between 1957 and 1990, with an age range from 3 to 70 years, and found a significant relationship between watching TV violence and aggression, the greatest effect being in pre-school children, and more in males than females.

Huesmann and Eron *et al.* carried out longitudinal research, starting in the 1980s, and found that

children who watched many hours of TV violence when they were in elementary school tended to show higher levels of aggressive behaviour when they were teenagers. Furthermore, the research found that children who had watched a lot of TV violence when they were eight years old were more likely to be arrested and prosecuted for criminal acts as adults.

The effects of computer games

Among adolescents in the USA aged 12–17, 97% play video games on consoles such as the Wii, PlayStation and Xbox, or on portable devices such as Gameboys, smartphones and tablets. Many of the most popular video games, such as 'Call of Duty' and 'Grand Theft Auto', are violent. Several meta-analytic reviews have reported negative effects of exposure to violence in video games.

Revision activity

Revise correlational research. If there is a correlation between watching TV violence as a child and aggressive behaviour as an adult, why can't we say that watching TV violence causes adult aggression?

Research: computer games

Anderson *et al.* (2010) concluded that exposure to violent video games is a causal risk factor for increased aggressive behaviour and for decreased empathy and pro-social behaviour.

Ferguson (2014) used data from the Entertainment Software Ratings Board (ESRB) to estimate the violent content of popular games from 1996 to 2011 and correlated this with data on youth

violence during the same years. The study found a correlation between falling youth violence and the popularity of violent games and that during the time period 'youth violence dropped despite high levels of media violence in society'. Ferguson noted that the narrative surrounding violent video games and youth violence may distract society from social concerns such as poverty, education and mental health.

Huesmann and Moiser (1996) suggested three ways that exposure to media violence may lead to aggression in children:
1 observational learning and imitation
2 cognitive priming
3 desensitisation.

Observational learning

Social learning theory: children observe behaviour of media models and may then imitate that behaviour, especially when the child admires or identifies themselves with the person on TV. The more real children perceive violent televised scenes to be, and the more they believe that they are like the characters, the more likely they are to try to copy the observed behaviour.

Exam practice answers and quick quizzes at **www.hoddereducation.co.uk/myrevisionnotes**

Cognitive priming

Cognitive priming refers to the activation of existing aggressive thoughts and feelings and suggests that immediately after watching a violent TV programme, the viewer is primed to respond aggressively because a network of aggressive memories is retrieved. Frequent exposure to violent scenes may cause children to store memories as cognitive scripts for aggressive behaviour, which may be recalled in a later situation. In effect, the theory of cognitive priming is that aggression shown in media can trigger other aggressive thoughts and that after watching a violent film, the viewer is 'primed' to respond aggressively.

Cognitive priming: the theory that immediately after a violent programme has been viewed, the viewer is primed to respond aggressively because a network of aggressive memories is retrieved.

Research: cognitive priming

Josephson (1987) demonstrated the importance of cognitive priming. In a study, a sample of 396 boys who were ice hockey players were split into two groups. Before a game, Group 1 watched a violent film and Group 2 watched a non-violent film. Impartial observers rated aggressiveness in the game. Those who saw the violent film behaved more aggressively, for example tripping and shoving other players.

Desensitisation (disinhibition)

This theory suggests that repeated exposure to violence in the media reduces the impact of the violence because people become **'desensitised'** to the violence and they become 'used to it' (habituated) so it has less impact on them. This theory also suggests that people who watch a lot of violent TV become used to it, so their emotional and physiological responses to violence decline and as a result they are more likely to engage in aggressive behaviour.

Bushman (2009) supported this theory as participants who played a violent video game for 20 minutes took longer to respond to an injured person (stooge) than those playing non-violent games.

Desensitisation: the theory that repeated exposure to violence in the media reduces the emotional impact of the violence because people become 'used to it' so it has less impact on them.

Evaluation

Do children learn pro-social or anti-social behaviour from watching TV?

The inhabitants of the tropical island of St Helena first got TV in 1995 and research contradicts many findings because very little changed in terms of anti-social behaviour. Most of the measures of pro- and anti-social behaviour either showed no difference or differences split between pro-social and anti-social behaviour. There were only two significant changes in anti-social behaviour scores and both scores were lower after the introduction of TV.

Research has usually focused on male-on-male violence, frequently carried out in artificial experimental conditions using unrepresentative samples (for example, male students).

There are methodological problems to overcome, such as ethical issues, demand characteristics and, in laboratory experiments, lack of ecological validity.

Much research into the association between media and violence is correlational, thus preventing statements about cause and effect.

Typical mistake

The Bobo doll study by Bandura cannot be used as a study of media influence on aggression.

Summary

You should be able to demonstrate knowledge and understanding of:

- neural and hormonal mechanisms in aggression, including the roles of the limbic system, serotonin and testosterone
- genetic factors in aggression, including the MAO-A gene
- the ethological explanation of aggression, including reference to innate releasing mechanisms and fixed action patterns
- evolutionary explanations of human aggression

- social psychological explanations of human aggression, including the frustration–aggression hypothesis, social learning theory as applied to human aggression and de-individuation
- institutional aggression in the context of prisons; dispositional and situational explanations
- media influences on aggression, including the effects of computer games
- the role of desensitisation, disinhibition and cognitive priming.

Now test yourself

TESTED ☐

1 (a) Which one of the following is not either a neural or a hormonal mechanism in aggression?
   A   Testosterone
   B   Serotonin
   C   Cortisol
   D   The amygdala
 (b) Which from the list below has the MAO-A gene also been called?
   A   The fighting gene
   B   The warrior gene
   C   The aggression gene
   D   The male gene
 (c) Briefly outline the function of the MAO-A gene.
 (d) Which one of the following is NOT true of ethological explanations for aggression?
   A   Are instinctive
   B   Are species specific
   C   Are learned
   D   Are adaptive
 (e) Briefly outline one evolutionary explanation for male aggressive behaviour.
2 Fill in the blanks:
 (a) Stimulation of the _____ increases aggressive behaviour.
 (b) Low levels of the neurotransmitter _____ may be linked to aggressive behaviour.
 (c) The basal model of testosterone proposes that the more testosterone someone has, the more _____ they will become.
 (d) Dabbs found that inmates who had committed violent crime had _____ than those who had committed non-violent crime.
 (e) Suggesting that high levels of testosterone causes aggressive behaviour is _____ as even if high levels of testosterone are associated with increases in aggression, aggressive behaviour is usually a response to _____.
 (f) Giving a genetic explanation for aggressive behaviour is _____ as it suggests that people do not have the free will to choose not to be aggressive.
 (g) Lorenz proposed that _____ is adaptive because the most aggressive animals control access to resources such as mates, food and territory.
3 TRUE or FALSE?
   A   An innate releasing mechanism (IRM) is nurture not nature.
   B   Animals can choose whether to engage in fixed action pattern behaviour.
   C   Fixed action pattern behaviour is genetic.
   D   Fixed action pattern behaviour is species specific.
   E   Imprinting in baby geese is an example of fixed action pattern behaviour.
4 Complete these sentences:
 (a) The frustration–aggression hypothesis suggests that aggressive behaviour _____.
 (b) The aggressive cues hypothesis suggests that _____.
 (c) The aggressive cues theory of aggression is useful because _____.

(d) The social learning theory of aggression is useful because _____.

(e) A person who is anonymous and deindividuated in a large crowd is more likely to _____.

(f) The dispositional explanation of aggression in institutions suggests _____.

(g) Cognitive priming of aggression refers to the activation of _____.

5 (a) What does MAO-A stand for?

(b) What is meant by fixed action pattern behaviour?

(c) Outline how evolutionary psychologists explain domestic violence.

(d) Outline the original form of the frustration–aggression hypothesis.

(e) Explain why cognitive factors are involved in social learning.

(f) In the Zimbardo prison study, why did deindividuation occur in both prisoners and guards?

(g) What is the difference between the dispositional and the situational explanations of violence in prisons?

(h) Give one reason why children who play violent video games may behave more aggressively.

Answers on page 245

Exam practice

1 (a) Outline and evaluate the findings of one research study into the aggressive cues hypothesis. [6]

(b) Explain how playing violent video games may cause aggressive behaviour in children. Support your explanation with psychological evidence. [4]

(c) Explain why attacking and shooting people while playing video games may result in the cognitive priming of aggressive behaviour. [4]

2 A psychologist who was interested in social learning theory showed a group of 11 boys aged 10–14 (Group A) a film of a football match in which there was an incident between two players who engaged in verbal and physical aggression. A matched sample of 11 boys of the same age and same IQ scores (Group B) was shown a film of the same football match but with the aggressive incident edited out. After watching the film, the boys in Group A were given a blue strip and the boys in group B a green strip. They were then observed for 40 minutes while they played a game of football. The observers counted how many times each group of boys (A or B) engaged in physical or verbal aggression (kicked, hit or swore). The data are given below:

	Incidents of aggressive language (swearing)	Incidents of physical aggression (kicking or hitting)
Group A watched aggressive football match	36	18
Group B watched non-aggressive football match	21	7

On questions a–d you must show your working.

(a) Calculate the ratio of physical to verbal aggression in Group A. [2]

(b) Calculate the ratio of physical to verbal aggression in Group B. [2]

(c) What percentage of the total number of 'physical aggressions' were carried out by Group A? [2]

(d) What percentage of the total number of 'verbal aggressions' were carried out by Group A? [2]

(e) Explain how observing people behaving aggressively may cause aggressive behaviour in children. Support your explanation with psychological evidence. [4]

(f) Explain two limitations of genetic explanations for aggression. [6]

Answers and quick quizzes 46, 47, 48 and 49 online

ONLINE

Forensic psychology

Measuring crime

REVISED

Defining crime

Crime might be defined simply as 'breaking the law', but some factors need to be taken into account when establishing a definition.

Historical context: what is defined as a crime at one point in time may not be considered a crime at another point in time. For example, sedition and witchcraft were crimes in Elizabethan England, and more recently, in the UK, homosexuality was a crime until 1967.

Culture: what is acceptable in one culture may be a criminal offence in another. For example, in some cultures it is acceptable to have more than one wife but in the UK bigamy is a crime. In some cultures, euthanasia is legal but in the UK euthanasia and 'assisting a suicide' are crimes.

Age: this is a factor in determining whether a person is a criminal – in the UK, if a person under the age of ten commits an illegal offence they cannot be charged with committing crime.

Official statistics: police figures

There are many reasons that the statistics gathered by the police do not reflect the true figures of crime. Farrington and Dowds (1985) found that different policing rules may affect the crime records in different areas. This study analysed crime reports in Nottinghamshire and two neighbouring counties and found that Nottinghamshire recorded crimes under a £10 value but the other forces did not.

Official statistics: victim surveys

The Crime Survey for England and Wales (CSEW)

The Crime Survey for England and Wales (formerly known as the British Crime Survey) is a face-to-face survey asking people in England and Wales about their experiences of crime in the past year. The survey was launched in 1982 and is conducted on a continuous basis, with around 35,000 adults and 3,000 children aged 10–15 years interviewed each year. The content of the survey is reviewed each year and new questions are added as required. The offences surveyed are violence, robbery, theft and criminal damage. The survey does not cover so-called 'victimless' crime, such as possession of drugs or motoring offences.

The CSEW provides a better reflection of the extent of crime than police recorded figures as the survey asks about crimes that are not reported to or recorded by the police. The survey is also unaffected by changes in police recording practices or levels of public reporting to the police, so it provides a more consistent measure over time. The survey provides a useful benchmark for police recorded crime. It also seeks the opinions of the public on a range of crime-related issues, such as public confidence in police and the criminal justice system, and fear of crime. The 2006 survey showed that overall, crime had increased by 3%; however, the official statistics showed a decrease of 2% (a 5% difference).

Offender surveys

Offender surveys use self-report methods to ask participants about their offending. These surveys focus on people previously convicted or at risk of offending. The 2006 offender survey showed that alcohol was a key factor in offending – the figures showed 27% of binge drinkers had offended in the past year. However, offender surveys are unlikely to collect valid data as many offenders will not want to tell the truth about crimes they may have committed.

> **Evaluation**
>
> Crimes may not be reported – perhaps because they are too trivial.
>
> Crimes are not recorded by police – perhaps to make their 'clear-up' statistics look good.
>
> Hollins (1992) estimated that the crimes reported account for only 25% of crimes committed. The other 75% are known as the 'dark figures' of crime.

Offender profiling

REVISED

Holmes and Holmes (1996) defined the goals of **offender profiling** as:
- **social and psychological assessments:** profiles should contain basic information, for example age, race, type of employment, marital status, etc.
- **psychological evaluation of belongings:** the profile should provide suggestions as to any possessions the offender may have that would associate him with the crime scene – these would be looked for if the police had a search warrant for the suspect's home
- **interviewing strategies:** to make suggestions as to effective ways to interview a suspect.

> **Offender profiling:** an attempt to describe the characteristics of an offender by analysing the behaviour of an offender at a crime scene or multiple crime scenes.

The top-down approach (USA)

The **top-down approach** developed and adopted by the FBI was two-pronged. First they used in-depth interviews on 36 sexually orientated murders, including those committed by Ted Bundy and Charles Manson. Second was the collection of detailed information from the Behavioural Science Unit in the area of sexual crime and homicide. They then combined the information with detailed examination of the crime scenes, the nature of the attacks, forensic evidence and any information relating to the victim to develop models that would result in a profile of the offender. On the basis of this they developed a classification system for several serious crimes, including murder and rape. Criminals are classified into either 'organised' or 'disorganised', the two types demonstrating different characteristics:
- The **organised offender** is socially competent. He is also sexually competent and is likely to be in a stable relationship. He has normal to high intelligence. At the time of the offences he is likely to have been angry, frustrated or depressed.
- The **disorganised offender** has poor social skills, is unlikely to be able to maintain a stable relationship and generally lives alone, probably close

> **Top-down approach:** a way of creating an offender profile in the USA.
>
> **Organised offender:** an offender who has planned the crime, thought to be socially competent, likely to be in a stable relationship and intelligent.
>
> **Disorganised offender:** an offender who has not planned the crime, commits crime on impulse, has poor social skills, generally lives alone and is of low intelligence.

to the scene of his crimes. He probably has poor personal hygiene. His level of intelligence is likely to be low and if employed, his work is likely to be unskilled. He may be suffering from a psychological disorder.

FBI profiling is called 'crime scene analysis' and is carried out as follows:

Stage 1: data assimilation – collection of as much information as possible from as many sources as possible, for example photos, autopsy reports.

Stage 2: crime classification – put the crime in a category (organised or disorganised).

Stage 3: crime reconstruction – development of hypothesis about behaviour of victims and modus operandi of criminal.

Stage 4: profile generation – should include details of possible physical appearance and demographic characteristics (such as age, race), as well as habits and personality.

Research: offender profiling

Ault and Reese (1980) reported a case in which seven rape case files were sent to the FBI's Behavioural Science Unit and an offender profile was constructed. The suspect was predicted to be a white male, probably in his late twenties or early thirties, most likely to be divorced or separated and to have a job as a casual labourer or similar. It was also hypothesised that he would have had a high school education and would live in the immediate area of the offences, have a poor self-image, and have convictions for minor sexual offences. Consequently, the police narrowed down their list of suspects to 40 local males who met the age profile. They then focused their investigation on one particular individual, who was arrested and later convicted of all the offences.

Mokros *et al.* (2002) investigated the idea that similar offenders will carry out similar crime scene behaviour. Analysing the crime scene behaviour of 100 male British offenders convicted of stranger rape, no correlation was found between any of the variables. In other words, rapists who offend in similar fashions are not similar with respect to age, socio-demographic features or criminal records. The authors concluded that the suggestion of socio-demographic similarity is too simplistic and they suggested that future research should consider a framework for offender profiling that is grounded in personality psychology.

Evaluation

This type of profiling may be effective when investigators have details about the suspect, such as in rape, arson and cult killings that involve odd or extreme practices such as sadistic torture or dissection of the body, but ordinary murder and non-violent crimes do not lend themselves to profiling as the crime scene does not yield sufficient information.

The bottom-up approach (UK)

Started in Britain by David Canter, the **bottom-up approach** is more scientific than the FBI's as it is based on psychological theories and methodology. It attempts to formulate psychological theories that will show how and why variations in **criminal behaviour** occur. Central to the bottom-up approach is the need to demonstrate consistencies *within* the action of offenders and identify differences *between* them. Canter (1989) outlined three aspects of criminal behaviour which may provide clues to other aspects of the criminal's everyday life:

Bottom-up approach: a way of creating an offender profile based on psychological theories in the UK.

Criminal behaviour: behaviour that breaks the law.

Interpersonal coherence: the degree of violence and control varies widely between offenders, although each offender tends to be consistent in his treatment of the victim. These patterns of behaviour may reflect the way the criminal treats women in everyday non-criminal life.

Significance of time and place: geographical profiling takes into account individuals' spatial behaviour and predicts the offender's residence based on the location of crimes such as victims' body dump sites, abduction sites, etc.

Forensic awareness: if police have previously questioned criminals for something similar, they need to check police records carefully because attempts to destroy evidence may suggest that the person has previous convictions.

Geographical profiling

Geographical profiling is a field of investigative psychology. It is the type of profiling method used in the UK, which involves generalising from the locations of linked crime scenes to the likely home/work/social base of the offender.

Canter and Gregory (1994) assumed that most offenders like to operate in areas they know well and that many offenders have a crime range of as little as two miles. A distinction has been drawn between:
- **marauders** who like to commit crimes in their own neighbourhoods
- **commuters** who travel to commit their crimes.

This method is based on the assumptions of cognitive psychology – that people store information about their lives in schemas/mental maps. According to Canter and Gregory, each person's mental map is highly individual and the location of crime scenes can be used to infer where the offender is based and also other information about the offender's likely interests and/or employment. The geographical technique uses a computer system called Criminal Geographic Targeting, in which crime data are analysed to produce a three-dimensional model known as **jeopardy surface**. The codes produced are superimposed onto a map where the crimes have taken place. A surveillance area for the subsequent crimes can then be set up.

> **Interpersonal coherence:** the theory that the way an offender behaves during criminal activity reflects the way the criminal usually behaves.
>
> **Geographical profiling:** the type of profiling used in the UK, which involves generalising from the locations of multiple (linked) crime scenes to the likely home/work/social base of the offender.
>
> **Marauders:** offenders who like to commit crimes in their own neighbourhoods.
>
> **Commuters:** offenders who travel away from the area where they live to commit their crimes.
>
> **Jeopardy surface:** the area identified by geographical profiling which is thought to be the home/work/social base of the offender and which should be focused on in an investigation.

> **Typical mistake**
>
> It is wrong to suggest that a weakness of profiling is that a profile does not identify the offender – this is not the purpose of profiling.

Research: geographical profiling

Canter (1986): geographical profiling was used to great effect in the case of the Railway Rapist. Between 1982 and 1986, 24 sexual assaults and 3 murders occurred in the London area. Canter's profile led to the arrest of John Duffy and key features of the profile matched Duffy's life.

Copson (1995) investigated whether offender profiling improves the effectiveness of experienced detectives. A survey was carried out into the opinion of 184 police officers who had used profilers (mainly murder cases) – 50% of respondents felt the profiler had been useful, providing an intelligent second opinion on the crime. Only 14% felt the profiler had helped

to solve the crime and fewer than 3% said that the profiler had 'identified the criminal'. It was concluded that in the UK there is no consistency of approach to profiling and thus it is difficult to measure its effectiveness.

Lundrigan and Canter (2001) studied the spatial behaviour of 120 serial killers in the USA by analysing the distances between the offenders' home locations and body disposal sites. They found that the offenders' homes were in the centre of the pattern. This study shows that spatial information about body disposal sites might be useful in locating an offender's base.

Evaluation

Geographical profiling is useful for a wide range of crimes, not just violent crimes. Geographical information is more useful than other information for linking cases.

Every profile is in effect a case study, so we cannot assume that just because one 'works' another one will be effective.

A profile cannot be used to identify 'the offender', only to identify a probable sample of the population in which the offender 'resides'.

The UK bottom-up approach is inconsistent. In the UK there is little consistency in profiling, compared with the FBI's approach which demonstrates a standard procedure.

A profile is a qualitative 'matter of opinion' and may be biased by the beliefs of the profiler. An inaccurate profile will mislead the investigation.

Revision activity

Draw up a chart comparing the strengths and limitations of top-down and bottom-up offender profiling procedures.

Biological explanations of offending behaviour

Historical approaches

Atavistic theories – Lombroso (1876)

In biology, an atavism is an evolutionary throwback, such as traits reappearing which had disappeared generations before. The term atavism is sometimes also applied in the discussion of culture to describe the return of older, more primitive tendencies.

According to Lombroso, criminal offenders are a biologically distinct group of people with primitive characteristics and are a separate species with the following features:
- narrow sloping brow and prominent jaw
- high cheek bones and large ears
- extra nipples, toes and fingers
- dark skin and hairiness
- insensitivity to pain.

Lombroso's evidence was based on a survey of criminals' heads and bodies (a sample of 383 dead skulls and 3,829 living ones). He claimed that 40% of crimes were perpetrated by **atavistic** people.

Somatotype – Sheldon (1949)

Sheldon proposed three main body types: **endomorphs**, **ectomorphs** and **mesomorphs**. Sheldon looked at 200 photos of criminals and 200 photos of a control group (students) and rated them on a scale of 1–7 for mesomorphy. According to Sheldon, delinquency is associated with mesomorphic body types:
- **Endomorph:** soft body, underdeveloped muscles, round shape and overdeveloped digestive system. Traits: tolerant, evenness of emotions, sociable, good humoured.
- **Ectomorph:** thin, delicate build, young appearance, tall, lightly muscled, stoop-shouldered. Traits: self-conscious, preference for privacy, introverted, inhibited, socially anxious, artistic.

Atavistic theories: historical theories that criminals can be identified by their primitive characteristics or body types.

Endomorph: a body type that is soft and round.

Ectomorph: a body type that is thin and delicate.

Mesomorph: a body type that is hard and muscular.

- **Mesomorph:** hard, muscular body, overly mature appearance, thick skin and upright posture. Traits: adventurous, desire for power and dominance, assertive, bold, competitive.

Evaluation

The Lombroso sample consisted of criminals only and there was no control group. Even if certain features did occur more often, it does not mean there is a causal relationship. There may have been other explanations such as disease, poverty or poor nutrition.

Stereotypes of criminals affect our judgement (revise the halo effect on page 107). Shepherd *et al.* (1978) asked participants to view a face for 30 seconds and then to construct a photofit. The description of the 'face' differed – half the participants were told the face was of a 'brave captain of a lifeboat', but half were told the face was of a 'mass murderer'. The resulting photofit pictures of the 'mass murderer' were judged to be more cruel, unpleasant and unintelligent by independent judges.

Sheldon rated the photofit pictures himself, which makes the study subjective and biased.

Genetic and neural explanations

A version of the MAO-A gene has been referred to as the warrior gene. There are several variations of the gene and a connection between a version of the MAO-A gene (3R) and several types of anti-social behaviour has been found. Research has shown that people with the low-activity MAO-A gene displayed higher levels of aggression than individuals with the high-activity MAO-A gene and that low-activity MAO-A could significantly predict aggressive behaviour in a high-provocation situation. Also, low MAO-A activity in combination with abuse experienced during childhood results in an increased risk of adult aggressive behaviour. Read through the Brunner syndrome on page 189.

Twin and adoption studies have been carried out to investigate the heritability of offending behaviour. In twin studies, concordance rates between monozygotic and dizygotic twin pairs are compared. Adoption studies involve comparing criminal features of adopted children with the criminal history of their biological parents and adoptive parents. The method assumes that if criminal behaviour is genetic, there is a greater similarity in the criminal behaviour of adoptees and their biological parents than adopted parents.

Research: genetic explanations

Christiansen (1977) studied 3,586 twins in Denmark and found concordance rates of 33% for MZ and 12% for DZ in a large sample study for male twins and 21% for MZ and 8% for DZ for female twins.

Mednick *et al.* (1984) used data from the Danish adoption data bank, which covers more than 14,000 children. Criminal conviction rates of male adoptees were compared with those of their biological and adoptive parents – 20% of adoptees who had convictions had a biological parent convicted of crime, but if neither the adoptive nor biological parents had criminal records, only 13.5% of adoptees were criminal. This suggests that criminality is genetic.

If offending is genetic, we would expect a higher concordance rate in MZ twins who share 100% identical genes than for DZ twins who share only 50%, but as there is not a 100% concordance rate there must be an environmental influence. Early twin studies did not control for the fact that MZ twins were more likely to share a more similar environment than DZ twins (due to being the same gender).

Children who are adopted tend to be placed in environments that are similar to those of their biological parents. If children are adopted later, their early experiences could cause later criminal behaviour.

The association between the criminality of the biological parent and the adopted child may be the effect of inherited emotional instability and/or mental illness rather than directly inherited criminality.

Deterministic explanations give criminals an excuse to argue that they are not responsible for their crimes.

Neural explanations for crime

Structures in the brain, specifically the limbic system and the amygdala, are associated with aggression. Different areas of the brain have been implicated in different types of aggression.

Anti-social personality disorder

People with anti-social personality disorder (APD) are called emotionless psychopaths as they lack emotion and feelings and are likely to offend. ECG of the brain activity of people with APD found abnormal patterns of slow wave activity typical of brain immaturity. Raine *et al.* (2000) compared the brain volume in people with APD and controls and found 11% less volume of grey matter in the prefrontal area for the APD group, suggesting there is a structural brain defect in people with APD.

Research: neural explanations

Raine *et al.* (1997) investigated brain abnormalities in 41 murderers (two female), all charged with murder/manslaughter in California. They were compared with a control group of 41 normal individuals (non-murderers) matched for sex, age and, in six cases, schizophrenia. PET scans were used to analyse differences in the brains of the murderers, with the following results:

- lower activity in the cortical and subcortical regions
- reduced activity in the prefrontal cortex and parietal region
- reduced activity in the corpus callosum
- less activity in the left brain hemisphere than the right
- abnormal asymmetries in the amygdala and the thalamus.

Both groups performed similarly on the performance task.

Raine *et al.* concluded that there is some evidence that murderers pleading not guilty by reason of insanity (NGRI) may have different brain functions to 'normal' people and that there may be a link between brain activity and a predisposition towards violence which should be investigated further.

No direct causal link can be found between neurological function and criminal behaviour.

Biological explanations are reductionist, attempting to explain complex criminal behaviour as the result of genes or neurology. There probably is no gene for shoplifting or breaking the speed limit!

Research on samples such as murderers or psychopaths is not generalisable to the majority of criminals.

Psychological explanations of offending behaviour

REVISED

Eysenck's theory of the criminal personality

Eysenck suggests that offending behaviour arises from personality traits that predispose us to offending. According to Eysenck, people vary across two dimensions, introvert vs extrovert and neurotic vs stable, and the criminal type is the neurotic extrovert, where:

- extroversion is associated with low autonomic arousal so the extrovert requires stimulation from their environment; also extroverts do not condition easily and do not learn from their mistakes
- neuroticism leads to unstable, unpredictable behaviour and high neuroticism scores show that an individual has high anxiety
- psychoticism is associated with uncaring, aggressive, solitary and cruel behaviour.

Research: Eysenck's personality test

McGurk and McDougall (1981) investigated the link between criminality and personality type. One hundred students defined as 'delinquent' and 100 control group students who were not delinquent completed the Eysenck personality test (EPI) and their extrovert and neurotic scores were calculated. There was a significant difference in scores, suggesting a relationship between personality type and delinquent behaviour.

Evaluation

It is possible to have a high extrovert/neurotic score and not commit crime, so there must be other reasons for criminality.

Eysenck's theory is reductionist – considering offending in terms of only two personality traits is oversimplistic.

Personality is a hypothetical concept that is difficult to measure.

Cognitive explanations

Criminal thinking styles

Research: criminal thinking

Mandracchia et al. (2007) aimed to identify the defining characteristics of criminal thinking.

The sample was 435 prisoners in six prisons in Texas, average age 36, age range 18–76 years, having committed a wide range of crimes, for example burglary, robbery, drug crimes, assault and sex crimes. The average sentence was 20 years and average time served was 5.5 years. Participants completed the Measure of Offender

Thinking Styles (MOTS), which measures 77 thinking styles. The findings suggest that criminal thinking is defined by three thinking styles:

- **control:** the need for power and control
- **cognitive immaturity:** for example, self-pity and overgeneralisation
- **egocentricity:** focusing on self and own needs and wants.

The research concluded that criminal thinking allows self-indulgent and rash behaviour that is contrary to accepted social standards, that is irrational and leads to immediate gratification.

Level of moral reasoning

Kohlberg (1958) proposed three levels of moral reasoning in which each level consists of two separate stages:

The pre-conventional level: during stage 1, goodness (or badness) is determined by consequences, so that an act is not bad if one can get away with it. At stage 2, children conform to rules in order to gain rewards. Stages 1 and 2 compose the lowest level of moral reasoning, in which the focus is on rules and the consequences for breaking them.

The conventional (conformity) level: this consists of stages 3 and 4, corresponding with increased understanding of others' intentions and the desire to win praise from others. Stage 3 is often called the 'good girl/ good boy' stage, when children obey rules to gain praise and because social order and authority are important.

The post-conventional (autonomous) level: in stage 5, moral actions are those that express the will of the majority (democracy). Stage 6 is marked by the development of a set of self-defined ethical principles that determine right and wrong based on ideas of universal justice and respect for human rights and dignity.

To determine a child's level of morality, Kohlberg asked children questions about hypothetical moral dilemmas and paid attention to the reasoning behind the answer rather than to the answer itself. For example, having heard a dilemma about stealing, a child might respond that stealing is wrong because it breaks the law and that laws should be upheld because otherwise no one will be punished.

> **Revision activity**
>
> Look at www.brainpickings. org/2012/03/29/heinz-dilemma-interactive/

Research: moral reasoning

Palmer and Hilling (1998) compared moral reasoning between male delinquents and male and female non-delinquents. The sample was 126 convicted male and female offenders in a young offenders' institution and 22 male and 210 female non-offenders, all aged 13–22 years. All participants were given the Socio-Moral Reflection Measure-Short Form (SRM-SF), which contains 11 moral dilemma-related questions (for example, not taking things that belong to others and keeping a promise to a friend). The delinquent group showed less mature moral reasoning. In the male group there was a difference on 10 out of 11 questions and in the female group it was 7 out of 11.

Hostile attribution bias

The hostile attribution bias is the tendency to interpret the behaviour of others, across situations, as threatening, aggressive or both. People who exhibit the hostile attribution bias think that ambiguous behaviour of others is hostile and is directed towards them. They often respond to the other person's behaviour in an aggressive manner because they perceive it as a personal threat. However, when they respond aggressively, their action is viewed as inappropriate because the other person's behaviour was not intended to be aggressive.

Dodge *et al.* (1990) gave 128 boys in a juvenile offenders' prison a task to assess hostile attribution bias and found that attributional biases are correlated with reactive 'angry' aggression.

We all justify and explain our behaviours using either internal or external attributions. An **internal attribution** is when a person accepts responsibility for their behaviour and sees the cause as being within themselves. An **external attribution** is when a person sees the cause of their behaviour as being an external factor, for example 'I was provoked so it's his fault I hit him'. A criminal is considered rehabilitated when they can make an internal attribution and accept their guilt.

> **Internal attribution:** a person accepts responsibility for their behaviour and sees the cause as being within themselves.
>
> **External attribution:** a person sees the cause of their behaviour as being external.

Research: internal versus external attribution

Gudjohnsson and Bownes (2002) examined the relationship between the type of offence and the attributions offenders make about their criminal acts. The research looked at:

- whether the offender made an internal versus external attribution
- whether the crime was explained in terms of a mental disposition
- whether the offender felt remorse or guilt.

Eighty criminals (20 had committed violent offences, 40 sex offences and 20 crimes against property) completed the blame attribution inventory. The offenders who had committed violent crimes were significantly more likely to make external attributions, the sex offenders felt most guilty but were also more likely to blame a mental disposition such as depression, and the offenders who had committed property crimes reported least guilt. The study concluded that violent criminals are more likely to make an external attribution for their crimes.

Cognitive distortion and minimalisation

Gibbs (1993) suggested that people use cognitive distortions to rationalise their behaviour that causes harm and distress to others. These cognitive distortions may blame others and/or mislabel one's behaviour and its consequences. Examples might be the rapist who suggests that the victim was at fault because 'she was wearing such a short dress she was obviously up for it', or the car driver who blames other motorists for his accident because 'they were all driving fast'. Another type of cognitive distortion is minimalisation, where the consequences of aggressive behaviour are minimalised or excused to protect the perpetrator from feeling guilt, for example the burglar who says that the victim 'is insured so won't miss much'.

> **Exam tip**
>
> Make sure you can explain why it is difficult to gain a valid measure of any cognitive processes that may cause crime.

Social explanations for crime – differential association theory

The theory states that criminal behaviour is learned during social interaction with others. Sutherland (1947) proposed that through

> **Revision activity**
>
> Revise social learning theory in Component 2 on page 39.

interaction with others, individuals learn the values, attitudes, techniques and motives for criminal behaviour. The principles of Sutherland's **theory of differential association** can be summarised as follows:

- Criminal behaviour is learned.
- Criminal behaviour is learned in interaction with other people in a process of communication.
- The learning of criminal behaviour occurs within intimate personal groups, for example within criminal gangs.
- When criminal behaviour is learned, learning includes techniques for committing the crime as well as the motives, drives and attitudes.
- A person becomes delinquent because they adopt the norms and values of the group in preference to the norms and values of non-criminal groups.
- Differential associations may vary in frequency, duration and intensity.
- The process of learning criminal behaviour by association with criminal groups involves all of the mechanisms that are involved in any other learning.

> **Differential association theory:** the theory that criminal behaviour is learned during social interaction with others.

Research: differential association

Farrington *et al.* (2006), starting in 1953, carried out the Cambridge Study of Delinquent Development, a longitudinal study of 511 boys from the East End of London. Results showed that 41% had criminal convictions between the ages of 10 and 60 years – 91% of those who started committing crimes aged between 10 and 13 years were reconvicted at least once, but at the age of 17, 50% of the convictions were by 5% of the sample. Farrington *et al.* identified the key risks for criminality as family criminality, poverty, poor parenting and low school achievement.

Evaluation

Social learning theory is deterministic because it suggests that criminal behaviour is the result of observation of role models but ignores the importance of free will.

Differential association theory can explain all types of offending, not just violent crime.

It is difficult to gain a valid measure of morality or thinking styles.

Differential association does not explain crimes of passion or impulsive crimes.

Farrington *et al.*'s study could be read as showing evidence for genetics as a high percentage of the sample had parents who were criminals.

Psychodynamic explanations

Psychodynamic explanations focus on the idea of:
- a weak or deviant superego
- defence mechanisms
- maternal deprivation.

> **Revision activity**
>
> Revise the psychodynamic approach in Component 2 on page 44.

Weak or deviant superego

The absence of a same-sex parent during the phallic stage means there is no chance to identify with the same-sex parent and internalise the parent's moral code, so the superego is not sufficiently punitive and does not cause guilt. Alternatively, the same-sex parent with whom the child identifies in the phallic stage is immoral so the child internalises a deviant moral code.

Defence mechanisms

Defence mechanisms are unconscious processes which defend the conscious self from unpleasant truths. For example:

- **Denial:** involves refusing to accept that an unpleasant event is happening as acknowledging it would be disturbing. For example, an abusive male may refuse to consciously acknowledge they are harming their wife/partner.
- **Sublimation:** involves redirection of primitive impulses into a more acceptable activity. For example, a person who wants to rape and murder might seek out the services of a prostitute to engage in violent sexual activity.

Revision activity

Revise attachment theory in Component 1 on page 17.

Research: maternal deprivation

John Bowlby (1946) formulated the maternal deprivation hypothesis that children who are deprived of maternal care during the critical phase of their development will suffer irreversible damage and may become affectionless psychopaths. Bowlby claimed that if a child loses a continuous and loving relationship with their mother in the first two years of their life, the results are irreversible affectionless psychopathy, intellectual retardation and delinquency. He compared 44 juvenile thieves with 44 non-thieves and found that the 'thieves group' had all experienced separation from their mother.

Evaluation

Many people without a same-sex parent with whom they can identify grow up to be perfectly law abiding.

Freud claimed greater fear in boys leads to stronger superego in boys than girls, so males should be more moral, but statistics show that males commit more crime.

The validity of the Bowlby theory is low because in longitudinal research there is a long time gap between the IV (the maternal deprivation) and the DV (delinquent behaviour). This means that other uncontrolled variables may have affected whether the person engaged in criminal behaviour.

Psychodynamic explanations are unscientific.

Dealing with offending behaviour

REVISED

Note: recidivism is the rate at which people re-offend after punishment.

Custodial sentencing

A **custodial sentence** involves the offender serving the time in either a prison or a young offender's institution. Custodial sentences are effective when they prevent recidivism. Custodial sentences aim to:

- protect the public – while in prison, criminals cannot commit dangerous crimes
- rehabilitate – help offenders change their behaviour
- show retribution – pay back the 'debt' to society
- deter – put offenders off offending.

Custodial sentence: involves the offender serving time in a prison.

Research: rates of re-offending

Cullen and Minchin (2000) tracked prisoners and found 57% of them re-offended within two years; for young males the rate was higher at 76%.

Walker and Farrington (1981) found the length of sentence made little difference to whether or not offenders re-offended.

Psychological effects of imprisonment

It is difficult to generalise the psychological effects of imprisonment because prison regimes vary and individuals cope with prison life in different ways. Bukshel and Kilmann (1980) found common reactions to imprisonment were restlessness, anxiety and sleeplessness.

Revision activity

Revise institutional aggression in prisons on page 196.

Suicide within prison

Within prison, 10% of suicides occur within the first 24 hours of imprisonment, 40% within the first month and 80% within the first year. Studies of prison suicide have highlighted the importance of both individual and institutional factors. In studies of completed suicides in England and Wales, risk factors have been identified as mental illness, a history of psychiatric contact, a history of single or multiple substance misuse, a history of self-harm, loss of social contact and relationship difficulties, victimisation by other inmates and difficulties in coping with the prison regime.

Evaluation

Recidivism rates after custodial sentences suggest that prison neither rehabilitates nor deters.

Prison can have negative psychological effects on mental health.

Loss of contacts and employment make it more difficult for the offender to stay out of trouble in the future.

Prison is sometimes referred to as a 'school for crime' and imprisonment gives younger inmates an opportunity to learn from experienced offenders.

It is difficult to measure the effectiveness of custodial sentences without in-depth longitudinal research.

Behaviour modification

Based on operant conditioning, desirable behaviours are reinforced and undesirable behaviours, such as fighting, are extinguished. A behavioural modification programme may be a token economy in which:
- the desired change in behaviour is clearly specified
- a baseline rate is measured over a period of days
- a reinforcement strategy is adopted
- all those in contact with the offender should adhere to the programme
- the offender progress is carefully monitored
- the target behaviour after treatment is compared with the baseline to measure improvement.

Revision activity

Read about token economy on page 159.

Research: behaviour modification

Cohen and Filipczak (1971) compared two groups of young male prisoners. One group was reinforced with tokens exchangeable for phone calls, tobacco, family visits, etc. and a control group did not receive treatment. The treatment group showed more desirable behaviour and less re-offending for up to two years.

Anger management

Anger management programmes in prison assume that offenders commit crimes because they cannot control their anger. Navaco (1974) described anger management as a form of cognitive behaviour therapy. The process of anger management involves three stages:

Stage 1: cognitive preparation – offenders learn to recognise feelings of anger and events that trigger their anger response.

Stage 2: skill acquisition – techniques to control anger response are taught, for example positive self-talk statements to keep calm.

Stage 3: application practice – anger-provoking situations are role played and the offender practises using learned techniques to control anger in a non-threatening environment.

The national anger management package was developed by the UK prison service in 1992. The programme is intensive and usually involves eight two-hour sessions.

> **Anger management:** anger management programmes in prison assume that offenders commit crimes because they cannot control their anger.

Research: anger management

Ireland (2000) investigated the usefulness of a group-based anger management programme with young male offenders. The treated prisoners attended 12 one-hour sessions. Pre and post programme they self-reported anger scores for an experiment group of prisoners and a control group of prisoners without treatment. The treated group showed significantly reduced anger, with 92% having improved on at least one measure and 48% having improved on two measures. It was concluded that the anger management programme successfully reduced anger and disruptive behaviour.

Evaluation

Anger management programmes are effective in reducing anger within prisons but only if they are well managed.

They give offenders insight into their anger and provide them with skills to control it.

If there is no link between anger and violent offences, the treatment will not be effective.

Anger management programmes require a high level of offender motivation so will be effective only with those who wish to change.

Revision activity

Read your test book and draw up a schedule for a typical anger management programme. How many sessions will it have? What will the offenders do during the sessions?

Exam tip

You could be asked to draw up or evaluate a behavioural modification programme. Can you explain why a token economy is a behavioural modification programme?

Restorative justice

Collaboration between offenders and victims is at the heart of restorative justice and therefore this is fundamentally different from all other forms of punishment. A meeting between victim and offender enables the offender to see the consequences of their actions and the victim to have their say. Restorative justice can be used as an alternative to prosecution, particularly in young offenders where it might serve as a final warning. The process can include face-to-face encounters and practical reparation, such as repairing a damaged garden fence.

Research: restorative justice

Sherman and Strang (2007) set out to review evidence of the effect of restorative justice, analysing 36 studies comparing restorative and conventional justice. Repeat offending was substantially reduced for some offenders. Recidivism rates were reduced for adults and young offenders. In victims, post-traumatic stress was reduced and desire for revenge was significantly lower.

Evaluation

Victims are often reluctant to meet the offender.

Some programmes identified as restorative justice schemes do not involve the victim, for example court-ordered restitution schemes.

It is difficult to measure the effectiveness of restorative justice without in-depth longitudinal research.

Typical mistake

In an exam do not state that biological explanations for criminal behaviour are reductionist because biological explanations ignore cognitive and social explanations. This is not what reductionism means.

Summary

You must be able to describe, discuss and evaluate:
- ways of measuring crime, including official statistics, victim surveys and offender surveys
- offender profiling, including the top-down approach, organised and disorganised types of offender, and the bottom-up approach, including geographical profiling
- biological explanations of offending behaviour, including historical approaches, genetic and neural explanations

- psychological explanations of offending behaviour, including Eysenck's theory of the criminal personality, cognitive explanations such as level of moral reasoning and hostile attribution bias, as well as differential association theory and psychodynamic explanations
- dealing with offending behaviour, including the aims of custodial sentencing and the psychological effects of custodial sentencing
- behaviour modification in custody, anger management and restorative justice.

Now test yourself

TESTED

1 (a) Which of these is the youngest age at which you can be charged with a crime in the UK?
   A 8
   B 12
   C 7
   D 10
  (b) Fill in the blank: Behaviour that is acceptable in one culture may be a _____ in another culture.
  (c) Briefly outline the purpose of the Crime Survey for England and Wales (CSEW).
  (d) Suggest one reason why the CSEW provides a more valid measure of crime in the UK than statistics gathered by police forces.

Exam practice answers and quick quizzes at **www.hoddereducation.co.uk/myrevisionnotes**

(e) What was the basis for the top-down approach for criminal profiling?

(f) Which of these is the correct order of procedures during a top-down profile creation?

    A   Crime classification; crime reconstruction; profile generation; data assimilation

    B   Crime classification; profile generation; data assimilation; crime reconstruction

    C   Data assimilation; crime classification; crime reconstruction; profile generation

    D   Data assimilation; crime reconstruction; crime classification; profile generation

(g) Canter (1989) outlined three aspects of criminal behaviour which may provide clues to other aspects of the criminal's everyday life. List these three factors.

(h) Canter (1989) suggested that when we study a violent crime scene, when thinking about a suspect we should consider interpersonal coherence. What does this mean?

2 (a) Is geographical profiling based on assumptions from:

    A   Biological psychology

    B   Social psychology

    C   Cognitive psychology

    D   Behaviourist psychology?

(b) What is the purpose of an offender profile?

    A   To identify the person who committed a crime

    B   To increase our understanding of violent criminals

    C   To describe the type of person who may have committed a crime

(c) Explain how geographical profiling is based on cognitive psychology.

(d) List two limitations of offender profiling.

3 (a) Which of these was not identified as a body type by Sheldon?

    A   Endomorphic

    B   Mesomorphic

    C   Lysomorphic

    D   Ectomorphic

(b) If the concordance rate for criminality is 33% for MZ male twins, can we assume that criminality is genetic? Why or why not?

(c) List two of the differences Raine et al. (2000) found when they compared the brains of murderers who pled NGRI to the brains of people who had never committed a crime.

(d) Which of these was not one of the personality traits suggested by Eysenck?

- Extrovert
- Introvert
- Neurotic
- Stable

(e) The Eysenck EPI is a psychometric test that measures personality traits. Give one reason why it is difficult to gain a valid measure of personality.

(f) Write a definition of the hostile attribution bias.

(g) Fill in the blanks:

    (i) An _____ is when a person accepts responsibility for their behaviour and sees the cause as being within themselves.

    (ii) An _____ is when a person sees the cause of their behaviour as being an external factor and so not their fault.

(h) Outline Sutherland's differential association theory.

(i) Why is the 'weak superego' theory of criminal behaviour unscientific?

4 (a) Fredd is a young offender who frequently engages in angry aggressive behaviour. Outline how Fredd's behaviour could be modified during a token economy programme.

(b) Suggest two reasons why anger management programmes may not reduce recidivism.

Answers on page 247

Exam practice

1 Give one reason why it is difficult to define crime. [2]
2 Suggest one cognitive bias shown by aggressive offenders. [2]
3 One method of offender profiling involves categorising offenders as either organised or disorganised. Explain one limitation of this method of offender profiling. [2]
4 Some research suggests that anger causes aggressive crimes. Explain one limitation of this theory. [2]
5 Prison staff compared two methods of managing aggressive behaviour in young offenders. One group of ten offenders (Group A) took part in a group anger management programme in which they participated in a one-hour session each weekday for a month. Another group of ten offenders (Group B) were treated with a token economy in which each offender was given a small reward for each pro-social act and allowed to swap each set of 10 rewards for an extra phone card, or each set of 20 rewards for an extra family visit. Five rewards were 'confiscated' for each aggressive act. The results are given in the table.

Aggressive behaviour in young offenders before and after token economy or anger management

	Aggressive acts in the week before the treatment	Aggressive acts in the week after the treatment
Group A: The ten offenders who were treated with token economy	60	45
Group B: The ten offenders who were treated with anger management	75	30

(a) What is the ratio of the aggressive acts of Group A to Group B before treatment? [2]
(b) What is the ratio of the aggressive acts of Group A to Group B after treatment? [2]
(c) In Group A, by what percentage are 'aggressive acts' lower after the token economy? [2]
(d) In Group B, by what percentage are 'aggressive acts' lower after anger management? [2]
(e) In what level of measurement are the data shown in the table? [1]
(f) Which inferential test would you use to analyse the significance of the difference between the token economy and anger management treatment? [2]
(g) Discuss the differences between token economy and anger management treatment programmes. [4]
(h) Suggest how the use of anger management programmes in prisons might benefit the economy. [4]
(i) Discuss biological explanations of offending behaviour. [16]

Answers and quick quizzes 50, 51, 52 and 53 online

ONLINE

Addiction

Describing addiction

Addiction is a repetitive habit pattern that increases the risk of disease and/or associated personal and social problems. Addictive behaviours are often experienced subjectively as a 'loss of control' – the behaviour continues to occur despite volitional attempts to abstain or moderate use. These habit patterns are typically characterised by immediate gratification (short-term reward), often coupled with delayed harmful effects (long-term costs). DSM-V includes 'substance use disorder' for drug addictions, including nicotine, and 'addictive disorders' for non-substance abuse. There is now a separate category for 'gambling disorder'.

Physical and psychological dependence

Dependence can be physical in nature and is usually experienced with addiction to substances, such as nicotine. Attempts to give up will lead to physical symptoms such as tolerance and withdrawal. It is possible to experience addiction without tolerance or withdrawal, which is still psychological dependence, for example from non-substance addiction to gambling or addiction to the internet. Additionally, individuals can experience both physical and psychological dependency – for example, the attitude and belief that they have about their smoking behaviour, such as 'smoking can reduce my stress levels'.

Tolerance

When a substance is used repeatedly over time the effects that were initially experienced will change. Once a person is addicted to a physical substance they will need an increasing amount of the substance to gain the same effect. A heroin addict will become 'tolerant' to a small amount of the drug and will need more and more to achieve the effect they initially experienced with a smaller amount. **Tolerance** is a symptom on the DSM-V to characterise substance abuse and may lead to increased amounts of the substance being consumed.

Withdrawal symptoms

Withdrawal symptoms are unpleasant feelings and physical effects that the individual suffers when they withdraw or stop the use of a substance. Symptoms can include shaking, moodiness, irritability and sleep problems, making it hard to cease substance use. Withdrawal symptoms in the past have been related to the removal of the chemical the person is addicted to. However, these effects have also been experienced by gamblers, so may be due to withdrawal of behaviours as well. Linked to tolerance, withdrawal symptoms can also be experienced when an individual tries to reduce the use of a substance to which they have become increasingly tolerant.

> **Addiction:** a repetitive habit pattern that increases despite attempts to give up the behaviour.
>
> **Physical dependence:** physiological state of adaptation to a substance, the absence of which produces symptoms and signs of withdrawal.
>
> **Psychological dependence:** an emotional state that develops as a result of an addiction to a substance or behaviour.
>
> **Tolerance:** addiction to a physical substance will lead to a need for an increasing amount of the substance to gain the same effect.
>
> **Withdrawal symptoms:** unpleasant feelings and physical effects that an individual suffers when they withdraw from or stop the use of a substance.

> **Revision activity**
>
> Write a glossary of the key terms for addiction.

> **Exam tip**
>
> When outlining key terms for describing addiction, be concise and provide a specific example from an addiction to show understanding.

Risk factors in the development of addiction

There is a need to identify the risk factors that can lead to the development of addictions in order to prevent or minimise their effects. This is particularly relevant as we have seen in the Eating behaviour section through dependence, tolerance and withdrawal. Not initiating the behaviour in the first place is preferable to trying to give up in the future.

Genetic vulnerability

The genetic model suggests that there is a genetic disposition towards addictive behaviour and that an addictive personality may be genetically determined. Research in this area analyses the genetic structure of the individual and their role in the prevalence of addictive behaviours. Additionally, research has focused on twin studies to show the genetic link between identical (MZ) and non-identical (DZ) twins. As MZ twins share exactly the same genetic make-up while DZ twins share only 50%, it allows psychologists to make useful comparisons measured using concordance rates as percentages. For example, is there a greater risk for becoming a smoker if you have parents who smoke?

Research: risk factors of addiction

Hughes (1986) compared two groups of adolescents. One group lived with family members who smoked, the other group lived with family members who did not smoke. Findings showed that 52% of those who lived with smokers smoked compared with 20% of those living with non-smokers.

Hall *et al.* (2002) reported on a recent adoption study which found a strong association between adoptees' smoking and that of their biological siblings. This association also exists between male adoptees and their biological mothers.

Stress

Stress is the perceived ability we have to cope with the demands placed on us during our lives. There is evidence to show a correlation between stress and addiction. This includes both extreme traumatic events and the everyday low-level stress that many of us experience. Post-traumatic stress disorder may lead to high levels of alcohol and drug addiction. Additionally, initiation of smoking or drinking alcohol may be due to the belief that the substance may help reduce everyday stress levels. It is suggested that addicts who are stressed are less likely to be able to give up the source of their addiction (Cleveland and Harris, 2010).

Research: stress and addiction

Nida (1999) found that people report that they smoke, drink, use drugs, gamble, etc. as a means of coping with daily hassles.

Cohen and Lichtenstein (1990) found that smoking actually increases stress levels, suggesting that it is an irrational belief that smoking decreases stress levels.

Driessen *et al.* (2008) found that 30% of drug addicts and 15% of alcoholics suffered from post-traumatic stress disorder.

Personality

Personality is defined as a set of characteristics that combines to make us who we are; it is an individualistic approach to explaining our behaviour. The trait approach to personality would define the risk of addiction as due to an individual having an addictive personality and measure the risk by identifying the specific traits. These include novelty seeking, sensation seeking and impulsivity. Eysenck's Personality Inventory (EPI) has been used to measure levels of psychoticism and neuroticism, both of which include the traits linked to addiction. One theory of personality and addiction is the tri-dimensional theory (Cloninger, 1987) identifying three personality traits that increase the risk of addiction: novelty seeking, harm avoidance and reward dependence.

Research: personality and addiction

Stein et al. (1987) found people with certain behavioural traits may be more disposed to addiction. For example, people addicted to drugs have been found to be more rebellious, impulsive and sensation seeking than those not addicted.

Loxton et al. (2008) found that chronic gamblers score higher on impulsivity than non-gamblers.

Family influences and peers

Young children are at risk from drug dependency in later life if their parents are ineffective and lack nurturing skills. The family's attitudes towards recreational drugs such as nicotine can also influence adolescent behaviour – for example, if parents have a positive attitude to smoking this can be a risk factor for adolescents to initiate smoking. Family and peers provide ideal role models on which to shape behaviour, particularly if reinforced as suggested by social learning theory. Peer pressure has been linked to first-time use of nicotine and recreational drugs. This is more prevalent in the teenage years and decreases as we get older.

Revision activity

With your friends, write your own scenarios of people with addictions and include elements of the risk factors in the description. Swap with your friends and answer each other's questions.

Research: family and peer influence

Moolchan et al. (2000) found that 75% of teenagers who smoke have at least one parent who smokes.

Wardle et al. (2007) found the prevalence of gambling was higher in individuals who had parents who gambled.

McAlistar (1984) found increased levels of smoking were linked to peer pressure and encouragement which is rewarding.

Evaluation

One problem with genetic explanations for addictive behaviour is that they are focused on the nature side of the nature/nurture debate and ignore environmental influences on addictive behaviour.

Alternatively, family and peers only suggest environmental risks.

Another weakness is that factors suggest a vulnerability and a link between factors and addictive behaviour, which means there is no cause and effect established.

Identifying risk factors such as the influence of family and peers has application as they can lead to educational campaigns in schools to help reduce the initiation of substance abuse in vulnerable teenagers.

Exam tip

When applying risk factors to scenario questions ensure you highlight all the important information and refer to the highlighted sections in your answer.

Explanations for nicotine addiction

Nicotine is a drug found in tobacco, mostly associated with smoking cigarettes. Nicotine addiction remains a serious cause for concern among health professionals as it has a high level of risk to the physical health of the individual and society as a whole. Nicotine addiction to the substance is found on the DSM-IV and is characterised as follows:

- Large quantities of tobacco over a long period of time are consumed, with unsuccessful efforts to quit or reduce intake of tobacco.
- There is a tolerance for nicotine, as indicated by the need for increasingly larger doses in order to obtain the desired effect and a noticeably diminished effect from using the same amounts of nicotine.
- There are withdrawal symptoms upon cessation of use, as indicated by the onset of typical nicotine-associated withdrawal symptoms and more nicotine or a substituted drug is taken to alleviate those symptoms.

Brain neurochemistry, including the role of dopamine

Neurotransmitters are brain chemicals necessary for the transfer of information within the nervous system: they transmit chemical messages across synapses. Nicotine affects the nervous system by increasing dopamine and levels of acetylcholine, a neurotransmitter which appears to be involved in reward processes. There are several dopamine systems in the brain; the one which seems to be most important for motivational processes is the 'mesolimbic dopamine system'. In order to maintain mood states the mesolimbic dopamine system releases small amounts of dopamine in the synaptic cleft. Biologically, nicotine has been shown to increase dopamine release within the brain reward system, giving the user a positive feeling. This positive feeling continues as long as the smoker maintains addictive smoking behaviour.

Neurochemistry and addiction

Altman *et al.* (1996) suggested that both alcohol and nicotine affect the nervous system by increasing dopamine levels.

Liebman and Cooper (1989) suggested that people who are susceptible to addictions might have inherited a more sensitive mesolimbic dopamine pathway.

Lerman *et al.* (1999) have shown that people with a particular gene are less likely to take up smoking than those without it. The gene, SLC6A3-9, works in the dopamine system.

Evaluation

Biological explanations explain individual differences, for example why one person may be more susceptible to addiction than another, and also why some people may find it more difficult to give up.

A change in brain chemistry explains why people become tolerant to a drug or experience withdrawal effects.

We do not yet have enough understanding of individual neurotransmitters and their roles in brain/behaviour function to be able to explain addiction and the effects of nicotine.

The neurochemistry explanation for addiction is reductionist as it focuses on only one neurotransmitter, dopamine, as the cause of addiction.

Typical mistake

When evaluating an 'explanation', writing a list of points that may be relevant but not explaining how they are strengths or weaknesses.

Learning theory as applied to smoking behaviour, including reference to cue reactivity

Learning theory suggests that smoking behaviour, as all behaviour, is learned through the process of association and reinforcement. Smoking is initiated and the smoker associates the positive feelings experienced with the behaviour. Smoking leads to changes in brain chemistry that provide rewards, leading to the smoking behaviour being repeated (positive reinforcement). Additionally, operant conditioning can explain why smokers who try to stop will relapse as they will experience withdrawal symptoms and will smoke again to remove the negative symptoms (negative reinforcement). **Cue reactivity** is linked to classical conditioning and explains how the smoker associates the behaviour with a variety of cues that strengthen the addiction. These may include lighters, ash trays and even locations where the behaviour usually occurs, such as at a bar. This results in the associated objects or locations leading to the conditioned response in the absence of the smoking behaviour.

> **Cue reactivity:** a learned response to situations and environment cues related to addictive substances or behaviours.

Smoking can also be explained by social learning theory: children and adolescents often model the behaviour of family, peers and the media. Learning is through imitation, observation and reinforcement. A teenager may start smoking because they have observed and imitated the smoking behaviour of their parents, peers or through the media; family and friends provide ideal role models. In the case of peers, smoking may be initiated to gain approval (positive reinforcement) from their peers.

Smoking as learned behaviour

Engelmann *et al.* **(2012**) provided findings from a meta-analysis of studies using fMRIs of smokers who were shown smoking-related cues compared with neutral cues. The smoking-related cues caused a larger neural response.

Akers and Lee (1996) found that modelling the behaviour of peers was one of the variables that influenced smoking initiation and abstinence in 254 adolescents in the USA.

Evaluation

Learning theory has application as it shows that in order to cease smoking the smoker needs to not only avoid the nicotine but also the objects and situations associated with the smoking behaviour.

Learning theory does not take into consideration individual differences as many people are able to quit smoking and do not associate in the way cue reactivity suggests.

Exam tip

As with other topic areas, the best way to evaluate theories as applied to smoking behaviour is to use evidence that supports and counter evidence. To make evaluation effective you need to show how the findings of the research support the theories.

Typical mistake

Providing a general description of social learning theory that could be used to explain any of the options, particularly when including Bandura's original research.

Explanations for gambling addiction

Gambling addiction is becoming more of a problem to individuals and society with the increase in accessibility of gambling opportunities. According to the DSM-V it now has its own category as a disorder and is seen as a 'persistent and recurrent problematic gambling behaviour leading to clinically significant impairment or distress including:

- need to gamble with increasing amounts of money in order to achieve the desired excitement
- preoccupation with gambling, for example having persistent thoughts of reliving past gambling experiences, and thinking of ways to get money in order to gamble
- has lost a significant relationship, job, or educational or career opportunity because of gambling.'

Learning theory as applied to gambling

Learning theory suggests that addictive behaviours are learned habits that are acquired through the process of classical conditioning, operant conditioning and social learning. Learning through association of the excitement experienced with gambling, if continued, will lead to strengthening the association. Gambling continues through the process of operant conditioning, which suggests that behaviour that is rewarded is more likely to be repeated. In gambling, the rewards can be either tangible in the form of money or intangible with the excitement of the potential win. Skinner (1953) found that varying rates of reinforcement affected the strength of the change in behaviour. This is known as **partial reinforcement** and the reward or punishment does not happen each time the behaviour occurs. In the case of gambling there is no way to predict when you will win or lose. Slot machines are manufactured to follow this format to ensure gamblers will continue to play. **Variable-ratio** schedules occur when a response is reinforced after an unpredictable number of responses. Scratch cards are a good example of a variable-ratio schedule of reward as there is no way to predict a winning pattern, and if your friend buys five cards and loses, the next card could be the winner. In a lab setting, this might involve delivering food pellets to a rat after one bar press, again after four bar presses, and a third pellet after a further two bar presses.

Meyer *et al.* (2004) found that problem gamblers' heart rates were significantly higher compared with those of non-problem gamblers, which shows that they have higher levels of excitement associated with gambling.

Positive reinforcement: the consequence of an action that is rewarding and increases the likelihood of the behaviour being repeated.

Partial reinforcement: any variation in the reinforcement of a behaviour. This can be fixed or variable

Fixed interval reinforcement: behaviour is reinforced after a fixed time interval providing at least one correct response has been made.

Fixed ratio reinforcement: behaviour is reinforced only after the behaviour has occurred for a specified number of times.

Variable-ratio reinforcement: behaviour is reinforced after an unpredictable number of times, for example fruit machine gambling.

Evaluation

Behavioural explanations have application as they suggest therapies are effective for addictive behaviours as part of CBT.

Learning explanations are based on a simple stimulus–response model and ignore the cognitive aspects of human behaviour, although most of the research evidence is based on the use of non-human animals, which cannot be generalised to humans.

Revision activity

Go back over operant conditioning in Component 2 on page 37 to remind yourself of the process of learning and the partial and variable learning schedules.

Cognitive theory as applied to gambling

The cognitive approach to psychology suggests that faulty thinking and cognitive biases are the cause of maladaptive behaviours found in gambling addiction. A **cognitive bias** is an error in thinking where a situation is explained through your subjective viewpoint. The faulty thinking involved in continuing these behaviours is that you will win (eventually) and balance the risk of losing. Rational choice theory suggests that people behave as they do as a result of weighing up the costs and benefits of a behaviour and then make a rational choice based on that evaluation. Gambling behaviour is maintained due to 'cognitive biases' as the gambler misjudges the amount that they have won or lost. This faulty thinking may also lead to addicts focusing on the positive features of gambling, such as winning, rather than the negative factors, such as losing. Frequent gamblers are more likely to have the 'illusion of control' over the outcome of events – for example, they believe that they are more likely to throw a six on a dice if they throw it themselves.

> **Cognitive bias:** a systematic error in thinking where situations are explained through your subjective viewpoint.

Research: Cognitive bias and gambling

Griffiths (1994) was interested in the cognitive biases that gamblers make which may encourage them to continue to gamble. The findings support the argument that regular fruit machine users do use cognitive biases when gambling.

Strickland et al. (2006) 37 participants – 10 frequent, 11 infrequent and 16 non-gamblers – completed the Gamblers' Belief Questionnaire (GBQ). Findings showed that frequent gamblers were more likely to hold beliefs consistent with cognitive bias and the illusion of control.

Ratelle et al. (2004) found that gambling addicts had persistent thoughts about gambling and had poorer concentration on daily tasks.

Evaluation

Cognitive explanations have application as they suggest cognitive behavioural therapy is effective for addictive behaviours.

Cause and effect of cognitive bias cannot be measured. Irrationality cannot predict addictive behaviour consistently.

Counter evidence from Griffiths has found that regular players do not have to think about what they are doing – they act 'on automatic pilot' – showing that cognition does not play a major role in maintaining the behaviour.

Revision activity

Draw a mind map for both learning theory and cognitive theory as applied to addiction to gambling.

Exam tip

You will have studied learning and cognitive theories throughout the A-level course. Take care when answering questions to link specifically to gambling addiction rather than using generic explanations that could be applied to other topics.

Reducing addiction

REVISED

Drug therapy

There are two main types of drug therapies: an **'agonist'** substitute or an 'antagonist' substitute. Addiction to nicotine is treated using an agonist substitution method where a safer alternative is provided to patients (nicotine replacement therapy). Nicotine medications such as nicotine

> **Agonist substitute:** a safer alternative to the substance that has caused the addiction, for example nicotine patches.

gum, patches and nasal sprays mimic or replace the effects of nicotine derived from tobacco and they help people to stop smoking in several ways. Once the habit of smoking has subsided, the dose in the gum or the patch is gradually reduced over a period of several months to help the person give up cigarettes.

A second biological method used in the treatment of substance addiction involves antagonist treatments, where drugs are given that block or counter the effects of the drug that the person is addicted to. These drugs work by blocking the action of neurochemicals that provide the person with rewarding feelings when they take the drug. **Antagonist** substitution is available for nicotine addiction as well as for a range of other addictive behaviour.

> **Antagonist substitute:** drugs that block or counter the effects of the drug to which the person is addicted.

Drug treatment for problem gambling

Zack et al. (2003) found that the effects of gambling on the brain are very similar to the effects of a psycho-stimulant such as amphetamine. They showed successfully that a dose of amphetamine given to problem gamblers can stimulate their motivation to gamble. They went on to indicate that an agonist that targets the action of these drugs may well be useful in helping gamblers control their motivations to gamble.

Kim and Grant (2001) showed that antagonist drugs could reduce thoughts about gambling, the urge to gamble and, in high doses, gambling behaviour itself.

Evaluation

Substitute drugs may help stabilise behaviour – methadone maintenance has been shown to be safe and very effective on a variety of measures, including preventing illegal drug use.

Studies have shown that both agonist and antagonist treatments have been very successful for smokers, alcohol and drug addicts.

Biological interventions may ignore the underlying reasons for addiction, so although the symptoms may be being treated, the underlying reasons for the addiction may be being ignored.

Addicts may return to their addictive behaviour when drug therapy is stopped. It is highly likely that the addict will return to the addiction if this is the only method of treatment used.

Behavioural interventions

Classical conditioning treatments for intervention include aversion therapy and the less extreme covert sensitisation. The therapies focus on cue exposure and relapse triggers such as sight and smell of alcohol/drugs. **Aversion therapy** is the pairing of an aversive stimulus with a specific addiction response. For example, alcoholics may be precribed an emetic so that if they drink alcohol, they will vomit. This will lead to nausea and vomiting being associated with alcohol, discouraging alcoholics from drinking. Covert sensitisation is a milder form of aversion therapy where the addict will use imagery to create a negative association with the behaviour. For example, a sugar addict may use imagery to visualise a slice of chocolate cake and then imagine it covered it covered in mud. If they carry out the exercise repeatedly, this should lead to the desire to eat chocolate cake lessening.

> **Aversion therapy:** the pairing of an aversive (unpleasant) stimulus with an addiction response.

Exam practice answers and quick quizzes at **www.hoddereducation.co.uk/myrevisionnotes**

Behavioural treatment for problem gambling

Meyer and Chesser (1970) found that when alcoholics were precribed a drug that caused nausea if combined with alcohol, 50% became teetotal in one year, which was a higher percentage compared with the control group of non-alcoholics.

McConaghy (1983) measured the effectiveness of covert sensitisation compared with electric shock aversion therapy for treating gambling addiction. After one year the group who had received the covert sensitisation were more likely to have reduced their gambling behaviours (90%) compared with the traditional aversion therapy (30%).

Evaluation

A strength of classical conditioning is that all of the therapies focus on cue exposure and relapse triggers. By repeated exposure to relapse triggers in the absence of the addiction, the addict learns to stay addiction-free in high-risk situations.

Another strength of covert sensitisation is that it provides a less extreme treatment for addiction and a more appropriate and ethical method than aversion therapy.

There is evidence to suggest that treating the symptoms means that the underlying problem is still present and that other addictive behaviours can replace the one that has ceased (Griffiths, 1995).

Another weakness is that once the therapy stops, the addiction could return.

Revision activity

Write one point of comparison between aversion therapy and covert sensitisation as behavioural interventions to reduce addiction.

Cognitive behaviour therapy (CBT)

CBT is a psychological technique used in the treatment of many kinds of psychological problems. For instance, it may be employed when someone feels anxious about flying, or when someone is suffering with mild depression. Essentially the goal of CBT is to help the client think differently about the object or behaviour that causes them difficulty. Smoking and drinking are both behaviours that people may seek psychological help to overcome. In both cases the addict may be helped to change their thoughts and beliefs about their addictive behaviours, with the aim of helping them stay away from such behaviours in the future. The techniques used include exploring the positive and negative consequences of continued use, and self-monitoring to recognise **cravings** early on. They might also be used to help the person recognise the situations where they may be at high risk of relapse, for instance stressful times. Once these high-risk situations have been identified, coping strategies can be learned. Anticipating problems addicts are likely to meet and helping them develop effective coping strategies is a key element of this approach. Research indicates that the skills individuals learn through relapse prevention therapy remain after the completion of treatment.

CBT: A psychological technique used in the treatment of psychological problems.

Craving: a powerful desire for a substance or taking part in an addictive behaviour. It can be physiological or psychological.

Cognitive treatment for problem gambling

Hajek et al. (2005) identified relapse prevention CBT as useful in helping people remain off cigarettes once they had managed to give up, while Echeburua et al. (2000) noted its value in helping pathological gamblers.

Carroll et al.'s (1994) research indicated that the skills individuals learn through relapse prevention therapy remain after the completion of therapy, suggesting CBT is an effective therapy for addiction.

Evaluation

A strength of using cognitive behavioural therapy for addictions is that the therapy can be tailored to the individual person compared with drug treatments that are more generalised.

A weakness of CBT is that the addiction can return once the therapy ceases.

Another weakness of CBT is that it may not be suitable for all addicts – for example, it may be more effective for addiction to gambling than to nicotine.

Exam tip

When explaining therapies to reduce addiction, ensure you show how they reduce addictive behaviour and make use of examples in your answer.

Typical mistake

When describing ways to reduce addictive behaviour such as CBT, drugs or behavioural therapies, not linking them directly to addiction, just describing them in a general way.

The application of theories of behaviour change to addictive behaviour

REVISED

The theory of planned behaviour (TPB)

The theory of planned behaviour is a cognitive theory that can explain why addiction occurs. It is influenced by our intention to behave in a certain way. Intention has three main factors: behavioural attitude, subjective norms and the perception an individual has over their behavioural control. Attitudes are the beliefs we have about a behaviour and can be positive or negative. Attitudes and intentions are underpinned by subjective norms and perceived ideas we have about how a behaviour will be viewed by others and by society as a whole. Finally, the more control the individual believes they have over a behaviour, the stronger their intention to actually perform that behaviour.

For example, for an individual wanting to make behavioural changes to stop smoking:

- **Personal attitudes:** an individual wants to give up smoking as they may hold the belief that smoking is a negative behaviour and they need to quit.
- **Subjective norm:** the individual may perceive that their family and friends have a negative attitude to smoking and are disapproving of their behaviour.
- **Behavioural intention:** their own attitude and the belief they have about the disapproval of friends and family leads to the intention to stop smoking.
- **Behavioural control:** the individual believes they have control over their behaviour and the likelihood is they will be successful in stopping smoking.
- **Behaviour:** the individual stops smoking.

Addiction and theory of planned behaviour (TBT)

Marcoux and Shope (1997) investigated the potential of TPB for predicting the use and misuse of alcohol among schoolchildren.

Goodie (2005) found that there are individual differences between addicts and non-addicts in terms of their perceived control – for example, gamblers were less affected by their level of control in betting decisions than non-problem gamblers.

Godin *et al.* (2006) examined the extent to which the TPB could explain smoking intentions and behaviours in adults intending to give up smoking. The researchers found that perceived behavioural control was the most important predictor of behaviour.

Evaluation

Ogden (2004) suggested that asking participants about their thought processes after the event may not directly identify how someone was actually thinking in the first place.

There has been criticism that the theory of planned behaviour is limited to conscious and deliberate behaviours and does not predict behaviours that are not consciously intended, including addictive behaviours.

The model fails to take into consideration that we may intend to stop an addictive behaviour though may not succeed.

Typical mistake

When answering exam questions that include a stimulus, you will lose many marks if you do not refer explicitly to the scenario presented in the question.

Prochaska's six-stage model of behaviour change

Prochaska *et al.* (1992) suggested that smokers commonly make three or four action attempts before they reach the maintenance stage. The Stages of Change Model (Prochaska, 1992) identifies an individual's 'readiness for change' and tries to get them to a position where they are highly motivated to change their behaviour.

- **Pre-contemplation stage:** the person has no intention of changing their behaviour and probably does not even perceive that they have a problem.
- **Contemplation stage:** the person is aware that they have a problem and thinks they should do something about it. This is related to the readiness the individual has to make the necessary changes to their behaviour, which may never happen.
- **Preparation stage:** the person is intending to take action in the near future and may well have already started to do something. This is an important stage in ensuring the individual is successful.
- **Action stage:** the individual will make the necessary changes to their behaviour. They will make changes to their situation and environment to help overcome their addiction. The action stage happens as soon as the individual alters their behaviour and gives up the addiction. This stage lasts for six months.
- **Maintenance stage:** the individual takes all the steps necessary to prevent relapse and to consolidate any of the changes they have made. The maintenance stage is after the individual is successful in abstaining from their addiction for more than six months.

Revision activity

Evaluation

One strength is that the model provides a holistic and dynamic perspective for behavioural change that can be applied to addiction.

One problem with the model is that due to the complex explanation of behaviour it is not a testable model, which reduces the validity.

One problem with Prochaska and TPB is that both models rely on self-report to measure the components and may be affected by response bias.

Revision activity

Draw a flow chart for both the theory of planned behaviour and Prochaska's six-stage model of behaviour change.

Exam tip

When applying the models of behavioural change to addiction, ensure you provide examples to show understanding.

Summary

You must be able to demonstrate knowledge and understanding of:
- describing addiction – physical and psychological dependence, tolerance and withdrawal syndrome
- risk factors in the development of addiction, including genetic vulnerability, stress, personality, family influences and peers
- explanations for nicotine addiction – brain neurochemistry, including the role of dopamine, and learning theory as applied to smoking behaviour, including reference to cue reactivity
- explanations for gambling addiction – learning theory as applied to gambling, including reference to partial and variable reinforcement; cognitive theory as applied to gambling, including reference to cognitive bias
- reducing addiction – drug therapy; behavioural interventions, including aversion therapy and covert sensitisation; cognitive behaviour therapy
- the application of the theory of planned behaviour and Prochaska's six-stage model of behaviour change.

Now test yourself

TESTED

1 Using Prochaska's six-stage model of behaviour change, fill in the blanks in the following sentences:
   (a) _____ is the stage where the person is intending to take action in the near future and may well have already started to do something.
   (b) _____ is the stage where the person has no intention of changing their behaviour and probably does not even perceive that they have a problem.
   (c) _____ is the stage where people change their behaviour, or their experience, or their environment so that they can overcome their problem.
   (d) _____ is the stage where the person works to prevent a relapse and to consolidate the changes they have made.
   (e) _____ is the stage where the person is aware that they have a problem and thinks they should do something about it.
2 Outline one explanation for nicotine addiction.
3 Outline the difference between learning theory and cognitive theory of gambling addiction.
4 (a) Outline evidence to support cognitive bias in addiction to gambling.
   (b) Evaluate evidence to support cognitive bias in addiction to gambling.
5 Explain the following terms:
   (a) Physical dependence.
   (b) Psychological dependence.
   (c) Withdrawal.
   (d) Tolerance.
6 Briefly outline two risk factors in the development of addiction.
7 Outline one strength of the drug treatment for reducing addiction.
8 Evaluate the learning theory as applied to smoking.

Answers on page 248

Exam practice

1 Explain one strength and one weakness for cognitive explanations for gambling addiction. [4]
2 Which of the following is not part of the theory of planned behaviour? [1]
   A Attitude
   B Subjective norm
   C Readiness
   D Intention
3 Explain stress as a risk factor in the development of addiction. [4]
4 Evaluate behavioural interventions to reduce addictive behaviour. [6]
5 Charmaine has always enjoyed new and exciting recreational activities such as white water rafting and visiting funfairs. A group of her friends recently suggested she join in an online bingo site. Now Charmaine has become a regular user and it is taking up all of her spare time.
   (a) Briefly outline risk factors related to Charmaine's addiction to gambling. [4]
   (b) Explain how cognitive behavioural therapy can be used to reduce her addiction. [4]
   (c) Evaluate the use of cognitive behavioural therapy to reduce her addiction. [4]
6 Discuss explanations for addiction to nicotine. [16]

Answers and quick quizzes 66, 67, 68 and 69 online

ONLINE

Now test yourself answers

Component 1: Social influence

1 (a) Internalisation occurs when a person conforms because he or she believes that a group norm for behaviour is 'right'.

(b) Normative social influence occurs when a person agrees with the opinions of others because he or she wishes to be accepted by them.

(c) Identification occurs when an individual conforms to the role that society expects them to play but does not change their private opinion.

(d) Majority influence occurs when a person's attitude is affected by the views of the dominant group.

(e) Compliance occurs when a person conforms to the majority opinion but does not agree with it.

(f) Informational social influence occurs when people look to others for information and may agree with the majority view.

(g) Minority influence takes place when a consistent minority changes the attitudes and/or behaviour of an individual.

(h) Deindividuation occurs when a person loses their sense of self-identity.

2 (a) FALSE – the emphasis is on social power.

(b) TRUE

(c) TRUE

(d) TRUE

(e) TRUE

(f) TRUE

(g) FALSE – they were not told the true purpose of the study.

(h) TRUE

(i) TRUE

(j) FALSE – Adorno gives a dispositional explanation.

3 (a) Authoritarian personality, external locus of control.

(b) Self-confidence, internal locus of control, high IQ.

(c) Being in a large group, being raised in a collectivist culture.

(d) The person giving the order has no legitimate authority; the person giving the order has low social status; the person giving the order is not physically present; other people refuse to obey.

(e) B

4 (a) Minority influence eventually changed attitudes to same-sex relationships.

(b) Consistency; they enter into discussion and avoid being too dogmatic; they take action in support of their principles (for example, take part in protest marches).

(c) The Moscovici study is a laboratory experiment and, in controlled conditions in a lab, people may be more likely to be influenced to change their opinions about the colour of a slide – which is not something they would have strong beliefs about. Persuading female students that a bluish slide is green is not representative of the effect of a minority opinion in everyday life.

Component 1: Memory

1 (a) STM has limited capacity, approximately 7–9 pieces of information, but LTM has unlimited capacity. Information in STM has limited duration, about 30 seconds, but information in LTM may last a lifetime.

(b) The primacy effect is when the first items from a list of information are remembered better and the recency effect is when the last items of information from a list are remembered better.

(c) The primacy–recency effect supports the multi-store model because the primacy effect happens because the first items of information have been transferred to LTM, and the recency effect happens because the last items of information are still in STM.

(d) Episodic memory is the memory of autobiographical events that are the collection of personal experiences that occurred at particular times and places. For example, remembering your 16th birthday is an episodic memory.

(e) Procedural memory stores information on how to perform certain procedures, such as walking, talking, typing, playing the piano, riding a bike. Procedural memories do not involve conscious thought.

(f) Semantic memory allows us to give meaning to words and sentences and to understand language.

(g) The central executive to process information from all sensory routes; the articulatory–phonological loop to process speech-based information; the visuospatial working area where spatial and visual information is processed.

(h) The articulatory–phonological loop processes speech-based information. The phonological store focuses on incoming speech and the articulatory process focuses on producing speech.

(i) The working memory model assumes that the articulatory–phonological loop has limited capacity. The interference task involves a participant being asked to perform two tasks that use the articulatory–phonological loop at the same time, such as reading a book while singing a song. If performance on both tasks is affected, this is because the articulatory–phonological loop cannot cope with both tasks at the same time and suggests that the working memory model is accurate.

2 (a) Retrieval failure is where the information is in long-term memory but cannot be remembered because the retrieval cues are not present, possibly because memory cannot be accessed as the context is not similar to when the memory was created.

(b) The limited capacity of short-term memory – holding seven plus or minus two chunks of information.

(c) Retroactive interference occurs when you forget a previously learned task due to the learning of a new task and would have occurred because after Ayesha revised her Spanish she revised her Italian vocabulary. Spanish and Italian are similar languages and revising the Italian vocabulary may have disrupted the memory of the Spanish, causing retroactive interference when Ayesha forgot the Spanish due to the learning of the Italian.

(d) When we store a new memory we also store information about the situation, called retrieval cues. When we come to the same situation again, these retrieval cues can trigger the memory of the situation.

(e) External retrieval cues are in the environment, for example the smell of the place where the memory was formed, but internal retrieval cues are the state inside the person, such as the mood we were in when the memory was formed.

(f) The students who were tested in the same room where they learned the city words would have had the same external retrieval cues to help them remember the words, but the students who were tested in a different room would have had no matching retrieval cues to help them remember the names of the cities.

3 (a) A leading question is a question that suggests a certain kind of answer. For example, 'Was the cat you saw black or ginger?' suggests that there actually was a cat.

(b) In Experiment 1, the participants who were asked the question using the verb 'smashed' reported the cars travelling at 9mph faster than the participants asked how fast the cars were travelling when they 'contacted' each other.

(c) The meaning of the verb smashed implies breakage. Loftus and Palmer suggest that when the students were asked to estimate 'how fast the cars were travelling when they smashed into each other', the meaning of the word smashed as breakage was added to the memory, creating a false memory that broken glass was shown in the film.

(d) Sample size – in Experiment 1 there were 5 groups of 9 students, 45 in all; in Experiment 2 there were 3 groups of 50 students, 150 in all.

Control group – there was no control group in Experiment 1, but in Experiment 2 there was a control group who were not asked a question about speed.

Measuring the DV – in Experiment 1 the effect of the leading question was measured immediately; in Experiment 2 there was a delay and the effect of the leading question was measured a week later.

(e) Low real-world realism – the witnesses were questioned immediately, the film was a 2D event rather than a 3D event, and there would have been no shock or surprise as there would have been for a witness to a real car crash. Also the participants were all university students who may have had better memories than most due to continual learning, thus a biased sample, all of which lead to low ecological validity.

(f) Duration of event – the longer we watch, the more likely we are to remember details.

Violence distraction – people have a better memory for non-violent events.

The amount of time between an event and recall – the longer the time, the worse the recall.

Anxiety – highly emotional events may be either more memorable or less memorable than everyday events.

(g) During the cognitive interview the witness is encouraged to relax and recall everything they can remember, no matter how trivial the information appears. During recall the police do not ask questions or interrupt the witness. The witness is asked to reimagine the sensory experience of the event and to describe the event from the perspective of another person, and in reverse, from the end to the beginning. Because the witness reimagines the sensory context and the timeline of the event, retrieval cues may trigger memories of the event.

Component 1: Attachment

1 (a) Attachment is a close emotional relationship between two people characterised by mutual affection and a desire to maintain closeness.

(b) Interactional synchrony is behaviour between caregiver and infant that is reciprocal – where the behaviour of the caregiver is a response to the behaviour of the infant or produced to elicit a response from the infant.

(c) Mother–infant pairs who were developing secure attachments were observed to interact in a reciprocal and mutually rewarding manner, but those developing insecure relationships were characterised by interactions in which mothers were minimally involved or unresponsive to infant signals.

(d) Up to three months of age, most babies respond equally to any caregiver. After four months, the baby learns to distinguish primary and secondary caregivers but will accept care from anyone. After seven months, the baby shows special preference for a single attachment figure and shows fear of strangers. After nine months, the baby becomes increasingly independent and forms several attachments.

(e) After the age of nine months.

(f) One was made of wire and gave milk and one was covered in soft terry towelling cloth and gave milk.

(g) Harlow supports the evolutionary theory of attachment (nature), in that it is the sensitive response and security of the caregiver that is important rather than the provision of food.

2 (a) Through imprinting, the chick immediately recognises and follows its parent, but attachment develops over time and up to the age of three months a baby does not recognise a special caregiver.

(b) Because it shows the similarities and differences between human and animal behaviour.

(c) Because human behaviour is complex and influenced by culture and society, so you cannot generalise from research involving animals to human behaviour.

(d) For behaviourist psychologists, attachments are learned and the basis for this learning is the provision of food. A baby forms an attachment because it learns to associate the feeder with the comfort of being fed and, through the process of classical conditioning, learns to find contact with the mother comforting.

(e) The caregiver carries the baby into a room, puts him/her on the floor and then sits in a chair and does not interact unless the baby seeks attention.

A stranger enters the room and talks with the caregiver, then approaches the baby with a toy.

The caregiver leaves. If the baby plays, the stranger observes unobtrusively. If the baby is passive, the stranger tries to interest him/her in a toy, and if the baby shows distress, the stranger tries to comfort him/her.

The caregiver returns and the stranger leaves. After the baby begins to play, the caregiver leaves and the baby is left alone briefly.

The stranger re-enters the room and if the baby plays, the stranger observes unobtrusively, offers the child a toy, or if the baby shows distress, the stranger tries to comfort him/her.

The caregiver returns and the stranger leaves.

(f) Separation anxiety; willingness to explore; stranger anxiety; reunion behaviour.

(g) The evolutionary theory of attachment is adaptive because it suggests that infants come into the world biologically pre-programmed to form attachments with others because this will help them to survive. The role of attachment is adaptive, as it promotes survival by maintaining closeness between infant and caregiver and provides the opportunity for learning through imitation.

(h) Because he suggested that infants are born with an innate drive to form attachments and that infants possess innate social releasers, such as smiles, that facilitate the caregiver's attachment to them.

(i) In the Strange Situation, a securely attached infant shows some anxiety when their caregiver departs but plays independently and is easily soothed, and greets the caregiver's return with enthusiasm. An insecurely attached infant may be indifferent or distressed when the caregiver leaves, may explore less and when the caregiver returns may not be easily soothed.

3 (a) Intelligence of parents.

(b) France.

(c) (i) Bowlby said infants form monotropic, rather than multiple, attachments.

(ii) Harlow said that continuous maternal care is essential to an infant's psychological health.

(iii) Lorenz said through imprinting chicks attach to the first moving object they see.

Component 1: Psychopathology

1 (a) It means that, if a type of behaviour is normally distributed, then people whose behaviour is more than two standard deviations above or below the mean will be defined as 'abnormal'.

(b) We are saying that a person whose behaviour does not fit in with social norms or meet social expectations is, or will be described as, abnormal.

(c) Any three from: a positive self-attitude and high self-esteem; a drive to realise self-potential; the ability to cope with stress; being in control and making your own decisions; an accurate perception of reality and the ability to feel for others; the ability to adapt to changes in one's environment.

(d) OCD, agoraphobia, arachnophobia (fear of spiders), claustrophobia (fear of enclosed spaces).

(e) Those who suffer from OCD have a persistent fear of a specific object or situation and recognise that the fear experienced is excessive. Exposure to the fear-provoking stimulus produces a rapid anxiety response, and the sufferer avoids the phobic stimulus to the extent that the phobic reactions interfere with their life.

(f) Diagnosis of unipolar depression requires five or more symptoms, including, for at least two weeks, extreme sadness, tearfulness, depressed mood and loss of interest in, and pleasure in, usual activities, as well as social withdrawal.

(g) Compulsive behaviour, anxiety, depression.

2 (a) A True; B False – this is learning by association; C True; D True.

(b) In flooding, the patient is confronted with their phobic stimulus, for example a spider or a snake, and their panic will be extreme but will not last long because eventually the body stops producing adrenaline.

(c) Flooding treatment causes the phobic patient harm and distress and so is unethical.

(d) The behaviourist explanation of phobia is helpful as it suggests that because a phobia is learned, it can be unlearned.

(e) A fear hierarchy is a series of stressful situations, described by a phobic patient, from the least stressful and increasing step by step to the most stressful – for example, holding a picture of a large spider, to having a large spider on one's body.

(f) One process involves classical conditioning, in which the fear is first learned by association. The second process involves operant conditioning, where because we avoid the fear-provoking stimulus, the fear is not unlearned and so continues.

3 (a) B and E

(b) Cognitive behavioural therapy is a treatment which aims to change both the way a person thinks and their behaviour, and assumes that it is the way people think about events, rather than the events themselves, that is important.

(c) The behavioural explanation of depression is reductionist because the disorder is explained in terms of stimulus–response learning and the biological causes of depression such as genetics and/or biochemistry are ignored, as are social and cognitive factors that may be involved.

(d) An advantage of cognitive treatment for disorders is that the treatment is hopeful. Cognitive treatments such as CBT have shown that depressed people can learn to control and change the way they think, leading to recovery.

(e) Recommending CBT suggests that patient could be 'normal' if they chose to think rationally, which could lead to people being blamed for psychological abnormalities.

(f) CBT may be appropriate only for a biased sample of depressed people – it may not be appropriate treatment for people who do not have strong verbal skills or who find it difficult to explain what they are thinking.

4 (a) Classical conditioning is involved because the fear (of spiders, for example) is first learned by association and operant conditioning because as the person avoids every fear-provoking stimulus (spiders), this prevents him/her from unlearning the fear, so operant conditioning explains why the phobia persists.

(b) Systematic desensitisation is a behaviour therapy where the person's phobia is broken down into small stimulus–response units. The patient is taught muscle relaxation and breathing exercises and then creates a fear hierarchy, starting at stimuli that create the least anxiety and building up in stages to fear-provoking images. The patient works their way up, starting at the least unpleasant and practising their relaxation technique as they go. The role of the therapist is to help the patient recognise the reason for the fear, and whether the fear is rational or not.

(c) Classical conditioning involves reflex behaviour but operant conditioning involves behaviour we can control.

(d) One advantage of the behavioural approach is that it is hopeful as it predicts that people can change (re-learn) their behaviour.

(e) The behavioural approach assumes that all behaviour is learned; that what has been learned can be unlearned; that abnormal behaviour is learned in the same way as normal behaviour.

(f) Beck believes that in the cognitive triad there are three processes and that depressed people get drawn into a negative pattern of viewing (1) themselves, (2) the world, and (3) the future.

(g) Depression may result from a deficiency of the neurotransmitter serotonin or a malfunction of its metabolism such as blocked serotonin receptors.

(h) **Strengths:** biological treatments, such as drugs, act rapidly to reduce symptoms so that patients can lead a normal life; drug therapy can be used alongside therapies such as CBT; drug treatments do not involve the patient changing their lifestyle or behaviour. **Limitations:** some drug treatments have unpleasant side effects; taking drugs may lead to addiction and dependency; drugs may only suppress symptoms and when treatment ends the disorder reappears.

Component 2: Approaches in psychology

1 (a) The learning approach.

(b) The biological approach.

(c) Conscious mental processes.

(d) It is a subjective theory that cannot be falsified.

(e) The id, the ego and the superego.

(f) Examine our own conscious mental processes.

(g) Subjective data.

(h) Biological explanations suggest that behaviour is caused by innate biological structures such as genes and that we have no free will to choose our own behaviour.

(i) The theory is based on Freud's opinion and cannot be scientifically tested or falsified –

unconscious minds are a matter of opinion rather than a matter of fact.

2 (a) TRUE

(b) FALSE – they demonstrated classical conditioning.

(c) TRUE

(d) TRUE

(e) TRUE – Bandura said that children must pay attention to the role model.

(f) FALSE – cognitive psychologists believe that conscious mental processes such as decision making cause behaviour.

(g) TRUE

(h) TRUE

(i) FALSE

(j) TRUE

(k) TRUE

3 (a) Because Maguire studied the effect of behaviour on the structure and amount of grey matter in the hippocampi.

(b) Because Loftus and Palmer studied the effect of leading questions on memory and remembering is a cognitive process.

(c) Because Watson and Rayner investigated the process of classical conditioning in Little Albert.

(d) Because the study looks at how children learned aggressive behaviour by imitating role models.

(e) The biological approach supports the 'nature' side of the nature–nurture debate but the behaviourist approach supports the 'nurture' side of the debate.

(f) Both the biological approach and the behaviourist approach reject free will and are deterministic. The biological approach says behaviour is determined by 'nature' while the the behaviourist approach says behaviour is caused by past experience.

(g) Both the humanistic approach and the psychodynamic approach are unscientific as both are based on subjective theories rather than objective evidence and neither can be falsified.

(h) The biological approach is scientific as experimental research usually gathers objective, quantitative evidence in controlled conditions.

(i) The cognitive approach is useful as it reveals hidden mental processes, usually in experimental research.

(j) The behaviourist approach rejects free will and suggests that all behaviour is caused by past learning experiences. The behaviourist approach is environmental reductionism, suggesting that all behaviour is caused by past learning experiences.

(k) The humanistic approach can be seen as 'blaming parents' for low self-esteem and mental disorders.

Component 2: Biopsychology

1 (a) C The memory

(b) (i) The central nervous system consists of the brain and the spinal cord.

(ii) The somatic nervous system and the autonomic nervous system are the two parts of the peripheral nervous system.

(iii) The biology of the fight or flight response is controlled by the sympathetic nervous system.

(iv) Information is carried between brain neurons by biochemical substances called neurotransmitters.

(v) Relay neurons relay information from sensory neurons to motor neurons.

(vi) Too little serotonin is thought to be the cause of depression.

2 (a) B and C.

3 (a) The set of glands that release hormones into the bloodstream is called the endocrine system.

(b) Just beneath the hypothalamus sits a pea-sized gland called the pituitary gland.

(c) Adrenaline is a hormone that acts quickly to prepare the body to act in an emergency.

(d) The brain has two hemispheres connected by the corpus callosum.

(e) There are two language centres in the brain called Broca's area and Wernicke's area.

(f) A person suffering from motor aphasia can understand language but cannot produce meaningful language.

4 (a) The frontal, the temporal, the occipital, the parietal.

(b) The brain and the spinal cord.

(c) Involuntary activity such as heart rate, breathing and blood pressure.

(d) The sympathetic nervous system.

(e) The sympathetic nervous system.

(f) Afferent neurons that relay information to the brain.

(g) neurons are afferent neurons and they only relay information to the brain, but motor neurons are efferent neurons and they carry information from the brain to the target.

(h) Dopamine – movement, attention and learning; serotonin – mood, sleep, appetite and aggression; epinephrine – energy and depression.

(i) The adrenal glands regulate moods, energy level and the ability to cope with stress. The pancreas performs both digestive and endocrine functions.

(j) If visual material was displayed in the right visual field, thus processed in the left hemisphere, the patient could describe it in speech and writing, but if visual material appeared to the left visual field, thus the right hemisphere, the patient could not describe it, which suggests that language ability is located in the left hemisphere.

(k) Post-mortem studies in which researchers study the brain of an individual who may have had some sort of illness.

Electroencephalogram (EEG), which records the electrical brain.

Functional magnetic resonance imaging (fMRI) measures the metabolic changes that take place in an active part of the brain.

(l) A biological rhythm that repeats over a period of less than 24 hours, for example the stages of sleep.

(m) Something external to the body that controls biological rhythms – examples are the amount of daylight, social norms and clocks.

Component 2: Research methods

1 (a) The extent to which the researcher can control extra variables – a lab experiment takes place in a specially contrived situation but a field experiment takes place in an everyday setting.

(b) The IV is not controlled or manipulated by the researcher.

(c) It is scientific because controls and standardised procedures can be used so statements about cause and effect can be made.

(d) Artificial settings can mean research procedures lack realism.

(e) Observational studies are difficult to replicate and usually involve small samples.

(f) The extent to which we can be sure that, if there is more than one observer, all observers are 'counting and recording' behaviours in the same way.

(g) Open questions collect qualitative data while closed questions collect quantitative data.

(h) Can be used to gather data from large samples of people.

(i) Self-report techniques such as questionnaires cannot assume that participants will tell the truth; bias such as social desirability bias may lead to invalid results.

(j) What the experimenter manipulates/changes between conditions.

(k) What is measured in the experiment.

(l) Because behaviour can be observed in its usual setting there are no problems with demand characteristics as participants may be unaware they are being observed.

(m) Usually an explanation for the observed behaviour cannot be gained because the observer counts instances of behaviour but does not ask participants to explain why they acted as they did.

(n) A case study is a detailed study of one person, or a small group, and one person is not representative of a population.

(o) If the source(s) used are biased, then the findings will also be biased.

Component 2: Scientific processes

1 (a) If students are under the age of 16, parental consent would need to be gained.

Bullying is a socially sensitive subject – questions should not be distressing or embarrassing.

Students should be told they have the right not to answer any of the questions if they do not want to.

(b) No informed consent – participants thought they were taking part in research into memory, not obedience.

Participants were deceived in many ways.

Participants were pressured into continuing when they said they wished to stop.

(c) No parental consent was gained – the children were under 16.

Harm and distress was caused – the children cried and were distressed.

(d) (i) Alternative

(ii) One-tailed

(iii) Directional

2 (a) Put the 53 students' names in a hat and pull out 20.

(b) Because the participants are approached by the researcher – all will probably live in the same geographic area and may be people the researcher knows.

(c) To gain a systematic sample select every fifth name from the list.

(d) A large sample – because the individual differences of the participants will have less effect.

(e) Can be used to identify the weaknesses or flaws in research procedures or questionnaires.

(f) In an independent design each participant experiences only one of the research conditions; in a repeated measures design each participant experiences all the research conditions.

3 (a) Because in a repeated measures design each participant experiences all the research conditions, so only one group of participants is needed.

(b) In research in which the experience in the first condition will improve (or make worse) the performance in a subsequent condition.

(c) To ensure that there was an equal number of more (and less) aggressive children in each condition.

(d) (i) Focal sampling records the behaviour of one person at a time.

(ii) In an event sampled observation … the observer records each time a pre-specified behaviour occurs.

(iii) In a time sampled observation … the observational period is divided up into time intervals, for instance every ten minutes, and the observer makes a note of behaviours once in each time sample.

(e) (i) TRUE

(ii) TRUE

(iii) FALSE

(iv) TRUE

(v) TRUE

(vi) TRUE

4 Being able to define variables in order to manipulate the IV and measure the DV – for example, performance on a memory test might be operationalised as 'the number of words remembered'.

5 Shoppers holding doors open for others.

People saying 'sorry' if they bump into someone in a crowded street.

6 (a) The research should be reliable as the rating scale was a consistent way to measure the interest in space research and the same questionnaire can be used again with either the same or a different sample.

(b) The research should have internal validity because a rating scale question gathers objective numeric data and the research has face validity because the question clearly does measure interest in space research.

7 Testable hypotheses, control of extraneous variables, objectivity, empirical evidence.

8 To decide whether research is good enough to be published.

9 The description of the participants is found in the Method section.

Component 2: Inferential testing

1 (a) When I make a TYPE 1 ERROR I decide to reject the NULL hypothesis, concluding that the IV did have a significant effect on the DV when actually the result was due to chance or some other factor.

(b) A TYPE 2 ERROR is deciding to retain the NULL hypothesis, concluding that the IV had no significant effect on the DV when actually the result was caused by the IV.

(c) Because she is allowing only a 1 in 1000 probability that the result (difference, correlation, association) is caused by something other than the factor being tested.

(d) Approximately 68/2 = 34% of the scores.

(e) 34% of 50 = 17 scores.

(f) **Possible suggestions:**

- The sign test because it is a test of difference suitable for use with related data – and in this case each participant gave their opinion before and after seeing the video on farming methods.

- The related T Test because it is a test of difference suitable for use with related data and with data that are at least ordinal (the attitude scores were numeric) and where the data are normally distributed.

- The Wilcoxen T test because it is a test of difference suitable for use with related data and with data that are at least ordinal (the attitude scores were numeric) and where the data are not known to be normally distributed and in this small sample there may be extreme scores.

(g) The Mann-Whitney U test because it is a non-parametric test suitable for testing the significance of the difference between two conditions when an independent design has been used and when the level of data collected is 'at least' ordinal and is not normally distributed.

(h) A related T test because it is a parametric test which tests the significance of the difference between two conditions when a repeated measures design has been used and the level of data collected is 'at least' ordinal and the data are normally distributed.

(i) The Spearman's Rho (Rank Order) correlation co-efficient because when correlation between two independent variables is being studied, the Spearman's test calculates the correlation co-efficient between ranked scores when both sets of scores are at least ordinal data (the memory scores can be placed in rank order) and the data set is said to be not normally distributed.

(j) The Chi-square test because it is a test of significance of association which is used when nominal-level data (frequency data) have been collected – the self-esteem levels categorised as high or low were nominal, and so were the cheerfulness, which was categorised as cheerful or not cheerful.

(k) There is an equal to or less than 1 in 100 (1%) probability that any difference or result is not caused by the factor being investigated (the IV, etc.).

(l) There is an equal to or less than 1 in 1,000 (0.1%) probability that any difference or result is not caused by the factor being investigated (the IV, etc.).

(m) There is only a 90% chance that difference or result is caused by the variable being investigated.

2 (a) An independent design – the participant either reads at least one book a week or does not read books.

(b) Repeated measures design can be used when participants experience all of the research conditions but it cannot be used in this study as the IV is either being a reader or not.

(c) Primary data – the spellings score was gathered directly from the participants.

(d) **Suggestions:** objective, allows comparisons, can be analysed statistically, matter of fact rather than opinion, can be displayed in a graph or chart.

(e) **Suggestions:** control for time of day, control for spelling test environment, all participants given the same amount of time to do the spellings, control for type of books read.

(f) Participants who read at least one book every week will score better on a test of 30 English spellings (such as embarrassing, accommodation) than participants who say they never read books.

(g) The higher range of 20 in the 'read books' condition suggests that although on average these participants spelled more words correctly, there were individual differences and more variability than in the 'does not read books condition' where the range was 17.

(h) The mean – the advantage is that the mean is the true arithmetic mid-point of the scores and takes into account the values of all the scores.

(i) The median of correct spellings in each condition could be calculated.

(j) Since the mean score of 22.4 is higher in the 'does read books' condition, we can conclude that reading does influence spelling ability.

(k) A bar chart to show the difference in the means of each condition.

(l) **Example answer:** Thank you for taking part in this study. You did really well on that spelling test. The aim was to see whether reading books influences spelling ability. Half of the participants in the study said they read at least one book every week and half said they never read books but all spelled the same 30 words. Don't worry if you made spelling mistakes – some of the spellings were difficult. Are you happy for your data to be included in the research? If not, don't worry, it can be withdrawn. When the study is completed the data will be published on our webpage at findmyresults.com/spellstudy. If you have any questions I will do my best to answer them; if not, thanks for your time.

(m) The SD is a measure of dispersion that is less easily distorted by an extreme score, and in both the 'does' and 'does not' read books there is an extremely low score. Also the SD takes account of the distance of each participant's spelling score from the mean spelling score instead of just the distance between the highest and the lowest spelling scores.

Component 3: Issues and debates

1 (a) It explains the behaviour of people from the cultural perspective (usually Western individualistic culture) of the researcher.

(b) An emic construct is a trait that is specific to one culture (for example, monogamy in Western culture) while an etic construct is a universal trait that is the same across cultures.

(c) When alpha bias occurs, research tends to emphasise and over-exaggerate differences between genders. When beta bias occurs, research tends to minimise or ignore differences between genders. Any research is beta biased if it is conducted with an all-male or all-female sample and then applied to both genders.

(d) Milgram – all-male sample; Asch – all-male sample; Zimbardo – all-male sample.

(e) Because it was done in 1956 and people were far more conformist in the 1950s than they are today.

2 (a) (i) FALSE

(ii) TRUE

(iii) FALSE

(iv) TRUE

(v) FALSE

(vi) TRUE

(b) Ideographic.

(c) Nomothetic examples are classification manuals such as the DSM-IV, which classifies people according to particular types of disorders; behaviourist experiments with animals (for example, rats, cats and pigeons) to establish laws of learning; Milgram used the nomothetic approach to draw general conclusions about obedience. Ideographic examples are Freud and the case study method (for example, Little Hans) in which patients are interviewed over a long period of time and qualitative records are kept of the interpretations.

(d) Biological determinism suggests that the cause of behaviour is inside the individual, for example the genetic make-up or the biochemistry of the brain; environmental determinism proposes that the causes of behaviour are outside the individual, for example a stimulus that evokes reflex behaviour in classical conditioning.

(e) The person level of explanation (individual differences).

(f) The biological level of explanation.

(g) Reductionism means explaining complex behaviours as being caused by simplistic single factors, such as inherited genes, so that scientific hypotheses about the causes of behaviour are easier to test.

(h) Usually nomothetic because a group (a sample) is studied and then generalisations based on this sample are made to explain how most people will behave.

Component 3: Relationships

1 (a) Evolutionary psychologists propose that mate choice is unconsciously guided by cues that indicate some survival advantage for offspring.

(b) Evolutionary psychologists suggest that women should be attracted to males who possess, and will share, valuable resources.

(c) Self disclosure is the act of revealing ourselves to another person.

(d) The halo effect means that we attribute positive characteristics to attractive people.

(e) The matching hypothesis proposes that we are attracted to people whom we perceive to be similarly attractive to ourselves.

(f) In the filter theory of relationship formation, the three stages of filter are – first the social and demographic variables, second is similarity of attitudes and values and finally the complementarity of emotional needs.

(g) B

(h) Equity theory proposes that an equitable relationship is one in which one partners' benefits divided by their costs is equal to the other partner's benefits divided by their costs.

(i) Rusbult's investment model consists of three processes that are positively associated with commitment, satisfaction level, quality of alternatives and investment size.

(j) B

(k) C

(l) In parasocial relationships, gating features (the physical or material barriers that may arise between people when they interact in person) are missing, such as physical appearance, race or class.

(m) In the addiction stage of the absorption-addiction model of parasocial relationships, the individual craves increasing closeness to the chosen celebrity and becomes delusional in thinking and behaviour.

(n) The attachment theory of parasocial relationships proposes that those with insecure attachments are more likely to become strongly attached to celebrities.

Component 3: Gender

1 (a) C
  (b) B
  (c) B
  (d) B
  (e) D
  (f) B
  (g) C

2 Fill in the blanks in the following sentences to outline the key features of social learning theory

  (a) A child is most likely to pay attention to a same sex model.

  (b) A child is more likely to imitate people if the imitative behaviour is rewarded

  (c) The child needs to have the ability to form a mental representation of the observed behaviour so they can later recall it.

  (d) Children need to have the ability to perform the observed action in order to reproduce it.

3 (a) One difference between social and biological explanations for gender identity disorder is the influence of upbringing. For example, Rekers linked GID in boys to an absence of a father figure, whereas Chung et al. (2002) argued

that prenatal hormonal influences might remain dormant until adulthood and then trigger a change, so there is no environmental influence.

  (b) Clinical discomfort in social situations and longstanding and strong identification with another gender.

4 Beeman (1947) castrated male mice and found that aggressiveness reduced. He later injected the mice with testosterone, which re-established their aggressiveness, which is arguably a male trait. This shows that as males have higher levels of testosterone than females, this will account for the difference in gender and aggression.

5 (a) Hopper (2005) found that teenage girls are more likely to read magazines than teenage boys, which shows a higher proportion of magazines are directed towards girls. However, this just shows a link between the availability of magazines and a higher proportion of girls buying them; this does not show reading magazines causes a change in gender role behaviour.

  (b) It is proposed that hormones have a significant effect on the development of gender. However, hormonal influences on behaviour are hard to establish, partly because behaviour is affected by social and other influences after birth. Therefore influences could be seen to combine the effect of both biological and environmental factors.

6 (a) Sex: an individual's biological status as male or female.

  (b) Gender: the attitude and behaviours related to an individual's biological sex.

  (c) Sex-role stereotypes: widely shared assumptions about the personalities, attitudes and behaviour of a particular gender group.

7 Turner syndrome is chromosome abnormality affecting only females, caused by the complete or partial deletion of the X chromosome (X0), that affecting the typical changes during puberty.

8 One strength is that it has application to real life. For example, as the influence of media shows the negative effects of role models, it can also have a positive effect on gender role stereotypes, to challenge stereotypical behaviour – for example, Rey, the lead character in the new Star Wars 'Force Awakens' film, is the female Jedi.

9 One strength is that there is evidence from Martin and Little (1990) suggesting that children place greater emphasis on gender-stereotyped behaviour. This shows the importance of schemas as an influence on gender. However, the theory cannot explain where schemas originate and overemphasises the role of the individual child's cognition.

Component 3: Cognition and development

1 Fill in the blanks in the following sentences.

(a) If a child has a new experience that does not match an existing then a state of disequilibrium is produced.

(b) Assimilation allows new information or experiences to be fitted into the child's current understanding of the world.

(c) Piaget proposes four stages of cognitive development.

(d) In the sensorimotor stage of cognitive development the child has not developed object permanence.

(e) Animism is the tendency to attribute feelings to inanimate objects such as dolls and teddy bears.

(f) In the pre-operational stage of development the child is egocentric and unable to see things from another person's perspective.

(g) A child has developed the ability to conserve when they understand that the quantity of an object does not change when its appearance does.

(h) The research by Samuel and Bryant supports Piaget's theory because as the age of the children increased the children made fewer errors of conservation.

(i) I bought a bunch of flowers, 6 were yellow and 8 were red. Are there more red flowers or flowers? According to Piaget, this type of question can be used to test class inclusion.

(j) For Piaget the child is a scientist but for Vygotsky the child is an apprentice.

(k) According to Vygotsky, each child has a zone of ability and a Zone of Proximal Development which is potential ability if the child is guided by a more able adult.

(l) In the picture four giraffes are walking past the window, if the tall giraffe did not 'appear' in the window frame Baillargeon would call this a violation of expectation.

(m) Scaffolding takes place when a child is helped with elements of a task that is beyond his/her capacity, thus permitting him/her to complete the parts of the task that are within his/her range of competence.

(n) Selman has developed a five-stage model of the development of perspective-taking.

(o) The Sally Anne test is a false belief task.

(p) Theory of mind is our understanding that we, and others, have mental states and that other people have mental states that differ from our own.

(q) The biological theory that mirror neurons are responsible for social cognition can be criticised as reductionist.

Component 3: Schizophrenia

1 (a) C
  (b) C
  (c) C
  (d) D
  (e) D

2 (a) The positive symptoms are abnormal behaviours, especially perceptual disturbances, such as hallucinations, delusions and disordered thinking, and as a result communication may be difficult. Negative symptoms are where normal behaviours are 'taken away', such as a reduction in the range of emotional expression (flattening of emotion) and reduction in speech fluency and in willingness to talk to others. Another negative symptom is avolition, which is a severe lack of initiative or motivation to do anything. In effect, positive symptoms are a distortion or excess of normal functioning, and negative symptoms are reduction or loss of normal functioning.

(b) Positive symptoms are perceptual disturbances, hallucinations, delusions; negative symptoms are lack of motivation, reduced range and intensity of emotion.

(c) A hallucination is a perceptual disturbance, such as a visual or auditory hallucination. A delusion is a false belief, such as the belief that you are being spied on.

3 **Suggested answers:** Gottesman (1991) compiled more than 40 studies in order to work out the risks of developing schizophrenia and found that those who share the greatest number of genes with schizophrenia sufferers have an increased risk of developing it.

Gottesman and Shields (1976, 1982) reviewed the results of twin studies and found that in identical (MZ) twins there was a concordance rate of 35–58% compared with non-identical (DZ) twin rates that ranged from 9–26%.

Kety et al. (1994) looked at schizophrenia in the biological and adoptive relatives of schizophrenic adoptees and compared these to a matched group of control adoptees. In the sample of adoptees with schizophrenia, the disorder was found exclusively in their biological relatives and not in their adoptive relatives.

4 (a) The concordance rate among MZ twins is not 100% and because even when people do share the same genes there is only a 50% chance of them both developing schizophrenia, the environment must contribute a significant

effect. The problem is that families, including twins, share the same environment, so if schizophrenia appears to run in families, this could be due either to genetics or to the shared environment and it is almost impossible to separate the effects of genes (nature) from the effects of the environment (nurture).

(b) If high levels of dopamine explain schizophrenia, then reducing the level of dopamine should reduce both positive and negative symptoms, but traditional antipsychotic drugs that reduce levels of dopamine reduce the positive symptoms only. This suggests that either the 'excess dopamine' hypothesis is wrong or that different types of schizophrenia have different causes. Drugs such as clozapine are an effective treatment for both positive and negative symptoms, but they affect both dopamine and serotonin levels, suggesting that excess dopamine may not be the only biochemical factor involved in schizophrenia.

5 Brown and Birley (1968) found that about 50% of patients experienced a stressful event in the three weeks prior to a psychotic episode. Hirsch *et al.* (1996) looked at the life events experienced by 71 schizophrenic patients over a period of four years and found that the cumulative effect of stressful life events in the 12 months prior to a schizophrenic episode had a significant effect. This suggests that the total stress experienced by the individual may be associated with an eventual schizophrenic episode.

6 Family dynamics have been found to be associated with schizophrenic episodes, especially expressed emotion (EE), comprising critical or emotionally over-involved attitudes displayed by one or more parents to their schizophrenic offspring. Cross-cultural research also suggests an involvement by family dynamics. Leff *et al.* (1987) found that high EE in Indian families was associated with relapse and that the significantly better outcome for Indian patients compared with a London cohort was due to the substantially lower proportion of high-EE relatives in the Indian study group.

7 Wright (2000) proposed that people with schizophrenia have a failing in a hypothetical cognitive filter that separates background sensory 'noise' from useful sensory 'signals' and that misinterpretation of this excess sensory input results in hallucinations. Frith (1992) suggests that the symptoms of schizophrenia can be explained in terms of abnormalities of cognitive processes. For example, because they are unaware of their own intentions, patients experience their actions, thoughts and speech as resulting from some source other than themselves, and the inability to correctly infer beliefs and intentions of other people results in delusions of persecution.

Component 3: Eating behaviour

1 Fill in the blanks in the following sentences.

(a) Eating sweet food is adaptive as ripe fruit contain large numbers of calories and would provide an easily accessible source of energy.

(b) Neophobia is a fear of new food, which is found in young children during weaning.

(c) Children learn food preferences when they observe and imitate their parents' eating behaviour.

(d) A change in attitudes and eating behaviour when people move to another country is known as the acculturation effect.

(e) Leptin is responsible for energy balance by acting as a hunger suppressant signal to the brain.

(f) According to family systems explanations for anorexia, problems arise for the child when family inter-relationships become dysfunctional.

(g) The cognitive explanation for anorexia nervosa states that the disorder is a result of maladaptive thought processes.

(h) Eating food that is forbidden can lead to the 'what the hell effect' and binge eating will occur. This is known as the disinhibition effect.

(i) Motivation is an important factor in dieting and several areas have been focused upon, including financial incentives and improved social networks.

(j) The lateral hypothalamus contains the feeding centre.

2 One explanation for the success of dieting is setting psychological and biological boundaries close to each other. As a result, the dieter will be less likely to go beyond their psychological boundary due to hunger or overeating.

One explanation for the failure of dieting is that when an individual tries to stop thinking about a desired food, the food becomes more appealing. This is known as the theory of ironic processes of cognitive control.

3 One difference between biological and social explanations for anorexia is the role of nature and nurture. Biological explanations suggest that anorexia is caused by inherited factors identifying a specific gene variant found in patients with anorexia. Social learning theory, meanwhile, suggests behaviour is environmental as it is learned through observation, imitation and reinforcement.

4 One study that supports the cognitive explanation for anorexia is MacKenzie *et al.*, who interviewed females to estimate their own size in relation to that of other women. Results showed that patients tended to overestimate their body weight. This supports the cognitive explanation as it shows that overestimation of body size is an irrational belief that patients hold that is contrary to reality.

5 **a)** One problem with using animals to research brain mechanisms in eating behaviour is that we cannot generalise findings to humans as we cannot be sure whether the dual control system works in exactly the same way in humans and therefore cannot explain human eating behaviour. However, it could be argued that we share genetic similarities with other mammals and using animals means we can precisely control the animal's environment in the way we cannot reliably control human eating behaviour, which makes research more objective and reliable.

b) Fisher and Birch found that when girls were given a standard lunch but then allowed to freely snack on calorific foods such as ice cream afterwards, they did not imitate the behaviour of their parents and ate foods that were discouraged at home.

6 **(a)** Taste aversion is an innate mechanism to recognise toxins in food, leading to avoidance and the person not eating the food that may be off.

b) Neophobia is the fear of new food found in children during weaning when they spit out and refuse unfamiliar foods.

c) Evolutionary adaptations occurred due to environmental demands when humans were hunter-gatherers and preferred energy dense foods that were free of toxins to ensure survival.

7 One neural explanation for obesity is the gene that codes for lipoprotein lipase (LPL), an enzyme produced by fat cells to help store calories as fat. If too much LPL is produced, the body will become efficient at storing calories, making obesity inevitable as the individual will gain more weight each time.

8 One strength of the family systems explanation for anorexia is that it has practical applications as a therapeutic approach and shows a way to work with families to improve interactions and to encourage autonomy. This will help the anorexic to gain control and reduce symptoms.

9 One strength of psychological explanations for obesity is that the boundary model is a good example of combining physiological and psychological factors to explain feeding behaviour. However, a weakness is that most of the research in this area is carried out under controlled conditions in the laboratory. Therefore this lowers the levels of ecological validity as we cannot generalise beyond the setting of the study.

Component 3: Stress

1 **(a)** General adaptation syndrome.

(b) The hypothalamic–pituitary–adrenal axis is responsible for arousing the autonomic nervous system (ANS) in response to a stressor.

(c) An acute stressor activates the ANS that secretes adrenalin.

(d) The ANS responds and releases adrenalin and stress hormones into the bloodstream.

(e) The stress hormone cortisol causes a physiological reaction of increased arousal levels increased heart rate raised blood pressure in readiness for a physical 'fight or flight' response.

(f) The ANS which causes stress hormones and adrenalin to circulate in the bloodstream.

(g) Reduces the effectiveness of the immune system (an immunosuppressive effect) because natural 'killer cell' activity is reduced.

(h) People who are stressed are more likely to engage in risky behaviour such as smoking, using alcohol, or overeating all of which have a negative effect on health.

(i) If stress continues for a long time, according to the GAS model – the body's resources are reduced, the immune system may be damaged and stress-related diseases caused by long term high blood pressure as well as cardiovascular disorders are more likely to occur.

(j) Stress causes people to change their behaviour, and engage in more risky behaviour such as smoking, or drinking alcohol, or over- or undereating – and these, rather than the stressor may influence health.

2 **(a)** Death of a spouse, marriage, divorce, losing one's job, Christmas.

(b) A life changing event happens infrequently, such as moving house, changing employment or getting married, but a daily hassle is a frequent occurrence, such as getting stuck in a long queue in a supermarket.

(c) The participant completes a questionnaire (the SRRS) indicating which of 43 life events they have experienced. Each of the 43 events has a fixed number of 'points' and the points the participant 'ticked' are added up to calculate the total number of life change (readjustment) points for the 12 months.

(d) Many of the 43 items relate to marriage, divorce, family problems, or changes in employment so the SRRS may only be appropriate to measure stress in mature adults and not appropriate to measure the stress of students and other young people.

(e) Both workload and control may be factors that cause Tom to feel stress. If Tom always has a queue of people waiting he will feel pressured to work as fast as possible, also the job is repetitive and he will have little control over his workload and research shows that jobs that are demanding but that involve low levels of control cause stress.

(f) Jobs that are demanding but that involve low levels of control have been found to be related to increased incidences of heart disease

(g) One advantage of using self-report to measure stress is that the data comes first hand from the stressed person, and since feelings of stress are private and subjective, only the individual can describe how stressed they are.

(h) One disadvantage of using self-report to measure stress is that people may not wish to disclose how stressed they are and thus may not tell the truth – leading to low validity.

Or: One disadvantage of using self-report to measure stress in the workplace is that people may fear that their responses will be disclosed to their employer and thus may not tell the truth about what stresses them at work.

(i) Measuring the amount of cortisol in saliva is a reductionist measurement of stress, because the amount of cortisol is a quantitative biological fact but a person's experience of stress is subjective and qualitative so biological measurement reduces psychological distress to biological 'fact' but does not tell us how the person feels.

(j) Many suggestions can be made. (a) Assure participants of confidentiality to reduce response bias; (b) Use physiological and self-report measurement and correlate the findings; (c) Use closed or rating scale questions to gather quantitative data.

3 (a) Type A people move rapidly; they try to do two or more things at one time; they are competitive; they are hard-driving, impatient and aggressive; they tend to be achievement-oriented.

(b) Usually, Type B people are not time pressured and hence do not become impatient, angry or irritable. They tend not to feel guilty about relaxing so their nervous system is less likely to stimulate the adrenal gland to release stress hormones into the blood stream.

(c) Physiological methods of stress management change the way the body responds to stress by reducing the physical symptoms of stress (e.g. reducing blood pressure) whereas psychological methods help people cope by getting them to think about their problems in a different way.

(d) Benzodiazepine drugs slow down the activity of the central nervous system (CNS) and reduce anxiety by enhancing the activity of a natural biochemical substance GABA which is the body's natural form of anxiety relief.

(e) The key traits of a hardy personality (known as the three Cs) are having a strong sense of personal control, a strong sense of purpose (commitment) and the ability to see problems as challenges to be overcome rather than as stressors.

(f) Drug treatments are fast acting; drug treatments do not require people to change their lifestyles.

(g) The person is attached to a machine that monitors changes in heart rate and blood pressure and gives feedback. The person learns to control the symptoms of stress by deep breathing and muscle relaxation and thus slows down their heart rate making them feel more relaxed. While they do this the biofeedback from the machine acts like a reward and encourages the person to repeat the breathing techniques. The person practises learns to repeat the breathing techniques in stressful situations.

(h) Stress inoculation training involves three stages. (1) Conceptualisation in which patients are encouraged to imagine stressful situations and analyse what is stressful about them and how they might cope with them. (2) Skill acquisition and rehearsal – in which patients practise how to relax, and how respond to stressors differently. (3) Application and follow-through in which patients apply their new skills while being supported through progressively more stressful situations.

(i) Offering emotional support (empathy); giving instrumental support (lending him money); giving informational support (advice about job hunting); giving companionship support (popping round to visit him).

(j) Any effect of social support will be subjective and qualitative and cannot be measured objectively. Also any effect of social support cannot be measured in a laboratory and will be correlational, thus no valid cause and effect statements can be made about the effect of social support on stress.

(k) Emotion focused strategies attempt to reduce the symptoms of anxiety by taking a physiological approach for example anti-anxiety drugs may be used, but problem focused strategies attempt to change how people respond to stressors by using cognitive therapies or by encouraging people to increase their social support.

Component 3: Aggression

1 (a) C

(b) B

(c) Monoamine oxidases (MAOs) are enzymes that are involved in the breakdown of neurotransmitters such as serotonin and dopamine and can influence the feelings and behaviour. MAO-A in humans is encoded by the MAOA gene and mutation in the MAO-A gene results in monoamine oxidase deficiency which has been associated with aggressive behaviour.

(d) C

(e) Evolutionary theorists propose that the reproductive challenges faced by our ancestors can explain aggressive behaviour. For example, because a man can never be certain that he is the biological father of his children he must prevent his female partner having relationships with other men, so male sexual jealousy causes aggression and domestic violence.

2 (a) Stimulation of the amygdala increases aggressive behaviour.

(b) Low levels of the neurotransmitter serotonin may be linked to aggressive behaviour.

(c) The basal model of testosterone proposes that the more testosterone someone has, the more aggressive they will become.

(d) Dabbs found that inmates who had committed violent crime had higher testosterone levels than those who had committed non-violent crime.

(e) Suggesting that high levels of testosterone causes aggressive behaviour is biological reductionism as even if high levels of testosterone are associated with increases in aggression, aggressive behaviour is usually a response to cues in the environment.

(f) Giving a genetic explanation for aggressive behaviour is biological determinism as it suggests that people do not have the free-will to choose not to be aggressive.

(g) Lorenz proposed that aggressive behaviour is adaptive because the most aggressive animals control access to resources such as mates, food and territory.

3 A False; B False; C True; D True; E True

4 (a) The frustration-aggression hypothesis suggests that aggressive behaviour is always the result of frustration.

(b) The aggressive cues hypothesis suggests that aggression will only happen if there is a cue to aggressive behaviour, such as a weapon, in the environment.

(c) The aggressive cues theory of aggression is useful because it suggests that if we prevent or reduce levels of frustration we can also prevent or reduce aggressive behaviour.

(d) The social learning theory of aggression is useful because social learning theory suggests that if, in society, we reduce the amount of modelled aggressive behaviour we can also prevent or reduce aggressive behaviour.

(e) A person who is a member of a large crowd becomes anonymous and deindividuated

and is more likely to engage in antisocial or aggressive behaviour.

(f) The dispositional explanation of aggression in institutions suggests that offenders enter prison with aggressive characteristics and personality traits which predicts they will be more likely to engage in aggressive behaviour.

(g) Cognitive priming of aggression refers to the activation of existing aggressive thoughts and feelings.

5 (a) MonoAmine Oxidase A which is an enzyme that degrades amine neurotransmitters, such as dopamine and serotonin.

(b) Fixed action pattern behaviours are instinctive, predictable behaviours that always happen in the same way and only in response to a specific signal known as an innate releasing mechanism. Fixed action pattern behaviours are not learned and the behaviour is seen in every member of the species.

(c) According to evolutionary psychologists, because a man can never be certain that he is the biological father of his children, fear of cuckoldry and sexual jealousy cause aggression and domestic violence.

(d) The frustration–aggression hypothesis is that aggressive behaviour occurs when a person's efforts to attain a goal is frustrated, that frustration always leads to some form of aggression.

(e) Social learning involves cognitive factors because to learn the behaviour the child must pay attention to the behaviour and attention is a cognitive behaviour, also the child needs to be able to remember and recall the learned behaviour and memory is a cognitive behaviour.

(f) In the Zimbardo study, the prisoners had to wear the same prison smock, had their hair hidden and were known by a number not a name, so they all looked the same and lost their sense of identity; The guards all wore military uniforms, dark glasses, and badges with numbers on, so they all looked the same and became anonymous 'just one of the guards'.

(g) The dispositional explanation suggests that offenders enter prison with characteristics that predict they are more likely to engage aggression. However, the situational explanation suggests that the prison situation causes inmates stress and frustration, which leads to aggression.

(h) Children who play violent video games may behave more aggressively because they see violence so frequently they become 'desensitised' so become less anxious about violence in real life because they become habituated (used to it).

Component 3: Forensic psychology

1 (a) D

(b) Behaviour that is acceptable in one culture may be a criminal offence in another culture.

(c) The Crime Survey for England and Wales is a face-to-face survey asking people in England and Wales about their experiences of crime in the past year. The offences surveyed are violence, robbery, theft and criminal damage and the aim of the CSEW is to provide trends for the crime types being carried out, the locations of the crimes, and the extent to which people worry about crime.

(d) Not all crimes are reported; the police do not record all crimes that are reported.

(e) Information was gathered from in-depth interviews on 36 sexually orientated serial murderers including Ted Bundy and Charles Manson.

(f) A

(g) Interpersonal coherence; significance of time and place; forensic awareness

(h) Interpersonal coherence means that the behaviour of a criminal during a violent crime will be consistent with (similar to) the way he (or she) usually behaves.

2 (a) C

(b) C

(c) Geographical profiling is based on the cognitive assumption that people store information about their lives in schemas/ mental maps and that because each person's mental map is different the location of crime scene(s) can be used to infer where the offender is based, is employed, etc.

(d) Every profile is in effect a case study, so we cannot assume that if one is successful the next will also be successful.

Profilers make inferences from looking at a crime scene and they may be biased by what they already know which will lead to an inaccurate profile and may mislead the investigation.

Profiling is only effective for serious 'serial' crimes.

3 (a) C

(b) No, we cannot assume that criminality is genetic because if offending is genetic we would expect a high concordance rate in MZ twins who share 100% identical genes but as there is not 100% concordance there must be an environmental influence.

(c) • Lower activity in the cortical regions and subcortical regions.
   • Reduced activity in prefrontal cortex and parietal region.
   • Reduced activity in the corpus callosum.
   • Less activity in the left hemisphere than right.
   • Abnormal asymmetries in amygdala and thalamus.

(d) Anxious.

(e) Personality is a hypothetical construct and as such may not even 'exist', also people tend to self-report the behaviours and traits they think they 'should have' rather than the behaviours and traits they do have.

(f) People who tend to make a hostile attribution bias interpret the behaviour of others as threatening or aggressive and directed toward them. For example, if a stranger looks at them they may think they are being targeted, stared at, or criticised.

(g) (i) An internal attribution is when a person accepts responsibility for their behaviour and sees the cause as being within themselves.

   (ii) An external attribution is when a person sees the cause of their behaviour as being an external factor and so not their fault.

(h) Differential association theory suggests that criminal behaviour is learned during social interaction with others, and that through interacting with other criminals, individuals learn the values, attitudes, techniques, and motives for crime. According to Sutherland, if we associate with groups whose norms and values are criminal we adopt these norms and values.

(i) Freud's theory that the human psyche is made up of the ID, ego and super-ego is based on subjective opinion not objective fact and his hypotheses cannot be tested or falsified.

4 (a) A reinforcement program can be designed in which each time Fredd engages in specific non-aggressive behaviours he is given a small reward, but each time he behaves aggressively a reward is taken away. Each time Fredd has collected 15 rewards he can trade them in for a special treat. Everyone who has contact with Fredd follows these rules and the number of aggressive behaviours Fredd engages in each day are counted. If the modification programme is effective Fredd will engage in less aggressive behaviour.

(b) Crimes may not be caused by anger, for example property crimes.

Offenders who commit aggressive crimes may not be willing to attend anger management programmes.

Anger management programs assume crime is caused by cognitive factors – but there may be biological reasons why people commit crimes.

Component 3: Addiction

1 Using Prochaska's six-stage model of behaviour change fill in the blanks in the following sentences.

(a) Preparation stage is the stage where the person is intending to take action in the near future and may well have already started to do something.

(b) Pre-contemplation stage is the stage where the person has no intention to change their behaviour and probably does not even perceive that they have a problem.

(c) Action stage is the stage where people change their behaviour, or their experience, or their environment so that they can overcome their problem.

(d) Maintenance stage is the stage where he person works to prevent a relapse and to consolidate the changes they have made.

(e) Contemplation stage is the stage where the person is aware that they have a problem and think they should do something about it.

2 One explanation for nicotine addiction is neurochemistry as nicotine affects the nervous system by increasing dopamine and levels of acetylcholine, a neurotransmitter which appears to be involved in reward processes. Nicotine has been shown to increase dopamine release within the brain reward system, giving the user a positive feeling. This positive feeling continues as long as the smoker maintains addictive smoking behaviour.

3 One difference between learning theory and cognitive theory of gambling addiction is the importance of thought processes. Learning explanations are based on a simple stimulus–response model, whereas cognitive explanations would that in between the stimulus and response comes decision assembly. For example, gamblers will weigh up the perceived costs/benefits before they adopt gambling behaviour.

4 (a) Strickland et al. (2006): 37 participants (10 frequent, 11 infrequent and 16 non-gamblers) completed the Gamblers' Belief Questionnaire (GBQ). Findings showed that frequent gamblers were more likely to hold beliefs consistent with cognitive bias and the illusion of control.

(b) One weakness of Strickland et al.'s study is the use of self-report with the Gamblers'

Belief Questionnaire, which may lead to biased responses from the participants as gambling is seen as a socially undesirable behaviour. This will reduce the overall validity of the study as it will not be measuring the gamblers' true beliefs. However, the questionnaire has high levels of test–retest reliability and the only way to measure beliefs is through the use of self-report.

5 (a) Physical dependence is usually experienced with addiction to substances, such as nicotine, and attempts to give up will lead to physical withdrawal.

(b) Psychological dependence is an emotional state that develops as a result of an addiction to a substance or behaviour and can remain long after the addictive behaviour has stopped. For example, after a person has given up smoking, the craving will continue.

(c) Withdrawal is the unpleasant feelings and physical effects that the individual suffers when they withdraw or stop the use of a substance. For example, giving up alcohol may lead to shaking and sweating.

(d) Addiction to a physical substance will lead to a need for an increasing amount of that substance to gain the same effect. For example, a heroin addict will become 'tolerant' to a small amount of the drug and will need more and more to achieve the effect they initially experienced with a smaller amount of the drug.

6 One risk factor is the family – for example, if parents have a positive attitude to smoking, this can be a risk factor for adolescents to initiate smoking. Another risk factor is personality – Cloninger (1987) identified three personality traits that increase the risk of addiction: novelty seeking, harm avoidance and reward dependence.

7 Studies have shown that both agonist and antagonist treatments have been very successful for smokers, alcohol and drug addicts. This is further supported by Kim and Grant (2001), who found that antagonist drugs could reduce thoughts about gambling, the urge to gamble and, in high doses, gambling behaviour itself.

8 Learning theory has application as it shows that in order to cease smoking the smoker needs to avoid not only the nicotine but also the objects and situations associated with the smoking. This increases the overall validity of the theory as it can be applied to everyday life and used in NHS programmes to help people quit smoking. However, learning theory does not take into consideration individual differences as many people are able to quit smoking and do not associate in the way cue reactivity suggests.